Fiction and Historical Consciousness

Fiction and Historical Consciousness

THE AMERICAN ROMANCE TRADITION

Emily Miller Budick

YALE UNIVERSITY PRESS
NEW HAVEN AND LONDON

Designed by Nancy Ovedovitz
and set in Electra type by American–Stratford Graphic
Services, Inc.
Printed in the United States of America by
Braun-Brumfield, Inc., Ann Arbor, Michigan.

Library of Congress card catalog number: 88–50433
International standard book number: 0–300–04292–2

The paper in this book meets the guidelines for permanence
and durability of the Committee on Production Guidelines
for Book Longevity of the Council on Library Resources.

10   9   8   7   6   5   4   3   2   1

For Sandy

Contents

Preface

The subject of this book is a series of literary works from Charles Brockden Brown's *Wieland*, through writings by Cooper, Hawthorne, and Melville in the nineteenth century, to works by Sherwood Anderson, Fitzgerald, Hemingway, Faulkner, E. L. Doctorow, and John Updike in the twentieth century. All of these works participate in a literary tradition that, loosely defined, we may call American historical romance. My focus is the relationship between this tradition's emphatic rejection of mimetic modes of representation and its equally strong insistence on specified settings in place and time (in what we generally call history). American historical romance, I argue, renders a double consciousness of interpretive processes. Its symbols and allegories enforce an awareness of the unknowability of material reality. Simultaneously, it presents a world that, however defamiliarized, is still intensely recognizable. These processes of defamiliarization and representation do not neutralize each other. On the contrary, the American historical romances insist on the reality of history and society in order to cast doubt on the mind's autonomy and to force the imagination to consider something outside itself. Focusing attention on past worlds, which, as historical entities, have already become fictions of reality, the romances heighten the tension between mind and world. In the tradition of American historical romance even a world remembered is still inarguably a world. What distinguishes the historical from the fictive imagination is that historical consciousness trains its subjectivity on a world that is, at whatever remove, decidedly not its own creation and not a replication of itself. In historical romance the reality of the past is verifiable through agencies outside the single perceiving self. What the self imagines, therefore, must always meet the test of someone else's evidence. In these fictions, the world of the past sooner or later confronts the individual with the limits of subjective interpretation. It also makes moral demands that subjectivity alone cannot meet. The historical romance tradition insists that we see things from someone else's point of view and that we accept a world constituted by differences, not similarities.

Central to the tradition of American historical romance is a specifically American reconstruction of the skeptical dilemma, what Emerson calls the noble doubt. From the late eighteenth century to the contemporary period a remarkable lineage of American writers produces a fiction that acknowledges the force of skepticism and yet allows writing to commit itself to history and society. Indeed, this fiction even requires writing to acknowledge the ethical imperatives implied by the difference between history and fiction. This burden of historical responsibility under the pressure of skepticism is, I believe, the distinguishing feature of American historical romance.

Let me state at the outset that my book focuses on a specific group of writings that participate in one particular literary venture. This venture is the identification of certain problems in the American imagination and the illumination of the broader issues of fictive representation implicit in those problems. My interpretation of the historical romance tradition has evolved, as have the works under discussion, from the intensity of interrelation that, within both literary and critical writing, constitutes one definition of tradition. The fictions I examine speak to one another. I consider my readings of these works a further element in that conversation. If it were not for the fact that the texts I treat constitute the canonical works previous critics have treated, and if I did not personally believe that it is the responsibility of critics to keep the canon open, I might feel it my privilege, within the realm of free academic discourse, simply to proceed with my readings. But the American historical romances I discuss are first and foremost invested in the openness of texts and society. They explicitly resist the tendency of the imagination to impose either inherited or private meanings on the world, foreclosing the possibility of different and competing points of view, and they attempt to create a literary tradition that will preserve its democratic responsibilities to society, history, and morality. Therefore, let me specify which works of American fiction I do not treat, and why.

I do not discuss works by major authors such as Mark Twain, Stephen Crane, and Theodore Dreiser. Much of the special quality of American realism derives from a tension between imagination and reason and between fiction and history, similar to that in the historical romance tradition. The realists, however, do not speak to the same issue of skepticism and its relationship to historical consciousness that occupies the historical romancers. I also do not explore the writings of Henry James. In James the issue of skepticism is very much in evidence and in terms consonant with the tradition of historical romance. But in James's writing, history and romance exist as impossible alternatives that even historical consciousness, properly romanticized, cannot mediate. The Jamesian protagonists who recognize the claims of history, like Isabel Archer at the conclusion of *The Portrait of a Lady*, must forsake the possibilities of their romantic readiness, while those, like Christopher Newman, who escape with their American temperaments intact, must give up the idea of entering history at all. In the latter part of the nineteenth century, American writing moved away from the particular formulation of the skeptical dilemma that characterizes the tradition of historical romance. It would be difficult to say why it returned to these formulations in the works of Fitzgerald, Hemingway, and Faulkner. However, the American historical romance tradition differs from British fiction in its choice of a romantic as opposed to a specifically realistic vehicle of representation. When American writers moved into the writing of realistic fictions, they necessarily transferred their attention—at least for a time—to radically different issues. Interestingly, at the end of the nineteenth and at the beginning of the twentieth centuries, just as American writers began to write in the mode of British realism, British writers, (Conrad, for example), under the influence of the American romance tradition began to adopt American modes of nonrepresentation. From this point of view, we can say that James is the most fully developed and brilliant writer of the tension between modes (and nationalities) of representation. His own career might be seen as reproducing the American development from romance to realism, moving from what James himself recognizes as the romance quality of *The American* to the more rigorous realism of his later writings. But this is beyond the scope of this book. In focusing on one particular line of development in the American canon, I exclude a large number of works with which this line undoubtedly intersects.

For similar reasons I do not trace two clear descendants of the romance tradition: the experimental writings of male authors such as John Barth, Thomas Pynchon, and Donald Barthelme; and the novels and stories of female authors like Carson McCullers, Grace Paley, and Toni Morrison, some of whom write experimental fiction, some of whom do not. In general, these writers differ from the historical romancers in the way that, like James (and Edgar Allan Poe, whom I also do not discuss), they turn the skeptical argument away from history and toward some other, more purely philosophical or aesthetic form of speculation. The case of the female writers is especially interesting. The women writers who inherit the romance tradition are as committed as the male romancers to the need to affirm and acknowledge an unknowable world and one's role in it. However, they preserve relatedness and community in ways not employed in the male tradition. Bearing the imprint of female marginality, the domain of women's fiction is any place but history. Therefore, the skeptical dilemma must be resolved on other grounds. While the male tradition is dualistic, the terms of female skepticism present themselves as the proliferation of multiple subjectivities that will not be consolidated into paired, stable alternatives. The male tradition identifies the terms of the skeptical dilemma as self and other, mind and world, imagination and history, and it proposes a dialectical relationship that takes into account the larger social and historical reality. In the feminist tradition, interpretations generate interpretations, relations beget relations. The text does not so much mediate or organize possibilities into a recognizable picture of the world as it collects or surrounds them. Finally, the female authors, because they are women, also respond to an additional set of precursor texts that are not (yet) incorporated into the major canon. They comment on the dominant male tradition and take it in new and interesting directions, but they do not participate directly in that density of interrelationship by which the tradition is defined. Their story is another one, one which I am beginning to explore elsewhere.

The revision of the American literary canon testifies to two salient features of the historical romance tradition: its concern with the moral contingencies in which the literary work exists and its commitment to affirming and acknowledging, even while changing, the tradition out of which new creativity emerges. Though our definition of the canon will likely undergo a series of radical alterations in the coming years, and though our terms of discussion are likely to experience similar revision, I nonetheless believe that the influence of the historical romance tradition will continue to be felt.

Acknowledgement and affirmation are largely the subjects of this book. It is appropriate, therefore, that I acknowledge here some debts that go beyond the standard footnote variety. In the early 1970s I studied Hawthorne with Michael Colacurcio. My excursions into Hawthornean romance have always been disciplined by Colacurcio's insistence that if Hawthorne had spent so much time and energy getting his history right, no reader who respected Hawthorne's achievement could afford to do less. I discovered in Hawthorne's historicity that respect for history was itself a key issue. In recreating the past, Hawthorne insisted that his readers take seriously matters completely outside themselves, matters that they might never fully know or understand or control. Meditating on this aspect of Hawthorne's interest in history, I became aware of the close connections between the problem of respecting the other and that of respecting history. Indeed, reading not only Hawthorne's writings (Colacurcio's *The Province of Piety* in one hand and Sacvan Bercovitch's *Puritan Origins of the American Self* in the other), but also the works of other American writers such as Brown, Cooper, Melville, Fitzgerald, Hemingway, Faulkner, Doctorow, and Updike, I saw emerging in the tradition of historical romance fiction a common concern. This is the concern with a dangerously egocentric, ahistorical imagination that seemed to these writers to reach far back into America's past. Through their historical fictions, these writers hoped to restore their readers to the historical consciousness they lacked and to shared responsibility in the national venture.

The work of Stanley Cavell took me yet another step in my understanding of the historical romance tradition. Hawthorne and his fellow authors wrote fictions, not histories, and these fictions opened up the interpretive process in ways antithetical, if not downright hostile, to the interests of historical analysis. Enforcing the idea of the undecidability or indeterminacy of language, Cavell demonstrates the need for individuals nonetheless to assume responsibility for their words. The American transcendentalist tradition, according to Cavell, is a profound instance of affirmation triumphing through doubt. For access to that power to affirm, without which the American romance would not be what it is, and without which I could not have written what I have written (and meant it!), I wish to thank Cavell. When I use the word *acknowledgment* in this study, it is with the special force of Cavell's presence behind it.

But these are not all my debts. Ellen Graham of Yale University Press has encouraged me throughout. I could not have proceeded without her valuable advice and painstaking care. Manuscript editor Carl Rosen edited diligently and with a flair for disentangling the knots of my academic prose. In 1982 the United States-Israel Educational Foundation, headed in Israel by Dan Krauskopf, paid my tuition at the Salzburg Seminar, where I first began to think seriously about contemporary American literature. The Foundation then provided funds that allowed me to continue my research in the States. The libraries at Princeton and Harvard made my work possible.

Finally, my husband, Sanford Budick, devoted himself, rigorously, unstintingly, and lovingly, to seeing this study through. He doubted nobly when necessary, affirmed wisely when possible, and, not least, shared with me in every way the enterprise of history and romance. Acknowledgment is also an expression of love. With that in mind I also acknowledge our children, Rachel, Ayelet, and Yochanan.

The following journals have kindly granted me permission to reprint materials from essays first published by them:

Hebrew University Studies in Literature and the Arts, where " 'American Israelites': Literalism and Typology in the American Imagination" appeared, vol. 10 (1982):69–107; this essay is reprinted in *Biblical Patterns in Modern Literature*, ed. David Hirsch and Nehama Ashkenazy (Chico, Calif.: Scholars' Press, 1985), pp. 187–208, which also granted permission to reprint; *PMLA*, for "The World as Specter: Hawthorne's Historical Art," 102 (1986):218–32; *Lamar Journal of the Humanities*, for "History and Perception: The Romance Epistemology of Hawthorne's *The House of the Seven Gables*," vol. 12 (1986):7–20; *University of Toronto Quarterly*, for " 'The Sun Also Rises': Hemingway and the Art of Repetition, 56 (1986):319–37; and Magnes Press for "Cooper's *The Spy*: Towards a Definition of Historical Romance," *American Studies Scripta*, ed. E. Miller Budick, Aryeh Goren, and Shlomo Slonim (Jerusalem, 1987).

Charting the Neutral Ground:
The Historicity of Fiction
in Cooper's *The Spy*

The Spy, by James Fenimore Cooper, is the first significant novel of America's first important novelist. *The Spy* thus occupies a cherished position in American literary history. "The Spy," writes James H. Pickering, "was an unabashedly 'American' novel [that] for the first time . . . made unapologetic use of authentic American character types, American scenery, American manners and customs, and American history."[1] Pickering's inclusion of American history in his list of distinguishing features is important. As Cooper's contemporaries recognized, "*The Spy* testified to what could be accomplished by a native writer of fiction who was willing to exploit the untapped riches of the American past."[2] History, the past, was to substitute for the romantic environment and even for the social coherence that America lacked. This lack, in the opinion of early literary critics, both at home and abroad, doomed the new nation to literary failure. An 1822 review of Cooper conveys the deep concern of many nineteenth-century intellectuals: "Where . . . are the romantic associations, which are to plunge your reader, in spite of reason and common sense, into the depths of imaginary woe and wonder?" The reviewer, however, quickly reassures intellectuals, "the truth is, there never was a nation whose history . . . affords better or more abundant matter of romantic interest than ours."[3]

But in designating the territory that American literature might hope to occupy, most critics did not define historical romance or the relationship between two inherently dissimilar or even incompatible kinds of imagination, the one fictional, the other historical. Until the nineteenth century, history and fiction had been considered alternative vehicles of the same narrative enterprise. By Cooper's time, however, they had already begun to emerge as different and even mutually exclusive disciplines.[4] The explicitly nonrepresentational, nonmimetic mode of writing into which American historical fictions were often cast highlights the differences that divided the historical and the fictional imaginations. Despite their anxieties about representation, nineteenth-century British novelists posited some point of convergence between the events of the world and the imagination's perception of those events. This abiding confidence in the powers of representational writing originated in the tradition of historical fiction developed by Sir Walter Scott. The American authors derived from this same tradition. They, however, wrote fictions that insisted on their freedom from the constraints of realism. Their romances severed whatever harmony world and mind might possess, dramatically emphasizing what lay outside the real and rational world of phenomenal occurrences. For the American historical romancers, the relationship between the reality of events and the fictional perception of those events was a self-conscious and somewhat anxious concern of the text.

Recently, critics of American literature have begun to dispute whether, in the nineteenth century, the term *romance* meant anything different from the terms *novel* or *fiction*. Since all of these terms have something to do with loosening the connection between imagination and reality, it is not relevant to my basic contentions about the American historical romance tradition whether we call these works historical romances or historical fictions.[5] Whether or not the term *romance* signified to nineteenth-century American writers and critics a difference between British and American fiction, American literature did evolve a form recognizably different from its British counterparts. The term *romance*, especially as it is used by Hawthorne, conveniently locates the American writers' intentional heightening of the disparity between realistic and nonmimetic modes of representation. The Americans make this disparity an even more pronounced condition of their writing by wedding their unrealistic fictional form to the investigation of history. Historical romance is a fact of American literary history, and it is by no means accidental.

Cooper is not America's first writer of fiction or the American romance (the first American romancer is Charles Brockden Brown, to whom Cooper refers in the preface to *The Spy*). And *The Spy* is certainly not the most impressive or even definitive representative of the genre (that will come from Hawthorne a generation later). Nonetheless, I begin this book on American historical romance with *The Spy* because it navigates the crossing from British to American fictionalizing, and it raises, almost schematically, the major theoretical issues of fiction writing that distinguish American from British literature. In addition, it hints at the form, and even the subject matter, adopted by the American tradition. As a *historical* romance, *The Spy* contemplates the relationship between fiction and the world, especially the relationship between a fantasy or romance of reality and a world ostensibly documentable and verifiable by the strategies of historical analysis. It begins to define then the kind of text in which history and fiction coexist or more to the point the kind of text in which history and a romance variety of fiction coexist. *The Spy* raises as a central issue what, finally, the subject of such a hybrid fiction will be: the romance of the mind or the history of the world.

THE FICTIONALITY OF HISTORY

It is useful to note that both history and romance provide the author with a form of textual derestriction not unlike the act of fictionalization itself. As Wolfgang Iser points out, the British writer of historical fiction to whom the American tradition, and especially Cooper, are most indebted was himself attracted by the marvelous and the supernatural. Sir Walter Scott, argues Iser, turned to historical materials because, like the devices of gothic literature to which Scott and his American counterparts were very much attracted, they extended the "limited sphere of action" and disclosed "forms of human conduct that had been excluded by the moral novels of the eighteenth century." History, however, could "make the extraordinary seem probable." It could "derestrict the natural" without, as Michael Davitt Bell puts it, sacrificing the relationship between the text and world. Bell argues that by "attributing to reality itself the 'romantic' or 'poetic' qualities of subjective imagination, American writers, influenced by associationist aesthetics and by the example of Scott, attempted to bridge the chasm between fantasy and experience, fiction and fact. . . . [H]istorical romance and romantic history . . . offered an apparent mode of reconciliation; they provided a rationale . . . by viewing 'romance' as a 'historical' or 'realistic' mode whose 'reality' just happened, luckily, to be 'poetic' or 'romantic.' "[6] For at least one large school of American historians, with whom we can associate Cooper, history was romantic art. It preserved the relatedness of fiction and the world.[7]

If American literature of the late eighteenth and early ninteenth centuries had evolved into the mimetic realism of nineteenth-century British fiction, Cooper could be cited as one more writer who dramatized a fortunate relationship between fictionality and historicity. This is the relationship that would provide prose fiction with the self-confidence it needed to resolve its anxieties about writing. But an important swerve takes place that sets the American tradition off in a different direction. This swerve is decidedly away from the real world that the nineteenth-century British novel would eventually offer and, instead, back to the gothic, marvelous, supernatural, romantic universe where fiction had originated and that had always seemed precisely the opposite of history and realism.[8] Cooper does not go the whole route to the historical romances of Hawthorne, either thematically or structurally. Nonetheless, he evidences the skidding away from the British path that would culminate in a distinctly American form.

The major difference between Scott and Cooper lies in what both of them call the "neutral ground" of writing. This is for Cooper, the place where the separation between England and its colonies occurs. It is also where the separate lives of American and British fiction begin. According to Iser, Scott developed the "extensive neutral ground, the large proportion, that is, of manners and sentiments that are common to us and to our ancestors" in order to forge "links . . . between the reader and historical reality."[9] Cooper's neutral ground initially constitutes the same kind of region of mediation. Indeed, *The Spy* enlarges the territory of that neutral ground. In Cooper's book the neutral ground stands not only between past and present but between two different national audiences, "natives of different countries" (p. 29), as Cooper calls them. Like Hawthorne's "neutral territory," Cooper's neutral ground of exaggerated melodrama would even seem to stand between the imaginary and the real.[10] It would seem to be the largest neutral ground there is.

But Cooper's is a strange neutrality. Even before he begins to explore the neutral ground of his fiction, he engages the problem of literary politics and finds it insoluble. What kind of book, Cooper asks in the preface to *The Spy*, should he, as an American author, be writing? Should it be a book written in America, about America? "There are several reasons why an American, who writes a novel, should choose his own country for the scene of his story": "the ground is untrodden," it will have "all the charms of novelty," and "an author may be fairly supposed to be better able to delineate character and to describe scenes, where he is familiar with both." But "there are more against it": "although the English critics not only desire, but invite works that will give an account of American manners, we are sadly afraid they mean nothing but Indian manners" (p. 31). As for his American audience, "familiarity will breed contempt" (p. 32). Cautiously surveying the territory his novel will traverse, Cooper realizes that there is no way that he can send his "compliments" equally to all of his readers (p. 34). There is no book that he can write that will satisfy all, or even most, of them.

Furthermore, if Cooper's goal were the reconciliation of his British and American audiences on some sort of neutral ground, he seems to have chosen an extremely odd way of attaining it. The British and the Americans both occupy the neutral ground of Cooper's book. But this is precisely the book's subject: the War of Independence in which the neutral ground exists as the field of battle. The past that Cooper's novel reconstructs is the time and place of the most keen antagonism between his two sets of readers. It hardly constitutes a safe position, and it is hardly neutral. Simply, Cooper's neutral ground is not an unspecified, transcendental space between here and there or now and then. It is the neutral ground itself, the particular place and time in the history of the nation when the English and the Americans battled for control. As the novel proceeds, it becomes the scene of intense violence.

The novel's very neutrality is one source of violence. Barbara Foley has suggested that Scott and Cooper imagined "historical process as affording a position of political and epistemological objectivism." She observes, however, that their works are "saturated with ideology."[11] I believe that this ideological saturation, the nonneutrality of the historical and fictional ground, is a major and explicit concern of Cooper's novel. As Cooper writes the neutral ground of American history into the presumably neutral ground of the fictional or historical imagination, he discovers no neutrality or simple commonality in historical or literary events. By definition, America's neutral ground represented politicization, ideology, and nonneutrality. It came into the world through a trauma of separation, a wrenching relocation of thought and feeling, that could not but issue in partisanship. And that condition of America's neutral ground originated and defined, for Cooper, America's continuing cultural and literary identity.

For Cooper, therefore, there is no neutral ground apart from the specific, geographical, historical ground of this particular country and of the tradition it established.[12] For the same reason, there is also in Cooper's view no writing that is not political. The neutral territory between the imaginary and the real was just as problematic for Cooper as the neutral ground between England and America. The problem for Cooper was not whether fiction could reproduce reality but whether writing could be made to reveal its biases and acknowledge its origins. Cooper believed the preference for fictional over historical composition itself represented a politics of writing, hardly neutral. As soon as Cooper introduces the tension between his British and American readerships, he momentarily entertains the idea of removing the novel from the natural, political, social universe altogether. He might, anticipating Edgar Allan Poe, write gothic romance or science fiction. "The moon," he suggests, might be "the most eligible spot in which to lay the scene of a fashionable modern novel, for then there would be very few who could dispute the accuracy of the delineations" (p. 32). But this is not the path Cooper chooses. Though gothic derestriction (like Scott's historical-fictional derestriction) could neutralize the text, placing it outside the sociopolitical reality that renders literary statements ideological, neutrality itself is a position as likely to alienate readers as any other literary choice. Gothicism could involve its own kind of literary politics. "When we suggested the thing to the original of our friend Caesar," Cooper records, "he obstinately refused to sit any longer if his picture was to be transported to any such heathenish place" (p. 32). Similarly, there are no lords and castles in his book not because "there are none in the country," which would be reason enough. Rather, he records, "we heard there was a noble within fifty miles of us, and went that distance to see him, intending to make our hero look as much like him as possible. When we brought home his description, the little gipsy who sat for Fanny declared she wouldn't have him if he were king" (p. 33).

Cooper playfully evades responsibility for his literary choices by declaring his preference for representational over gothic literature, patriotically relocating the sources of his mimetic representation from England to America. He reveals that, according to some "European notions of our States," America *is* the moon (p. 32) as American manners are "Indian manners" (p. 31). Thus he focuses attention on two particularly knotty problems of fictionalization—its relationship to history and its claim for neutrality between the mind and the world. Through gothic and historical-fictional derestriction, literature feigns neutrality, a story with no political implications. There are, however, *originals* that lay claim to the author's imagination. Authors, then, ultimately are responsible to someone or something. Cooper's tale of the neutral ground is a story of the dangers posed to both literature and history by the pretense to neutrality. Cooper's neutral ground *is* history. Specifically, it is the history of the lack of neutrality that inheres in every human decision, even the decision to remain neutral.

The originals to whom Cooper owes his patriotic loyalty are, of course, as fictive as the fiction he goes on to write. Even as he concedes his political purposes, Cooper seems to retreat from them. He appears to opt for the moon, though his moon is a psychological inner space (like Poe's) rather than a region of cosmic or historical otherness. By agreeing that America is not the moon, that it possesses no lords and castles, and that American literature will therefore have to find other topics and figures worthy of literary representation—subjects like the American Revolution, characters like black servants and tender young patriots—Cooper simply restates the common assumption of nineteenth-century American intellectuals: the subject of an American fiction would have to be America. But in relocating the sources of mimetic representation from what actually exists in America to fictive originals, Cooper takes a critical, theoretical step toward what will be the prevailing characteristics of American fiction in the nineteenth century. Romantic fiction is intensely preoccupied with fictionality itself. It is concerned with the originating idea out of which a literary work evolves and with the responsibilities that this imposes on authorship. Cooper recognizes the politicization of reality. Yet he will not withdraw from the world. Rather than resolve the conflict between life and fiction, his originals preserve the tension between them. They are originals both insofar as they are unique unto themselves and as they are creations of Cooper's creative intellect.

Cooper's fiction of his reasons for writing a book that explicitly acknowledges its Americanness does nothing less than recast mimesis. Cooper locates the sources of fiction's depictions and the rules that govern its representational processes within the imagination. But literature, he insists, cannot directly transcribe the pure contours of the imagination that produces it (by disentangling the imagination from the sociopolitical realities that restrict and define it). Neither can it portray absolutely the sociopolitical reality that lies beneath its interpretations. It has become fashionable in literary criticism to argue for the essential fictionality of history.[13] In *The Spy*, Cooper explicitly refuses to dwell on this indeterminate intermingling of fact and fiction. Instead, he explores the tensions between factuality and fictionality that are not resolved, either by claiming the superiority of one kind of representation over the other or by meta-arguing the synonymity of the two. Cooper's text does not simply play between restriction and derestriction. It specifically recognizes the indeterminacy of historical perceptions and literary statements, and then it self-consciously undertakes to restrict what has been derestricted. Much critical discussion of the American romance tradition has assumed that history and romance are synonymous in American fiction and that often the romantic elements conceal ideological content and disguise literary motives.[14] Cooper is aware of the relationship between history and fiction that *The Spy* dramatizes.

FICTION AS CONCEALMENT

The Spy is one of America's first detective novels, a spy novel that, like Poe's tales of ratiocination two decades later, attempts to spy out the processes by which knowledge of the world is acquired, individual identity is achieved, and stories and histories are written.[15] For Cooper, as for Poe, reality wears the garb of fiction, and vice versa. It is almost impossible to distinguish the one from the other, to assign a point of origination, and to give the story a beginning or, equally important, an end. Nonetheless, for Cooper (if not for Poe), it is imperative to do just this: to prevent history and fiction from merging into a sea of phenomenological, epistemological, and moral relativism that totally obliterates the separateness and uniqueness of people, nations, ideas, and stories themselves.

It is no accident, and therefore it comes as no surprise, that this novel about the relationship between imagination and the world should focus on the theme of concealment and revelation. The book almost seems to side with history against fiction. Proceeding through numerous disguises and masks, hidden identities, deceptions, and role playing, the book concludes with a series of recognition scenes, affirming the role of the historical imagination in clarifying the meaning of human events. It would seem to identify, once and for all, who is who and what is what, in relation to the Revolution and its aftermath. Birch's interview with Washington (pp. 420–25), which is concurrent with the events of the book; the conversation of Wharton Dunwoodie and Lieutenant Mason, thrity-three years later (pp. 426–32), in which the very appearance of Wharton Dunwoodie's name reveals the subsequent and heretofore unknown history of the Wharton and Dunwoodie families; and, on the last page of the book (p. 432), the final revelation of Birch's and Harper's identities, withdraw many masks and solve many mysteries. These discoveries evolve as historical knowledge generally does: through narratives, both fictional (like the scene between Birch and Harper) and factual (as in Dunwoodie's and Lieutenant Mason's conversation within the world created in the fiction); and through documents, like the letter, which are history's own written records:

> *Circumstances of political importance, which involve the lives and fortunes of many, have hitherto kept secret what this paper now reveals. Harvey Birch has for years been a faithful and unrequited servant of his country. Though man does not, may God reward him for his conduct.*
>
> George Washington. (p. 432)

The book concludes: "It was the spy of the Neutral Ground, who had died as he lived, devoted to his country, and a martyr to her liberties" (p. 432).

But one mask is not withdrawn: the ontological status of the text itself. Is Cooper's novel imitating, emulating, or interpreting history? Is the fiction simply the mask history must wear, reluctantly perhaps, in order to cater to the need for coherence and what Frank Kermode calls "followability"?[16] Or does the fiction compete with history, engulfing it so fully as to threaten to displace real events and real people with a story far more coherent and compelling than any story history alone might tell? The end of the book is a web of uncomfortably interlocking historical and fictional structures even more troubling, perhaps, than the actual deceptions that occur within the story. Birch is a wholly fictional character who acts out the problems (and some of the solutions) inherent in a world of masks and deceptions, in which some disguises are honorable and some are not. But inhabiting a text that is defined by real historical events (like the Revolution) and populated by real historical figures (such as Washington), Birch is also a fiction masquerading as a fact. Indeed, he is a fiction so powerful in his authority that he reduces historical figures to his own lesser status of fictionality. As a character within the book, Birch is subordinate to the equally fictional Harper. But he—and Harper—are not subordinate to the historical George Washington. Within the world of the novel Washington exists only as Harper. When the name George Washington appears as the signature on the letter written by Harper to verify Harvey Birch's identity, it is as if the fiction did not exist to flesh out and confirm the reality, but the reality was at hand to lend its signature to the fiction. In the figure of Mr. Harper, which disguises equally two George Washingtons, one fictional, the other factual, the ontological collapse is total. The George Washington whose name appears on the final page of Cooper's novel represents not only Harper's real fictional identity but his real factual identity as well. It makes no difference, finally, whether a fictional identity conceals another fictional identity or a historical one. In either case, disguise functions to confound the reader's knowledge of the world, whether it is a mimetic representation of the world within a text or a world that is a text or a historical world that is outside the text. *The Spy* treads on a perilous quicksand that only subsequent generations will begin to learn how to cross.

Whatever else is going on, this depiction of ontological indeterminacy does not portray a happy coincidence of perceptual modes. Various kinds of seeing do not conspire to confirm one another. Conspiracy of another sort is the book's subject. In the world of *The Spy*, everyone and everything (including history and fiction) wear masks. The ontological status of the masks cannot be determined. Neither can their moral quality. Birch and Harper are noble spies, but what are we to do with Mr. Wharton's opportunistic neutrality, the cowboys' and skinners' exploitative misrepresentations, Isabella's destructive misstatement of her relationship to Dunwoodie, and in perhaps the most dramatic example, Wellmere's painful deception of Sarah? In a neutral ground, there is no clear inside or outside to fiction or history. There is also no simple mechanism for distinguishing one kind of disguise from another. A historical identity cannot be so easily distinguished from a fictional one, a moral purpose from an immoral one, a Tory from a patriot, or, indeed, a patriot from a rebel. A spy, after all, is a real individual with a "real" identity who consciously adopts a fictional one; as Cooper's spy is himself fictional, one is reminded of Thomas Pynchon's dizzying whirlpool of actors becoming lawyers becoming actors once again.

This tension between the apparent revelations of history and the endless undecipherability of experience is the major preoccupation of this novel, which is also about the American Revolution. In the story of Henry Wharton, even more than the story of Harvey Birch, we discover the link between Cooper's theoretical interests and his political purposes. Henry Wharton dramatizes the problem of the spy on the neutral ground. The Tory brother of the patriotic Fanny, Henry disguises himself in order to visit his family. Eventually he is arrested (and rearrested) as a spy. He is tried and sentenced to death, and to escape hanging, he assumes still another disguise, designed by the archspy of the novel, Harvey Birch. The plot is intricate, even absurd. The movement of the book toward this scene can only strike the reader as curious if not downright perverse. From the beginning of the novel there is no particular reason to sympathize with concealment as a general strategy of life. Henry Wharton's own disguise in the opening pages is so foolish and disagreeable as initially to alienate even his own family (p. 43). And it is so poorly contrived as to be immediately penetrated by Mr. Harper. Harper's advice would seem to make both immediate and long-range moral good sense: "You really look so much better in your proper person. . . . I would advise you never to conceal it in future. There is enough to betray you" (p. 69). Disguises, especially in wartime, raise problems, as Henry himself realizes: "It is true my purposes are innocent; but how is it to appear? My visit to you would seem a cloak to other designs" (p. 55). The seriousness of the issue of disguise and the subjectivity involved in defining who or who is not a spy—that is, who is on the wrong side and who is on the right—can be seen in the example of Major André:

> "When men like Major André lend themselves to the purposes of fraud [explains Henry's father], it is idle to reason from qualities, much less externals."
> "Fraud," cried his son quickly; "surely, sir, you forget that Major André was serving his king, and that the usages of war justified the measure."
> "And did not the usages of war justify his death, Henry?" inquired Frances. . . .
> "Never!" exclaimed the young man. . . . "Frances, you shock me; suppose it should be my fate, even now, to fall into the power of the rebels—you would vindicate my execution—perhaps exult in the cruelty of Washington."
> "Henry!" said Frances, . . . "you little know my heart." (Pp. 72–73)

"Ain't one spy as bad as another?" asks the simple-minded but perceptive Katy (p. 322).

But the problem is even more difficult than knowing how to designate and judge spies during times of military crisis. Harry B. Henderson has suggested that "the Revolution presented a thorny problem for Cooper the fierce patriot and for Cooper the lover of good social order: how to distinguish the process of national growth from the accompanying throes of dangerous philosophies and social upheaval. . . . The book's central conflicts . . . concern the problem of honorable behavior in a chaotic historical situation."[17] But for Cooper, the unnatural state of war is also the natural state of existence. Disguise is a condition of reality; concealment, a fact of life. The problem with Henry's trial is that he is judged and punished not for what he himself has done, but for what someone else, namely, Major André, has done. The radical error that results from this trial suggests the dangers of historical analogizing.[18] Harper recognizes this when he first confronts Henry's family with the fact of Henry's concealedness: "Had I motives for betraying him, they could not operate under present circumstances" (p. 68). As a guest in the Wharton home, Harper, also in disguise, will not betray circumstances, even to expose a spy. Moral decision making cannot be generalized and made applicable theoretically or analogously. It depends on a particular context that demands specific moral judgments.

These moral judgments are, however, an even more complex matter still. The "heart," mentioned by Fanny, implies a truth that can be reached. Once reached, this truth will insure that justice will prevail. Cooper, however, makes the opposite case in describing Henry's escape from prison. In a slapstick scene, abounding with concealed jokes and puns as if language itself is as ambiguous as everything else in Cooper's universe, one of the rebel officers says to the peddler, "Off with you, for a hypocritical, psalm-singing, canting rogue in disguise." He does not realize how close to the mark he is. "He goes," says the peddler of Henry, who is now disguised as his black servant, "to return with a book of much condolence and virtue to the sinful youth above [Henry], whose soul will speedily become white, even as his outwards are black and unseemly" (p. 362). Birch's strategies and maneuvers are far from inspiring—if anything, they are a form of cheap and deceptive humor, and they place Birch, not to mention Henry, in extreme danger. Henry voices what could also be the reader's hesitations: "If the risk to yourself be so heavy, retire as you came, and leave me to my fate" (p. 355). He knows that this is no make believe, no frivolous drama. Henry trusts in the power of the heart and in the possibilities of human justice. "Dunwoodie," he argues, "is making, even now, powerful exertions on my behalf; and if he meets with Mr. Harper in the course of the night, my liberation is certain" (pp. 355–56). He believes that Harper, knowing the truth, will reveal the truth, and that he will be saved.

Harvey Birch, the seasoned spy, understands otherwise. Harper, who, as Henry knows, is a rebel leader, and, as we know, is Washington himself, must conceal his identity in order to keep functioning. Even if Dunwoodie locates him, he will not be able to reveal or use his "power" on Henry's behalf. "If I fail you," says Birch, "all fail you. No Harper or Dunwoodie can save your life; . . . no other power on earth, not even Washington, can save you" (p. 356). Birch knows how elusive and unstable the truth is. His gratuitous addition of the phrase "not even Washington" does not serve simply to emphasize his point nor is it simply an aside to the reader, sharing the private knowledge that Harper is Washington. Rather it emphasizes the hopelessness of Henry's situation. Henry does not even know that in calling on Harper he is invoking the supreme authority of the American Revolution, and that even this authority cannot help him. Birch's statements stress how rarely an authority or power exists that will verify the truth of a human situation and address it. His reference to Washington alludes to the gap between stable, locatable truth and human action. Reality itself seems to conspire to conceal truth, or at least to repress it. In order to be Washington, that is, to fulfill the role of rebel leader, Washington must pretend that he is someone else, less powerful than himself. As Harper, he is further required, by historical contingencies, not to use whatever power he might possess. Birch knows that there is no true authority or power to which Henry can turn. The phrase itself, "not even Washington," coming as it does almost from outside the text and transgressing the ontological barriers between American history and Cooper's fiction of that history, suggests that not even the power of history is real enough to save Henry. Were history itself to enter this novel and try to wield its authority, Henry would still be lost. Cooper is claiming that just as fiction cannot bail out history by rewriting and recasting the traumas of the historical past on some kind of neutral, because fictional, ground, so history cannot redeem fiction, coming in to resolve or neutralize fiction's dilemmas. History and fiction cannot validate each other. There does not exist within history, as separate from fiction, any kind of authority or true identity to which the rest of history may appeal, and similarly for fiction. There is no simple transcendent, metaphysical truth in Cooper's world to which either history or fiction or a mixture of the two can attain.

This does not mean, however, that human beings do not live in history, or that fiction may not achieve historical accuracy, either in its own terms or in terms of historical events outside itself. Caught between their own powerlessness and the world's, Birch and Henry do precisely what every human being does, whether in life or in literature. They conceive and enact a plot that is simultaneously a factual involvement in human existence (with origins in and consequences for the real world) *and* a rather trivial, absurd indulgence in the costumes and roles of play acting that only tangentially, imitatively, touch human existence. They enact a story, and they make history.

The scene of Henry's escape from prison may be ludicrous. But it is also full of care: "In the manner of the peddler there was an odd mixture of care and humor; the former was the result of a perfect knowledge of their danger and the means necessary to be used in avoiding it; and the latter proceeded from the unavoidably ludicrous circumstances before him, acting on an indifference which sprang from habit, and long familiarity with such scenes as the present" (p. 358). Perfectly aware of and totally familiar with their danger, the peddler authors what is simultaneously a real-life event, serious and urgent in the extreme, and a self-conscious, parodic fiction that expresses his awareness of how comic and ludicrous the attempt to evade life's dangers really is. It is not that the peddler doesn't care. He does, anxiously. But Birch is indifferent—he is detached and therefore reflective. He recognizes the dilemma for what it is and he determines to proceed as best he can. Like the neutrality of Cooper's not-so-neutral ground, indifference momentarily turns away from the conflict between history and fiction or between truth and action. It acknowledges and accepts that while no plot can promise that it will succeed in promoting the cause of truth and justice—indeed, while no plot can assure us that there is a truth to be justly unfolded—the enactment of plot positively affirms and reinvests the processes of living and writing.

As the political connotations of the word *plot* suggest, plot depends on the concealments that the search for truth would want to overcome.[19] The literal plotting of a historical event like the American Revolution, for example, requires that a man like Washington not use his power to expose secrets or to reveal identities. To do so would damage, even halt, the plot through which the historical events are realizing themselves. Because a plot depends on its impenetrable secrecy, to expose it would be to put an end to it. "The veil which conceals your true character cannot be raised in years—perhaps never," says Harper to Birch, "in me you will always have a secret friend; but openly I cannot know you" (pp. 423–25). Only after his death is Birch's identity, let alone his relationship to Harper and Harper's true identity, revealed to his world, in the note that Harper writes for him and that Birch then conceals on his person for the duration of the story. Throughout the story, Birch's identity is as genuine a historical identity as anyone can ever possess. It is even documented, literally inscribed within him or, at least, on him. But this identity depends on its remaining concealed. Like Harper, what Birch is depends on who he is not known to be; his apparent identity enables him to perform a true function. Not accidentally, the revelation of the note (such as it is) coincides with the conclusion of the book. What is true about historical plots is also true of fictional plots: without the secrets of plot there is no more plot; and when the secrets are revealed, the plot comes to an end; that is, historical events and fictional events—and the identities that emerge through them and on which they depend for their own enactment—cease.

THE NEUTRAL GROUND OF POLITICS AND DIFFERENCE

History involves the acting out of plots. And the acting out of plots involves the concealment of the so-called truths that would legitimate plots. Plots cannot therefore verify some imagined transcendental truth. They can only serve to activate a relationship between individuals and their world that is comic, serious, and finally, meaningful. Writing also involves constructing a plot. This plot, like the plots of history, is to some significant degree a deception, a concealment of something else. And yet the plots of fiction, like the plots of history, can also establish meaningful relations with their world. They do so precisely by managing their plots in the way of history.

Like Birch, Cooper possesses "perfect knowledge" of his world, past and present. He has a "long familiarity" with the dangers, physical, intellectual, and cultural, posed by the English to the new nation.[20] *The Spy*, like Birch's attempts to help Henry, is a perfectly serious endeavor both to promote the American cause and to extricate the British from their unfortunate entanglement in America. But, as Birch is indifferent to the plot he enacts, so Cooper, through strategies of humor and melodrama, preserves a kind of indifference to the story he tells. Cooper knows that, for all its deadly seriousness, the not-so-neutral ground of American history and fiction is a playground, where the Americans dress up as rebels and pretend to be something other than British. The American Revolution might be no more than the presumptuousness of overly self-confident upstarts. Even the idea of writing a distinctly American literature in English is represented in Cooper's novel as a foolish ambition fuzzily conceived. The originals to whom Cooper claims to owe his conception are represented by an illiterate black man, who imagines the moon is some heathenish place near Guinea, and a little gypsy, who is only a cute little Fanny.[21] Leaving racism and sexism aside, Cooper's conception of an American story has to do more with an interest in nether regions than with any carefully formulated literary program or conception of nationhood. As Cooper's preface makes clear, and as the escape scene reiterates, there are no genuine originals. There is nothing that does not have antecedents—in history or in fiction. Nothing is wholly unique, different, or individual. Everyone is a disguised version of someone else, an imitation of another reality or fiction. Thus it is absurd to privilege one original over another.

Cooper's novel self-consciously declares itself American and insists that it is telling American history. Cooper believes origins are ontologically indistinguishable, and plots are only concealments of truths, which cease to be true when they lose their secrecy. Differentiations, however, can be made; identities can be claimed. Indeed, difference, or differentiation, not superiority or transcendence or priority, as ideologues on both sides of the American Revolution had supposed, is Cooper's objective in the war for separate identity and independence. If the American nation erred in imagining itself utterly different from the British from whom it had separated itself, it was only balancing off the British perception of the Americans as imitation British. Difference or separateness was precisely what British rule denied to America. It was therefore what America had to acquire in order to become a nation: "It was only after the establishment of their independence that the American people seemed to consider themselves as anything more than sojourners in the land of their nativity. Before that era, their inventions, their wealth, and their glory centered in the isle of Britain as unerringly as the needle pointed to the pole. Forty years of self-government has done for them what a century and a half of dependence was unable to achieve" (p. 317). For Cooper, the story that precisely transcribes another is just what America and its history are not about. Cooper's description of the American landscape (p. 317) makes the case for American individuality. If America pursued the straight and narrow path, it would arrive only at what has already been thought and written. It would condemn itself to be a poor imitation of England, without any independent life. Cooper's main point is affiliated with his specification of the neutral ground itself: history and fiction, the world and the self, justice and truth are not interchangeable. These terms exist only as differentiations from each other. Cooper writes a historical fiction of differences, not a metaphysics of equivalences or transcendent truths.

America and England might be similar, but they have different groundings. In order to be its own nation, and to convey its unique intellectual and cultural content, America must project its difference, and England must recognize it. America may not yet be fully formed. Its plots, like all plots, and its landscape can partake of comic distortions and chaotic randomness, and they can recall other plots that are not even American. But there is no America separate from its "uneven surface" (p. 317). Henry's farcical escape to freedom, or Cooper's witty tribute to his literary and spiritual originals, is no more than the honest confession of this unevenness. It is a recognition of the absurdity of trying to make ends and means coincide. Only by expressing the lawlessness of an untamed and unruly nature, giving full credit to the accidents and circumstances of life on the new continent (p. 317) and playing out the charade of history, can America voice its genuine independence. The nation must exaggerate, not conceal, its difference from England.

In a curious scene toward the end of the book, Cooper renders the American situation, and the demands that it places on its writers of history and fiction, with all of its comic seriousness. A British clergyman whom Lawton finds wandering in netural ground admits of being "so little acquainted . . . with the rebel uniform" as to be unable to distinguish the Americans from the "natives."

> "Natives!,", says Lawton, I have that honor, I do assure you, sir."
> "Nay, sir, I beg that I may be understood—I mean the Indians—they who do nothing but rob, and murder, and destroy. . . ."
> "And did you expect to meet those nose-jeweled gentry in the Neutral Ground?"
> "Certainly," returned the chaplain, confidently; "we understand in England that the interior swarms with them."
> "And call you this the interior of America?" cried Lawton. (Pp. 312–13)

Lawton proceeds to demonstrate the impossibility that the British, "at a distance of three thousand miles" (p. 313), can accurately perceive the American continent. For this reason, the American spokesperson, whether it be Lawton or Cooper, must enlarge the image he projects, even to the point of comic absurdity. America had to self-consciously assume its costumes, act out its plots, and embrace its history, even if these were only versions of other stories and histories back through an indeterminate series. Cooper self-consciously addresses his novel to "natives of different countries" in order to stress the unique nativeness of all his readers. This "nativity" (p. 313), in a particular place and time, is the source of differences. It is also, however, what people must recognize about each other to insure mutual respect and a proper perspective. British rule had made the Americans into subjects. Through the Revolution, America turned away from the British mirror world in which it had become trapped. The Revolution signaled the invention of a new, large, independent American self-image.

Three thousand miles effectively concealed America from the British, but it would take a mere "thirty-three years" (p. 426) to disguise America from itself. The "old war," which comes cloaked in rumor and whisper (p. 428), is veritably incomprehensible to Wharton Dunwoodie. And if it seems, in 1812, a mere "difficulty" too insignificant to be discussed (p. 429), how much more indistinct it must have been for Cooper's readers, both American and British, even in 1821. If Cooper wooed his readers of opposing national factions not by forgetting past conflicts but by remembering them, he cultivated his American audiences by reminding them of these same conflicts through which their ancestors had carved out the national identity. The job of history, in Cooper's view, was to preserve the record of the past. History had to keep alive its difference from the present, so that the present would not subsume and absorb the past as the subject over which it ruled.

Like Sir Walter Scott, Cooper wanted to reconcile his readers to each other and to the past. He recognized that in order to engage readers a text must establish some means of promoting sympathy and identification. He could not, however, discover any genuinely neutral ground, either in history or in literature. The relationship between America and England (and between the American generations) thus depended on the recognition and acceptance of the differences that divided them. For Cooper, the neutral ground between here and there, then and now, is not determined by a theory of history but by history itself. In Cooper's case, this is the history of a nation coming into being on a neutral ground that does not stand between history and the imagination but is reality, a reality of conflicts, poses, and irreconcilable alternatives. Cooper's grand, if somewhat comic, epic of the American Revolution charts with a bold stroke the clamor of this neutral ground where individuals competed not only for political power but for perceptual authority. What authorized American history would authorize American literature as well. This was the recognition of the idea of America as inseparable from the story of America, from the genuine historical facts costuming that story. Cooper viewed the crossroads of America with great affection and no small measure of plain good humor. His benevolent disposition distinguishes Cooper from most of America's other nineteenth-century writers of historical fiction. But Cooper touches the heart of the American subject. Directing his steps away from the path pointed to so unerringly by America's magnetic attraction to England, he commits himself to the uneven, intersected surface of America and makes his home on the neutral ground of historical, cultural, and epistemological conflict.

Literalism and the New England Mind: Charles Brockden Brown's *Wieland* as American History

In *The Spy* Cooper establishes the conditions of political, ideological, and cultural nonneutrality that for generations of American authors will define the neutral ground of fiction. *The Spy* dwells on the fictionality of all human endeavors—the costumes and plots that constitute all stories, whether fictional or real, and make all stories, to some extent, versions of each other. But *The Spy* insists on the differences that distinguish stories from each other, finally separating fact from fiction. For Cooper, the emergence of a genuinely American history and literature depended on the recognition and acknowledgment of these differences, not only between the histories of nations but between a story and the reality in which it is set. However much Cooper plays with the American Revolution in his text, costuming his characters and composing witty dialogue, he must yield to the demands of a real world far more potent than his fantasy can ever be. Writing history into his fiction, Cooper commits his story to the reality from which it originated and which it serves. He recognizes that, for American authors, the story of the neutral ground must be the story of the specific place and time when a unique entity called the United States of America came into being. The nation's fiction, like its history, would have to express its utter difference from all other stories to be truly American. Cooper's novel is no more pure romance than it is simple history (or even realistic historical fiction). It is historical romance, attending to the differences between history and fiction and activating the relationship between them.

The Spy, however, does not go the full route of the American historical romance tradition. Cooper does not understand, or at least does not admit, that American independence was threatened by more than the lure of England and English history. Rather, an independent and self-sufficient America was equally endangered by a conception, a fiction, of America that originated precisely in the rejection of America's British origins. For a certain group of writers it seemed that America functioned under the dangerous illusion that American history did not originate in human history at all, that it was, from the beginning, the product of an original conception that transcended or predated human history. This anxiety of the historical romancers who succeeded Cooper (and even one who preceded him) was far more radical than Cooper's concern that, without a proper consciousness of the subjectivity of historical narratives and without an appropriate commitment to acting out the specificity of the uniquely American situation, American history might simply become an imitation or conclusion of some other—namely, British—history. These writers wondered if the American national consciousness had ever entered history or if it conceptualized American history as separate from its romantic fiction of history. *The Spy* posits a cooperation between reality and fiction in order to create history on the one hand and historical romance, or literature, on the other. The historical romances of other nineteenth- and twentieth-century writers explore the lack of this cooperation, examining the failure of historical consciousness to penetrate the fictions of the American mind. They trace the consequences to American history and literature of a romantic perception of reality, which seemed to be history itself to their American protagonists.

In a long series of historical romances, from Charles Brockden Brown's *Wieland*, Hawthorne's "Roger Malvin's Burial," and Melville's *Billy Budd*, through Sherwood Anderson's "Godliness" and Flannery O'Connor's "A View of the Woods," one type of scene structures the investigation of the relationship between history and romance. This is the scene of the sacrifice of the son by the patriarchal father. what is called in the Hebrew Bible the *akedah* or binding of Isaac. Although many critics have noted that these texts contain versions of the Old Testament narrative of the binding of Isaac (and its New Testament reenactment as the sacrifice of Christ), only one critic has remarked on the recurrence of this biblical episode in all five works, and no one has suggested what this recurrence might mean.[1] In all of these works, I believe, the scene of the *akedah* dramatizes the moment when, in the view of these writers, America failed to step meaningfully into history. As I demonstrate below, it is a moment that they believed was destined to occur in America, and that had to be represented in the enactment of this particular biblical scene, because of a special American-Puritan relationship to the *akedah* that had made the *akedah* a key event, not only of Old Testament history and its New Testament reinterpretation, but of American history as well. American fiction contains what we can call, playing off the Arcadian myth of America, an *akedian* romance of America. This is not the story of America as a New England, nor is it the story of an American Eden, creating a new history for the world as well as for itself (though it has to do with an ironic reversal of this story). Rather it is the story of an America that attempts to secure for itself a special covenant with God through an act of sacrifice like the akedah. This act of self-sacrifice, which follows out a transcendent and (by definition) nonhuman historical plot, loses the human dimensions of history for America. Not only does it fail to secure the special American covenant that would make America a continuation of Christian scripture, but, in killing off the generations on which continuity depends, it threatens to put an end to national history. Even in stories like *Billy Budd*, where a literal end to America is not imagined, there is the strong suggestion that American history is doomed to become nothing more than a repetition of poorly understood archetypes of destructive tendencies. The akedian romancers inherit the scene of the akedah as a figure for covenant from the American Puritans. Akedah was wrought up in the Puritans' expectations for America, not as a New England, but as a New Israel. In the view of the historical romancers, the Puritan attempt to project American history as a culmination of scriptural events stood in the way of the new history that America might come to enjoy. It produced a pattern of repetitions that seemed to the historical romancers more like gothic tales of terror than a national epic. The akedian romances, which I discuss in the next three chapters, record this gothic tale. They restore to public consciousness the historical events and the commitment to the life in history sacrificed by the akedian heroes.

COOPER'S *THE PRAIRIE*

In *The Prairie*[2] Cooper confronts the failure of American historical consciousness that will occupy historical romancers throughout the nineteenth and twentieth centuries. He also hits on the scene of the akedah that will be the medium of their investigation. He stages this scene curiously and obliquely, not deciphering its relevance to the problems of American history and American historical consciousness that he himself recognizes. Cooper's failure to follow through on his own insights contributes to a perpetuation of the ahistorical, mythic imagination that troubles his inheritors in the literary tradition.

The Prairie dramatizes the new nation's overreaching of its destiny. Cooper does not put a fine point on the fact that the family of Ishmael Bush does not reincarnate the line of Abraham. Indeed, like the other Ishmaelites of the desert, the Indians (p. 39), Bush and his family reverse the direction of Christian history. They substitute a law even older than the old law for the new law they have left behind in the settlements (p. 70). The trapper justly resents their invasion of the prairie. These Ishmaelites would wrest American history out of the control of the Mosaic law, entrusted to the trapper, whose dying word, "Here" (p. 460), recalling Abraham's and Moses's responses to God, invokes the covenantal tradition interrupted by Ishmael Bush. (The prairie is referred to as a desert, thus recalling the forty-year wanderings of the Israelites.)

The death of the patriarchal trapper, uttering the word *here*, markedly contrasts with the death scene that immediately precedes it. This scene concludes the history of the lawless, barbaric Bushes. It also seals off the possibility that these new settlers of the American deserts will complete the contours of a new history of the promised land. Having discovered that his brother-in-law Abiram White has murdered his "first-born son," Ishmael exacts what is explicitly identified as biblical justice: he kills the murderer of his child. But the manner of Abiram's death, bound on a rock, suggestively recalls a familiar biblical moment that has nothing to do with punishment but is related to covenant. This is the moment of Abraham's binding of Isaac (pp. 428–30). In *The Prairie*, the terms of the analogy are clearly wrong. This is Ishmael binding a brother-in-law whose name recalls the very Abraham for whom Ishmael (brother of Isaac) now substitutes himself. Abraham's first-born is not sacrificed in the biblical story. In Cooper's story, he is literally killed by Abiram, as Abiram is later killed by Ishmael. Other imprecisions abound. In the Bible, before he is called Abraham, Abraham's name is Abram. The name Abiram evokes Abraham's earlier identity. But whereas Abram's name is eventually changed to Abraham, adding to it a *ha*, which represents the name of God, Abiram undergoes no transformation. His consciousness remains godless from beginning to end. Even the name Bush suggests the fraying of the biblical thread. Like the Mosaic revelation, Ishmael's also issues from a bush. In a story containing a Mosaic figure like the trapper and an Ishmael Bush, it is unclear which bush Cooper wishes us to recall. Therefore, we cannot easily decipher Cooper's message concerning the nature of the American covenant. We can only conclude that Cooper's story signals the end of America's special covenantal relationship to God, not its beginning. The Ishmael Bushes disappear, never to be heard from again, and the trapper dies heirless.

American history, Cooper seems to suggest, in this story and in other of his works as well,[3] enacts a story strangely reminiscent of Old Testament history yet dangerously, painfully oblique to the meaning and tenor of biblical events. Cooper did not perceive that the American failure to incarnate scriptural history might be the result of more than the avarice and godlessness of America's pioneers. It instead could have resulted from the tendency to imagine America in biblical terms, the cast of mind that Cooper himself unselfconsciously demonstrates in *The Prairie*.

SENTIMENTAL FICTION, GOTHIC ROMANCE

Hawthorne's "Roger Malvin's Burial" realizes fully the larger problems of historical consciousness that the scene of the akedah raises (and in which Cooper may unwittingly have conspired). "Young Goodman Brown" links that problem with the larger issues of skepticism and faith to which it is related. Nonetheless, Charles Brockden Brown's *Wieland, or the Transformation: An American Tale*[4] is the first American historical romance to construct this scene of the akedah and to begin to fathom its deep implications for American history. Wieland's sacrifice of his family is doubtless the most striking action of the book. This is the event that spurs Clara to write her memoirs. It is the action against which we measure all of the lesser evils, misapprehensions, rationalistic errors, and religious crises that punctuate the novel. What is far from clear, however, is how Brown intends the reader to understand Wieland's quasi-divine, consummately destructive action. Is the book, as one critic has argued, an "enlightenment sermon against credulity and religious fanaticism?" Or does it constitute a diatribe against enlightenment complacency, playing out a vibrant allegory of a godless eighteenth-century world being made to acknowledge the essentially Calvinistic terms of human existence?[5] The answer, I think, is that the object of Brown's attack is a variety of literalistic imagination that mistakes the fictions of the mind for the actualities of human experience. This literalism, in Brown's view, characterized both the fanaticism of American Puritanism and the rationalism of the eighteenth-century enlightenment. *Wieland* is a history of the evolution of this literalism through the seventeenth and eighteenth centuries. It is a literalism, Brown almost perceives, that had to do with the lack of historical consciousness implicit in reenacting the scene of the akedah.

The ostensible theme of *Wieland* is as universal as it is enlightened, and it does not seem intent on undermining rationality, which the book ultimately succeeds in doing. Clara's memoirs are a sentimental, moral fiction of eighteenth-century vintage. The theme Clara announces in the novel defines a set of conventional and totally unremarkable, moral, psychological, and epistemological assumptions that hardly seem the stuff of gothic romance: "Make what use of the tale you shall think proper. If it be communicated to the world, it will inculcate the duty of avoiding deceit. It will exemplify the force of early impressions, and show the immeasurable evils that flow from an erroneous and imperfect discipline" (p. 11). She rearticulates these themes in the final lines of the book:

> I leave you to moralize on this tale. That virtue should become a victim of treachery is, no doubt, a mournful consideration; but it will not escape your notice, that the evils of which Carwin and Maxwell were the authors owed their existence to the errors of the sufferers. All efforts would have been ineffectual to subvert the happiness or shorten the existence of the Stuarts, if their own frailty had not seconded these efforts. If the lady had crushed her disastrous passion in the bud, and driven the seducer from her presence when the tendency of his artifices was seen; if Stuart had not admitted the spirit of absurd revenge, we should not have had to deplore this catastrophe. If Wieland had framed juster notions of moral duty and of the divine attributes, or if I had been gifted with ordinary equanimity or foresight, the double-tongued deceiver would have been baffled and repelled. (Pp. 275–76)

How Clara can address the extraordinary events that have befallen her own family in the same breath that she discusses the conventional and clichéd Stuart tragedy is jarring at best, unfathomable at worst. The relation between the two stories, a gothic romance and a traditional eighteenth-century sentimental fiction, is far from obvious. But it is clear from the tone of Clara's discourse as well as from the content of her statements that she sees them both as lessons in reason and moral order. Her memoirs fulfill her rational, didactic needs. Significantly, she addresses "no supplication to the Deity" (p. 11). Clara is a late eighteenth-century rationalist, spokesperson for the unassailable principles of enlightenment reason. She believes in the causalities of human events and in the rational underpinnings of experience. She pens her memoirs to identify the links in a chain of events that has culminated in the story at hand (p. 65).

But Clara is like the famous Poe narrator who also sets out to write a "most homely narrative," "a series of mere household events," and who addresses his story "to some intellect more calm, more logical, and far less excitable . . . which will perceive, in the circumstances . . . nothing more than an ordinary succession of very natural causes and effects."[6] Poe's narrator discovers that the inherent logic he seeks is grotesque illogic. Similarly, Clara cannot discover principles of universal reason. Despite her best efforts to the contrary, the tale she writes is a hysterical rehearsal of the gothic romance that, throughout her story, she resists. Michael Davitt Bell has argued that, "making finally explicit the tensions implicit in the works of his more conventional fiction-writing contemporaries,"

Brown's novel renders "the conventional fear of fiction [its] overt preoccupation."[7] In a similar vein, Nina Baym has suggested that Brown intends *Wieland* as a "hoax" or "melodrama." Clara, she argues, is not a real character but a device by which Brown tricks his audience. This trick, I believe, logically results from the dangers of fictionality as Bell describes them. "Each mistake Clara makes," says Baym, "leads her plausibly to the next, so that her story achieves a specious, ungrounded, consistency. Diverted from its original task of conveying Wieland's madness [which would have produced a tragic novel], the novel is experienced as a continuous sequence of mysterious events, systematically misread by a narrator motivated to make sense of her world." "The structure of her reasoning, beginning from false premises and making continual reference to wrong facts, is . . . grotesquely . . . logical."[8] But Brown is not Poe. He is not primarily exploring the disjunctive fictions of a diseased intellect. The grotesqueness of logic is itself Brown's subject. The first object of Brown's attack, then, is not Wieland the murderer but "Wieland," the peculiarly rationalistic story Clara thinks she is telling.

It is not difficult to establish the serious limitations of reason in *Wieland.*[9] One need only consider that Wieland himself is the product of an enlightenment education. Though "there was an obvious resemblance between him and [his] father in their conceptions of the importance of certain topics, and in the light to which the vicissitudes of human life were accustomed to be viewed . . . the mind of the son was enriched by science and embellished with literature" (p. 31). This is the American-enlightenment dream come true. But even if we were to dismiss Wieland as hereditarily diseased and therefore not susceptible of the medicinal influences of reason, we would have to deal with the failure of the novel's archrationalist and archatheist, Pleyel, to utilize reason appropriately. Whereas "moral necessity and Calvinist inspiration were the props on which [Wieland] thought proper to repose . . . Pleyel was the champion of intellectual liberty, and rejected all guidance but that of his reason" (pp. 33–34).

Pleyel can no more explain the phenomena of the mysterious voices than can Wieland. Under the influence of inexplicable phenomena, he draws all the wrong conclusions. Throughout the novel Pleyel is confidently rational and stupidly imperceptive. It is difficult to blame Pleyel for being unable to understand what is going on. The reality that Brown creates defies rational interpretation. The voice that rouses Clara from her dream proceeds flawlessly from a narrative context to which Carwin has absolutely no natural access. The voice prophesies events in the future, and Clara's salvation literally proceeds from the same voice, articulating the same words. In the dream sequence itself, the flow from natural to supernatural is eerily perfect, and chilling. We cannot naturalize or rationalize it:

> The lulling sounds of the waterfall, the fragrance, and the dusk, combined to becalm my spirits, and, in a short time, to sink me into sleep. Either the uneasiness of my posture, or some slight indisposition, molested my repose with dreams of no cheerful hue. After various incoherences had taken their turn to occupy my fancy, I at length imagined myself walking, in the evening twilight, to my brother's habitation. A pit, methought, had been dug in the path I had taken, of which I was not aware. As I carelessly pursued my walk, I thought I saw my brother standing at some distance before me, beckoning and calling me to make haste. He stood on the opposite edge of the gulf. I mended my pace, and one step more would have plunged me into this abyss, had not some one from behind caught suddenly my arm, and exclaimed, in a voice of eagerness and terror, "Hold! hold!"
>
> The sound broke my sleep, and I found myself, at the next moment, standing on my feet, and surrounded by the deepest darkness. Images so terrific and forcible disabled me for a time from distinguishing between sleep and wakefulness, and withheld from me the knowledge of my actual condition. (Pp. 74–75)

The novel remains slippery, purposely ambiguous, on all the major issues. The text does not even indicate definitively whether the voice of eagerness and terror originates within Clara's dream. Like Cooper's *Spy*, Brown's *Wieland* presents a world of undecipherable masks, concealing other equally unfathomable masks and fictions.

The moment that confounds interpretation is not an isolated occurrence. It has roots deep in the Wieland family history, in Wieland's father's strange premonitions of his death by fire. Indeed, Clara's dream surfaces throughout the story, dragging its romantic possibilities into the light of day and overshadowing events that are unquestionably real. Carwin, who cannot possibly know the content of her dream, warns her:

> Fear me not: the space that severs us is small, and all visible succour is distant. You believe youself completely in my power; that you stand upon the brink of ruin. Such are your groundless fears. . . . The power that protects you would crumble my sinews and reduce me to a heap of ashes in a moment, if I were to harbour a thought hostile to your safety.
>
> Thus are appearances at length solved. Little did I expect that they originated hence. What a portion is assigned to you! Scanned by the eyes of this intelligence, your path will be without pits to swallow or snares to entangle you. (Pp. 107–08)

Pleyel independently conjures up the image of the same dream, ironically associating Carwin with the image of the pit: "I had thought to have been the first to disclose to thee his infamy; to have warned thee of the pit to which thou art hastening" (p. 121). "Should I not haste to snatch you from the talons of this vulture? Should I see you rushing to the verge of a dizzy precipice, and not stretch forth a hand to pull you back?" (p. 150). The pattern of spine-tingling coincidence of thought and language—divine intention or demonic artifice—haunts the novel. It prevents the story from settling into the simple moral narrative that Clara wishes she were writing.

Brown's point is that reality is unfathomable and that its unfathomability is terrifying. But the faith in reason that motivates Clara is itself so reasonable that the reader must wonder why Brown feels compelled to attack reason so strenuously in this novel. Surely, reason is not in itself a bad thing. No matter how seriously Clara and Pleyel fail to understand reality, their misperceptions never culminate in Wieland's murderous deeds. Yet Clara's faith in reason is not only the occasion of interpretive error but in some way the source of the tragedy that overtakes her and her family.

As Clara's memoirs draw to a close, the repressed object of her story surfaces. The story that emerges from the crevices of Clara's psychological inattentiveness points us to the problems of Clara's enlightenment philosophy, echoed in the previously quoted words that conclude the book. The story that Clara would like to be telling, which is analogous to the story of Maxwell and the Stuarts, is the story of a clever ventriloquist who so muddled the characters' rational faculties as to cause them to act impetuously and immorally. Had the participants to the tragedy, Clara insists in her conclusion, provided themselves with proper access to the facts, and if they had bothered to learn the origins of the voices they hear, the tragedy could have been prevented. Appearances, Clara believes, do express realities, if only we know fully how to interpret them. Like Henry Wharton, Clara believes in a saving truth. But Clara tells the story of *Wieland* no more than the ventriloquist's voices express unambiguous truths that can be deciphered with the right tools. When Clara tries to make her rational, sentimental story emerge, she is made to confront what her rationalistic assumptions would preclude: the double-tongued deceiver. This appearance of the double-tongued deceiver (the "grand deceiver" or "devil" as he is called elsewhere [pp. 216 and 222]) exposes the story Clara tries to avoid.

BROWN'S "AMERICAN TALE"

Wieland is the first of many American tales to record the story of the new American Eden and the fall that took place there.[10] Some critics have suggested that *Wieland* is an allegory of the inevitable, divinely ordained repetition of biblical history in America. This is contradicted, however, by the nature of Clara's (and Wieland's) fall. Their fall is caused not by the double-tongued deceiver (Carwin or devil), but by their faith in reason, which would deny the devil his due. Blessed with a new rational understanding of reality, Pleyel and Clara would free America from history, especially from the history of scripture. America would be not the Eden of scripture, which marked a moment in history before the fall, but an Eden immune from history, existing eternally within an ever-renewable moment of recreation.

The seventeenth-century Puritans would seem utterly different from these naive eighteenth-century rationalists. They were not so foolish as to imagine they might reconstruct paradise in the new world. Indeed, the American Puritans were not interested in evading biblical history. Fully recognizing the implications of the fall, the American Puritans dwelled on the covenant of grace that promised personal and national redemption from the sin and evil that America's eighteenth-century rationalists did not believe existed. But in imagining themselves what Edmund Morgan has called "visible saints," capable of directly interpreting their experience as evidence of divine providence and therefore competent to construct a community of saints, the Puritans laid the groundwork for the assumptions of enlightenment reason that Clara and Pleyel so forcefully express.[11] The second scriptural story to which *Wieland* recurs, the akedah, is the same event that figured prominently in the Puritans' covenant theology. The superimposition of this other moment of biblical history onto the story of Eden-America does not simply reinforce Brown's feeling (like Cooper's) that American history only ironically, or parodically, reproduced the contours of biblical history. Rather it associates the religious fanaticism of Wieland, with its attempt to reproduce literally scriptural experience, to the ahistorical enlightenment rationality of Clara and Pleyel, which ignores biblical events altogether. Both seventeenth- and eighteenth-century mentalities, Brown suggests, incarnate similar tendencies of imagination. Enlightenment reason, in Brown's view, is a direct descendant of the most troubling feature of Puritan orthodoxy: its belief in visible sanctity, in the possibility of judging the condition of a human soul on the basis of external appearances in order to construct a community of saints. This tendency reemerged in eighteenth-century America as a belief in sense evidence as problematical and destructive as the old Puritan attitudes.[12]

Wieland deals with the issue that, according to several interpretations (including Hawthorne's), toppled the American theocracy in the seventeenth century, the issue of visible sanctity. During his testimony at the murder trial, Wieland explicitly raises this issue:

It is strange: I am known to my judges and my auditors. Who is there present a stranger to the character of Wieland? who knows him not as a husband,—as a father,—as a friend? yet here I am arraigned as a criminal. I am charged with diabolic malice. I am accused of the murder of my wife and my children!

It is true, they were slain by me: they all perished by my hand. The task of vindication is ignoble. What is it that I am called to vindicate? . . . You charge me with malice; but your eyes are not shut; your reason is still vigorous; your memory has not forsaken you. You know whom it is that you thus charge. The habits of his life are known to you; the soundness of his integrity, and the unchangeableness of his principles, are familiar to your apprehension; yet you persist in this charge. . . . Think not that I speak for your sakes. . . . I make not an effort to dispel your illusion; I utter not a word to cure you of your sanguinary folly; but there are probably some in this assembly who have come from far; for their sakes, whose distance has disenabled them from knowing me, I will tell what I have done, and why.

It is needless to say that God is the object of my supreme passion. (Pp. 187–88)

Wieland assumes that because he is known to the community as a good father and husband and because they know him to have a "single and upright heart," he must be a saint. Like many a Christian before him, Wieland has spent his days "searching for the revelation of [God's] will" (p. 188). But Wieland craves to prove himself through literal "sacrifice" (p. 189). He desires more than a private, internal revelation. When Wieland prays, "Oh, that I might be admitted to thy presence! that mine were the supreme delight of knowing thy will" (p. 190), we can imagine that he wishes what any devout congregant might want. He longs for a chance to prove himself faithful to the divine commandments. But Wieland also desires the "privilege of direct communication" with God and of "listening to the audible enunciation" of His pleasure (p. 190). The difference between Wieland's prayer and the prayer of any other religious person could be one of nuance. In context, however, Wieland's special conditions of divine intercourse cannot be ignored. Wieland is decidedly not a typical seventeenth-century typologist who applied "scripture to the self" in order to discover "spiritual paradigms and . . . the workings of Divine Providence in one's own life."[13] Rather he is like an American Puritan, interested in reliving the biblical moment.

Wieland's prayer is answered, as psychologists of wish fulfillment would not be surprised to discover, in the materialization of the vision he so desires: "I opened my eyes and found all about me luminous and glowing. It was the element of heaven that flowed around. Nothing but a fiery stream was at first visible; but, anon, a shrill voice from behind me called upon me to attend" (p. 191). Ann Kibbey has pointed out in a recent study of Puritan rhetoric that for the Puritans "conversion was an alteration of the hearer's system of reference . . . from one system of meaning to another." Meaning was specifically associated with "material shapes," in the form of words, natural events, and people.[14] This is Wieland's situation exactly. In a typically Puritan way, he needs to have his visible sanctity visibly revealed. As spirituality is made visually and audibly manifest, Wieland responds to the vision by literally murdering his wife and children in sacred sacrifice to the divine behest.

Wieland's behavior surely exaggerates Puritan precepts. But he expresses a disposition of mind that is consummately Puritan. Indeed, the Puritans themselves recognized it as a danger. In Puritan terminology, Wieland believes that "justification" precedes "sanctification." Election to the divine community of saints puts the saved individual out of reach of human law:

> My motives have been truly stated. If my judges are unable to discern the purity of my intentions, or to credit the statement of them which I have just made; if they see not that my deed was enjoined by heaven, that obedience was the test of perfect virtue, and the extinction of selfishness and error, they must pronounce me a murderer.
>
> They refuse to credit my tale; they impute my acts to the influence of demons; they account me an example of the highest wickedness of which human nature is capable; they doom me to death and infamy. Have I power to escape this evil? If I have, be sure I will exert it. I will not accept evil at their hand, when I am entitled to good; I will suffer only when I cannot elude suffering.
>
> You say that I am guilty. Impious and rash! thus to usurp the prerogatives of your Maker! to set up your bounded views and halting reason as the measure of truth!
>
> Thou, Omnipotent and Holy! Thou knowest that my actions were conformable to thy will. I know not what is crime; what actions are evil in their ultimate and comprehensive tendency, or what are good. Thy knowledge, as thy power, is unlimited. I have taken thee for my guide, and cannot err. To the arms of thy protection I intrust my safety. In the awards of thy justice I confide for my recompense.
>
> Come death when it will, I am safe. (P. 201)

America's Puritan ancestors, interested in realizing a federal as well as a spiritual authority in New England, had been aware of the primary danger that this kind of strict orthodoxy posed to Puritan theocracy. Hence their strenuous, even fanatical, opposition to the antinomianism of Anne Hutchinson and the Quakers. The American Puritans, Michael T. Gilmore states, protected a "middle way."[15] Much of their rhetoric and policy making concerned preserving the path between the single, sanctified soul and the social entity.

Michael Colacurcio maintains the American Puritans could barely glimpse that the real and ultimately deadly danger to their theocracy was not the potential anarchy of antinomianism but the concept of visible sanctity itself. This visible sanctity underlay both the antinomianism they rejected and the federal theology to which they subscribed. The ultimate breakdown in covenant (or federal) theology, according to Colacurcio, occurred when visible sanctity no longer represented a viable mechanism for realizing the Puritans' political and social objectives. Following close on the heels of the halfway covenant, which itself represented a serious compromise on the issue of visible sanctity, the Salem witch trials of 1692 called into question whether sanctity could be proven on the basis of appearance. As the argument ran in 1692, if a devil could assume the guise of a saved person, then how could witches be distinguished from saints?[16]

Wieland, the saint-as-murderer, poses the same problem of spectral evidence that bedeviled the seventeenth-century Salemites. Wieland himself points to this problem in his final words to Clara: "Neither thee nor myself have I cause to injure. I have done my duty; and surely there is merit in having sacrificed to that all that is dear to the heart of man. If a devil has deceived me, he came in the habit of an angel. If I erred, it was not my judgment that deceived me, but my senses. In thy sight, Being of beings! I am still pure. Still will I look for my reward in thy justice!" (pp. 253–54). When devils can parade as angels, when the senses must interpret unreliable, nonsense data, then sanctity must not be relegated to the realm of the visible and sensual but, as Augustine had always recognized, and as Roger Williams had reiterated for the American polity, to the realm of the spiritual community of God's invisible church.

In *Wieland* Brown asks, simply, what if the appearances one witnesses are motivated by evil rather than good spirits? What if the voice is not Catherine's but Carwin's, the vision not a manifestation of the divine but rather the foggy emanations of an overheated imagination? Or, to put the question in the Puritans' own terms, can the devil assume the body of a saint? and if so, how can one interpret spectral evidence? what is the meaning of visible sanctity? By forcing external realities to conform to internal and highly subjective images of reality, Wieland disallows the possibility of human error and divine inscrutability. He closes the saving distance between divine perfection and human fallibility.

Wieland's story recapitulates the evolution and demise of the American theocratic ideal and the visible sanctity on which it was founded. But Wieland is not, like Hawthorne's Young Goodman Brown, educated to seventeenth-century Puritan ideals. He is trained to become an eighteenth-century rationalist. Thus *Wieland* also suggests how the tendencies of thought that first established the dangerous new world covenants survived the demise of Puritanism and resurfaced not only as Great Awakening revivalism but as enlightenment reason. Wieland's heinous deeds have two significant antecedents in the novel. The first is the inheritance of his father's religious fanaticism. The second is his enlightenment education in reason, that is, in the criterion of indubitable sense-data to which Wieland also refers in his defense testimony. Thus, for example, when Theodore Wieland is first accosted by his wife's voice on his way to the Temple (the novel's first instance of a voice articulating wild injunctions), he argues for the "testimony of [the] senses." He presents the universe in an unambiguous disposition of either-or alternatives that recall Puritan bifurcations and disjunctions. "I must deny credit to your assertions," he tells Pleyel and Clara, "*or* disbelieve the testimony of my senses. . . . One thing . . . is true: *either* I heard my wife's voice at the bottom of the hill, *or* I do not hear your voice at present" (p. 41; italics added). What is true must be true in all places and at all times. The evidence of the senses is unchallengeable. One must credit the voice in the flame as being an accurate spokesman of the divine and not a deviant or satanic pretender or a psychotic longing after divinity.

Wieland's inability to separate appearance from fact, his insistence that the two are the same, suggests the persistence of the old Puritan problem into the eighteenth century. We can now specify even more precisely the unresolved tensions in Clara's language as she attempts to beat back the devil in whom she refuses to believe. We can also identify the cast of mind and the language of Pleyel's own brand of enlightenment wisdom. Despite Pleyel's secularism, he reincarnates the most rigid aspects of the Puritan mentality. He applies its most stringent doctrines precisely where the Puritans themselves had brought the pressure to bear. Pleyel knows, intellectually, how shaky appearances can be. He allows Clara to defend herself because "adverse appearances might be numerous and specious [and] false" and "some error may possibly lurk in those appearances which I have witnessed" (p. 141). Like the Salem witch trial judges, Pleyel understands the problem of spectral evidence. He cannot, however, allow anything "to outweigh the testimony of his senses" (p. 129). He cannot believe he is "deceived" (p. 138). When the "blackest of crimes," "witchcraft" (pp. 137 and 140) occurs, what other evidence can be applied? Pleyel insists that he is "not constituted [Clara's] judge." His "office is to pity and amend and not to punish and revile" (p. 138). Nonetheless, he judges the "bewitched" Clara (p. 144) and her "fall" (p. 138) automatically, unconsciously reenacting judgments similarly sweeping and unfounded. Pleyel is not literally accusing Clara of covenanting herself with the devil, but the language of his accusation so strongly evokes this other context of witches and devils that we cannot help but close the gap between the seventeenth- and eighteenth-century rehearsals of the same controversy. Like Arthur Miller two centuries later, we are forced to look for the devils in our political and sexual behavior while recalling that politics and sexuality precipitated witch-hunts in the first place.[17] Pleyel's experience complements Wieland's by exploring the sexual innuendoes of religious fanaticism. And together Pleyel and Wieland anticipate Hawthorne's Young Goodman Brown, who like Pleyel is "precipitate and prone to condemn" and who "instead of rushing on the impostors and comparing the evidence of sight with that of hearing . . . stood aloof, or . . . fled" (p. 137). Charles Brockden Brown knew Young Goodman Brown before Hawthorne ever invented him; and Hawthorne may well have acknowledged this fact in the rhythms and details of his protagonist's name. There are, then, two causes of what Clara later identifies as an "erroneous and imperfect discipline" such as Wieland's. The two might appear to derive from diametrically opposite sources. But both the theological assumptions and experiences of the elder Wieland that reappear, almost atavistically, in the younger Wieland and the enlightenment educations of Wieland, Jr., and Pleyel converge in one overriding principle: outward and visible signs evidence inward and spiritual meaning. Puritanism and the American enlightenment narrate a single intellectual history.

THE SEPARATION THAT CONFOUNDED CHURCH AND STATE

To understand the line of descent that Brown traces, from the Puritans to the eighteenth century, it must be pointed out that Wieland himself is a son. Wieland's story begins when his father fails to perform the act of sacrifice that his son eventually enacts. The commandment is never specified in relation to Wieland, Sr., but the accumulated evidence of the story—the allusion to the elder Wieland's temple as the "'rock'" (p. 23), the statement that the commandment is "transferred . . . to another" (p. 20), and the fact that the elder Wieland, though "a fanatic and a dreamer" (p. 19), finds himself unable to execute it, suggests that it is the same sacrifice of the son, or of the family, that the younger Wieland finally brings to a conclusion. Wieland's father, a Calvinist of the most rigorous variety, represents an intensification of certain aspects of Puritan belief. However, he also represents a withdrawal from some of Puritanism's most dire characteristics.[18] Coming to America to escape religious persecution, he would have liked to establish a visible church. But Wieland, Sr., recognizing the limitations of visible sanctity, builds the only visible church whose purity he can guarantee, the church of which he is the only member: "He allied himself with no sect, because he perfectly agreed with none" (p. 18). Incapable of making judgments about others, he extends to them an "invincible candor" and "invariable integrity."

"Few men, equally sincere in their faith, were as sparing in their censures and restrictions, with respect to the conduct of others. . . . Other modes [of worship], if practiced by other persons, might be equally acceptable" (p. 19). He even attempts to educate the Indians, an activity that did not interest most American Puritans.

As both a rigorous Puritan and a proponent of religious tolerance, Wieland, Sr., evokes the American pilgrim who insisted, most vociferously, on the "typical uniqueness" of the Israelites and argued with the Puritan establishment that "only the spiritual Israel and seed of God, the newborn, are . . . one."[19] For Roger Williams, the antitypological moments of Christian history—the birth and resurrection of Christ—had already occurred. The American Puritans, therefore, like the Israelites before them, could only stand in a typological, or figurative, and spiritual relationship to the major events of divine history. To think otherwise was heresy: the New England Puritans, he suggested, were under the dangerous misapprehension that "the letter [is] yet in force, and *Christ Jesus*, the *mystical* and *spiritual King of Israel* is not yet come."[20]

By the time Theodore Wieland, Jr., is confronted with the same theological choices that his father faced, the safeguards of typological thought controlling Puritan belief had fallen away. This had happened, however, not only because of strong forces within Puritanism itself, but, ironically, because of the separation of church and state for which liberal-minded and enlightened people like Williams had argued.[21] The liberal Christian or deist or atheistical world of the eighteenth century, in Brown's view, retained the Puritans' faith in visible evidences. It manifested the Puritans' desire to construct an ideal community. Indeed, the eighteenth century was much more radical than the seventeenth. The seventeenth century had only thought to rebuild Israel. The eighteenth century wished to recreate Eden. Under the pressures of secularism and liberalism, the antinomianism that the Puritans had held in check was fully unleashed. *Wieland* traces the belief in visible sanctity as it moved from the highly controlled theological environment of the seventeenth century to the more secular and enlightened world of the eighteenth century, where the seeds of Emersonian transcendentalism, the creed of American individualism, and the violent conflagrations of the Revolution were already beginning to evidence themselves in another dramatic religious episode, the Great Awakening.[22] It is no accident that the Great Awakening occurred when it did: Locke may have legitimized the premises of Puritanism for Jonathan Edwards, but he did not invent them.[23] The line from Edwards to Franklin, and from Edwards to Emerson and Thoreau, is, as several critics have suggested, more direct that we might imagine.[24] According to Brown, the logical outcome of Edwards' Great Awakening might just be a Theodore Wieland, elevated to the role of saint, or, indeed, to the role of biblical type or even antitype, by a relocation of the typological moment in a natural universe understood as controlled by eschatological patterns. Wieland prophesies a line of egocentric selves that represent a conflation of the worst aspects of Puritan and Transcendentalist thought.[25]

Wieland, Jr., untutored in theology, fails to understand that Christ has interceded on man's behalf. The Old Testament has been supplanted by the New Testament. The covenant with Abraham has been replaced by the covenant of grace. Wieland's act is the consummate expression of hubris and misconceived religious passion. It represents an atrophy of both proper religious understanding and human sensitivity. In literally reenacting the sacrifice of the son, in literally imagining himself the heir of Abraham, as Bradford and Winthrop and others had literally imagined themselves heirs of Moses, Wieland exceeds playing Abraham to his family's Isaac. He vaunts himself into the role of God and plays deity to the crucifixion of his family. The Old Testament story concerns Abraham's reverence and respect for God. His is the sacrificial willingness that ultimately paves the way for human salvation. But Wieland's rehearsal of the biblical episode disastrously closes the gap between the Old Testament and the New Testament, between type and antitype, and between the self and God. Wieland is archantinomian and, in Hawthorne's description of Young Goodman Brown, an arminian "to boot."[26] He is the ultimate literalist. The consequence of his deed is a lethal blow to theocracy, even though the deed logically extends Puritan theology. The more guarded Puritans had always suspected the internal contradictions of their theology. Dialectically, Wieland is also the consummate secularist or pagan, an American rationalist who has eliminated God and grace from his universe of self. The story he enacts is as gothic as anything of which the enlightenment thought it was ridding itself.

Wieland is not a sentimental fiction appropriating scriptural themes or a gothic parody of biblical materials. Nor is it a typological reaffirmation of America's biblical plot. It is not an allegory of either an American fall or an American redemption. Rather it is the record of a misrelationship to history that began with a desire literally to unwrite scripture and rewrite it as American history. This desire became, in the eighteenth century, a wish to dispense with history altogether. In this way, the novel is a history of American thought. Its subject is a certain kind of imagination, which Brown identifies as an enlightenment recasting of a Puritan mentality. This kind of imagination repeats the most horrendous aspects of human experience because it interprets the world literalistically. It is an imagination, Brown realizes, though less vividly than Hawthorne, that also fails to take into consideration historical realities. Clara would like to historicize her brother's experience. She wants to produce memoirs that mimetically reproduce experience and that provide an appropriate moral message. But Clara cannot believe that her story has historical precedents. "The experience of no human being can furnish a parallel," she claims (p. 12). Her story, therefore, lapses into the reductive language of a hysterical gothic text because she cannot recognize the history in which her story participates. She cannot grant the primacy of history's consequences for human behavior, preferring to retreat to a prehistorical and ahistorical Eden of her own making. Nor can she see in Wieland's actions and in her own perception of reality remnants of the immediate American past, which she would also like to eclipse. Effacing the past, she repeats its perceptual errors. Brown's text is historical where Clara's is not. "If history furnishes one parallel fact, it is a sufficient vindication of the writer," Brown records in the preface. "Most readers will probably recollect an authentic case, remarkably similar to that of Wieland" ("Advertisement," p. 8).[27] That authentic case may in fact be one of several cases, from Eden and the akedah through the interpretation and reconstruction of these events in Puritan ideology and history. Even in the adjudicating of moral law, then, precedents exist that must be taken into account.

Brown's purpose in telling (or rather, retelling) the biblical archetype and the story of its endless reenactment is decidedly not to assert the inevitability of a certain pattern in American history but to suggest that repetitions occur because of a failure to recognize these archetypes of human experience. Repetitions result from an unwillingness to temper the archetype with the individual differences that convert myths of history into meaningful, self-conscious and self-willed historical realities. There are primal scenes in historical as well as personal development: historical analysis and psychoanalysis may not be so far apart. Like Hawthorne after him, Brown sketches this primal scene to restore it to conscious memory. Like his descendant in the art of historical romance, he can only hope that his readers will be better historians and psychologists than his characters.

3

Covenant, Sacrifice, and the Loss of Eden in the Promised Land: Historical Consciousness in Hawthorne's "Roger Malvin's Burial"

In recalling the biblical paradigms that correspond to events in the Wielands' lives, Brown employs what Karl Keller has described as a structure of typological thinking. Brown does not, however, use this typological structure to assert an identity between American and biblical history. Nor does he subvert typology to dramatize the ambiguity of human experience.[1] Rather he presents a critique of a literalistic American imagination that would interpret human events as unambiguous and visible evidences of another reality (natural or supernatural), the dimensions of which are known and to which American history can be made to conform. The origin of the typological urge concerns Brown, as it does Hawthorne, who employs a similar strategy of typological figuration. Brown is worried about the consequences of suspending the Puritans' own severe typological controls, whereby God would be made referrable and answerable to the single secular self. As typology moved from religion to romanticism to transcendentalism, the danger of reversal or collapse seemed to become extraordinarily intense to Brown, threatening to close down the life in history and to preclude the possibility that America would be anything more than the setting for a terrifying reenactment of biblical paradigms. Taken out of their scriptural contexts, these paradigms would become tales of sheer gothic terror.

Wieland is a history of a problem in American consciousness. From Brown's point of view, American Puritans and eighteenth-century rationalists evidence the same tendencies of mind, and the problems of the American enlightenment originate in the problematics of Puritanism. For all their apparent differences, especially in relation to scripture, the American rationalists and their seventeenth-century ancestors express the same troubling attitude toward history. Embedded in the moment of sacrifice on which Brown constructed his novel is another problem that Brown only glimpses: the lack of historical consciousness that his characters also exhibit. In recapitulating the story of the fall, *Wieland* records the story of America's dawning ahistoricity and its dangers. However, in reenacting the story of the akedah, the binding of Isaac, *Wieland* records the origins of this ahistorical imagination in what only appeared to be a different kind of historical consciousness.

In the Old Testament, the story of the sacrifice stands between the fall and the promised land. It establishes the covenant with Israel that, in the New Testament, became the type of the new covenant secured by the sacrifice of the divine son, Christ. For the American Puritans, the sacrifice of Isaac locates the transitional moment between the loss of Eden and the covenant with Israel and with the saints. It also defined and guaranteed the essential movement of American history, from its exodus from England through its entry into Canaan to its establishment of a Puritan theocracy in the new world. The moment of the akedah, then, is the point at which Old Testament, New Testament, and American history begins and begins anew—or ought to begin. In American history as recorded in the akedian romances, something goes wrong. Isaac lives to keep history going. The Wielands, and, as we shall see, the Bournes, the Bentleys, the Fortunes, and the McCaslins all die out, leaving no redemption in the wake of their deaths. The history and salvation that might have been perish with these families.

According to the writers of akedian romance, the original Puritan conception of America as Israel and of Americans as Old Testament patriarchs determined that it could not be otherwise. Building on what Perry Miller labeled the "narrow-minded literalism" of the American Puritans and on what Charles Feidelson also identified as their literalness and narrowness, Sacvan Bercovitch has described the essential features of the American Puritan interpretation of scripture that account for the budding ahistoricity of the American nation.[2] For the Puritans, the Bible was not merely the historical record out of which American history unfolded, a record of historical events simply more sacred than the history of America's ties with England. Instead it was the plot or transcript or prophecy of what American history would be. It was history written before the fact. This literalistic antitypological interpretation of scripture, Brown, and later Hawthorne, perceived, was essentially an ahistoricizing of the biblical text that could dispossess America of history altogether. Bercovitch writes:

The national covenant emphasized the Lord's promise to Abraham, which material-ized in the Israelite state; after the Hebrews' apostasy, the promise was renewed, this time *in aeternum*, by Christ to His Church. The renewal antitypes the earlier agree-ment; historically it establishes a developmental connection between two elect com-munities. Seen in this double aspect, the New World theocracy became a collection of saints whose public contract reflects the progress of human history and by the same token is mystically foreordained, like the covenant of grace. . . . This correspondence between "Israel" and the "new Adam" (and by extension between the "new Israel" and the "second Adam") can be made to serve, from the standpoint of historical typology, as an implicit justification of the New England doctrine of a "visible" church-state.

The Puritan colonists loudly proclaimed their orthodoxy, but when they announced that "America" was a figural sign, *historia* and *allegoria* entwined, they broke free of the restrictions of exegesis. Instead of subsuming themselves in the *sensus spiritualis*, they enlisted hermeneutics in support of what amounted to a private typology of current affairs. They were not only spiritual Israelities. . . . They were also, uniquely, American Israelites, the sole reliable exegetes of a new, last book of scripture.[3]

In the evolution of biblical exegesis, the Church had developed strategies to protect the Bible from forms of interpretation, such as allegory or figuralism, that might compromise its historicity. Historical typology was devised to prevent the reduction of scripture into an everyman's compendium of spir-itual rules and regulations, a divine *Poor Richard's Almanack*. Samuel Mather wrote that real types are "not bare *Allegories* . . . but they are a true Narration of Things really existent and acted in the World, and are literally and historically to be understood."[4] The American Puritans claimed to be historical typologists. But identifying themselves so thoroughly and literally with the ancient Israelites as to become "American Israelites," the nation of Israel incarnate, they essentially erased the historical dimension of the text. They allowed for no difference between Old Testament and new America. Therefore they eclipsed the historicity that historical typology intended. Rendering the biblical text in their own image, they converted the history of scripture into the history of self. They considered themselves visible saints for whom the invisible covenants of grace had been realized in a physically manifest church covenant that had, in the founding of America, culminated in a new federal covenant such as Israel had enjoyed.[5]

Wieland spawned a whole line of American progeny who confused per-sonal identity and desire with divine revelation. In trying to reestablish the promised land or recreate Eden they destroyed the possibility of a genuine and meaningful American history. Like their ancestor in *Wieland*, Reuben Bourne of Hawthorne's "Roger Malvin's Burial," Captain Vere of Melville's *Billy Budd*, Jessie Bentley of Sherwood Anderson's "Godliness," Grandfather Fortune of Flannery O'Connor's "A View of the Woods," and Isaac Mc-

Caslin of Faulkner's *Go Down, Moses*, all interpret their lives' experiences as if they were antitypes enacting great originating events. More important for American history, they imagine themselves capable of restoring paradise and of redeeming the promised land. Specifically, each character (except the bachelor McCaslin, who is the exception to prove the rule) imagines himself a biblical patriarch, securing the covenant through the sacrifice of the son. And in each story, the consequence of the misinterpretation of the covenantal promise is personal and communal disaster.[6] The sacrifice results in the unraveling of history back to some primal scene of self-destruction, which destroys the possibility of history in America.

ANTITYPOLOGICAL LITERALISM ON THE AMERICAN FRONTIER

In "Roger Malvin's Burial,"[7] Hawthorne explores America's antitypological ahistorical imagination and its implications for the nation's history. He recovers the elements of the American past that its ahistorical consciousness would forget or ignore, and in recording and acknowledging these events of history, he marks the crucial differences between the delusive fantasies that destroy history and the historically conscious modes of attention that help to create it.

Surviving an Indian battle, which, as several commentators have noted, was not just a type of Christian battle with the antichrist but a specially antitypological continuation of Christian as American history, Reuben Bourne and his "father" (actually, his father-in-law-to-be) are confronted with a moment pregnant with profound scriptural and American-historical portent. As many critics have pointed out, battles such as Lovell's Fight were seen by the colonists in the double aspect pointed to by both Bercovitch and Colacurcio. It was a type and therefore a historical instance of the ever-continuing battle of the saints for Christendom. It was also America's special antitypological continuation of Christian history, its rewriting of the text, as the battle moved from the Old Testament to the New Testament and then to the new American continent. The American interpretation of the Indian wars was not just a generalized providential or typological rendering of historical reality. It was an attempt to make American history coincide with biblical history, to convert current into scriptural events, as Bercovitch puts it.

In the case of Lovell's Fight, Cotton Mather had preached a sermon in which the typological relationship between the Old and New Testaments and the special, antitypological relationship between the Old Testament and America were carefully spelled out in relation to the central event in Hawthorne's story, the sacrifice of the son. Ely Stock explains:

In his sermon Mather had urged the Puritans to forget the selfish, worldly, ends which he thought were then uppermost in their minds and recall the terms of the covenant which God had entered into with Abraham, and which, according to Mather's typological reasoning, Christ, by the sacrifice of his life, had renewed. He had couched his call to faith in language appropriate to the covenant theology he was expounding: ". . . you will approve yourselves the Genuine children of Abraham: and to prove your claim to the blessings of the covenant, if you overcome the Reluctaines [sic] of Nature to it—Withhold not the Child whom thou hast loved when God calls you." The "blessings" of the covenant as enumerated in Genesis 17 were to have made Abraham a "father of many nations," "exceeding fruitful," and would have given the "land of Canaan" to him and to his "seed."[8]

In Hawthorne's story, both Reuben and Roger are seriously wounded as a result of their encounter with the Indian antichrist. If Reuben, the "son" (pp. 339 and 343), continues to minister to his father's, Roger Malvin's, needs, he will effectively lie down with him upon the "rock" (the word is repeated throughout the story) and perish with him in the wilderness. He and Roger will "withhold not the Child" and receive the "blessings" of the covenant. But the text immediately recognizes the problem of this solution. The "sacrifice," it suggests, would be "useless" (p. 346). Leaving Roger heirless, Reuben's death would effectively halt the providential destiny that the Indian wars were intended to secure. Therefore, with Roger's blessing and encouragement, Reuben returns to the community to marry Roger's daughter Dorcas and to perpetuate the race of which Roger is the patriarchal figure. But Reuben cannot reconcile himself to what he has done. This is in part because of the guilt that is borne as the inevitable consequence of his having survived (which is exacerbated by his failure to return to bury Roger and by his inability to tell the whole truth to Roger's daughter).[9] More important, however, it is the consequence of Reuben's antitypological view of history. Reuben, like Wieland, must complete the suspended act of sacrifice. Returning to that same rock, where he once almost laid down his life, now a father with his own son, Reuben (like Wieland) completes the sacrificial moment.

In "Roger Malvin's Burial," Hawthorne examines the ahistorical, antitypological literalism that both Bercovitch and Colacurcio locate in early American theological consciousness. He traces it to its disastrous consequences for both the individual and the nation. Furthermore, he links it to the biblical story that, simultaneously, set the Old Testament plot into motion, determined the relationship between the Old and New Testaments, and provided the basis for the American redefinition of covenantal history: God's covenant with Abraham.[10] Hawthorne acknowledges that it is every man's dream to be a "patriarch of his people," to be "dimly glorious" and "godlike" (p. 352). But for Reuben, under the pressure of his covenantal historiography, this fanciful craving for leadership in the national history becomes a desire literally to reenact patriarchal events. This impulse for patriarchal and ultimately divine experience originates, as it does for Wieland, with the father. Roger instills within Reuben the fervor for the covenantal relationship to the land that ultimately makes the confession of his sins impossible.[11] Godlike, he articulates for Reuben the course of providential history, including the meaning of the battle they have just fought. Scholastically he relates the typological episode in his own biography that justifies Reuben's leaving him in the wilderness, even though he admits to himself the "wide dissimilarity between the two cases" (p. 342).

But Roger Malvin is not God. He is not even an Old Testament patriarch. He is a frail human being who, no sooner than speaking the words of prophetic wisdom, encouraging Reuben on his way, lays on Reuben the burden of guilt that causes Reuben to distort his understanding of biblical texts and kill his own son. " 'And Reuben,' added he, as the weakness of mortality made its way at last, 'return, when your wounds are healed and your weariness refreshed, return to this wild rock, and lay my bones in the grave, and say a prayer over them' " (p. 344). When Reuben recalls their parting in the woods, he cannot remember the "weakness of mortality" that separates men from gods. He can remember only the "kind and generous" man who, it seemed, "had not a thought for his own welfare" (p. 346). Deifying Roger, he can only aspire to be "godlike" himself. He is his father's son and, as Fitzgerald puts it, he must be about his father's business.

Reuben errs because, like his "father," he imagines that he and Roger and later he and Cyrus are literally reenacting the moment when the covenant is granted to Israel-America. And in rewriting biblical history as human history he unwrites both of them: the divine father (Roger) having refused the sacrifice of the earthly son (Reuben), the earthly father (Reuben) imagines himself divine and sacrifices the earthly son (Cyrus). When Reuben's conscience, "a continual impulse, a voice audible only to himself" (p. 350), commands him to go forth and redeem his vow, the Puritan antitypologist in Reuben can only imagine that this voice is a "supernatural power [calling] him onward" (p. 356). Reuben is "unable to penetrate to the secret place in his soul, where his motives lay hidden" (p. 356; cf. p. 343: "the hidden strength of many another motive"). Like Wieland, he cannot see and respect the difference between his mortal self and the spirit of the divine, which, after the manner of the antinomians, he believes to be indwelling. Like Wieland, he conflates self and God and imagines himself a biblical patriarch, if not the deity incarnate. The promised land is not secured. And the plot, unraveling backwards, threatens to jeopordize Eden itself, where the innocent first of all sons was slain in the woods. Rather than subordinate himself to history Reuben Bourne makes history an extension of self. Divine history born of man, we might say, can only die an excruciating, self-sacrificial death.

One way of interpreting "Roger Malvin's Burial," which also pertains to *Wieland*, has been as an affirmation of the antitypological relationship between Israel and America. Hawthorne's story, it has been argued, demonstrates how only continuous renewal of the covenant, through sacrifice, can secure for America uninterrupted scriptural blessing.[12] Like *Wieland*, "Roger Malvin's Burial" not only recalls the issues of type and antitype, it also develops its own internal set of typologically related moments that are linked to each other in the same relationship and sequence as the original Old Testament and New Testament events. Just as Wieland's sacrifice of his family completes the sacrifice deferred by his father in relation to his son, so Reuben's killing of Cyrus brings to fruition the sacrifice that Roger does not complete in relation to him. But the story is clearly *not* an allegory of Christian history which would confirm America's special relationship to the covenant. The paradigm of sacrifice inhabits a text replete with a whole range of biblical allusions that collectively contradict and negate one another and that specifically invalidate the straightforwardness of the Abraham-Isaac motif as it emerges in the story.[13] Also, the death of Cyrus is too disturbing to support such a reading. Reuben is no saint. What he does (largely by accident) results from mental anguish and dementia rather than clear spiritual purpose. And the silent figure of Dorcas, prostrate over the body of her dead son, undercuts any more conciliatory or affirmative readings of the text.

Roger's and Reuben's reading of history has gone awry.[14] The problem lies in the appropriation of scriptural history in human history and in directing one's life by biblical paradigms. Hawthorne wrestles with a tension related to Cooper's undertaking in *The Spy*. He is concerned with separating the fiction of history from the events of history. He wishes to locate the specificity of human experience, which distinguishes among events and provides the moral basis for choice and responsibility. What is more disturbing about Roger's and Reuben's antitypological literalism is not so much the fatalities (in both senses of the word) that it causes, but rather how it evades the human contextualization of historical events, which would claim those events as human choices with mortal, moral consequences. Reuben and Wieland and the line of protagonists in which they exist attempt to evade history by embracing a mere fiction of history, absolving themselves of all responsibility for the history that they create.

For Hawthorne, divine history, despite the many repetitions and parallelisms of its plot, is not a set of interchangeable, repeating stories. It does not function either as a paradigm of human history (American or otherwise) or as a moral example transcending historical context. Rather, scripture is a continuously evolving story of human beings and their faulty, wavering relationship to God and each other.[15] Scripture is history, however divine. Though Abraham and Moses may type each other, and other characters as well, each is a separate historical figure whose story is important in and of itself. Similarly, though Christ antitypes both Abraham and Moses, he is a unique actor whose story depends on the stories of the figures who precede him. The new scriptural story of Christian revelation may repeat, reinterpret, and reinvest Old Testament events, but it does not displace those events or substitute for them.

Old and New Testament events exist on opposite sides of an ontological barrier separating the human from the divine. The completed sacrifice of Christ is different from the binding of Isaac, in which the act of sacrifice is suspended, and their typological relationship is defined by a historical movement, which at a critical moment shifts gears and leaves the purely historical universe of human circumstances behind. If, from the Christian point of view, the world of the Old Testament is primarily a human universe infused with divine meanings, the world of the new scripture is essentially a divine universe enacted by human players. The difference between type and antitype, the human and the divine, is essential.

Scriptural history, in Hawthorne's view, demands a historical typological reading that depends on two things: first, respect for the literal historicism of the Old Testament; and second, acceptance of the fact that there is only one antitype of Old Testament history, the new scriptures. Reuben Bourne does not abide by either of these demands of historical typology. He lives neither in the historical-temporal world that permits the actual unfolding of divine history, nor in the spiritual universe of the antitypological reinterpretation of the Old Testament. Historical typology creates two different temporal dimensions, each of which is equally important to the task of biblical interpretation and both of which must be preserved in order for the new and old scriptures to maintain their sacred relevance to each other and to the world. Reuben Bourne does not understand these dimensions or that on the temporal-historical axis, the axis of the real world running from past to present, divine history moves inexorably forward, each step a real step, moving toward a real goal. He fails to comprehend that the New Testament also moves forward in time, continuing the making of history, rewriting but not unwriting prior history. Reuben, like Wieland, reverses historical direction. He attempts to journey back through time, from New to Old Testament. When biological and historical necessity forces his life to unfold nonetheless, he repeats all the moments of sin and error that have characterized human history, from the Old Testament to the New Testament and into the contemporary period. These are the events, with their consequences for human history, that Reuben, repeating the moment of sacrifice, would have evaded. They become inevitable because of the biblical mode into which he has cast himself. Indeed, misrepeating the sacrifice of the son, Reuben and his fellow antitypologists catapult themselves back further than the covenantal moment with Abraham. They discover themselves repeating the original moment of sin and loss, as well as the explusion from Eden and loss of the covenant between Adam and God. Failing to take up their proper residence between scriptural and American history, and between God and self, they fail to discover a felicitous congruency between scriptural and American history, and they find that, unwriting scripture, they have also undone America.

What Roger Malvin and Reuben Bourne disastrously disrupt in their miniscripture is the historical dimension of the Hebrew Bible and of its relationship to the Christian Bible. They could have been allegorists, anathema to the Puritan tradition, or they could have become dreamers, partaking of a Freudian nightmare, for whom all realities are the same reality, all times one time. As in many of his stories, Hawthorne unearths a fatal contradiction in Puritan theology. Treading the fine line between arminianism and antinomianism, the Puritans expressed antinomian tendencies nonetheless. They held the fort against allegory through a typology so literal that it ultimately betrayed symbolic thinking and substituted in its stead a decompositional atomistic logic. Hence, they undid typology and blatantly allegorized. The Puritans' antinomian antitypologism was nothing more than a radical form of allegorization in which the biblical story was retold as if the self were God, and the Book autobiography.[16]

In sacrificing the son that their own fathers had not sacrificed, Reuben and Wieland (each succeeding generation apparently understanding the text less well) ignore the intervention of the antitypological moment (the crucifixion of Christ) and reverse the biblical direction. They repeat, rather than complete, the akedah, the binding of Isaac, with one fatal error. According to Christian interpretation, the Old Testament sacrifice could be left suspended because it looked forward to its completion in Christ, as, analogously, the sacrificial act need never be repeated because all subsequent moments would look back to an event already performed. Like Roger Malvin contemplating the death of Reuben on the rock, Abraham recognizes the implicit contradiction between God's promise that his seed will endure and

His demand that the covenant be sealed through the sacrifice of the son (the giving of the covenant in Gen. 15.3–8).[17] But Abraham is willing to grant what neither Reuben nor Roger will allow: divine and human logic are not the same, the laws of cause and effect in one realm do not necessarily pertain to the other. The world of the Old Testament is not reduced, as was Puritan America, to a set of either-or options.[18] Abraham evidences this knowledge within the biblical text itself. When Isaac asks his father "where is the lamb for a burnt-offering?" Abraham answers: "God will provide Himself the Lamb for a burnt-offering, my son" (Gen. 22.7–8). Abraham seems to know, or at least believe, that a divine substitution can occur, even if he does not know exactly how it will take place, and he certainly risks being mistaken.[19] As many biblical commentators have pointed out, it is not remarkable that God demands human sacrifice. In the Old Testament world such sacrifice was common. And the Old Testament is a historical document. What distinguishes this text from contemporary analogues is that the request is withdrawn.[20] In the Christian account, God justifies Abraham's faith and fulfills both his promise and his demand when he shifts ontological gears and sacrifices his own son, who is not wholly mortal, instead of Abraham's purely human offspring.

Hawthorne intuited what many midrashic commentators have stressed in this affecting and painful biblical moment. Crucial to the story, and emphasized in the text, is the fact that God and Abraham, and more importantly perhaps, Abraham and Isaac, are of one mind in relation to the divine demand. When Isaac questions Abraham about the missing lamb, Abraham answers him with the phrase he uses at two other junctures to signal his willingness to perform God's will, the famous *Hineyni*, "Here am I" (Gen. 22.7; Gen. 22.1 and 11: Moses responds the same way in Exod. 3.4). Abraham is as present for his son as he is for his God (the full phrase reads: "Here am I, my son"; the phrase "my son" also repeats throughout the passage). And Isaac is also there for his father. The passage ends with a verbatim repetition of a phrase that is itself emphatically repetitious, as much in the Hebrew original as in the English translation: "So they went both of them together" (Gen. 22.8; cf. Gen. 22.6). The story stresses unity of purpose and shared love among all three participants. There is no doubting that God understands and sympathizes with the human situation: "Take now thy son, thine only son, whom thou lovest, even Isaac, and get thee into the land of Moriah; and offer him there for a burnt-offering" (Gen. 22.2).[21] In the biblical stories God and Abraham and Isaac respect and love one another in proper measure, recognizing the difference between the human and the divine. In the Old Testament type, a mortal Abraham treats with a divine

God. In granting God the absolute authority due Him, Abraham is rewarded with humane consideration. Abraham is not asked to sacrifice Isaac. In the New Testament antitype of the same event, a divine God treats with a son who is not simply mortal, and the sacrifice is effected within a realm of existence that is only tangentially, covenantally related to human affairs. The introduction of the divine context in the New Testament enables God to preserve the human context of the Old Testament.

Reuben's (or Wieland's) attempt to understand and act on a logic that only God could comprehend must result in a disastrously human conclusion. The saving substitution can occur only in a universe that is, in Charles Feidelson's terms, symbolically conceived; that is, in a world that recognizes multiplicity and multivalence of meaning.[22] Abraham knew that God would provide the lamb, but by *lamb*, He might have meant a son who is lamblike or a literal ram, who will take the son's place. The exegetes of the New Testament knew that the lamb might be the son after all, if only we understand what the text means by the word *lamb*. Reuben, unfortunately, is a literalist who confuses and collapses ontological states and misunderstands the symbolism of their interaction. For Reuben, substitution is the simple substituting of one thing or one word for another. His universe is allegorical, not symbolic, according to the Coleridgean distinction. He misunderstands the terms of the relationship between the human and the divine, the Old and the New Testaments, eradicating the temporal dimensions whereby biblical history accomplishes its divine purposes and renders the biblical text fully symbolic.

Reuben does not understand that the "sacrifice" of Cyrus will be just as "useless" as his own death would have been. Neither of the sacrificial moments of his life, first with his "father" and later with his son, is antitypological, or for that matter, typological, either in a personal, biographical sense or in a national, religious one. According to Hawthorne events in human history, such as Reuben's first decision on the rock and his second, do not repeat. Every event, every meaning is a unique and individual occurrence. Reuben errs in not being able to acknowledge the uniqueness and individuality of historical moments. He cannot see the difference between one historical moment and another, even within his own life.

Indeed, Reuben's problem is more than an inability to confront national history. It is an unwillingness to confront his own history, his own movement toward becoming a responsible human being with an identity in and responsibility to the world. Robert Hollander maintains that typological thinking is not a theological construct imposed from outside human psychology but a natural response to inherent features of human experience.[23] Reuben is seduced by life's inevitable repetitions and duplications. Human conscious-ness would prefer to dwell in sameness, to reassure itself with duplications affirming its continuity in time, both past and future. Antitypological liter-alism, Hawthorne realizes, is a response to the problems of life in history, in which the temporality and uniqueness of one's experience brings one face to face with one's own mortality. The problem in "Roger Malvin's Burial" is not only that, in Michael Colacurcio's words, "The Divine Masterplot will *not* repeat,"[24] but also that nothing in God's universe will repeat. Yet one constantly strives to make things repeat or at least appear to repeat, as if sameness insured the perpetuity of the self into eternity.[25] The issue of repetition and substitution as strategies for guaranteeing the continuity of self in time is at the heart of Hawthorne's historiographical art.

REPETITION AND ACKNOWLEDGMENT

The text provides an important narrative repetition that is not thematic or structural but textual and linguistic. The following is the story's first view of the tree and the rock where Roger, and later Cyrus, die. This setting evokes Reuben's serious typological misreadings of human history and also provides the psychological backdrop for his more personal misperceptions:

> The early sunbeams hovered cheerfully upon the tree-tops, beneath which two weary and wounded men had stretched their limbs the night before. Their bed of withered oak-leaves was strewn upon the small level space, at the foot of a rock, situated near the summit of one of the gentle swells, by which the face of the country is there diversified. The mass of granite, rearing its smooth, flat surface, fifteen or twenty feet above their heads, was not unlike a gigantic grave-stone, upon which the veins seemed to form an inscription in forgotten characters. On a tract of several acres around this rock, oaks and other hard-wood trees had supplied the place of the pines, which were the usual growth of the land; and a young and vigorous sapling stood close beside the travellers. (P. 338)

In the second view:

> The thicket, into which Reuben had fired, was near the summit of a swell of land, and was clustered around the base of a rock, which, in the shape and smoothness of one of its surfaces, was not unlike a gigantic grave-stone. As if reflected in a mirror, its likeness was in Reuben's memory. He even recognized the veins which seemed to form an inscription in forgotten characters. (P. 356)

The text echoes itself ostensibly to replicate the experience in Reuben's memory: "as if reflected in a mirror, its likeness was in Reuben's memory."

But the repeating text does not simply reproduce the character's internal psyche. It expresses the tendencies of life, language, and especially the narrative toward duplication and repetition. Outside the frame of Reuben's consciousness, the text insists that the gravestone and its forgotten characters still look the same. The storyteller can find no other words in which to describe them except those already used. This is textual mirroring as well as psychological mirroring. And as the mirrors proliferate—the text mirroring itself mirroring the world mirroring the biblical text, which is itself a bifurcated mirror of Old and New Testaments, mirroring Reuben, whose imagination is already interpreting through the mirror of the biblical text and of some other innate mirroring memory—the reader is made to feel the pressure of cosmic likenesses. Like Cooper's world in *The Spy*, everything conceals something else; everything is a mask or a disguise. Reuben Bourne is lost in the funhouse before John Barth constructs it.

Everything is indeterminately the same, yet everything is also utterly different:

> everything remained the same, except that a thick covert of bushes shrouded the lower part of the rock, and would have hidden Roger Malvin, had he still been sitting there. Yet, in the next morning, Reuben's eye was caught by another change, that time had effected, since he last stood, where he was now standing again, behind the earthy roots of the uptorn tree. The sapling, to which he had bound the bloodstained symbol of his vow, had increased and strengthened into an oak, far indeed from its maturity, but with no mean spread of shadowy branches. There was one singularity, observable in this tree, which made Reuben tremble. The middle and lower branches were in luxuriant life . . . but a blight had apparently stricken the upper part of the oak, and the very topmost bough was withered, sapless, and utterly dead. Reuben remembered how the little banner had fluttered on the topmost bough, when it was green and lovely, eighteen years before. Whose guilt had blasted it? (Pp. 356–57)

Hawthorne's text stresses what Reuben cannot see, and never could see: the differences that prevent likeness from being sameness. The dead man is gone. The sapling is now a full-grown tree, and even now, despite what has occurred, it represents "luxuriant life" as much as it records withering and blight. Reuben, however, can only see death, which he has seen from the beginning, symbolized by the gravestone rock. For Hawthorne, all parts of the scene exist and have always existed inseparably. Growth and maturity, blight and withering, all dwell under the aspect of the giant gravestone. Reuben takes refuge in this indeterminacy and converts doubt into certainty. For him life is death. His fate, therefore, was sealed the moment he and Roger arrived at the rock.

In tying his red badge of courage on the branch, Reuben does not mark the reality of death so that he might remember his relationship to it or to the dead. Rather he makes the young sapling into a site of death, a prophecy of doom. In Reuben's view, the gravestone always marked a blasted sapling; youth and its possibilities never existed; it was not the case that an old man died, youth flaunting itself in the form of a red banner above his head. Rather youth was "wounded" (p. 338) from the start, blasted by the inevitabilities of mortality, which Roger embodied.[26] In binding the branch, Reuben would ensure the certainty of his conviction that life was never a viable option for him. He ties his consciousness to a changeless place of death. Therefore, his mind suffers the same conditions of blight as the tree. This is Hawthorne's definition of fixation. It is a process of intense identification with the ruined image of oneself, whereby one wills self-fulfilling prophecies; for what kills the branch is not, of course, the enemy death, biological necessity taking its course, but Reuben's binding of it. When Reuben again confronts the tree after so many years, two potentially contradictory pictures, the one with a young vigorous sapling, the other with the branch destroyed by blight, jar Reuben's fixation. Two trees, two sites, and multiple interpretations begin to emerge. Therefore, once again, Reuben must reconcile the irreconcilable. He must blur the determinate differences between the strikingly similar realities of life and death. The one portrait of the young sapling and the second picture of the blighted tree cannot exist side by side as determinately different views of the same tree. If they do, Reuben must accept the interval that has transpired between the one moment and the next. He must acknowledge life and history and the responsibilities that they imply.

The confrontation with the consequences of "time" (p. 356) and moral choice is made even more painful by the presence of another version of the young sapling, and of himself—his son Cyrus. In the first scene, the sapling serves as Reuben's substitute in the scene of the akedah, just as in the original story the ram served as Isaac's. In the second scene, Cyrus serves this same purpose. Reuben's motivations may originate in human psychology (Hawthorne may not possess the Freudian terms, but he knows well enough about the conflict between fathers and sons), but there is more to the story than an unresolved psychological problem. Thinking he recognizes the pattern of substitutions in which he participates, Reuben cannot deal with events on any other terms except those already given in scripture. He cannot imagine that substitution may be just that: deferral or delay or the substitution of a symbolic act or object for a real one. Therefore, he must bring the story to its predetermined biblical climax. In killing Cyrus, Reuben provides the blasted sapling with a cotemporal human counterpart. Thus he satisfies both his psychological and theological needs. He redraws the original portrait and climaxes what he believes is its scriptural meaning, excusing himself for both the desertion of the father and the killing of the son. He obliterates the differences and chronologies of life in history that not only enable human action but require it. In Reuben's psyche, the fault does not lie with unmade moral decisions but resides with his father's legacy of death, which has kept him heirless and sterile. Jay Gatsby, Jake Barnes, and Isaac McCaslin have it easy compared to Reuben: they never have to sacrifice sons in order to return to childlessness. Reuben's self-preservation as a human being depends on the obliteration of historical time and of the concomitant responsibilities of moral action. He unwrites his own story, substituting Cyrus for himself as once he had substituted the branch. He delivers his story back to his failure to enter historical time. In Reuben's view this was not a failure of his own making. His father had set the conditions that made his entry into history impossible.

The text, repeating itself, seems to confirm Reuben's logic. But there is something wrong, even, or especially, on the textual level. I refer again to the opening and closing descriptions of the rock. All of the physical details from the first scene repeat in the second, except for one, "the bed of withered oak leaves" with which the first description begins. A small detail perhaps, an authorial oversight or insignificant aspect, except that the withered oak leaves are not forgotten. They return to the scene through a substitute, the same substitute that both the storyteller and Reuben use to symbolize Reuben. By the end of the second scene "the withered topmost bough of the oak loosen[s] itself in the stilly air, and [falls] in soft light fragments." Textually, the two scenes would seem to have been made identical with each other, the withered bough in soft fragments replacing the withered oak leaves. Exhibiting an unrelentingness of textual memory, a kind of law of the conservation of narrative, the literal leaves reappear, as if they were there from the start. Like Reuben, the text can forget nothing, can leave nothing behind.

This kind of substitution, however, is not mindless obsession. Whereas Reuben would bury difference under the cloak of repetition, the text will repeat to reveal what is not the same. The passage enumerates what the tree bough covers; and it is not the scene of eighteen years earlier. The passage in full states, "At that moment, the withered topmost bough of the oak loosened itself, in the stilly air, and fell in soft, light fragments upon the rock, upon the leaves, upon Reuben, upon his wife and child, and upon Roger Malvin's bones" (p. 360). Reuben would understand the falling bough as covering over and obliterating time and change and moral decision making. His response to the bough's loosing itself in the "stilly" air (recalling the small, still voice of his own conscience and the still biblical voices that it invokes, as well as the "stillness" [p. 346] in the air when he leaves Roger Malvin earlier), and its falling on the rock, the leaves, his wife, child, father, and self—the whole dramatic company, past and present—is to conclude that the historical record has been wiped out and that he is forgiven. The story closes: "Then Reuben's heart was stricken, and the tears gushed out like water from a rock. The vow that the wounded youth had made, the blighted man had come to redeem. His sin was expiated, the curse was gone from him; and, in the hour, when he had shed blood dearer to him than his own, a prayer, the first for years, went up to Heaven from the lips of Reuben Bourne" (p. 360). History and time would seem not to matter at all. The second sentence, so terse and compelling, apparently asserts an irrefutable identity between the wounded youth and the then blighted man, Roger, and the now blighted man, Reuben. Hawthorne's sentence might well seem to begin without the comma, "The vow that the wounded youth had made the blighted man." No time, it seems, is lost, no moment has intervened. But something has escaped Reuben that the text insists on restoring to consciousness—the reader's consciousness, if not the protagonist's.

The conclusion of Hawthorne's story is perhaps one of the most troubling moments in his fiction. It seems to concur in Reuben's interpretation of his experience and to confirm his understanding of the terms of covenantal existence, both on the public and private levels. By all rights, this Abraham should see his seed inherit the promised land. Cyrus should rise up from the grave and redeem humankind. But Reuben's repentance, his tears flowing like water from a rock, evokes a second biblical type, which foresees the exclusion and lack of salvation that concludes "Roger Malvin's Burial." Hawthorne refers, in the final moment of the story, to the figure of Moses.[27] He invokes a type that was widely popular in nineteenth-century literature. Quoting a prominent Victorian preacher, George P. Landow explains that "it is generally allowed that this rock in Horeb was typical of Christ; and that the circumstances of the rock yielding no water, until smitten by the rod of Moses, represented the important truth, that the Mediator must receive the blows of the law, before He could be the source of salvation to a parched and perished world." Furthermore, "a second, perhaps less strictly orthodox type occurs when poets use the image of Moses striking the desert rock to pre-figure, not the Old Law bringing forth the New by means of the crucifixion, but rather Christ himself bringing forth tears of repentance from the stony heart of the individual worshiper."[28]

But all rocks are not the same rock. Indeed, Moses strikes two different rocks in the desert, one that God commands him to strike, which he strikes once, drawing forth water for the people of Israel, and one to which he is commanded to speak, but which he angrily strikes nonetheless, twice, again producing water for the people but in the process losing the covenant for himself:

> Moses cried unto the Lord, saying: "What shall I do unto this people? they are almost ready to stone me." And the Lord said unto Moses: "Pass on before the people, and take with thee of the elders of Israel: and thy rod, wherewith thou smotest the river, take in thy hand, and go. Behold, I will stand before thee there upon the rock in Horeb; and thou shalt smite the rock, and there shall come water out of it, that the people may drink" (Exod. 17: 4–6)

> And the Lord spoke unto Moses, saying, "Take the rod, and assemble the congregation, thou, and Aaron thy brother, and speak ye unto the rock before their eyes, that it give forth its water; and thou shalt bring forth to them water out of the rock. . . . And Moses took the rod from before the Lord, as He commanded him. And Moses and Aaron gathered the assembly together before the rock and . . . Moses lifted up his hand, and smote the rock with his rod twice; and water came forth abundantly, and the congregation drank. . . . And the Lord said unto Moses and Aaron: "Because ye believed not in Me, to sanctify Me in the eyes of the children of Israel, therefore ye shall not bring this assembly into the land which I have given them." (Num. 20: 7–12)

In the first episode, to which the major typological tradition recurs, Moses does as he is told, and the rock abundantly produces water. In the second episode, however, Moses disobeys the divine injunction. He substitutes his own earlier action for what God demands. And he expresses anger at God and the people, and perhaps at himself, causing him to lose the reward he most desires. In God's second utterance, almost everything repeats, except that, significantly for Hawthorne's creative purposes, God tells Moses to speak to the rock, not to strike it. But Moses, never a confident speaker, and here motivated by intense personal vexation, substitutes action for words. He inserts his own will into the divine commandment. That Moses hits the rock twice could suggest to Hawthorne not only the intensity of Moses's feeling and his lack of control, but also the principle of repetition. His refusal to speak suggests the difference between the Old Testament and the New Testament, the substitution of the word of the New Testament for older scriptural actions. Like Reuben, Moses repeats blindly his own earlier actions because he does not recognize what Reuben will not recognize, the importance of speaking the word, the need for conscious thought and speech within a universe of perilously repeating actions and feelings, which can treacherously seduce us into patterns of mindless repetition.[29]

Like Moses, Reuben does not follow his "father's" instructions. When he returns to Dorcas and the community, he refuses to speak. He ignores not only the meaning of the characters engraved on the rock, which suggest anything from the ten commandments to the Old Testament itself, but the act of speech itself.[30] When he is again confronted with the rock and its forgotten characters, he strikes out, in total silence, substituting action for words. Literally reenacting what he could better interpret exegetically, he sacrifices his son. In another incarnation of the rock story, the son's blood would spill, not literally, like blood or water from a stone, but figuratively, in the death of the greater son who is no mere mortal man and whose death was intended to secure the salvation of both Reuben and his progeny. Reuben is a false Moses as well as a false Abraham. Just as he would single-handedly secure God's covenant for America, he would author God's story. But Reuben misreads the Mosaic text, and he forgets that Moses received the book, of which he is the ostensible author and major protagonist, fully written by the hand of God. Misreading *the* text, Reuben misenacts and miswrites his own.

We can imagine that Reuben's prayer at the end of the story will be much like Moses's own prayer at the end of his life. It will be a futile plea to be allowed to do what God has already stated he may not do—to enter the promised land, and hence to rewrite the already completed story. Perhaps the Bradfords and Winthrops of American history ought to have paid more attention to the terms of the Exodus they thought they were reenacting. The moment they led their people into the promised land they violated the divine identities into which they had transcribed their historical being. Rewriting biblical history their own way, they had unwritten it, and the next generations of Americans would discover themselves not in Israel but in an Eden they were destined to lose. In Hawthorne's view, human authors are better off sticking to human texts, and human history does best when it reflects mortal concerns. The only story for Reuben to write is his own. The only history America can have is its own, though when it lives its own unique experience, it may well become a part of the scriptural history that it would have taken as its own private possession.

In repeating its own language, insisting on repetition as a natural cosmic phenomenon, Hawthorne's text momentarily threatens to collapse into the sameness that overtakes Reuben. All fiction seems to be an allegory, disguising or concealing (to adapt Cooper's insights) the same enduring archetypes. But "Roger Malvin's Burial" refuses the consolidation into the single story, the single truth, that obsesses its protagonist. Multiple stories abound, including the biblical, the historical, the psychological, and the strictly Hawthornean. When they come together, they produce only this story, this specific text. The potential parallelism and sameness explode in a fury of differences that tell Reuben's story and no other. Hawthorne's are interpretive repetitions. They reveal the differences among plots that provide the spaces in which human history occurs. Because Reuben is not Abraham (or Moses), and Cyrus is not Isaac, and the "rock" is not the "rock" (indeed, the rock in Genesis is not the rock in Exodus, and the Mosaic rock in Exodus isn't even the Mosaic rock in Numbers), the end of the story is not the redemption of anyone or anything. It is no one's salvation, no new law. The story records a falling away from grace, the finale of the failure to enter the promised land. Reuben's story is, finally, a nonstory, spoken to no one. Dorcas's own response to her husband's cold exegesis can stand for the reader's. "This broad rock is the grave-stone of your near kindred, Dorcas," he explains, "Your tears will fall at once over your father and your son" (p. 360). Dorcas "heard him not. With one wild shriek, that seemed to force its way from the sufferer's inmost soul, she sank insensible by the side of her dead boy" (p. 360).[31] There are no words to express the horror of what has occurred. Explication empties meaning into a restatement of imponderable paradoxes. It simply cannot convey the dimensions of human tragedy or even of human history.

It is fitting that Reuben's expiation, such as it is, should issue in a prayer that remains silent, voiceless. The last words of the story do not record his prayer. They assert his name, his partial, limited, and by now highly qualified human identity, his marking of the bourne or boundary between our fictions of history and history itself. What remains must be our Dorcas-like outrage and Reuben Bourne's inescapable, undeniable specificity, as a personality, as a fictional character, and as a shorthand for the story itself. "Roger Malvin's Burial" could have been titled, "Reuben Bourne." Properly speaking, Roger Malvin is never buried, except in Reuben's consciousness. And the ceremony of burial at the end, if that is what the falling bough represents, is at best a mock funeral. The story is about the son's substitution for the father, the substitution of Reuben Bourne for Roger Malvin's burial. Like all substitutions, especially those that concern the birth of one consciousness or personality at the expense or death of another, it involves a forgetting and a remembering. Reuben forgets. Hawthorne's story remembers. This remembering stresses the importance of the differences that create human history, personal identity, and the story itself. The story thus assumes responsibility for actions that it refuses to forget. Historical romance fiction, for Hawthorne, is the remembering text, as it traverses the not-so-neutral ground between history and fiction, between this world and God. Reuben Bourne refuses to speak; his prayer is silent and issues in nothing. Hawthorne does not refuse to speak: he speaks the utterly singular and specific name "Reuben Bourne"; and out of his spoken acknowledgment, American history and literature evolve.

4

Type, Antitype, and the Burdens of History: The Akedian Romance of America

In "Roger Malvin's Burial" Hawthorne locates the origins of the akedian myth of America within a literalistic, antitypological, ahistorical imagination, which would prefer, even at the cost of destroying the possibility of genuine history in America, to project American history as the unfolding of another, supernatural story. Hawthorne associates this tendency of the American mind with a desire to dwell in the indeterminate mingling of all realities, past and present, real and fictional. The fulfillment of this desire would preserve the individual from the need to differentiate between kinds of realities and to enter a history that is not a self-contained and self-referential fiction. Finally, Hawthorne prophesies the consequences for the nation and the individual of entangling themselves in these theological and psychological fantasies. He believes that American heroes verge on endlessly reenacting a moment of deadly self-sacrifice and self-destruction by unselfconsciously reenacting a desire for sanctification. By disowning their real history, they seemed at the point of discovering only that there was nothing to be said, no one left to say it. For Charles Brockden Brown the primary danger of the antitypological imagination was an explosion into gothic horror. For Hawthorne it was a withdrawal into silence, which was even more terrifying.

Though Hawthorne discovers in "Roger Malvin's Burial" the psychosexual origins or correlatives of the American fantasy of uncreating the world, he does not generalize this fantasy into an abstract principle of all life and all writing. Like *Wieland* and *The Spy*, "Roger Malvin's Burial" is a historical romance. It recovers the exact historical moment, in all its uniqueness and specificity, that has eluded Theodore Wieland and Reuben Bourne, and it makes that moment the occasion of an act of speaking and writing. This, implicitly in Hawthorne's view, is what Cooper, for all his insights in *The Spy*, did not achieve in his mythic romances. Cooper's leatherstocking tales only exacerbated the basic problems of American ahistoricity, reassuring American readers that their faith in Edenic beginnings was warranted, that America surely would escape history to begin anew.

THE PRAIRIE, REVISITED

Several critics have suggested that the pioneering Cyrus, cut down in his youth, offers an ironic portrait of Cooper's leatherstocking figure.[1] In "Roger Malvin's Burial," Hawthorne, I believe, offers more than a veiled response to what he saw as the failure of Cooper's fictions to read the American story correctly. As I suggest, Cooper's *The Prairie*[2] almost discovers the American story and almost constructs the scene of the akedah. It provides, I think, the site where at least part of the action of "Roger Malvin's Burial" takes place. The ceremony of burial at the end of Hawthorne's story reinterprets the two death scenes that conclude Cooper's novel. It buries, once and for all, the mythological promises that issue from *The Prairie* despite the disappearance of its major characters. These mythological promises, Hawthorne realized, were dangerous to American historical consciousness.

In *The Prairie*, the description of the dead body of the slain son Asa, "seated nearly upright, the back supported by a mass of matted brush, and one hand still grasping a broken twig" (p. 159), anticipates the posture of the dead Roger Malvin. Esther, her "voice frozen in grief," throwing "herself on the earth, and receiving the cold and ghastly head into her lap . . . in a silence far more expressive than any language of lamentation" (p. 158), prophesies the fate of this other mother whose pioneering son is lost in the wilderness, also at the hands of a relative. And in what is perhaps the oddest of these echoes, the normally phlegmatic, atheistical Ishmael Bush reacts to the execution of his brother-in-law with a religious mysticism that is almost more appropriate to a characterization of Reuben Bourne than of Bush:

> At the spot where he and Esther had conferred he reached the boundary of the visible horizon from the rock. Here he stopped, and ventured a glance in the direction of the place he had just quitted. The sun was near dipping into the plains beyond, and its last rays lighted the naked branches of the willow. He saw the ragged outline of the whole drawn against the glowing heavens, and he even traced the still upright form of the being he had left in his misery. Turning the roll of the swell, he proceeded with the feelings of one who had been suddenly and violently separated from a recent confederate forever. . . .
>
> The wind had risen with the moon, and it was occasionally sweeping over the plain

in a manner that made it not difficult for the sentinel to imagine strange and unearthly sounds were mingling in the blasts. Yielding to the extraordinary impulses of which he was the subject . . . he strayed towards the swell of land . . . For the first time, in a life of so much wild adventure, Ishmael felt a keen sense of solitude. The naked prairies began to assume the forms of illimitable and dreary wastes, and the rushing of the wind sounded like the whisperings of the dead. It was not long before he thought a shriek was borne past him on a blast. . . . The teeth of the squatter were compressed, and his huge hand grasped the rifle, as if it would crush the metal. Then came a lull, a fresher blast, and a cry of horror that seemed to have been uttered at the very portals of his ears. A sort of echo burst involuntarily from his own lips.

Ishmael Bush returns to bury his brother-in-law and say a prayer over his dead body (pp. 430–33).

The shriek of Abiram White, the silence of Esther Bush, and the haunted and frantic desire of Ishmael Bush to comprehend the sacrificial deaths of both Asa and Abiram are "borne past'" Cooper's novel into Hawthorne's story. There they are revised into a careful critique of the biblical paradigms they casually reflect. According to Hawthorne's story, the problem with Cooper's rendition of these moments was his failure to consciously engage and thereby disengage the biblical texts that his story echoes. Cooper would suggest that America was wracked by two competing covenants, the covenant of Ishmael and the covenant of Abraham/Isaac/Moses. Although the pur-veyors of both covenants disappear, the covenant of Moses, the trapper, prevails: "The grave was made beneath the shade of some noble oaks. It has been carefully watched to the present hour by the Pawnees of the Loup, and is often shown to the traveller and the trader as a spot where a just white man sleeps. In due time the stone was placed at its head, with the simple inscription which the trapper had himself requested. The only liberty taken by Middleton was to add, 'May no wanton hand ever disturb his remains!' " (p. 460). "Roger Malvin's Burial" disentangles the elements of Cooper's story. The "rock" and the binding, the "boundary," and the "bush" are all made to reveal the difference between the contours of the story that the protagonists think they are enacting and the story that they are indeed enacting. Hawthorne's story also concludes with a gravestone and an oak. But the oak tree is "blighted." And the gravestone is the rock of sacrifice itself. Its inscription is incoherent, uninterpretable. No covenant or myth remains, leaving only the history that witnessed the events, and the story, which Hawthorne wrote to separate events from the mythologies into which they have threatened to dissolve.

Cooper claims that Ishmael and his family are never heard from again. But Hawthorne knows that the ancestors of Moses mirror the ancestors of

Ishmael. They are twins, in the long tradition of biblical twins, who go their separate and unequal ways. Inheritors of diametrically opposite covenants, the Israelites and the Ishmaelites reincarnate the same problems of covenantal history: the subordination of the details of human experience to a scriptural contract imposed from outside human events. Hawthorne revises Cooper's vision in order to revise the scriptural vision on which Cooper's was based. Ishmael Bush's descendants, he suggests, did not disappear. Indeed, they reappear in every generation, veiled behind the identities of biblical types who seem their very opposite. In Faulkner's *Go Down, Moses*, the alternatives of Mosaic and Ishmaelite history form the focus of the critique of covenant theology, as Ike McCaslin tries to return history to the moment before the akedah, the moment before Isaac and Ishmael received their different covenants and set out on their separate historical courses.

Before we can understand Faulkner's mammoth undertaking in *Go Down, Moses*, or proceed to readings of the other two novels that constitute the final reaches of this line of akedian romances (*The Great Gatsby* and *The Sun Also Rises*), more details must be sketched into the historical romance picture.

THE CONTINUED LIFE OF THE AKEDIAN ROMANCE: *BILLY BUDD*, "GODLINESS," AND "A VIEW OF THE WOODS"

It can be objected that *Billy Budd*[3] is not a story about America in the same way that *Wieland* and "Roger Malvin's Burial" are. The action of the story takes place on a British ship in a situation fraught with special significance for British and European history. Yet the devices of the story and its conclusions are strikingly similar to those of *Wieland* and "Roger Malvin's Burial." Scholars have long recognized the Calvinistic influences in Melville's fiction, especially in *Billy Budd*. The story is a veritable treatise on the three central tenets of Calvinist theology: innate depravity (suggested by the inherent imperfections of both Claggart and Billy); determinism (the "fated boy" [p. 99] is an "angel of God. Yet the angel must hang" [p. 101]); and salvation through Christ (represented by Billy's death). In fact, the final sermon delivered by Vere is explicitly likened to a "Calvinistic text" to which the sailors listen like "a seated congregation of believers in hell" (p. 117). The universe of Melville's text seems to bear basic affinities with a Calvinistic worldview. But the events on board the *Indomitable* do not, I believe, endorse the terms of a Calvinistic universe. Rather, the tragic events of the story represent the handiwork of a mortal and limited captain who acts as if he were responsible for rectifying original sin and personally determining the course of human history. Vere acts as if he were God.

Vere enacts this divine role as a Calvinistic deity. Given the Puritan origins of the American predisposition toward antitypological literalism, his assumptions about the unfolding of cosmic events come as no surprise.[4] We are not provided with abundant information concerning Vere. The evidence, however, suggests that he is a dry, egocentric literalist who sees the universe and himself in antitypological historical terms, like Wieland and Reuben. "In this line of reading [i.e., history and biography] he found confirmation of his own more served thoughts." He is a man of "settled convictions," "positive convictions which he forefelt would abide in him essentially unmodified so long as his intelligent part remained unimpaired" (p. 62). "In illustrating of any point touching the stirring personages and events of the time [Vere] would be as apt to cite some historic character or incident of antiquity as he would be to cite from the moderns" (p. 63). Convinced that experience will always confirm his basic suppositions about life, Vere is decidedly fatalistic in his views. Billy, he knows, is an angel of God; yet he knows equally that the angel must die. Even Vere's name associates him with the exegetical tradition in a particularly skewed way. It is only a linquistic accident that provides his nickname, the "Starry Vere" (p. 61). The name itself signifies nothing but Vere embraces it as if it were intentional and meaningful. The designation of Vere as the Starry Vere establishes typology as a structure of cosmic relationships that is essentially meaningless, mechanical, and arbitrary.

The issue of typology opens the story. In the preface, Melville introduces the subject of mutiny, which informs the entire story not simply in its specific historical context but as a generalizable universal phenomenon. In the phrases "Revolutionary Spirit" and "Spirit of [the] Age" the term revolution signifies not only revolt against tyranny but the cycles of tyranny and freedom themselves.[5] The French Revolution and the Great Mutiny are presented as types of one another, and as we are led into the story, we are made to realize that these revolts are also types of another mutiny or revolution, the original insurrection in the Garden of Eden. The consequences of that first rebellion are, of course, well known, and they are recorded in the primary allegorical plot of Billy Budd. God (represented by Vere) punishes sinning Adam (Billy) with death (p. 94). But in condemning humankind to death God also provides for its redemption in Christ (again represented by Billy). In the Old-New Testament sequence of events, and in Melville's allegory, the fall leads directly to the resurrection, Adam to Christ. The two events and their two major figures have significant typological affinities within the Christian tradition. Christ is the second Adam, both of them innocents, favored sons of God, bound to him through special covenantal relationships. But in

Melville's story Adam is Christ. The fall is the resurrection. Some critics have argued that Melville collapses typological distance in order to accentuate the particularly vicious character of Christian history. In a Poesque gesture, he seems to condemn God for a strikingly cruel masterminding of a gothic cosmic plot.[6] Yet the failure, according to Melville, lies not with God but with Vere. It resides in Vere's peculiarly literalistic imagination and the course of action on which it takes him.

Conceiving of himself as the center of law and order on the ship, Vere manipulates events in order to create the conditions for a tragedy that is for him inscribed in the events. Vere stages the confrontation between good and evil; he conducts the trial of innocence; he sentences mortal humanity to death. Melville stresses throughout the story that Vere is under no legal or moral obligation to conduct the affairs of the case in this way.[7] It is suggested that duty may well require that he defer the trial to the "admiral" and the naval courts or at least that he try Billy by a jury of his peers. The legal system does restrict Vere's role in the trial. Vere knows this. Nonetheless he functions simultaneously as "sole witness," prosecutor, and judge. "A sense of the urgency of the case overruled in Captain Vere every other consideration." Thus he stages the trial to reap maximum benefit from his rank, even deviating from law and "general custom" to do so (pp. 104–06).

The urgency that motivates Vere is his sense of both the inevitability of events and his inescapable centrality in them. Because of his belief in typological cosmic relationships and his special antitypological historiography, law and order on his ship become the natural, necessary culmination of law and order outside the ship (the law and order of the nation, for example, or beyond that, of God). Therefore he forsakes the strict letter of military and civil law. He speaks of the mutiny on the *Nore* as if it were a type of mutiny on the *Indomitable*, even though mutiny has not been proven on his ship and is in fact not in the offing. "In Adam's fall / We sinneth all," read the New England primer. "Billy's intent or non-intent is nothing to the purpose," explains Vere (p. 112). In terms of Puritan theology, Billy is damned simply because he is not saved.[8] He is hanged for the original disobedience, the mutiny on the *Nore*, not for any mutiny or insurrection or even murder of which he himself is guilty. Indeed, the trial carefully misfocuses attention from the crime that Billy did commit, which could have been handled in a number of ways, to the crime he did not commit, which is punishable only by death. (The situation recalls Henry's trial for treason in *The Spy*.) For Vere, the ship is antitypological. He proceeds as if his judgment and his judgment alone can determine the outcome of national and Christian history.

But Vere forgets that the fall has been atoned for. The mutiny on the *Nore* has been put down. The critical action of the story appears in the competition between a typological and an antitypological interpretation of human events; that is, in language more familiar in Melville criticism, it is a conflict between a literalistic definition of Billy's crime as murder and a more humane consideration of it as inadvertent manslaughter. The two sets of terminologies, biblical-exegetical and human-legalistic, are related. The tragedy of *Billy Budd* is not precipitated by the contours of Christian history. God works in mysterious ways, insuring the perpetuation of the line and yet demanding the sacrifice of the son who inaugurates that line. Human beings must follow the laws of a rationally unfolding history, already infused with divine grace. The tragedy of Billy Budd is caused by human pride and a failure in theological imagination by an individual who would ignore redemption as the primary fact of postlapsarian Christian history. In Christian history, Adam and Christ are not one and the same figure. The fall and the resurrection are different events, and their relationship is carefully controlled by Christian history and typology. Vere's failure to understand the controls of historical typology precipitate the crisis. Vere sees Billy and the mutiny not as types but as antitypes, and herein lies the problem.

Melville, like Brown and Hawthorne, provides two type-antitype relationships to make his point on the connection between the fall and the resurrection. After he has sentenced Billy to death, Vere, "letting himself melt back into what remains primeval in our formalized humanity, may in the end have caught Billy to his heart, even as Abraham may have caught Isaac on the brink of resolutely offering him up in obedience to the exacting behest" (p. 115). The second type of Christ, Isaac, transmits the theological and human message that Vere cannot understand. Mediating between types (Vere and Billy and Abraham and Isaac) is the true antitype: God and Christ. The existence of this antitype invalidates Vere's compulsion to sacrifice his "son" in expiation of a sin and a rebellion that have been atoned for. Christ's crucifixion restored the universe to love and compassion, which Vere chooses to ignore.

In *Billy Budd* Melville carefully explores the implications of America's antitypologizing imagination for its role in the international community. Americans were not content to see themselves as Adamic creators, new men and women in a new Eden. They desired also to be Christ, the savior. For the American, the land was Eden and Canaan both, the individual, Adam, Moses, and Christ. America's role, therefore, would be both prophetic and evangelical. Melville presents his version of America's wildly erring, antitypological, ahistorical concept of self on a British ship, with a British cast of characters. He suggests that the American passion to export salvation had not issued in the resurrection of Christian faith but in the repeated crucifixion of Christian faith. If Americans were trapped in an Eden of their own making, doomed to replay the fall, Americanism abroad crucified the faith it intended to save. Another revolution related to the French Revolution and the Great Mutiny that is left unnamed in the preface is, of course, the American Revolution.[9] And the American Revolution, as Alan Heimert and Mason Lowance have pointed out, might well have constituted a political expression of the same kind of typological, or literalist, antitypological, thought that characterized American Puritanism from the beginning.[10] If America did antitype something, it might be neither creation nor redemption but disobedience. Thus *Billy Budd*, in Melville's words, is about a "crisis for Christendom."[11] It is about the ever-constant, ever-present threat of rebellion, which is directed not against the king or the navy but by the civil authority against God Himself. In usurping God's power, in making himself into a god, Vere repeats the act of rebellion that necessitated the human history through which the covenant of grace succeeds the covenant of works. But in denying that history, rolling it back to the moment before it began, Vere evades the historical consequences and moral responsibilities by which grace can be achieved.

In Anderson's "Godliness" and O'Connor's "A View of the Woods,"[12] several generations later, the "father" figures have become, appropriately, grandfathers, who stand in an even more oblique relation to biblical events than did their ancestors. The social conditions no longer reflect a nation and a culture growing into civil and religious maturity. Rather they testify to a highly industrialized, materialistic society trying to preserve wealth and progress. The issues of these stories, therefore, are somewhat different from those in *Wieland*, "Roger Malvin's Burial," and *Billy Budd*. Yet both Anderson and O'Connor focus on characters who strongly evoke Wieland, Reuben, and Vere. Both grandfathers Bentley and Fortune long for patriarchal authority and divine election, view their lives providentially, quest for visible confirmation of their sainthood, and believe that within their own persons and in their progeny, they will secure God's covenant for the land. Latter-day typologists, Anderson's and O'Connor's grandfathers manifest a continuing brand of Americanism. They act out an American tendency to prefer grand, mythic reenactments of sacred events to the limited human actions that bespeak moral commitment and responsibility.

Jesse Bentley's religious fanaticism, for example, provides an object lesson in the relation between material greed and the tradition of an ahistorical, antitypological reading of nation and self. Jesse's problems concern his being a second generation American. His ancestors in Winesburg are characterized by a different kind of religious passion altogether: "As they worked in the fields, vague, half-formed thoughts took possession of them. They believed in God and in God's power to control their lives . . . The churches were the center of the social and intellectual life of the times. The figure of God was big in the hearts of men" (p. 71). But Jesse forgets the bigness of God and the power of the church. He appropriates these things to himself. He does not remember that human nature is puny and that Christ's church, not the self, secures salvation. Consequently, he confuses material signs with spiritual meanings, or, to put the problem in the language of the story, he allows avarice and self-interest to determine his relationship to God. The issues at hand, as in the following passage, are the recurring issues of visible sanctity and federal theology:

> Jesse's mind went back to the men of Old Testament days who had also owned lands and herds. He remembered how God had come down out of the skies and talked to these men and he wanted God to notice and talk to him also. A kind of feverish boyish eagerness to in some way achieve in his own life the flavor of significance that had hung over these men took possession of him. Being a prayerful man he spoke of the matter aloud to God and the sound of his own words strengthened and fed his eagerness . . . "Oh God, create in me another Jesse, like that one of old, to rule over men and to be the father of sons who shall be rulers." (Pp. 69–70)

But the motivation for such palpable, visible expressions of sanctity is located, according to Anderson, not in nationalistic aspiration but in avarice and greed:

> A fantastic impulse, half fear, half greed, took possession of Jesse Bentley. He remembered how in the old Bible story the Lord had appeared to that other Jesse and told him to send his son David to where Saul and the men of Israel were fighting the Philistines in the Valley of Elah. Into Jesse's mind came the conviction that all of the Ohio farmers who owned land in the valley of Wine Creek were Philistines and enemies of God. "Suppose," he whispered to himself, "there should come from among them one who, like Goliath the Philistine of Gath, could defeat men and take from me my possessions." . . . Jumping to his feet, he began to run through the night. As he ran he called to God . . . "Jehovah of Hosts," he cried, "send to me this night . . . a son. Let Thy grace alight upon me. Send me a son to be called David who shall help me to pluck at last all of these lands out of the hands of the Philistines and turn them to Thy service and to the building of Thy kingdom on earth." (Pp. 72–73)

"Thy service" and "the building of Thy kingdom on earth" are inextricable from the fear of defeat and the desire for wealth that fire Jesse Bentley with religious passion. The repetition of the word *possession* throughout the description of Jesse suggests not only Jesse's demonic relationship to the world but also the source of this demonism in the desire for material goods.

Jesse's failure, like Wieland's, Reuben's, and Vere's before him, is morally and psychologically a lack of humility. Theologically, it is a failure of faith and historical-typological sensitivity. Jesse cannot accept that biblical times are over, that he is Jesse Bentley, grandfather to David Hartley, brother of Enoch. As in "Roger Malvin's Burial," the biblical allusions prevent a neat paralleling of historical and scriptural events. Thus, while Jesse sees the citizens of Winesburg as Philistines, it is Jesse who is Goliath when David shoots him with his slingshot. Jesse acts as if he were Saul. But he is Jesse, David's physical father, or rather, grandfather.

Nor is Jesse, Abraham, or David, Isaac. When Jesse first takes David into the woods to pray, he becomes so possessed of his Old Testament vision of himself as biblical patriarch that he terrifies his grandson, who hits his head and falls unconscious. Jesses's response to David's wound is human and sympathetic. He cradles the "boy's cut and bleeding head . . . tenderly against his shoulder" (p. 86). But Jesse does not fundamentally understand what has occurred. He cannot see that David's terror derives from his own ranting and raving about the biblical patriarchs. He does not realize that his religious fanaticism has not transformed him into that other Jesse whom he so desires to emulate and has made him a "dangerous" usurper of the body of the real and "kindly" Jesse whom David loves (p. 85). For these reasons Jesse cannot forebear taking his grandson into the woods once again on a related but even more disturbing mission. This mission does not result in injury to David, but rather in psychological and physical injury to Jesse. Jesse's failure to perceive the meaning of the first encounter in the woods mirrors Jesse's misconceived relation to biblical history. He cannot see contained in the first moment a hint of what the second antitypological moment would have to be and cannot be, because human beings are not scriptural types and were never meant to be. Jesse's error in typological understanding is fully exposed when he fails to comprehend that the need to sacrifice the lamb (and by implication, the son or grandson who is identified with the lamb [pp. 100–01]) has already been eliminated in the Christian universe by the one authentic sacrifice of *the* Lamb, who substitutes for the human son and also for the ram that is slain in Isaac's stead. Even animal sacrifice cannot work in the modern world (and it is not called for). In attempting to reproduce biblical events, Jesse severs himself from the only valid covenant, the covenant of grace. The patriarch reverts to his pagan origins, and the budding messiah, David, strikes him down with his slingshot, to disappear until some later, unimaginable second coming. If the second-generation zealots, like Theodore Wieland and Reuben Bourne and Jesse Bentley, lose their grasp of the new covenant, which restricts their fathers' similarly antitypological desires, their offspring of the third and fourth generations leave the fold altogether, annihilated or released into a future that can in no way be foreseen. Another third generation son of the chosen people, Isaac McCaslin, makes explicit David's repudiation of his inheritance, dramatizing the demise of the messianic estate.

Grandfather Fortune in "A View of the Woods" is a similarly erring antitypologist who refuses to admit that the climax of Christian history has already occurred. He will not accept that a "view of the woods" is the only fortune we possess and that we inherit it from God as the medium of salvation. In Grandfather Fortune's occluded view, he and his granddaughter Mary must save the world from the mortal Pitts, who would, sentimentally, cling to those woods and would not see beyond them to the future of wealth and power that sacrificing the view of the woods might provide. Grandfather Fortune's mistake, reaching back down the line of akedian heroes, is no simple greed. It is, rather, that he would secure his own fortune, distinct from the historical inheritance to which he is entitled and which requires his full and willing participation in order for it to succeed from generation to generation. He will not recognize the sources of salvation in the present world, and therefore, he will not take his appropriate place, or allow Mary to take hers, in the line of human descent whereby salvation is secured. Grandfather Fortune, in amassing a material fortune for the child to inherit (p. 57), would devise a plot whereby he will determine who will inherit his earth (which he will deface by building parking lots and gas stations where there was once nature). The inheritor, furthermore, will be himself, reincarnated in the child. Grandfather Fortune prefers Mary to all of his other grandchildren, even to his own daughter (Mary's mother), because she is "a small replica of the old man." From the beginning she bore an "unmistakable likeness" to him (p. 57); she is a "throwback" (p. 56), "thoroughly of his clay" (p. 58). More important, she is "like him on the inside too." She reproduces his most salient features: "his intelligence, his strong will, and his push and drive" (p. 55). So powerful is his identification with the child that when her father beats her, "it was as if it were *he* that Pitts was driving down the road to beat and it was as if *he* were the one submitting to it" (pp. 61–62).

But Mary is not his child, as David is not Grandfather Bentley's. And she no more reproduces her grandfather than she does her father. Fortune sees in Mary the possibility of a clean, asexual, immortal line of private generation, as if he himself were capable of the virgin birth that will yield the savior. (This idea recurs in *The Great Gatsby*.) " 'Are you a Fortune,' he said, 'or are you a Pitts? Make up your mind' " (p. 74), as if the two could be separated, and the matter decided. But Mary is "Mary—Fortune—Pitts," a child of multiple fatherings, a Mary who contains or conveys or transforms "Fortune" within (or between) her personal and family identities, as Mary, and as Pitts. When Grandfather Fortune insists that he is "PURE Fortune!" (p. 74), he denies his relationship to the child and forces her to become precisely what he would not have her be, "PURE Pitts" (p. 80). As pure Pitts, Mary excludes the possibilities of fortune, in all of its various biological, psychological, and spiritual meanings. Grandfather Fortune would defy the power of blood and lineage. He would convert the child into a vehicle and image of his exemption from the claims of family and parentage and human community. But, like David in "Godliness," this child rebels. Mary Pitts is not the "saint" or "angel" Fortune claims (p. 66). She is only the earthly child who would preserve the view of the woods for herself and her family.

Mary Pitts fights back, and when she asserts her identity as her human father's child, her grandfather must destroy her. Being pure Pitts she all too well reflects her grandfather's own PITiful, limited humanness. "The old man looked up into his own image. It was triumphant and hostile. 'You been whipped,' it said, 'by me,' and then it added, bearing down on each word, 'and I'm PURE Pitts' " (p. 80). The moment repeats an earlier instance, when Mary loses the battle of names: "For an instant she looked completely defeated, and the old man saw with a disturbing clearness that this was the Pitts look. What he saw was the Pitts look, pure and simple, and he felt personally stained by it, as if it had been found on his own face" (pp. 74–75). Whether Pitts defeats Fortune, or Fortune defeats Pitts, the result is the same. Murder is suicide, for in either case Fortune's image of self is destroyed. What Fortune desires is the absence of Pitts from his self-imagining, the freedom to confront the world without constantly confronting the claims of the blood. This is death, as Edgar Allan Poe had made clear in the American tradition. Grandfather Fortune will not acknowledge that whether as conqueror or vanquished, he is tied to Pitts. He will not admit that his role as purveyor of the fortune can be no more than intermediary, as he stands between the generations through which inheritance must flow. If Mary is genuinely a "throwback" to the "clay" of her grandfather, she can indeed escape the problems implicit in the complexities of generation. But she will do this only by becoming a force of degeneration, which is even more terrible. She will make Fortune conscious of something even worse than his marriage to the the fleshly Pitts. She will unearth the clay out of which the earth itself and all its creatures were created. History will be rolled back to its absolute pre-Christian origins, and all that will remain will be neither

Fortune nor Pitts but the "one huge yellow monster which sat to the side . . . gorging itself on clay" (p. 81). Consuming the flesh of his flesh, this prehistoric monster consumes Fortune's fortune, material and spiritual, as well. Fortune and Mary die. Their clay returns to clay.

Just before the terrible consummation of his dream of immortal wealth and power, Grandfather Fortune is given a final opportunity to recognize his place within Christian history. Before he takes his granddaughter into the woods, he sees the trees "as if someone were wounded behind [them] and [they] were bathed in blood" (p. 71). But this potentially saving vision does not penetrate his warped religious sensibilities. Possessed of the conviction that his fortune is his to determine and to pass on, he plays out the story of the covenantal moment. He fails to see what the woods have put before his view. Denying God, he discovers that no God will stay his hand. When at the end of the story he gazes at his dead granddaughter, a "little motionless figure with its head on the rock" (p. 80), he has indeed actualized the biblical event. But the blood of the dead Mary, like the deaths of the Wielands and of Cyrus, will not bring salvation. It not only seals off the possibility of the continuity of Old Testament, New Testament, and American history, but it prevents any entry into history altogether. This Mary will bring no David/ Christ into the world: born into an Eden of parking lots and huge monster machines, hers will be the virgin death that will restore chaos and uncreate the universe.

O'Connor, of course, is a Catholic and not a Protestant writer, and her stories have a decidedly Roman message: "Underlying demonic destructiveness is pride," explains David Eggenschwiler, "the pride that enables man to reject God and to establish idols. . . . If one will not have faith and will not accept grace . . . one becomes estranged and demonic—the philistine trying to imprison the possible in the probable; the anti-Christ, asserting himself in defiance or self-pitying spite; the rationalist, refusing to admit his animal nature . . . because man's spiritual nature is inseparable from other aspects of his being, . . . the man in rebellion against God is also in rebellion against himself."[13] But these comments about the story's Catholic point of view easily recall the old antitypological historiography of the Puritans that had engaged a series of writers preceding O'Connor. As well as deepening the insights of the akedian romance, "A View of the Woods" opens up the patterns of the American imagination to new and different kinds of scrutiny. By the twentieth century, the peculiarly Puritan patterns of the American sensibility had fully penetrated the national consciousness—an important point, given the Catholic tendencies of two of America's major twentieth-century figures, Hemingway and Fitzgerald. The antinomian literalism of

American historiography and antitypological thinking was not simply a particular instance of a universal problem. For Brown, Hawthorne, Melville, Anderson, and O'Connor, in these stories and in other of their works as well, the fall and the resurrection had been made especially relevant to the American experience because of an American appropriation of these stories as the paradigms of American experience. As products of the literary realism of the late nineteenth and early twentieth centuries, Anderson and O'Connor point to the continuing relevance of a historical romance mode, which was the formal expression of this American theme. If American characters consistently forgot their human history, American authors would not forget their origins within a particular textual reality. They would create the literary history that would remind their American readers of the necessity for history itself.

THE COVENANT OF ISHMAEL: GO DOWN, MOSES

Faulkner's Isaac McCaslin is "an Isaac born into a later life than Abraham's" (p. 283), as Faulkner's Go Down, Moses (1942)[14] is written at a later time than most other akedian works (except for "A View of the Woods," which comes later). Ike repudiates "immolation," as the other protagonists in the line do not. But Ike, "fatherless and therefore safe declining the altar because maybe this time the exasperated Hand might not supply the kid" (p. 283), like his ancestors, chooses to pursue the life of the Nazarene, "because if the Nazarene had found carpentering good for the life and ends He had assumed and elected to serve, it would be all right too for Isaac McCaslin even though," as Faulkner acknowledges, "Isaac McCaslin's ends, though simple enough in their apparent motivation, were and would be always incomprehensible to him" (pp. 309–10). In an extreme compression of the akedian myth (Faulkner's Isaac is his own Christ, and his own childless Abraham as well), and with a significant reversal of some of its major elements, Go Down, Moses, brings forward the major elements of the akedian tradition: the obsession with biblical history, the compulsion to rewrite American history as Old Testament scripture, and the deadly consequences of mistaking the human for the divine.[15]

But Faulkner's novel does more than reconstruct the elements of the akedian romance. By having Ike consciously refute the pattern of sacrifice that obsessed preceding generations and yet still fulfill it, Faulkner accentuates the deep hold of this kind of imagination on the American mind. By having Ike decide on his mistaken course of ascetic renunciation because of a romantic commitment to nature transcendentally defined, Faulkner suggests how the tendencies of American thought became even more dangerous when they escaped the tethers of their scriptural origins and became infused with a certain notion of self. Like Charles Brockden Brown and Hawthorne, Faulkner traces the history of an American psychosis. Like Hawthorne in "Roger Malvin's Burial," he ties it to Cooper's myth of the frontier.[16] What he discovers is not only the continued life of the akedian impulse but its intensification in the secular ideologies to which it was joined. The akedian myth, Faulkner realized, raises questions not only about the direction of American history but about the place of self in American society. It concerns the sources of authority in America and the distribution of physical wealth and imaginative power. It concerns acknowledging and accepting one's place in history and taking responsibility for the story that tells that history.

Faulkner criticism has been sensitive to the major issue of the book: whether Ike's repudiation of the McCaslin estate is an affirmation of a wilderness ideal or an escape from history and responsibility. Though some have argued for the essentially Emersonian or Coopnerian bias of the book, most critics have seen the novel as an explicit repudiation of the wilderness experience. John Hunt has expressed the latter position best: "From Isaac's point of view . . . his relinquishment of the land . . . is the active expression of what was latent in his wilderness experience. . . . He believes his decision is commensurate with God's purpose in history, which is to set man free, free of the consequences of his prehistorical fall." But Ike, Hunt continues, "is compounding sin rather than expiating it, evading responsibility for the human condition rather than accepting it and suffering for it, denying the continuity of historical experience rather than recognizing and acting within it."[17]

Ike falls victim to two competing myth systems, the biblical and the Emersonian or Coopnerian. These myth systems collaborate to doom Isaac to a process of endless self-sacrifice, which paradoxically perpetuates the sacrificial act that Ike specifically avoids. The original sin of racism and of disinheritance repeat, and Ike directly contributes to that repetition. Rejecting his cousin's illegitimate black child (who is the only offspring, except for one unspecified descendant, of either the white or black Mc-Caslin lines), Ike foreswears any and all progeny. He completes the akedah twice. As the great patriarch of the McCaslin line, he sacrifices the son. As uncle to everyone and father to no one, he sacrifices the very idea of progeny. He is the Miltonic Adam taking Eve's advice and failing to produce the generations that would constitute human history and its redemption. Bypassing sacrifice the first time by repudiating the land, then bypassing sacrifice again by never bearing the son whom he might be asked to remit, and finally rejecting the son of his cousin, leaving both the male and distaff branches of the family essentially heirless, Ike becomes the most absolute of America's angry fathers, a veritable personification of the concept of sacrifice itself.

If the Old Testament text consists of the chronologies and genealogies that insure inheritance and tradition, Ike McCaslin's story is constituted by what he is not. His history is the prophecy of what will not be. His story therefore does not record moments of birth. It catalogues occasions of sacrifice and childlessness. Ike is " 'Uncle Ike' . . . a widower now and uncle to half a country and father to no one" (p. 3), "husband but no father, unwidowered but without a wife" (p. 281). And the essence of his story is that

> if he couldn't cure the wrong and eradicate the shame, who at fourteen when he learned of it had believed he could do both when he became competent and when at twenty-one he became competent he knew that he could do neither but at least he could repudiate the wrong and shame, at least in principle, and at least the land itself in fact, for his son at least: and did, thought he had: then (married then) in a rented cubicle in a back-street stock-traders' boarding-house, the first and last time he ever saw her naked body, himself and his wife juxtaposed in their turn against the same land, that same wrong and shame from whose regret and grief he would at least save and free his son and, saving and freeing his son, lost him. (P. 351)

Ike unwrites history.

The source of Ike's error is his essentially correct insight into an aspect of the akedian myth that troubles Hawthorne as well. Ike realizes that the essential problem in the Old Testament-New Testament vision of Hebraic history, especially as it was adapted in America, is the concept of covenant. The rite of inheritance perpetuated injustice and inequality, no less in the world of the Old Testament than in Ike's own South. As one critic has observed, Isaac might not have been so "fortunate in receiving his father's lands and heritage. The benighted pride of civilized man was (and is) unable to see that Ishmael, not Isaac, had the valuable inheritance . . . the wilderness."[18] This may overstate the case; the wilderness is not, for Faulkner, a solution to basic human problems, and the powerlessness of an Ishmael is certainly not a condition to be envied. But Go Down, Moses does deal, directly and powerfully, with the problem of covenant. It treats the tendency of a certain kind of history to eclipse other histories, to privilege itself, and to disenfranchise competing claims.

Ike's major action is the abrogation of the covenant that the akedah would secure. Given the consequences of that covenant for human, and especially Southern, history, Ike's solution would seem ideal. Given the effects of Ike's abnegation—Ike's prideful isolation, the extinction of the family line, the rejection of Zack's child, and the continuation of exactly the separation between the lines of family descent that annihilation of the covenant would seem to repair—clearly it is not. This is so, in part, because of the human relatedness that covenant secures and that the breaking of the covenant destroys. Ike McCaslin considers himself "fatherless." Repudiation, therefore, seems to him to offend no one. It appears to destroy no set of relationships, evade no personal responsibilities. Yet Ike is the son of no less than four fathers whom, in rejecting the covenant, he also disinherits. There is his literal father from whom he inherits the plantation; Sam Fathers, from whom he gains mastery over the wilderness; Cass Edmonds, "rather his brother than cousin and rather his father than either" (p. 4), who articulates for him the philosophy of historical responsibility, which is also a part of the biblical text; and God Himself, with whom Cass is loosely connected: "I am what I am," Cass says to Ike, echoing the tetragram and the divine definition of self. In refusing to take on himself his covenantal destiny, Ike abrogates four times over his relationship to his parentage.

Critically, he abrogates four separate covenantal possibilities, any one of which could have provided the means for assuming and executing the burdens of his history. Like other American heroes, Ike would reverse scriptural history and go back to the Edenic moment before history came into being. He would unwrite the history of the South to return to the moment before his grandfather had founded his dynasty of black and white McCaslins. This is the moment before Ike's ancestors established the covenant with their white descendants and doomed their unacknowledged black children to eternal enslavement. Ike would unwrite even the history that preceded his grandfather's ownership: "I cant repudiate it. It was never mine to repudiate. It was never Father's and Uncle Buddy's to bequeath me to repudiate because it was never Grandfather's to bequeath them to bequeath me to repudiate because it was never old Ikkemotubbe's to sell to Grandfather for bequeathment and repudiation. Because it was never Ikkemotubbe's father's fathers' to bequeath Ikkemotubbe to sell to Grandfather or any man" (p. 256). In other words, Ike would retreat to the moment before Abraham secured the covenant through the akedah. He would recover the moment before Isaac and Ishmael went their separate ways, the moment that in a sense necessitated the akedah as a way of ensuring or marking (like circumcision) the difference between Isaac and Ishmael.

But in unraveling the covenants, which seem to him the source of so much human error, Ike does not change the structure of covenantal thought.[19] The problem is not simply that, escaping the accumulated errors of history, Ike evades the possibilities for redemption that history also provides. Rather, Ike fails to see that his theory of history replicates covenantal history in reverse. Most painfully, it dooms the black McCaslins to pursue the course of covenant to the same disastrous ends that the white McCaslins have pursued it. Ike does not remember, as he returns to the moment before the akedah, that Ishmael also received a covenant. In the Old Testament text that Ike would undo, the moment of separation between peoples is constantly reiterated, as if the separation of history into histories, some of which are excluded and some of which are told, is itself a part of the Old Testament story. Isaac and Ishmael are not the only brothers to go their different, unequal ways. So do Isaac's sons Jacob and Esau in the third generation, and Jacob's sons Joseph and his brothers in the fourth, and Ephraim and Menasseh in the fifth. When Ike goes on to construct a new history, in which Ishmael and not Isaac carries on the line of descent, he discovers that he is writing covenantal history all over again. The history of Ishmael that he begins to write mirrors the history of Abraham, Isaac, and Moses that he thinks he is undoing.

If American whites were not, finally, the chosen people, perhaps, Ike considers, black Americans were. "Go back North," Ike tells the racially mixed mother of Zack's illegitimate child, "Marry: a man in your own race. That's the only salvation for you" (p. 363). What is important here is not so much Ike's racism, linked with an anti-Christian lack of love (" 'Old man,' she said, 'have you lived so long and forgotten so much that you don't remember anything you ever knew or felt or even heard about love?' " [p. 363]), but his fixation on a salvation and redemption analogous to those guaranteed in white history. Ike imagines a "plan" (p. 300), inexorably moving him toward the clearly defined goal of renunciation. This same plan moves the blacks into the position of inheriting the covenant that he has rejected:

> Not enough of even Father and Uncle Buddy to fumble-heed in even three generations not even three generations fathered by Grandfather not even if there had been nowhere beneath His sight any but Grandfather and so He would not even have needed to elect and choose. But He tried. . . . Absolute which contained all and had watched them since in their individual exaltation and baseness and they themselves not knowing why nor how nor even when: until at last He saw that they were all Grandfather all of them and that even from them the elected and chosen the best the very best He could expect . . . would be Bucks and Buddies and not even enough of them but in the third generation not even Bucks and Buddies but . . . Yes. If He could see Father and Uncle Buddy in Grandfather He must have seen me too. . . . So He turned once more to this land which He still intended to save because He had done so much for it. (Pp. 282–85)

Ike is chosen for his role. So are the blacks, who are now the chosen people on whom American destiny depends. "They will endure . . . they will endure" (p. 294), he proclaims of the blacks, quoting his author in *The Sound and the Fury*, as moments earlier he alludes to the title of that work and another of Faulkner's early novels, *The Sanctuary*: "He had rescued them but this new one too which He had revealed and led them to as a sanctuary and refuge were become the same worthless tideless rock cooling the last crimson evening except that out of all that empty sound and bootless fury one silence, among that loud and moiling all of them just one simple enough to believe that horror and outrage were first and last simply horror and outrage and was crude enough to act upon that" (p. 284). The blacks will inherit what the whites have despoiled, their Bible, their God, their land, even their texts.

But if the blacks were really the chosen people, might not their history unfold as white history had unfolded, as an ironic misrepresentation of the major facts of redemption? Might not their "sanctuary" and "refuge" be the same worthless, tideless "rock" that has witnessed "horror and outrage" in more than one generation? Furthermore, might not the imposition of white paradigms of history onto black consciousness be itself a form of enslavement? "The curse you whites brought into this land has been lifted," the black minister tells Ike. "It has been voided and discharged. We are seeing a new era, an era dedicated, as our founders intended it, to freedom, liberty, and equality, for all, to which this country will be the new Canaan" (p. 279).[20] The founders whom the black minister quotes are the "the melliluous [choir] of self-styled men of God" "to whom the wilderness itself began at the top of the tide and who looked, if at anything other than Beacon Hill, only toward heaven" (p. 287). These are the same white men who first enslaved the white imagination and who now threaten to enslave the black imagination as well.

Faulkner saw black history poised in the same perilous position that white American history once occupied. It seemed to him about to leap into the same self-destructive error of patterning itself on something else and denying its own history. The earlier patterns were directly responsible for black history's disenfranchisement as history. If Faulkner's fiction constitutes violent activity, as one critic has suggested,[21] its violence is directed as much against the enslavement of the black community's historical imagination as against the enslavement of the historical community itself. It is not because Faulkner is so entrapped in stereotypes of the black that he cannot produce black characters who are not imitation whites. Faulkner sees that black language, like white language, has fastened itself to the language of the biblical paradigm. History for American blacks, as for American whites, has become an invocation of the Exodus. "Go Down, Moses": in the words of the Negro spiritual; in the words of Bradford and Winthrop; in the words of a white Old Testament God.[22]

Many critics have discussed Faulkner's attitudes toward blacks and the implicit racism, or at least stereotypical approach to blacks, that permeates his writing.[23] In *Go Down, Moses* Faulkner self-consciously grappled with the problem of white imaginings of blacks. Racism, he realized, had been caused largely by the enslavement of the white imagination to certain biblical paradigms of covenantal theology. Those same paradigms, he understood, were being employed to redeem black history, to trace the line of descent that white history had eclipsed. But in the gesture to locate the black axis of biblical history, whites continued to reflect a white rather than a black perspective on human history. Irving Howe has eloquently described the progression in Faulkner's writings from a sentimental portrayal of the "white man's longing" for fraternity with blacks to a "personal vision" and "ideology" that are moving also toward a realization of the impossibility of a white person understanding blacks: "As Faulkner discovers the difficulty of approaching Negroes, he also develops an admirable sense of reserve, a blend of shyness and respect; trusting few of his preconceptions he must look at everything afresh."[24] Several critics have cited Lucas Beauchamp as Faulkner's most "memorable" black character, who achieves, especially in *Intruders in the Dust*, a "complexity," that far surpasses that of Faulkner's other black characters.[25] Even Myra Jehlen, who makes a strong case for Faulkner's racism, acknowledges that "There is . . . evidence in *Go Down, Moses* that Faulkner had somehow extricated his extraordinary imagination from racial attitudes which previously (and again later) bound it to stereotypes." Jehlen notes, "One of the stories in the collection, 'Pantaloon in Black,' is explicitly critical of white men who refuse to recognize the common humanity of a black."[26] *Go Down, Moses* understands deeply an American impulse to dissolve history into myth. It is, like Brown's and Hawthorne's romances, quintessentially historical. Specifically, *Go Down, Moses* is Faulkner's history of American blacks and of the threatened dissolution of that history into white myth.

Go Down, Moses is Faulkner's historical romance. Faulkner recognizes that as a white author he cannot with total accuracy tell black history. As a limited mortal human being, he cannot accurately tell any history. Yet the telling of history is all that stands between human beings and the eclipse of history, which would deliver them back to primal, ahistorical scenes of self-sacrifice and destruction. For Faulkner, then, genuine historical telling requires the recognition of the historical specificities that distinguish history from myth and the further acknowledgment that historical understanding is limited. There are things that we simply cannot know or understand about the historical past, and these must form a part of the historical undertaking as well. The confession that we do not know prevents history from becoming myth. In "The Negative Structures of American Literature," Terence Martin has argued that America traditionally defines itself by what it is not, producing a kind of apophatic history.[27] Faulkner employs this strategy to produce not a positive valuation of America but a critique of America's overly self-confident sense of itself as chosen, negating all of the evils of world history. Thadious M. Davis has explained, "The 'solid South' had one clearly defined conception of what 'the Negro' was: he was *not white.*' "[28] Despite his difference from other Southern writers, Faulkner shared this basic assumption. For Faulkner, however, addressing what was *not white* expressed his willingness to acknowledge the difference between presumption to absolute knowledge and knowledge of qualified uncertainty. Richard Wright had charged white writers with using the American Negro as a metaphor for its own problems. Faulkner is no exception to this charge, but he ennobles the awkward relationship between white writers and their black subjects. For Faulkner, the world is decidedly *not* everything that is the case.[29] All one can say for sure is what is not the case.

There are two kinds of unwriting going on in Faulkner's novel. Ike's unwriting produces only a pale and sickly imitation of the story it would unwrite. It renounces what Ike must learn to accept, the covenants that bind us to history and to other people, and it dooms black history to do the same. The other unwriting, Faulkner's, also peels away historical layers, but it does not deny or repudiate the historical past. It confesses its own impotence to possess history. The book begins with "Was." It begins with what it was that one must accept as a part of one's history, and, critically, with what was not, for which one must also assume responsibility: "This was not something participated in or even seen by himself, but by his elder cousin, McCaslin Edmonds, grandson of Isaac's father's sister and so descended by the distaff, yet notwithstanding the inheritor, and in his time the bequestor" (p. 3). Like Ike, Faulkner reverses or unwrites genealogy. "Isaac McCaslin" is " 'Uncle Ike' . . . a widower now and uncle to half a county and father to no one" (p. 3). He is "the boy . . . the man, repudiated denied and free . . . and husband but no father, unwidowered but without a wife, and found long since that no man is ever free and probably could not bear it if he were" (p. 281). But even as Faulkner negates identity, he reminds the reader that such an unwriting of events does not erase their consequences. Not only does

McCaslin Edmonds inherit and bequeath Ike's property, almost as a consequence of his participation in the events and Ike's absence from them, but Ike, too, who only hears the story, or perhaps even occasionally listens to it (p. 4), will have to assume responsibility for its consequences. One of these consequences is no less than his own birth into the world. What was may be not much of anything at all. And Faulkner's story "Was," as both comic and horrific, is certainly one of his most whimsical evasions of reality. But what is cannot be evaded. Indeed, "Was" is only the first in a series of stories that constitutes *Go Down, Moses*. What is, is a direct consequence of what was and was not; so is what is not.

Ike's birth into the world is not even the main point of the story. By beginning with "Isaac McCaslin," Faulkner seems to be declaring that this is a story about Ike. Much critical attention has been devoted to explicating this story. But by decreating Ike even as he introduces him, Faulkner removes him from the center of the history that he tells. This *was* Ike's story, but no more. It never really was Ike's story because Ike was not even there. Buck and Buddy may think that they and the white McCaslins rule the roost, so that all stories are finally their stories. But Tomey's Turl and Tennie control the action in "Was" and, in the final crisis, Tomey's Turl shuffles the deck on which the destinies of all the McCaslins depend.

Faulkner knows this, but as a white writer he is doomed to write only white history. Like Buck and Buddy, who record the lives of their black slaves in the ledger that appropriates black history to white, Faulkner can only repeat white history's simplistic notions of black history. He can only, like Ike and Cass, quote what he knows to be reductive.[30] Carl E. Rollyson has suggested that Ike's interpretations of the concrete data of the ledgers stand for the difference between historical facts and their interpretation.[31] But Ike's efforts to decipher the ledgers do little to solve the basic historical problems they record. Like Ike, Faulkner was not there when history began. But also like Ike, he has heard, sometimes actively listened to, or read fragments of that history. Faulkner cannot dismiss history as what was and cannot be recovered, because one was excluded from it. But he also cannot tell it as if it were his own history, a history either about or culminating in himself.

When Isaac McCaslin rewrites the story of the South he puts himself at the center of consciousness. Critics are correct to see in "The Bear," and in *Go Down, Moses* as a whole, the story of a young man's initiation into evil; his loss of romantic innocence; his decision to disentangle himself from the sins of the past. This is Isaac McCaslin's story, and it is as proto-, stereo-, in short, plain typical as they come. But Ike's story is not Faulkner's, and it is for this reason that "The Bear" cannot be read in isolation from the whole novel. (Faulkner repeatedly claimed that he considered *Go Down, Moses* a novel.) Nor is it unimportant this book is followed by *Intruder in the Dust*, the story of Lucas Beauchamp. *Go Down, Moses* begins and ends with black characters, and it is superseded by them. Tomey's Turl sets "Was" and the history that follows into motion. His daughter-in-law, "Aunty" Mollie, and not Uncle Ike, concludes the book.

Critics have pondered the highly experimental form of *Go Down, Moses*. The book went through many revisions. It consists of semi-autonomous stories, all of which are associated with one another through theme and image, and all but one of which concern the extended, multigenerational McCaslin family. But the stories never seem to coalesce into a single unified work.[32] Critics have tried to understand what this book is finally about. I believe the book is about the ways in which the human imagination causes things to be about other things, the ways in which plots of various kinds dominate human freedom and the historical unfolding that would witness that freedom. Casting the plot of the historical South (that had itself cast itself as another plot) as a fiction not following any particular plot, Faulkner breaks the frozen art of a chronological, genealogical narrative. He writes, as it were, a new kind of testament. This testament, which is the testimony of history, makes no promises. It testifies to the haphazardness of human experience, the inexplicability of stories, and their inapplicability to one another. "Pantaloon in Black" has no match in *Go Down, Moses*, either among the stories of the white McCaslins or among the stories of the black McCaslins. That it is not literally about the McCaslins is not the important point. It defies any attempt to integrate it rationally into the novel. In fact, any attempt to relate it to the other stories seriously compromises its stunning uniqueness and power. Other blacks love in the course of the novel: Tomey's Turl and Tennie, Mollie and Lucas. Other blacks murder and are hanged. But these analogies get us nowhere. There is no love and no pain that can equal Rider's. We can no more conclude from the fact that Tomey's Turl and Tennie produce Mollie and Lucas who in turn produce the murderer at the end that the point of Faulkner's novel is that love begets murder than we can use Rider's fate to prove anything about Southern history. There are no easy causalities in these stories, no way of collecting family, or human, history and making it cohere. Faulkner's wisdom, which is not Isaac's, is to resist coherence on all levels. There are, he knows, only particular stories to be told, one at a time. And these stories, rather than specify what events mean and what they signify, can only state the facts that defy even the storyteller.

Faulkner writes the only kind of black history a white man can write because it is the only kind of history any man or woman can write. As Ike says of the scripture itself: "There are some things He said in the Book, and some things reported of Him that He did not say. And I know what you will say now: That if truth is one thing to me and another thing to you, how will we choose which is truth? You don't need to choose. The heart already knows. He didn't have His Book written to be read by what must elect and choose, but by the heart" (p. 260). At the end of the novel, Mollie asks the editor of the newspaper if he is "gonter put hit in de paper?" Gavin Stevens' response is not the one Faulkner chooses.[33] Stevens says, "And I wanted to say, 'If I should happen to know how he really died, do you want that in too?' And by Jupiter, if I had and if she had known what we know even, I believe she would have said yes. But I didn't say it. I just said, 'Why you couldn't read it, Aunty.' And she said, 'Miss Belle will show me whar to look and I can look at hit. You put hit in de paper. All of hit,' " (p. 383). Like scripture itself the newspaper will report truths and lies and will not necessarily enable us to choose between them. The white man will not accurately record black history, getting less of it rather than more, as the white editor supposes. But the written record is important in and of itself. Without the ledger of the past, there is nothing for human consciousness to own, no record to interpret or on which to act.

Like the title of Hemingway's *The Sun Also Rises*, which I discuss below, Faulkner's book echoes scripture after all. *Go Down, Moses*, it tells its reader, and, it says once more in the final story, "Go Down, Moses." But, as the repetition of the phrase within the book itself suggests, not all sayings, even when they directly quote others, are the same. The words of the Negro spiritual, "Go Down, Moses, / 'Way down in Egypt land / Tell ole Pharoh,/ To let my people go,"[34] no more reproduce the original Old Testament text than Faulkner's titles reproduce the words of the Negro spiritual. Freedom, for Faulkner, requires more than the absence of physical enslavement. It demands freedom from the constraints on language and imagination that would make history into the quotation of scripture or anything else. The phrase "Go Down, Moses" is, however, an imperative to action. It is a personal address to participate in the emancipation of the human intellect. "I wants hit all in de paper. All of hit," Aunt Mollie insists. What matters to Faulkner is the publication of the written word, however faulty and imprecise. We must record the human events that we must acknowledge and take onto ourselves as the personal imperatives of history.

5

The Spectral Evidence of History: Skepticism and Faith in Hawthorne's "Young Goodman Brown"

Go Down, Moses is the culminant akedian romance. More dramatically than his predecessors in the line, Isaac McCaslin attempts to unwrite history. He tries to retreat to an originating moment, before biblical or national or personal history began, so that he can author a story of heroic redemption patterned on the biblical text. But the differences accumulated in human history render this repetition impossible. Failing to acknowledge the genuine configurations of his own more limited and personal history and his scriptural responsibilities within them, the hero fails to achieve his goals. His story slips into repetition of psychological archetypes of obsessive and compulsive behavior and of vaguely biblical moments of sin and error, which represent versions of these mortal failings within the scriptures themselves. The hero, therefore, redeems no one and nothing. He repeats acts of pride, presumption, and a painful disregard for divine authority. The history that he inadvertently produces is only an oblique and distorted reflection of the history he wanted to create, threatening to make American history into a perpetual reenactment of his and the nation's obsession with uncreation.

The akedian romances concern the neutral territory or bourne separating history from fiction, one history from another, biblical history from human history, and black history from white history. They retrieve the facts of a real history in order to restore to consciousness both those facts and the almost primal moments in the nation's past, when the conception of a scriptural America had occasioned a painful pattern of repression and forgetfulness. According to Hawthorne, Faulkner, and others, America's Puritan origins directly threatened moral imagination in America. This was true, not primarily because of the Puritans' ethical teachings, which were problematical enough, but because of their insistence on the literal identification of America with Israel. This ahistorical literalism prevented historical events from coming to signify their own unique human meanings. It closed down the interpretive space in which the human imagination acknowledges and assumes moral responsibility for its history. The historical romancers therefore write *historical* romances. They reopen the human space in which a historical imagination contemplates the past and interprets it.

The historical romancers realized that they could only live and write in the specificity of concrete human actions and events. Only in the recognition and acknowledgment of their place within history could they assume the moral responsibility required by biblical redemption and human ethics. But the recurrence of the biblical story in over two centuries of American fiction cannot be explained simply as a critique and revision of the American mind. Wolfgang Iser has argued that the modern novel evolved in response to the thematic restrictions imposed by the fatalistic determinism of Calvinistic Protestantism. Unable to change the future, consciousness turned inward to explore and record itself.[1] The akedian romances arose out of a similar pressure writ large. Because it seemed to reenact a predetermined plot, American history (and therefore American literature) seemed to many Americans impossible to write because it had already been written. Therefore, many Americans mindlessly repeated historical patterns they did not fully comprehend. The romance writers could have chosen to ignore this flight from history, which led only to the hellish sterility of a Reuben Bourne or an Isaac McCaslin, but they did not. Rather than write gothic romances or didactic or sentimental or realistic novels of social manners that evaded such issues, Brown, Cooper, Hawthorne, Melville, Anderson, O'Connor, and Faulkner recognized that American history and literature could no more be separated from America's special brand of imagining than they could be made to coincide with it. Divine history might not have determined American history, but an American history of interpreting itself as a reflection of the divine had accomplished its own kind of prophetic fatality. With certain large patterns of American history thus determined, the historical romancers explored the awful implications of the American obsession, hoping through a process of self-conscious reflection unavailable to their protagonists, to moderate this obsession. Despite a tragic and misguided fanaticism, the characters of historical romance embody genuinely American impulses. The historical romancers take upon themselves, as a condition of their own imaginative being, the same contours of biblical history that their protagonists stretch to painful absurdity. The writers acknowledge and accept what their characters cannot—the burdens and errors of American history. By assuming responsibility for the events of their history and for its psychological cogency, the historical romancers provide the possibility for self-aware reflection, which could ultimately effect the revision of American history.

In entering sympathetically into their protagonists' misguided views of history, the historical romancers do more than acknowledge and review a problem of America's ahistorical imagination. The American historical romancers write fiction, not history. These fictions are not even historical in the sense of their being either mimetic or representational; they are romances. Though the historical romances reclaim, often in painstakingly precise historical detail, America's lost historical past, they emphatically do not commit themselves to the objectivity and rigorous neutrality of historical writing. The romances often seem like versions of their heroes' own worst obsessions. They seem to blur the distinctions between the real and the imaginary, representing history in an allegorical or symbolic mode, tottering on the same verge of collapse into horror or silence that engulfs their heroes. The protagonists are not wrong to suspect that all stories and all histories are masks or mirrors of each other, concealing rather than projecting differences. If Reuben and Ike are victims of this omnipresent indeterminacy of the real and the imaginary, who can blame them? (As I suggest above, many critics have not only not blamed them but have pronounced them heroic.) Hawthorne's and Faulkner's blends of the fictional and the historical would seem simply the furthest reaches of the undecidability of experience that often traps their characters.

History and romance can appear to be versions of each other, confirming the impossibility of interpreting human experience. American historical romance discovers in the situation of American history and the nation's ahistorical imagination a representation of the problem of interpretation, the subjectivity of perception. The American historical romance explicitly acknowledges this subjectivity, which makes all stories and histories romance fictions. At the same time, however, it refuses to abandon the reality of a world that is, at its core, historical and not romantic. The writers of historical romance sought a philosophy of fiction and history that could become, like historical consciousness or as a result of historical consciousness, a force of moral imagination capable of distinguishing the elements of the life-literature relationship. This historical romantic mode enabled authors to write texts that did not ignore the problems of undecidability and yet allowed them to produce and accept a history of determinate moral meanings.

INDETERMINACY AND THE TRADITION OF AMERICAN ROMANCE

In "Freud and the Scene of Writing," Jacques Derrida has suggested that there is no primal text of which written language is the transcript. Instead,

"everything begins with reproduction. Always already."[2] The American historical romancers were explicitly responding to this recurrent displacement or
deferral of meaning in the furthest reaches of human speech and action.
Because of this American response, the critical predilections suggested by
deconstructionism have found fertile ground in American literary criticism,
as did text-centered New Critical formalism before it. American fiction,
especially the romance tradition, has been absorbed with a tension between
repetition and origination, in history as well as in literature, and with the
problem of the indeterminate text.[3]

Marked by what Richard Poirier has called "style" over action, American
writing has been understood by generations of American critics as deliberately privileging text over world. "The only possible environment for [the
American experience]," writes Poirier, "is in a context invented by the
writers, the initial proposition being that they are only antagonistically received, if indeed they aren't obliterated, in the real world, or in literature
which allows itself to be merely a mirror of that world."[4] Michael Davitt Bell
argues that "self-conscious American romance, which began in a radically
deviant conception of fictionality and soon took to experimenting with the
possibility of making imaginary or irrational subjective states the objects of
literary mimesis, eventually became . . . in the works of Poe, Hawthorne,
and Melville, a means for scrutinizing the disrelations or dissociations beneath the aesthetic, epistemological and metaphysical assumptions of American Romanticism."[5] American romance, in the views of Bell and others
(including Henry James), sacrifices the relation between the text and the
world just as the protagonists of American historical romance sacrifice their
relation to history. The sacrificial moment seems to be not only the great
subject of American romance but its modus operandi. At most, as Evan
Carton has argued in an extremely sensitive study, powerfully informed by
the principles of Derridean deconstruction, the romance approach to reality
represents a dialectical confrontation, persistently redramatized, between the
impossible alternatives of presence and absence, immanence and transcendence, artistic representation and historical mimesis.[6]

Recent trends in "marketplace" criticism and other forms of socially
conscious and new historicist scholarship have begun to counter the more
theoretical readings of American fiction. The nineteenth-century romancers
from Brown, Irving, and Cooper through Hawthorne, Melville, and James,
they demonstrate, were hardly oblivious to the pressures of society, politics,
culture, and even economy that impinged on their worlds.[7] In writers like
Cooper, Hawthorne, Melville, and Faulkner, an explicit engagement with
historical events occurs, neither independent of nor hidden beneath the

romantic elements.[8] Like the "Neutral Ground" of Cooper's *Spy*, the so-called neutrality of American romance is neither as neutral nor as pacific as it might at first appear. Furthermore, in one whole family of American romances, which includes such works as Charles Brockden Brown's *Wieland*, Hawthorne's "Roger Malvin's Burial," and Melville's *Billy Budd*, the text occupies a place that is clearly not a transcendentalization or relocation or negation of the real world.[9]

By self-consciously placing wildly fictional events within verifiable historical contexts, the historical romances go out of their way to insist on the difference between history and the imagination. They remind the reader of what the stories' protagonists have failed to recall or understand: likeness is not sameness. Again, the recurrence of the biblical story of the akedah and of other biblical materials throughout American fiction is a part of the American writers' acceptance of their historical situation. It acknowledges both the events and the psychological disposition of American history and attempts to deal with their many implications. But the scene of the akedah does more than crystallize a particular failure in American historical imagination. It also engages the larger, more theoretical problem of consciousness itself, and the apparent impossibility of deciding whether experience can be decisively interpreted or whether it must be left as an infinite series of inadequate interpretations, constantly displacing each other.

The akedian romances recognize a paradox in the relationship between fiction and history, which becomes for the tradition at large an insight into the comprehension of human experience. In perceiving themselves as biblical figures, and American history as scriptural history, Wieland, Reuben, Ike, and the others had forced the meaning of American history. They had made human history conform to some other story, which was reflective of an indisputably higher moral authority. In thus determining the meaning of history, the historical romancers realized, these American "historians" had made history into a kind of fiction. By making human history into divine history, which they could only imperfectly understand and which functioned according to rules and laws that transcended human logic, they had converted it into something that could never finally be explicated or judged by human beings. The antitypological literalists had made the meaning of history as indeterminate as any romance could be. Henceforth, one could never decide whether an action was right or wrong, divinely decreed or humanly misunderstood. One could not, then, distinguish an actual human event from an allegory or symbol of some other kind of reality. This falsely imposed indeterminacy, the akedian romancers understood, was what threatened the identity of the nation, its consolidation into a concrete, moral entity. It was also, however, what made American history so intensely relevant to the problems of fictionality. For the alternative to the indeterminate text could not, in America, be the historical text (or the newspaper reports and ledgers in Go Down, Moses). Not entertaining the problem of decidability made interpretation as indeterminate as casting events as fictions pure and simple.

Like Poe, the historical romancers are committed to exploring perceptual and experiential disjunctions. But they also tie their romances to rigorously grounded historical investigations. They do this, not to suggest that the indeterminacies of fiction must be controlled by the determinate meanings of history, but to place in irresolvable opposition the two forces that must control our perception of the world. What emerge with equivalent power in their fictions are the disrelation and dissociation of the world and the text, on the one hand, and, on the other, the firmness of a nonverbal reality of people and events. The historical romancers will not allow their works to depart from this reality, even to achieve a moment of expanded self-consciousness or to get beyond duality and dualism. The effort to pass beyond dualism is what many of the historical romances thematize and criticize. At the center of Hawthornean romance, and the historical romances that succeed it, is the basic problem of the skeptical dilemma, of determining whether or not the elements of the dualism, the self and the world, exist at all. It is this dilemma that these writers, bringing fact and fancy face to face, hope to confront. By consistently confounding the reader's sense of reality through the perplexities of a symbolic and allegorical language that never departs from a historical context, the historical romances dwell on duality and our strategies for evading it. They redivide, as it were, a world artificially unified by history, philosophy, and above all, fiction. A key element in negotiating this skeptical dilemma is not so much the facts of history as historical consciousness. This is a consciousness of the world as remembered, and therefore as a story or fiction of indeterminate origin or meaning. Yet the world of history, because it is remembered and not simply imagined or invented, is also indisputably and undeniably other and real. It is an aspect of the world itelf, not merely a fantasy of the world as self. And it makes explicit demands on the individuals who inhabit it. In the next two chapters, I explore Hawthorne's historical romance treatment of the skeptical dilemma and prepare the ground for the Emersonian philosophy of history that Hawthorne evolves in The House of the Seven Gables and that Fitzgerald inherits from him in The Great Gatsby.

PLAYING THE DEVIL WITH HISTORY

Toward the end of "Young Goodman Brown,"[10] Hawthorne raises the question at the heart of historical romance. This question points to the tortuous relationship between imaginative and historical truth, the dream reality that is romance and the implacable reality of actual events. "Had Goodman Brown," Hawthorne asks, "fallen asleep in the forest, and only dreamed a wild dream of a witch-meeting?" (p. 89). Reader responses to this question reveal exactly how the question's philosophical nature and historical concerns have consistently been evaded. For moral-allegorical readers, for example, Young Goodman Brown's excursion into the forest to attend a witches' sabbath is real in the same way that any allegorical experience is real.[11] Throughout the story fiction serves fact. It exposes moral hypocrisy, the dishonesty of human beings (with the historical setting merely an incidental backdrop) or of the New England Puritans in particular (necessitating the specific historical details). The story seems to be historical interpretation cast as universal moral allegory or fiction.

But this answer to Hawthorne's question, which decides in favor of the primacy of reality over fiction, does not satisfy a majority of readers. This is so for the reasons cited by psychologically oriented critics who note the story's powerful concern with perceptual subjectivity. To Hawthorne's question, these critics answer that Brown's witches' sabbath does represent a pure and unadulterated dream, a warped projection of the protagonist's demented imagination. For Hawthorne, the central issue seems to be the mind's grasp of the world, not the world's relationship to the mind. "Hawthorne's interest in history," writes Frederick Crews, "is only a special case of his interest in fathers and sons, guilt and retribution, instinct and inhibition. . . . [The] history of the nation interests him only as it is metaphorical of individual mental strife." The story, therefore, does not embody a moral. Explains Crews, Hawthorne's plots "follow a logic of expression and repression that bypasses or undercuts moral problems."[12] Not all critics of a psychological persuasion share Crews's conclusions. A good many of them do, however, and their effect on the historical and moral analyses of the story cannot be ignored.[13]

Psychoanalytic readings give rise to the most radically indeterminate interpretations of Hawthorne's story. These dissociate the story totally from its historical setting. Perhaps, this group of critics suggest, Hawthorne's question articulates the impossibility of decidability, and it does not matter in the least whether Hawthorne's story records a dream or a reality. As one critic has put it, "the ultimate effect on Brown is the same."[14] When the story is seen in terms of what Crews calls "psychological necessity,"[15] it does not seem to matter whether events occur outside, in the real world of contemporary or historical fact, or inside, within the equally real world of the mind. The reality is the dream. History and fiction are synonymous and both are equally unrelated to any objective, external reality.

But "Young Goodman Brown" is an inherently moral tale, as it is a thoroughly historical one. It insists on the existence of a real world that has a real history and in which moral choices matter. Michael Davitt Bell has argued that "the question of whether or not Goodman Brown's vision is 'real' . . . is not irrelevant to the meaning of the story. If Brown's experience in the woods is real, then this is a tale about the depravity of mankind; and Brown's reaction, however excessive, is morally justified. But if the experience in the woods is dreamed . . . then the story is hardly moral at all."[16] Though Bell's conclusions about the story are not, I think, wholly accurate, his demand to decipher the story, to decide between reality and dream, is correct. The story's historical backgrounds do not simply enlarge its psychological investigations or illuminate them by placing them within a specific historical context. American history did not just happen to raise certain moral issues that were less conspicuous elsewhere. Rather historical consciousness emerges as a factor in the mind's capacity to struggle between good and evil. The tale intends us to judge Brown and his historical community and to recognize that his failure in moral decision making stems directly from his own lack of proper historical consciousness. The tale is decidedly not indeterminate.[17]

Michael Colacurcio has dealt with the pervasive attempts to allegorize or psychologize "Young Goodman Brown." According to Colacurcio, the story explores the problems of visible sanctity and specter evidence. It examines the meaning of faith in a universe of ambiguous, spectral evidences.[18] Any interpretation of the story must begin by crediting the seriousness of Hawthorne's involvement in the historical concerns that the tale raises. To do otherwise would be to forfeit much of the story. The reader must accept the premises of Brown's seventeenth-century mentality, that is, must grant the story a literal, historical plausibility. Brown may indeed have entered a real forest, with a real devil, and that devil may have conjured real specters. The reader who fails to journey with Brown may misunderstand the issue of specter evidence, which, if not the rich center of the story as Colacurcio and David Levin claim,[19] at least constitutes a vital component. From a modern point of view, belief in witches may well seem unfounded; Brown may certainly be hallucinating in the woods, and he certainly can be faulted for a lack of theological sophistication when he fails to question whether the devil might not assume the person of an angel of light. But there is nothing inherently demented or warped in seventeenth-century Brown's willingness to believe in witches and devils. Hawthorne's story, therefore, struggles with real and serious historical issues, examining how an individual makes difficult moral decisions in the light of what seem firm and irrefutable evidences.

One necessary, albeit partial, answer to Hawthorne's question is the old moral-allegorical answer reconstructed as a historical answer: Brown did not dream a dream of a witch meeting. He witnessed a spectral performance directed by a competent and real devil. Claiming that Brown is dreaming compromises the story's seriousness. As Levin has put it, discussing another literary work that refers back to the Salem witch trials, "Stupid or vicious men's errors can be appalling; but the lesson would be even more appalling if we realized that intelligent men, who tried to be fair and saw the dangers in some of their methods, reached the same conclusion and enforced the same penalties."[20] Similarly, arguing that it does not matter whether Brown's vision is hallucination or revelation can simply reproduce Brown's disastrous insensitivity to the difference between the mind and the world. Therefore, readers must refrain from overly concerning themselves with Brown's psychology, however interesting it might be. They must consider instead how one makes moral choices predicated on visible evidences of good and evil in an ambiguous universe.

The story is neither pure allegory, in which the whole story renders reality a dream (historically interpretive or not), nor psychological analysis (in which, while Brown himself is not a figment of the imagination, his perceptions are). Rather "Young Goodman Brown" is history, or, more precisely, historical fiction, in which all the events also have a historical reality. Crediting the historicity of the tale nicely complements the allegorical and psychological possibilities. Even if the witch meeting is a dream (and might not a dream in the post-Freudian era be thought of as a specter conjured by the devil within?) the issue can still be whether, given the psychological imperatives of the human mind, Brown can do other than respond to this spectral demonstration as if it were indisputable fact instead of highly subjective and suspect fiction.[21] And if this is so, then what can or must be his decision after he has seen what he has seen? If Brown is not guilty merely of sexual awkwardness or self-delusion or vain self-righteousness, then of what else is he guilty and how might he have avoided his terrible destiny?

Most readers agree that, whether or not he correctly assesses his fellow Salemites, Brown responds to them inappropriately. He dooms himself to becoming "a stern, a sad, a darkly meditative man" on whose tombstone "no hopeful verse" is carved (pp. 89–90). And yet if we examine his behavior in the light of his conviction and the possibility that he is witnessing real events (that is, either real citizens as witches or at least real specters pretending to be real citizens as witches), then it is difficult to find fault with his responses. If all of us were revealed to be in league with the devil, then would it not be every individual's responsibility to resist? Religion and ethics would demand at least this much. It is important to remember that we are viewing the story momentarily from Brown's point of view, as if the vision were a genuine and unambiguous revelation. We are seeing the tale with an emphasis on history and not on romance. Like Brown, we are not taking into account that this vision could be a dream or even that, while what he is seeing could be real (real specters conjured by a real devil), it might not mean what Brown thinks it means. Hawthorne provides the reader with the clues necessary for a sophisticated understanding of the relationship between perception and reality. But how can Brown, locked within a culture and a mindset in which he is not an enlightened spectator but an imprisoned actor, accede to the irony and moral complexity with which his story reverberates? Is there any way that Brown, too, could have become an intelligent reader of his experience?

If Brown had been a philosopher or a psychologist or if he had read or been able to read Spenser or Brockden Brown or Hawthorne or a number of other writers, he might have understood the subjectivity of human perception. If he had been a better theologian he might have comprehended the complexity of specter evidence. But there is one further way in which Brown could have escaped the hermetic seal of his psychosociological determinism. He could have been a better historian. This possibility figures strongly in Hawthorne's decision to write historical fiction and not unanchored allegory or psychological fantasy. Historical consciousness, Hawthorne insists, enables human beings to resist the self-reflexive prison of their own prejudiced perceptions. Hawthorne does not write his story of a young man's descent into psychological hell as historical fiction because history provides a distance from which to examine a contemporary problem or because he wants to suggest that Americans suffer from a special obsessive psychosis. Rather, he wants to reveal the ways in which history mediates between the demon of psychological and cultural determinism and the emancipating savior of moral free will.

In *The Province of Piety*, Colacurcio analyzes Hawthorne as a "moral historian." But it is not enough to say as Colacurcio has claimed, that history is as philosophical as literature.[22] One still needs to ask, why render the philosophical fictional? Why render it historical? And one still needs to record the consequences for the literary text of its involvement in a historical as opposed to a purely fictional form of philosophizing. Even if one grants the depths of Hawthorne's historical analyses, as Colacurcio explicates them, it is still necessary to discover why or how deciphering the stories as historical fictions is different from explicating them as allegories, symbolizations, or flights of fancy, as if the contexts, places, people, and events derived, as they usually do in a work a fiction, from the imagination of the author or from the literary tradition, and not from the historical record. What difference does it make that Hawthorne writes historical romance, that he chooses to communicate through the events of the past?

Hawthorne encodes the importance of historical consciousness as distinct from historical knowledge at a critical moment in the text. The devil, himself playing moral historian, reveals two precedents that will help Brown justify his excursion into evil:

> "Too far! too far!" exclaimed the goodman, unconsciously resuming his walk. "My father never went into the woods on such an errand, nor his father before him. We have been a race of honest men and good Christians, since the days of the martyrs. And shall I be the first of the name of Brown, that ever took this path and kept—"
>
> "Such company, thou wouldst say," observed the elder person, interpreting his pause. "Well said, Goodman Brown! I have been as well acquainted with your family as with ever a one among the Puritans; and that's no trifle to say. I helped your grandfather, the constable, when he lashed the Quaker woman so smartly through the streets of Salem. And it was I that brought your father a pitch-pine knot, kindled at my own hearth, to set fire to an Indian village, in King Philip's war. They were my good friends, both; and many a pleasant walk have we had along this path, and returned merrily after midnight. I would fain be friends with you for their sake."
>
> "If it be as thou sayest," replied Goodman Brown, "I marvel they never spoke of these matters. Or, verily, I marvel not, seeing that the least rumor of the sort would have driven them from New-England. We are a people of prayer, and good works, to boot, and abide no such wickedness." (Pp. 76–77)

Many critics have cited this passage as evidence either of Brown's psychological weakness or of his theological innocence. Brown immediately believes that his ancestors received help from the devil. Furthermore, he accepts judgments that may only represent the devil's willingness to use moral argumentation in the cause of evil.[23] Problematically, Brown fails to question the sweeping and unsubstantiated claim that his ancestors willingly accepted the devil's help, that they performed deeds that they (and not a subsequent generation) considered the devil's work. This final failure of moral imagination is the key to the problem. It takes only a modicum of historical knowledge (and Brown surely possessed it) to understand that to Father and Grandfather Brown, perhaps even to Goodman Brown himself in another frame of mind, lashing a Quaker woman through the streets or setting fire to an Indian village would hardly have constituted devilish activities. From the perspective of the earlier Puritans, and some of Brown's generation as well, such deeds would have been quite the opposite of wickedness. Therefore, though Father and Grandfather Brown have sinned, their sin does not evidence that they are the devil's "good friends." Their sins only exhibit the inevitable imperfection of all fallen humankind, the inescapable interference of the devil in postlapsarian life.

When Brown judges his father and grandfather guilty of collaborating with the devil, he is not thinking as a seventeenth-century Puritan (of the first, second, or third generations). Nor is he identifying with or making allowances for the moral norms of another society. He is judging them from the standpoint of a detached, objective, ahistorical morality. One would think that such a moment of absolute moral conviction is just what Hawthorne is advocating in this story of abundant human prejudice and nastiness. Yet, ironically, Brown's sudden revelation does not set him on the course to moral action. It ensures his damnation, psychologically, theologically, and historically. This is so because Brown fails at the critical task of sympathizing, even accepting, moral perceptions different from his own. Hawthorne is not amoral. He believes in a set of moral values that transcend the whim of individual preference. But moral action, apparently, cannot be directly defined. Brown's misreading of history mirrors his misunderstanding of specters. He cannot acknowledge the interdependence of the absolute and the subjective. Therefore, he leaps for judgments that, in their utter simplicity, distort and then replicate the errors they seem at first to reveal.

Since it is unlikely that Brown did not know of his father's and grandfather's historical exploits, the unspoken matters that the devil reveals to Brown must be not the deeds themselves but their devilish aspect. Since Brown initially resists the devil's enticements on the basis of his reading of history (the fact that his father and grandfather "never went into the woods on such an errand"), what essentially happens here is that the devil changes Brown's reading of history. He converts it from a reading of absolute identification, blind to moral nuance ("We have been a race of honest men and good Christians") to one of equally imperceptive condemnation and not a small measure of self-righteousness. Brown, simply, loses faith in his ancestors; that loss of faith beomes a loss of faith in religion because, for Brown, theological truth and human truth are the same. For Brown, the world is an allegory, and good and evil, can be made manifest, revealed spectrally, to the satisfaction of any rational intellect. Brown's error is that he confuses reason and faith. If, for Hawthorne, faith is not blind allegiance to the past, it also does not depend on the paltry powers of human reason to judge the past. Rather, faith accepts the special terms and conditions of Christian history, which, though enacted and recorded by human beings, expresses a divine reality not circumscribed by the limits of human comprehension. Faith cannot depend on rational demonstration. It must bind an identification and sympathy with the past to a knowledge that human history is fallen, that it only imperfectly expresses the divine history in which it participates.

Not accidentally, in seducing Brown into abandoning faith in his ancestors and in his religion, the devil is portrayed as reasoning with Brown as they proceed to journey through the woods of moral complexity (p. 76). A language of uncharitable, faithless reason colors Brown's pronouncements and conclusions throughout the rest of the story. "Friend," says Brown at one point, "my mind is made up. Not another step will I budge on this errand. What if a wretched old woman do choose to go to the devil, when I thought she was going to Heaven! Is that any reason why I should quit my dear Faith, and go after her?" (p. 80). But the devil admonishes him, "You will think better of this, by-and-by" (p. 80), and he proceeds to conjure or to appear to conjure a wealth of evidence, including horsemen and conversations and the infamous pink ribbon, that gives Brown just the "reason" he needs to abandon faith. The devil's apparently logical demonstration of the wickedness of the whole Salem community, past and present, results in Brown's reasoned formula: "My Faith is gone! . . . There is no good on earth; and sin is but a name. Come, devil! for to thee is this world given" (p. 83). When evidence flies in the face of faith, we can, according to the logic of Brown's position, reasonably conclude that evil is our only reality and the devil our only God. Brown's syllogistic logic and his either-or cast of mind, reminiscent of Wieland's, seal his fate.

Brown fails to realize that God has provided humankind with faith so that it might resist the devilish snares of an unfeeling logic. As Colacurcio has put it, "Finally, in a way Goodman Brown had little expected and is totally unprepared to accept or even comprehend, everything *does* depend on Faith,"[24] though faith, for Hawthorne, includes a historical as well as a doctrinal understanding. Faith mediates between rationality's mutually exclusive alternatives and the ambiguity and mystery of Christian salvation. Reason and the desire for the gifts of reason caused the fall; only the suspension of rational judgment allowed a justifiably angry God to sacrifice His son to secure salvation for humankind. Faith is the belief in the covenant of grace that accounts for the redemption of sinful human souls despite their wickedness and that magically transforms sinners into saints. Faith demands a basic acceptance of a transcendent Christian history as recorded in scripture. This history Puritan Brown ignores. In addition to his other, more human sins, Brown is an arminian, as he inadvertently admits when he confesses to his "good works, to boot" (p. 77). Brown foolishly forgets the facts of redemption. He ignores what he must surely have known: that even the saint is a sinner. As I have suggested, the Puritan historiographers, emphasizing visible sanctity and positing a federal ideal based on such sanctity, tended toward an antitypological rather than a historically controlled, typological reading of history. The result was that they elevated their place in the ongoing story of scripture and eclipsed all history preceding them. This corruption of the historical sense, which put the self and the community at the center of the interpretation of history, had resulted in the profoundly anti-Christian moral absolutism and egocentrism exposed in Hawthorne's story.

In less theological terms, morality, according to Hawthorne, is dialectical, not absolute. It is controlled by a sympathy that, like faith, modifies purely rational judgment. Therefore, though moral or immoral deeds may be isolated objectively, moral nature and conscience must be defined subjectively. Logical argumentation can demonstrate that Brown's father and grandfather are guilty of wickedness, that some devil participated in their misconceived exploits. But the dictates of moral relativism, the lessons of history, require us to recognize that, according to their own moral lights, they were no more in league with the devil than Brown is or believes himself to be. Hawthorne does not intend to license all deeds enacted in the name of God or morality. The devil correctly argues that Brown's father and grandfather have sinned in their persecution of the Quakers and the Indians; we are appropriately sensitive to Brown's even more dramatic moral exclusivity, his lunatic hatred of all humankind. But Hawthorne wishes us to see in Brown's readiness to pronounce judgment on his ancestors and his community the more general moral principle that morality must be interpreted through historical consciousness. It is not impossible to make distinctions. The proper lesson of history, however, is not that Father and Grandfather Brown have sinned (we all do). Rather, it is that their sin proceeded from an ahistorical moral absolutism. In the theological sphere, they forgot the fundamental mystery of their own salvation (which depends on faith and not works). On the secular front, they carelessly disregarded the pressures of a real world that inevitably alters the definition and manifestation of right and wrong.

The incorporation of the historical moment within the historical tale of fiction is crucial. We cannot require of Brown that he have read Hawthorne or Freud or even Cotton Mather. But we can demand that, when confronted with the record of history in which the historical figures (his own father and grandfather) define morality one way and the contemporary reader of history defines it another way, he will see that morality and perception are subjective phenomena. To take this view is to regard history as more than moral exemplum or illustration or even allegory. It is to see history as the respectful examination of the complexity and variety of the human spirit. The historian who uses history to render facile and superficial judgments, to see the past through the limited and limiting lens of self, is a false historian who can play the devil with our moral sense. The false historian can conjure specters like Grandfather Brown or Father Brown or even Young Goodman Brown, which reduce the multidimensional historical world to an allegory of good and evil and convince us of our objective moral superiority. This devil writes history as fiction and leaves real historical contingencies behind.

Using a self-consciously fictive romance to ask the epistemological, historical, and theological question that had plagued Salem in 1692, Hawthorne does more than plumb history for insights into the world or establish a neutral ground of human feeling. He forces history to probe the determinants of historical and artistic truth. The storyteller as Puritan historian asks, what is a specter? Does it accurately represent the real world, faithfully translating material reality into cerebral construct? Or does it devilishly distort truth, willfully seducing the perceiver into a demonic perspective? Does a specter make visible what is concealed by the material world? Or does it impose a devilish fiction that itself conceals reality? As psychological and fictive elements qualify and modify this question, it metamorphoses into a quandary even deeper and more compelling. What, asks the romancer, is an image, any image, whether conjured by devil, artist, or historian?[25] Do images enchance our knowledge of truth, or do they substitute for truth and make it inaccessible to genuine human knowing?

Knowledge of both past and present inevitably flows through images. Young Goodman Brown errs because he does not understand technically what a specter is. He cannot fathom its relation to realms of reality that are not purely physical but that are subject to interpretation and manipulation. He does not comprehend the spectrality implicit in any act of perception and accentuated and dramatized in the actual specters of literal devils. But Brown's problem exceeds even this lack of theological and epistemological sophistication. Hawthorne does not fault Brown simply for mistaking specters for real persons and for misreading the mind's fictions, whether the mind is his own or the devil's. Rather he condemns Brown for treating those fictions, to which he has already ascribed the status of real human beings, as if they were solely his own creations. Having assigned the specters a historical validity that removes them from the purely self-reflective realm of mind, Brown behaves as if they were objects or subjects produced by and for his own intellect and moral sense. Human beings perceive the world through images, whether those ghosts and specters of another reality are created by some force outside the self, demonic or divine, or whether they are the internal products of human consciousness. Paradoxically, however, the world, for all its spectrality, is not a fiction. It is not a dream. It is solid and unalterable, a physical and historical entity that cannot be made to accommodate anyone's subjectivity.

Hawthorne's historical romance explicates this perceptual, moral problem by reconstructing it. Brown, too, is a specter. The narrator conjures him in much the same way that the devil conjures his father and grandfather and, one might be tempted to conclude, for much the same purpose: to moralize on our Puritan fathers. If we judge the miscomprehending Brown too harshly, if we treat him as he has treated his own ancestors, as a disembodied figure symbolizing evil or psychosis rather than as an individual who tried to resist the Evil One and did not wholly succeed, we make Hawthorne into one more devilish historian. Ignoring the historical context that makes Brown a complex human being, we repeat rather than expiate the sins of the fathers. The historical reality so faithfully reproduced in the story, which prevents our grandly dismissing Brown's belief in witches, helps us to sympathize with his dilemma in relation to spectral evidence. Had Goodman Brown "fallen asleep in the forest, and only dreamed a wild dream of a witch-meeting?" Hawthorne's answer is, "be it so, if you will" (p. 89). We seem to have no more authority to go on than if the world were but a dream, a projection of our internal desires and fears. But whether the subjectivity of perception expresses itself as specter or dream or fiction, the question remains, how must individuals act in the world?

For Hawthorne a proper approach to history—that of historical romance perhaps—fortifies the individual against the devil's wiles. Hawthorne's historical romance dramatizes the differences among moral judgments in different generations. It insists that these differences result from the spectral quality of perception and judgment. And it declares that, for all its spectral evidences, the world is not a figment of the imagination. Puritan history provided a rich field for the examination of this relation between imaginative and historical truth. The crisis that weakened the New England theocracy seemed to Hawthorne to hinge on the community's twofold failure to register the spectral quality of reality and to acknowledge a past and a present outside its private definitions of them. The Puritans, whose federal theology was predicated on visible sanctity, had committed themselves to interpreting all specters, natural and supernatural, epistemological and psychological, as concrete and irrefutable evidences of a spiritual reality that they themselves defined.

Puritan history provided the inevitable setting for this American story. Other historical realities, however, could also have been made to serve Hawthorne's purposes. For in Hawthorne's view, history, as the story of the past, embodies the essential conflict between the spectrality of human perception and the necessity for nonetheless regarding the people and objects of our perception as objectively real.[26] History is a spectral, not a physical, evidence of human action. It records a world that has already disappeared and it must project that world as story, as imaginative construct. But history, raising the possibility that the world is revealed spectrally, does not abandon the world to the solipsistic self-indulgence and egocentricism of an ahistorical Goodman Brown. Proper history, despite its insistence on interpretive subjectivity, respects the objective separateness of the story that it narrates, the flesh and blood of the world that it projects.

If Brown and his Puritans err in accepting as real their highly questionable perceptions of the world, they also sin in treating the objects of their perception as lacking substantial humanness. Thus they dismiss as fantasy the similarly spectral but equally legitimate perceptions of others. Hawthorne rejects the Puritan orthodoxy of his ancestors, with its literalizations of its imaginings, its absolute divisions of right and wrong, saint and sinner, and its subsequent intolerance for those who see differently. He does so, however, by employing the sympathy and Christian charity that they did not possess. While Hawthorne rejects the Puritans' unshakable conviction in the reality of their perceptions, he does not reject the reality of the Puritans themselves and of their differently defined historical world. History does not reveal a string of disconnected acts of moral tyranny and dishonesty. Rather it exposes a continuous pattern of self-deception in which conviction in the reality of the self and in absolute moral dictates forces individuals to repeat the acts of immorality they despise. As a counterforce to these indeterminacies, history also posits the concrete existence of those individuals whose corporeal presence demands respect and sympathy. Michael Bell argues that Brown's (and the Puritans') sin is the "unpardonable Sin of allegory, subjugating life . . . to abstract notations." Historical fact breaks the force of the propensity to allegorize. Like Hawthorne's own stories, which as Bell observes employ an allegorical mode to express an anti-allegorical intention,[27] history projects the symbolic outlines of reality without forsaking the substance that gives reality its unique, human identity.

In blending romance with history, Hawthorne analyzes both the Puritans' explicitly federalist assumptions, with the attendant implications for the reading of history, and their often denied but just as pervasive antinomian tendencies, which are reborn in nineteenth-century America in the transcendentalists.[28] Though Hawthorne seems to postulate a popular transcendentalist conception of the inseparability of world and self, he significantly revives the Emersonian insistence on the necessary tension between idealism and a raw love of nature that verges on materialism. Only the frivolous, Emerson knows, make themselves merry with the idealist philosophy. But idealism creates problems, and Hawthorne addresses these problems. "Know then that the world exists for you," Emerson wrote in *Nature*. "Build therefore your own world." "I . . . require of every writer . . . a simple and sincere account of his own life . . . some such account as he could send to his kindred from a distant land; for if he had lived sincerely, it must have been a distant land to me," explains Thoreau in *Walden*.[29] That each self's world is built by and exists only for itself, that there is a distance between any two worlds, makes the Emersonian and Thoreauvian positions problematic. If all individuals are Neoplatonic first causes of a universe of their own, they are also the created beings of other individuals' similarly private, exclusive, and separate creations. How, in such a multitude of worlds, does one create sympathy? For Hawthorne, the solution lay in part in the will to moral action that followed from the knowledge of historical reality. "Had Goodman Brown only dreamed . . . a wild dream . . .?" "Be it so, if you will," he answers his own question. Sympathy depends on the awareness of the dreamlike and yet insistently real quality of the past, in which we see others dreaming the same illusion of reality and mistaking it for reality itself. It resides in our own willingness to conjure history's spectral entities and to acknowledge them, not as ghosts and shadows but as real persons.

In so formulating his argument Hawthorne significantly reverses the here and now direction of Emersonian historiography.[30] He returns history to its proper discipline, which both the Puritans and the transcendentalists were inclined to forget: the study of the particularity and uniqueness of the past, the record of change over time. Though the view that Emerson stood outside history and disputed its importance has recently come under revision, Quentin Anderson's notion of an Emersonian self decidedly different from a historical Hawthornean or Jamesian self locates an important aspect of the transcendentalist tradition. Writes Anderson: "The moment Emerson chose to say that we are not bound by time, that we could start afresh, was a critical moment in the national consciousness."[31] It was this moment that troubled Hawthorne. It is no accident that Anderson's description of Emerson's (a)historicity articulates a version of the sacrifice of relation that worried James and that forms the basis for one whole view of American romance. "To bind the dreamer on the wheel of cause-and-effect was to make him a part of history. Simply by denying a single providence, Emerson stood aside from all this."[32] The explicit, almost mind-boggling thoroughness of Hawthorne's historicity prevents our entertaining, even for a moment, the transcendental solution that was at moments plausible for Emerson.

In Hawthorne's view, it is impossible, and dangerous, to imagine that each individual mind repeats the whole of human history and that history therefore exists to confirm the self in its knowledge of itself. In a sense Puritan historiography had done just this. Father and Grandfather Brown dismiss the Indians and Quakers, Young Goodman Brown dismisses his father and grandfather, because each one wishes to see the world as confirmation of his own specialness, his own saintliness. Of this reading of history the devil is the consummate historian and Goodman Brown his most accomplished student. As Milton understood all too well, Satan would not only substitute himself for God, he would permeate the creation with his essence. This is not to say that for Hawthorne, Emerson is the devil. As I discuss below, in *The House of the Seven Gables*, Hawthorne actively adapts many of Emerson's positions, substituting history for nature as the place in which human beings learn about their relationships with the world and with each other. But there is a danger in Emersonian historiography that had been transmitted along the line of American historical (or ahistorical) thinking.

For Hawthorne, as for Emerson, human life exists under the injunction of the "noble doubt," the skeptical imperative that questions the existence of the world and the self and then chooses, notwithstanding the uncertainty, to forge a relationship between them.[33] History, for Hawthorne, records the world from a point of view that is not the self. It demands that the self acknowledge a world it did not create, cannot transform, and cannot finally even verify. Present and historical reality are both specters. But so is the self. We can never, therefore, know for sure who is the specter and who the spectral perceiver, who is being written into whose text. Specters, therefore, must be conceived of as possessing the same solid and inaccessible selfhood that we all possess. Goodman Brown errs because, like other witch hunters, he fails to respect the integrity of other human beings. He cannot grant them the same perceptual freedom he claims for himself. By simultaneously breaking the hold of Brown's perceptual authority and sympathetically recreating the world Brown believes in, Hawthorne's historical romance provides the grounds for just that sympathetic identification that Brown denies.

History's Veil and
the Face of the Past:
Acceptance and Acknowledgment in
Hawthorne's Historical Romances

The necessity of coming to terms with the essentially spectral and yet insistently human quality of the world is one of the great arguments of Hawthorne's historical romances. For Hawthorne, all action in the world, past and present, reflected the subjective perceptions of the enactors of events, who, necessarily viewing themselves and their world through private optics, largely determined the configuration of their reality.[1] But if individuals are all proto-Neoplatonic first causes who generate personal and private realities, they also, in Hawthorne's view, constitute the objects of the imaginative constructs of others, who go about the same business of fabricating a world out of the varied fragments of perception. Goodman Brown damns his ancestors and his fellow Salemites because he cannot see beyond the veil that isolates his vision from the vision of others. He imagines that there is no perception, no way of perceiving, that is not identical with self. Embodiments of this perceptual problem recur in much of Hawthorne's fiction, most notably in "The Minister's Black Veil." The veil that stands between the mind and the world seems to doom the mind to viewing only itself. At best, it seems to project only the distant and hazy outlines of a reality that it can never verify or affirm.

In recent studies, Sharon Cameron and Myra Jehlen have explored an American tendency to realize selfhood and national identity through what Cameron calls a process of corporealization and Jehlen an incarnation of the self.[2] These insights, which bring into new and interesting focus a view of the American self that permeates American literary criticism, identify an important feature of the historical romance tradition. For the historical romancers the central liability of fictionalizing is not only that it often blurs its social-historical origins and the ideological contents that these determine.

Equally troubling for them is its tendency to privilege its own perception of the world, to dissolve the boundary between self and world and spill over into the border that prevents their disastrous conflation. Writers from Brown and Cooper through Hawthorne and Melville and into the twentieth century are explicitly concerned with the authority of authorship and with its decided authoritarianism as well. They deal with the designs that the subjective self has on its world and the ways in which, especially in America, it incorporates or incarnates itself in the world and as the world. By overdetermining meaning in a whirl of indeterminacies, fiction would eclipse the distance between the fiction and the world and between the self and the other on which moral, historical, and philosophical interpretation depends.

And yet, the veil that separates the self and the world and that seems to lead to the problems of subjective perception could also function to preserve autonomy, to protect the other from the predatory activities of the self. Historical consciousness, which prevents the evaporation of reality into dream, also ensures the distance between the perceiving self and the world. It restrains the imagination from engulfing a reality largely at the mercy of the individual's perceptual authority. History, Hawthorne suggests, presents reality through a veil that simultaneously acknowledges the indeterminacy of human perception and protects the objects of that perception from dissolving into fictions of the omnipotent imagination.

THE APPEAL TO INDETERMINACY

Not every appeal to history will successfully balance the claims of mind and world. A history that is made too present to the world can actually engulf reality with its own presence. That kind of history is just as spectral and just as deadly as the imaginings of a mind that would dematerialize the past. In "Alice Doane's Appeal,"[3] Hawthorne writes the devil's kind of historical romance in which romance yields to the powerful forces of indeterminacy that historical consciousness, properly understood, can control. The artist-historian of "Alice Doane's Appeal" does not intend to play a devilish role. His "appeal" is admirable enough: "it is singular, how few come on pilgrimage to this famous hill; how many spend their lives almost at its base, and never once obey the summons of the shadowy past, as it beckons them to the summit. Till a year or two since, this portion of our history had been very imperfectly written, and, as we are not a people of legend or tradition, it was not every citizen of our ancient town that could tell, within half a century, so much as the date of the witchcraft delusion" (p. 267). The narrator believes in the value of historical knowledge—and not just for personal or financial gain (p. 267). He knows that every community, to ensure its soul, needs to acknowledge its collective responsibility for past and present. Like the story of "Young Goodman Brown," the story of Leonard Doane debates the essential issues of the Salem witch trials, and it suggests how future generations stand on the same perilous ground when they look back into the past and fail to recognize that its monsters inevitably reflect the projected images of themselves.[4] Like "Young Goodman Brown," the story does more than psychoanalyze history. It insists on the necessity for historical consciousness in the analytic process.

The story, both in the narrative of Alice Doane and in the description of the Salem witch trials, makes its point only by creating a "historical influence" (p. 267) as ghastly as the events themselves. This historical influence is as dangerous as the lack of historical imagination that it is meant to correct. Blurring the distinction between past and present, the speaker traps his listeners and readers in an almost spectral web from which there is no simple escape. Like Matthew Maule and his descendant Holgrave in *The House of the Seven Gables*, he casts a dangerous, potentially deadly, spell. In an eerie voice, which proceeds by a fascinating blend of direct and indirect narration, in which past and present, self and other, become inseparably intertangled, the narrator tells the story of his own ascent to Gallows Hill and of his reading the story of Alice and Leonard Doane (a story that he himself has written). He also reads from the story, quoting himself, as it were, and also quoting the major protagonist Leonard, as if Leonard were also a narrator of the story. It is impossible to determine who is speaking and where we are, in the story or outside it, in Salem 1692 or nineteenth-century Salem. The narrator begins, "I had brought the manuscript in my pocket. . . . After a little hesitation on my part . . . I began the tale, which opened darkly with the discovery of a murder" (p. 269). Then the narrator—or is it the storyteller within the story?—begins to narrate the story proper: "A hundred years, and nearly half that time, have elapsed since the body of a murdered man was found, at about the distance of three miles, on the old road to Boston" (p. 269). The confusion continues, becoming more ghastly still, as the very voice of Leonard Doane merges with the narrative voice: "Searching . . . into the breast of Walter Brome, I at length found a cause why Alice must inevitably love him" (p. 271). This undifferentiated flow from narrator to storyteller, within the story, to fictive character as narrator causes a total collapse in the distinctions between reality and imagination, present and past, and artistic control and psychotic compulsion. Auditors and readers (both literal and implied, outside the story and within) are all drawn into the confusion:

By this fantastic piece of description, and more in the same style, I intended to throw a ghostly glimmer round the reader, so that his imagination might view the town through a medium that should take off its everyday aspect, and make it a proper theatre for so wild a scene as the final one. Amid this unearthly show, the wretched brother and sister were represented as setting forth, at midnight, through the gleaming streets, and directing their steps to a grave yard, where all the dead had been laid . . . As they went, they seemed to see the wizard gliding by . . . But here I paused, and gazed into the faces of my two fair auditors . . . Their bright eyes were fixed on me; their lips apart. I took courage, and led the fated pair to a new made grave, where for a few moments, in the bright and silent midnight, they stood alone. But suddenly, there was a multitude of people among the graves. (Pp. 274–75)

The two auditors are as hypnotized by the scene as are Alice and Leonard within it. They are as much subject to the storyteller/narrator's dramatic direction as his characters. And when the wizardlike narrator, who has thrown a ghostly glimmer around the town, takes courage and leads the "fated pair" to the grave where they stand alone, the reader—both the literal reader and the implied reader in the tale within the tale, around whom Hawthorne also intends to throw that ghostly glimmer, both of them bewitched by the language's imprecisions—cannot be sure if the narrator is referring to Alice and Leonard or to his "two young ladies." Every reader will have to decide for himself or herself how much he or she is under the story's spell. But Hawthorne unmistakably confuses the interpretive process. We cannot even decide whether the narrator's language is figurative or literal. Does he actually lead the fated pair to a newly made grave or does he only take them there through his story? Is it the case that "suddenly there was a multitude of people among the graves," or that imaginatively speaking it was as if such a multitude had appeared? And who is the wizard who glides by: the wizard who authored the original tragedy; the wizard whom the narrator has written into his story; or the narrator/storyteller himself, who is also a kind of wizard? Ontological barriers collapse and the conclusion of the scene brings the indeterminacy to a horrific climax: "Each family tomb had given up its inhabitants . . . All, in short, were there; the dead of other generations . . . all whom black funerals had followed slowly thither, now re-appeared where the mourners left them. Yet none but souls accursed were there" (pp. 275–76). Where and when is this taking place? It could be in Salem 1692, before the gaze of Alice and Leonard, or on Gallows Hill in the nineteenth century, in front of the storyteller and his two auditors, for whom Alice and Leonard are themselves the dead of another generation, souls accursed, or in the mind of the reader for whom not only Gallows Hill 1692 is a specter, but for whom the storyteller and his two young ladies (not to mention the literal author of the tale) are also ghosts. And if the reader is also there, is his or her soul also accursed? The possibilities are as Poesque as the story itself seems to be.

But Hawthorne is no Poe. Indeterminacy, this story tells us, is no simple philosophical or epistemological or literary critical matter. Hawthorne, therefore, will not continue to entertain the frank, raw horror of gothic literature.[5] He will reject the gothicism of Poe and of his own early achievements, because he recognizes that the indeterminacy on which gothic literature depends, like the textual derestriction it affords, is double-edged. He does not doubt the power of the imagination so much as he fears it, his own every bit as much as the imaginations he investigates in his fictions. But he also knows that authorial genius can be tamed. In the evolution from witches to artists that he describes in a work like *The House of the Seven Gables*, he shows how one kind of craft can be made over into another. In stories like "Young Goodman Brown," and in "Edward Randolph's Portrait" and "The Minister's Black Veil," Hawthorne draws the bottom line that contains textual indeterminacy and limits the repetition of an endless self-absorption. He draws the curtain between fiction and the world, the past and the present, that protects each domain from the encroachments of the other and that keeps the author a saving distance from his listener/reader, firmly on the other side of the veil. This veil also concerns history.

"EDWARD RANDOLPH'S PORTRAIT"

The veil of imagination that Hawthorne throws over the story of "Alice Doane's Appeal" (p. 268) differs dramatically from the veil of history that he describes in "Edward Randolph's Portrait" (pp. 258, 261) and "The Minister's Black Veil."[6] In these stories, Hawthorne does more than suggest the similarities between historical and subjective perception. He indicates how the veil of history qualifies the veil of imagination. He records the process by which history's veil teaches us how to escape the blinding or suffocating effects of our own subjectivity and to reach out and establish the network of community that characters like Goodman Brown and Minister Hooper never achieve. The portrait at the center of "Edward Randolph's Portrait," "if picture it can be called—which is no more visible, nor ever will be" (p. 261), a "black waste of canvas" (p. 259) and a "void blackness" (p. 258), pictures the historical past in its present spectrality. The portrait is the absence of a picture. It is the nonrepresentation of a reality. Ostensibly what has obliterated the picture's lineaments and cancelled its powers of representation is "time" (p. 258), the "mist of years" and the "duskiness of time" (p. 261), which have "thrown an impenetrable veil over [the picture], and left to tradition, and fable, and conjecture, to say what had once been there portrayed" (p. 258). The picture is as gothic as they come, so horrible, so indeterminate, so derestrictive that it seems to contain any and all projections, any and all horrors. The major action of the story concerns the maneuvers by which individual viewers attempt to interpret the painting. This story, linked to the picture, might seem to be a conventionally romantic-gothic dematerialization of reality, with time serving as the source of the "veil," which obscures and thereby projects reality with the appropriate indefiniteness.

But in "Edward Randolph's Portrait," as in "Young Goodman Brown," the veil of subjective imagination does not become the range and content of the world. The nonrepresentational aspects of the portrait cannot be separated from its explicit acknowledgment that a reality once existed, that a flesh-and-blood world, which could be described and painted, still lies beneath the surface of the canvas. Like so much of Hawthorne's fiction, the story comes replete with historical facts that are the opposite of fancy or legend.[7] Alice, as artist, is more interested in the painting than its history. As a historian, however, she must produce a living picture from behind time's veil.

In "Edward Randolph's Portrait" Hawthorne explores the role of the veil in defining the relationship between past and present and even future. He examines the veil between history and fiction, representation and romance. The portrait is simultaneously and equally the historical, representational picture of Edward Randolph beneath the surface of the canvas and the "black waste of canvas" (p. 259), which is a picture in its own right, hanging for generations in the governor's mansion. The veil of time obscures the face of the past. It is, however, also the only face of the past that exists. Alice has to discover some way of getting behind the veil without dislodging or destroying it. Like an archaeologist she must respect the layers of historical accretion, one of which is the veil itself. Each layer will have to be pushed aside to reveal the one beneath. But each layer will also have to be treated and preserved as a separate and legitimate record of the past.

Hawthorne reveals that even before the "duskiness of time had so effectually concealed it," "a veil had . . . hung down before the picture" (p. 261). The portrait has always worn a veil. Its early owners had concealed what had not yet faded away. Indeed, a fragment of that veil, "ragged remnants of black silk," survives (p. 261). It is a reminder of the portrait's past, and of the fact that in the past, it was an instrument of concealment. Alice's technique in restoring the portrait and thus unveiling history involves two almost antithetical activities. To make the image of the past visible (p. 267), she, like every historian, wipes away the deposits of time that hide historical reality. She removes the apparently "impenetrable" veil (p. 267) or "cloud" (p. 269) of history to reach a mimetic picture of the world. Simultaneously, however, to restore the portrait fully, she recovers the veil it has always worn and reveils it with "a black silk curtain . . . suspended before the mysterious picture, so as completely to conceal it" (p. 266). This curtain, which is associated with a "painter's art," a "spirit of intrigue," and the "tricks of stage-effect" (p. 268), acknowledges that which can never be made visible or subject to "ocular demonstration." It recognizes and commemorates the veil that has "covered the canvass since the memory of man" (p. 269), the veiledness of all reality and representationality. Alice's veil does not obscure meaning. It conveys it, expressing its own meaning. Though the literalistic Hutchinson needs to have the veil withdrawn in order to perceive what the curtain conceals, Alice knows that the portrait's veil is inseparably part of it. "Pressing one hand across her eyes," veiling her vision, Alice "snatch[es] away the sable curtain that concealed the portrait" (p. 266). She unveils the picture for her more literalistic uncle, while keeping it veiled for herself. For herself she knows that to see the veil is to see the portrait.

The veil acknowledges the limitations of interpretation. It protects the separate existence of realities that can never merge and that conceal and are concealed by each other. Like history, which the veil also images, it demands that viewers recognize something beneath it that is not pure interpretation but substance, fact, and multiple interpretations controlled by perceptions other than the viewer's. Alice's historical romance art reveals by reveiling because the image in the portrait represents a concealed meaning and always has. The face in the portrait hides another face, that of the real Edward Randolph, whose face almost certainly masked a complex human identity never to be captured in a painting. But that series of interpretive spirals unravels from a historical ground unlike subjectivity's bottomless maelstrom. Hutchinson, a conventional realist and historian, is not wrong when he informs Alice that the picture is "the portrait of Edward Randolph, the founder of this house, a person famous in the history of New England" (p. 261). That is the simple and true fact of the matter. And Randolph's historical identity is a crucial aspect of the picture's meaning, as Colacurcio's reading suggests.[8] Just as Hutchinson's "antiquarian researches" (p. 261) are limited by his inability to recognize that simple declarative identifications of names and places cannot define reality, so Alice's and Colonel Lincoln's legends require the knowledge a conventional historian provides. In the end, art's truth and Hutchinson's "Historical truth" (p. 262) do not oppose each other. This is so, not only because historical truth largely depends on the stories (p. 260) that accrue to history but because the stories could not exist without the history.

It is not that history is story. History narrates the events of a vanished world, but it does not expose reality to endless fictionalizations, which subsume the real and the remembered. History and story hang as veils over our knowledge of past and present. Like the veil of subjectivity, the veil of history can and must, on occasion, be lifted. But the veil of history is not simply a perverse obstacle to historical knowledge. It is, in and of itself, a portrait of the past. And it defines the necessary relationship between past and present. A veil has two sides. Each of them is equally valid. Each is equally inaccessible to the other. Yet each is the only optic through which one side can view the other. The veil of history does more than acknowledge the limited access from one side to the other. It draws the curtain that protects each side. It preserves the reality of things threatened by the mind's endlessly fictionalizing activities. The remnants of this veil, therefore, must never be extracted from the frame that delimits our perception of the world. The frame that supports the veil is also important. Historical frames, such as those employed in Hawthorne's own fiction, including the fictional and historical frames around "Edward Randolph's Portrait" (that is, both the "Legends of the Province House" in which the story is set and the historical circumstances by which both of "The Legends of the Province House" and the individual stories are framed) do not clarify or dispel obscurity. They contain it, and they make it part of the picture.

"THE MINISTER'S BLACK VEIL"

The minister's black veil is not Alice's (or Hawthorne's) kind of veil at all,[9] and the story abounds with hints as to how the reader should interpret it. Despite the veil's occasional effectiveness at funerals and during the preaching of certain kinds of sermons, it clearly hinders the minister's office. From the moment that he assumes the veil, it begins to throw "its obscurity between him and the holy page, as he read the Scriptures; and while he prayed, the veil lay heavily on his uplifted countenance. Did he seek to hide it from the dread Being whom he was addressing?" (p. 39; the minister himself calls its effect "miserable obscurity" [p. 47]). It also adversely affects his congregants. Many of them leave the church in "indecorous confusion" and "with ostentatious laughter" (p. 40), while the newly married bride and groom can only feel the veil as a portent of evil (p. 43).

We might be tempted to associate the veil and its ill effects exclusively with the minister, as it begins to cause him to see the world as if everyone in it wore a veil. "I look around me," he confesses at the end, "and, lo! on every visage a Black Veil" (p. 52). But the veil belongs to the community as well. Even the most sympathetic and loving of the community's members, Elizabeth, his fiancé, is not above putting on the veil. Ignoring the minister's appeal not to leave him in "miserable obscurity forever," "frightened" and "alone behind [the] black veil" (p. 47), she "covered her eyes with her hand, and turned to leave the room" (p. 47). Elizabeth's action recalls Alice Vane's similar gesture in "Edward Randolph's Portrait." But whereas Alice veils her vision in order to corroborate the necessity for veils, Elizabeth turns away simply in order not to see. Her final "shuddering gaze" seals both the minister's isolation and her own.

We might conclude from this pervasiveness of veils that the minister is correct in his desire to communicate the essential veiledness of reality. If veils are an inescapable part of our world, shouldn't they be made a conscious part of every perceptual act? Indeed, the art of romancer like Hawthorne, whose words and symbols are as dark and veiled as the minister's, seems to depend for its structure on the fact of veiledness. It seems to declare this fact in every word it utters. Richard Harter Fogle captures the textual dilemma, and its implications for the reading of literature: If "the veil is emblematic of the common plight of man, why should it isolate its wearer with a poignancy unfelt by other men and leave him lonely and alone? . . . [or] is it possible . . . that the message of the veil *is* representative and universal: that the failure to recognize it is simply the last and most chilling proof of man's imprisonment in himself. . . . The discrepancies between the two interpretations must go unreconciled."[10]

Colacurcio also powerfully argues the case for the undecidability of Hawthorne's story. The veil is the minister's humble, penitent acknowledgment of his essentially sinful nature. It is an emblem of the "true sight of sin" under which he and his community must stand. "His veil is nothing but the metaphor for his awakened Puritanism." But the veil is clearly a strategic and human error. It hopelessly, painfully, confuses literal fact and metaphoric meaning, symbol and spirit, the external and the internal self. It permanently isolates Hooper from his community, blocking love and sympathy and communion.[11] Colacurcio's reading, however, does not leave the story undecidable. It locates the matrix of historical fact, which, however subject to interpretation, is outside the story's own system of indeterminacies. If the painful paradoxes of Hooper's veil make it a model of the impossibility of fixing meaning in signs and symbols, Hawthorne's veil, both as literary symbol and as literary language, differentiates between meanings and between problems of representation. From the initial footnote on the historical

Reverend Moody through the increasingly complex historical allusions, which Colacurcio carefully explicates, the story unceasingly reminds the reader of the factual universe from which Hawthorne's veil was derived. Hawthorne's veil is neither accidental nor arbitrary. It does not express Hawthorne's private, solipsistic view of the world. It is not his obsession or his religion. And he does not intend it to symbolize a unified reality. Hawthorne's veil, reconstituting some of the salient features of the minister's veil, is a critique of the qualities that it reconstructs. Hawthorne's veil, then, is a self-conscious attempt to register the problems of the veil and to sympathize with it, to reach out into another reality and embrace a dissimilar and yet related consciousness. Hawthorne identifies with Hooper's and the Puritans' veiledness. He recognizes the force of the veil, and, refusing to leave the past in "miserable obscurity forever," he brings forth a veil that conjures those that exist behind it.

In some sense every meaning in the story generates an opposing meaning. Even literary devices such as symbol and allegory self-cancel. Yet the story does take a stand. It positions itself somewhere outside the epistemological and philosophical uncertainties it activates. "What tips the balance against Hooper," according to Colacurcio, "is some sense of his too-powerful partialness" and "his perpetual and finally self-convicting insistence on his own exemplariness": "the veil [becomes] an object of unique concern in itself," mirroring his obsessive self-absorption.[12] The text must separate itself from the possibilities of endless self-reflection and self-projection that afflict its minister. Textual ambiguity must be prevented from bringing about a process of infinite play. To put it another way, "The Minister's Black Veil" must be prevented from collapsing into the minister's black veil. Hawthorne achieves this distance between his story and its subject by substituting the veil of history for the veil of the Minister's obsessive self-concern. Hooper's problem is that symbol and self become hopelessly intertwined, so that in ministering to the symbol, he ministers to himself. Hawthorne's genius is to release both self and symbol back into the world from which they have derived. History unsettles the allegory of self. It calls imagination back into the world. The minister's black veil is not Hawthorne's, not even as invented symbol. The veil existed, somewhere back in the past, in a true story, whatever that story meant or might seem to mean today. Hooper is acting out some sort of childish regression. He is converting the world and the self into reductive allegories of biblical and spiritual truths narrowly conceived. Like the akedian heroes to whom he is related, he would reconstruct salvation on his own terms and make himself the central character in its unfolding. He would remove himself from the communal intercourse that creates society and history, preferring the black veil to the wedding veil that Elizabeth might have assumed for him. Hawthorne, however, in historicizing allegory, is participating in society and history. He is breaking the self-sufficiency and self-referentiality of the allegorical structure and turning it back toward the historical reality from which, in this particular instance, it has itself broken away.

Responding to claims that Hawthorne's writings are only allegorical, critics have recently suggested that Hawthorne's art is in fact antiallegorical.[13] But Hawthorne's stories do allegorize. Hawthornean allegory, however, is historical-typological. It assents to the fact that reality and fiction can both be read as allegorical structures. But it also insists that there is more to fiction and the world than the allegories they enact. In "Figura," Erich Auerbach distinguishes between historical types and conventional allegories and symbols: "Figural interpretation," admits Auerbach, "is 'allegorical' in the widest sense. But it differs from most of the allegorical forms known to us by the historicity both of the sign and what it signifies." Similarly, "symbolic or mythic forms [of interpretation] have certain points of contact with figural interpretation; both aspire to interpret and order life as a whole; both are conceivable only in religious or related spheres. But the differences are self-evident. The symbol must possess magic power, not the *figura*; the *figura*, on the other hand, must always be historical, but not the symbol. . . . Figural prophecy relates to an interpretation of history—indeed it is by nature a textual interpretation—while the symbol is a direct interpretation of life and originally no doubt for the most part, of nature." The activity of figuration, then, exists somewhere between *"littera-historia* and *veritas,"* between history and truth.[14] Hawthorne's allegory is figural allegory of the kind Auerbach describes. As in the akedian romances, he is concerned with a breakdown in historical typological thinking that had had serious consequences for American history and literature. He does not appropriate the essential tenets of an ahistorical literalism and write historical fictions that allegorize or symbolize events. He does not try to suggest how history reflects transhistorical or divine realities. Nor does he simply historicize an allegorical or symbolic imagination in order to criticize a certain Puritan or American mentality. Hawthorne's symbolic and allegorical histories reveal the ways in which allegory and symbol only seem to unveil and thereby transcend history's deepest contours. He demonstrates how history only appears to unmask what allegories and symbols, as structures of concealment, hide from view. In dramatizing this fluidity of meaning, however, he does not celebrate a veiledness (whether of history, allegory, or symbol) that hopelessly confuses the interpretive process. Rather he attempts to show how veiledness can function to separate and protect disparate regions of experience and knowledge. No one will ever get behind the minister's black veil, to know beyond a shadow of a doubt either what it means (to Hooper, to the community, to Hawthorne, or to the reader) or what it is (historical artifact, invented symbol, historical symbol, or mere word).

In Hawthorne's fictions, history, allegory, and symbol seem to draw one another back into obscurity beyond the possibility of any determinate meaning. But, while Hawthorne fully intends to convey the tensions generated by veiledness and the (often thwarted) expectations of revelation, he does so in order to make the veil part of what history and fiction portray. Hawthorne's veiled meanings do not conceal fictions veiling other fictions. Rather they figure specific historical events that can be identified. Even if the allegorical or symbolic or literal meanings of these events cannot be summed up or determined, decades or centuries after the fact, their ontological existence cannot be disputed. Like Alice, and unlike Hooper, Hawthorne veils in order to affirm reality and acknowledge its claims on him.

"The Minister's Black Veil," therefore, reproduces the minister's veil. It makes it the central figure of a narrative that creates equally perplexing linguistic and narrative veils, which, in seeming to validate Hooper's mode of symbolizing, at least sympathize with what Hooper hopes to accomplish. In thus veiling Hooper's reality, the story evokes that reality. It enables the reader to accept not only Hooper but the historical community that he embodies. The Puritan community of Reverend Hooper did see the world through veils. It veiled itself through its oblique relationship to reality; and it was veiled by time, as it was forced, inevitably, to withdraw into the historical past. At some moments, it is as if Hawthorne's story has taken up residence on the other side of the veil. It is as if it has taken upon itself the veil that the community wore and continues to wear, though now through no conscious will of its own. Hawthorne's story also, at moments, seems veiled in miserable obscurity, as the history of Hawthorne criticism will attest! But even as he assumes the minister's veil, Hawthorne separates himself from it. He ascribes it to the minister, even titling the story "The *Minister's* Black Veil." He restores it to history.

In writing "The Minister's Black Veil," Hawthorne is definitely not writing a black veil of words—that is, he is not creating the linguistic equivalent of the veil. He is only writing a story on the veil, about the veil. What he produces is no more the minister's black veil than are the critical writings on his story "The Minister's Black Veil." Writing on the veil is not, however, Hawthorne's way of evading taking a stand. Hawthorne positions his consciousness in the only place it can be, on the neutral territory between its subjectivity and the world's otherness, between what it knows about itself and what it can never ascertain about the world. If the story were to take up permanent residence behind the veil and present itself from the other side, it would risk contaminating itself with whatever lies there, obscuring itself as thoroughly as everything else behind the veil. It would violate the minister's right to remain behind a veil that, as the story demonstrates, no one can ever wholly penetrate. It would expose history the way Goodman Brown exposes it: as a set of hypocritical lies and acts of violence against which a more enlightened contemporary reality can only rebel. Hawthorne understands that it would be as impertinent for him to demand of history or reality or fiction to cast aside its veil as it is for Hooper's community to ask Hooper to do the same thing, as if we ourselves do not wear and see the world through veils. We are meant to resist the shudder that concludes story: "but awful is still the thought, that it mouldered beneath the Black Veil!" (p. 53). For, as the syntax makes clear enough, Hooper's affrighted auditors have suffered his identical fate: "Still veiled, they laid him in his coffin, and a veiled corpse they bore him to the grave" (p. 52). They are just as veiled as the minister. They are still veiled today, corpses of history. Hawthorne will protect the veil that protects the privacy of individual and historical conscience, his characters', his world's, even his own. Veils are the most natural things in the world (even the earth wears a veil). And if this is the case, is any man or woman less entitled than the author himself to "keep the inmost Me behind its veil," as Hawthorne claims in *The Scarlet Letter*?[15] Hawthorne believes in sympathy and love. In the "Custom House" sketch, which prefaces *The Scarlet Letter*, a novel that specifically concerns the veiling of secrets, he courts his reader with a promise of direct and unmediated communication. But as the relationship of Chillingworth and another minister not so different from Hooper makes clear, total intimacy and self-revelation are destructive forms of human intercourse.[16] Although Hawthorne willingly acknowledges a story-writing "I," he avoids voyeuristic self-confession. He thus protects himself and his reader, and, finally, secures their relationship. He promises to stay on his side of the veil, and, if the reader will not peer too indecently at him, he will not peer too indecently at the reader. Only from that kind of mutual respect on either side of the veil can the relationship between individuals emerge. Veiling the past, Hawthorne not only sympathetically reproduces it, he accepts and protects it. So doing, he establishes the bases for the human intercourse (denied by Hooper and Brown) on which social and historical community depend.

"LADY ELEANORE'S MANTLE"

Veils can be miscomprehended and misapplied, as they are by Hooper and by the reader who would insist that "The Minister's Black Veil" and the minister's black veil are one and the same. They can facilitate tendencies toward solipsism, detachment, and smug self-righteousness, which are perhaps the latent other side of American individualism and self-reliance.[17] Even history's veils can become instruments of arrogance and self-congratulation. "He may have been a wise man in his day," Hawthorne writes in his "Old News," "but, to us, his wisdom . . . appears like folly, because we can compare its prognostics with actual results."[18] This is the arrogance of a certain kind of imagination that is happy to remain on its side of the veil of history or the text, blithely reducing the world outside to frivolous indistinctness. This pride of the present moment is the subject of "Lady Eleanore's Mantle" and "My Kinsman, Major Molineux."

Like so many of Hawthorne's stories, "Lady Eleanore's Mantle" seems hopelessly reduced when it is read as a universal allegory that just happens to be set in prerevolutionary America.[19] The tale's allegorical meaning is blatantly dramatized in the aristocratic Eleanore's shabby treatment of her American cousins. Eleanore herself spells it out: "I wrapt myself in PRIDE as in a MANTLE" (p. 287). But Eleanore's pride is more than aristocratic snobbism. It is also associated with youth and beauty. It represents, most simply, the smugness of the living over the dead. The main image of this pride is not Eleanore's stepping on Jervase Helwyse, an "emblem" of "aristocracy and hereditary pride, trampling on human sympathies" (p. 276). It is defined by the juxtaposition of her haughty entry into the community and the tolling of the funeral bell that one of her admirers suggests ought to be silenced in deference to her astonishing vitality (p. 275). This association of pride with youth and the defiance of mortality is reinforced by the major symbol of pride in the story, the mantle. The mantle is the material object of Eleanore's vanity. It lent "a new and untried grace to her figure each time that she put it on" (p. 278). It secures her position in the community, separating her from the contagions of mass fashion and the humble attire of the colonists. Drawing "the rich folds of the embroidered mantle over her head, in such a fashion as to give a completely new aspect to her beautiful face" (p. 281), Eleanore asserts her pride in the endless versatility and inexhaustibility of her youth. But if Eleanore's "grace" is as yet "untried" (p. 278), her entry into Puritan America will try it, for the mantle is "the handiwork of a dying woman" (p. 278). It is intimately interwoven with the implications of mortality. It does not protect her from death. It wraps her in the contagion (p. 284) she would use it to guard against. By the time of the ball, the mantle has become her shroud, her "feverish flush," revealing the power of its infection (p. 278).

The story proves Eleanore as mortal as everyone else. But Eleanore is not the only character in the story convinced of his or her immunity to time and death. She is not the only one who wraps herself in a mantle of self-delusion and pride. Eleanore's mantle descends to new hands at the end of the story. Throwing open the curtains that conceal the dying Eleanore in her bed, exposing her as a "thing," a "heap of diseased mortality," Helwyse Jervase brings Eleanore out from behind her mantle (p. 287). But he does so through the most cruel and vicious lack of sympathy demonstrated in the story. Like Chillingworth in *The Scarlet Letter*, Jervase serves the interests of truth only by the most indelicate exposure of his victim's deepest vulnerabilities. If Eleanore has exempted herself from the chain of human sympathies, Helwyse Jervase has done no less. Jervase "snatch[es] the fatal mantle" for himself (p. 288). He inherits the symbol of pride, assumes the mantle of British power, which he then wraps around an effigy of Eleanore and burns.

At first Jervase, the representative of the American people, is the foolish slave of British imperiousness, as enacted in the opening scene of the story. By the end of the story, he has not freed himself from the yoke of authority, although the sources of the new order of rule are different and more dangerous. At the conclusion of the tale, Jervase has become the foolish slave to the power of "King Death" (p. 275). Helwyse, who has worshipped "Lady Eleanore" as a British aristocrat, now worships her as the "Princess," the "Queen of Death": "Let me look upon her," Jervase pleads, "Let me behold her, in her awful beauty, clad in the regal garments of the pestilence! She and Death sit on a throne together. Let me kneel down before them!" (p. 286). "Death, and the Pestilence," he declares, "who wears the aspect of the Lady Eleanore, will walk through the streets to-night, and I must march before them with this banner" (p. 285). Dr. Clarke, who knows much about the legitimate claims of death on the living, correctly diagnoses Jervase as deluded. He accuses him of worshipping his "destroyer": "Thus man doth ever to his tyrants" (p. 286). Jervase is still a slavish "Bedlamite" (p. 275). He has simply changed his allegiance from England to the Death of England.

The red banner and the procession prefigure the American flag and the Revolution, as the new nation proceeds to free itself from British authority, represented in the story by both Eleanore and her mantle. But as the final scene plays itself out, we see that Eleanore and the pride she represents have given way only to another kind of pride that is just as insane and sick and that is also symbolized as a veil. The mantle of her disease now envelops someone else. The story represents the American Revolution as contagion, the flag as the "red flag of pestilence" (p. 288). (The images recur in "My Kinsman, Major Molineux.") It is a story that sees revolution as *Billy Budd* sees it: an endless enfolding of oneself in a mantle of pride and perceptual distortion. Jervase is mad. Because of his bitter hatred for Eleanore, he worships her destroyer. That destroyer becomes his new tyrant, his new king. The people's effort to burn the past, their desire to destroy the image of British history, is itself a kind of pride in which they wrap themselves as in a mantle, asserting self-sufficiency, independence, and arrogance. Believing they can escape history by destroying it, they repeat history. As a result, the new history of America, in the tradition of akedian romances, replicates just what it would disown and disavow. Eleanore's mantle has not been discarded. It has simply changed hands and been hoisted aloft, where it is as dangerous as it was when Eleanore used it to deny the legitimate claims of sympathy and mortality. The mantle of pride has descended on new and perhaps even more frail shoulders.

"MY KINSMAN, MAJOR MOLINEUX"

To achieve real freedom the American nation will have to release itself from the pride not only of class and preferment and material wealth but of youth and newness and self-reliance. It will have to see beyond the mantle of the present to a past just as vital and dynamic as itself. America, in Hawthorne's view, had neither owned nor owned up to its history. In "My Kinsman, Major Molineux,"[20] Robin's main problem is not his misguided desire for his kinsman's patronage. It is rather that he lacks the wherewithal to interpret his experience.[21] In the beginning of the story Robin's faulty perceptions reflect his youth and ignorance. By the end, however, his inability to understand what has happened to him and to his fellow citizens has become part of the larger condition of youthful arrogance from which the entire community suffers. Willfully cutting himself off from his roots, Robin mirrors his society. His society has come to institutionalize the "shrewdness" of a country bumpkin.

Robin searches for an angle of vision from which to understand his highly perplexing experience. As he sits on the church steps, he "endeavor[s] to define the forms of distant objects" (p. 221) and "to fix his attention steadily upon the large edifice which he had surveyed before" (p. 223). But Robin's attempts to grasp reality fail: "his mind [keeps] vibrating between fancy and reality," until he is not even certain whether he is at home with his family or in the town of his kinsman, "here, or there" (p. 223). Like Brown, Robin views a defamiliarized world: "a deeper sleep wrestled with, and nearly overcame" Robin (p. 223). "It is as if a dream had broken forth" (p. 228), and both Robin and his gentleman friend wonder whether in fact Robin isn't dreaming. The early Robin is an innocent realist who, out of ignorance, exempts himself from the phantasmagoria that surrounds him. Robin is firmly outside the dream, resisting it. He is trying to bring a reality that is not a dream into focus. Like the ordinary reader of history he prefers a Hutchinson's "long and dry detail of colonial affairs" (p. 209) to a Hawthorne's feverish dream of the same events (p. 228). Hutchinsonian history demystifies reality. It reassures its readers that if only they are rational and "shrewd" enough they will find the world recognizable, knowable (the word *shrewd* repeats on pp. 211, 216, 219, 225, and 231).

But as experience overtakes Robin, and he recognizes that he too is "to bear a part in the pageantry" of the evening (p. 228), his relationship to the dream world changes. The experienced Robin perceives that he is continuous with the "strange" world that had heretofore resisted his efforts to penetrate it (pp. 215 and 220). He understands that the dream somehow represents the world, despite its strangeness. Were Robin to consent to the world's strangeness, were he able to accept that he might never penetrate its masquerade, then he might truly have been able to understand the terms by which human beings fix (p. 223) their vision of the world. But Robin is still determined to bring things into focus. He takes the process of familiarization one fatal step forward. Having accepted that the dream reveals a reality, he assumes that the dream is reality, unambiguous and pure. He naturalizes the strangeness that first signaled to him that there was something he did not understand, that reality consists of something other than clearly ascertainable and assimilable facts. He continues to interpret the world with the same shrewdness that has characterized him from the beginning. This is no nightmare, he concludes. This is a world of real citizens, in costume. The people, he understands, have shrewdly transformed reality into allegory in order to achieve real political objectives. Like "Howe's Masquerade," the world for Robin is a kind of masked ball in which all are willing and eager players. That the world could be nightmare and reality both, that the masked ball might mark the supernatural as well as the natural, as it does in "Howe's Masquerade," does not occur to Robin.

For Robin, reality is a single homogeneous substance—call it quotidian or fantastic—that he can turn inside out at will, with little or no damage, like an expertly sewn reversible coat. But the fabric of reality, Hawthorne suggests, is highly fragile. It is not to be fashioned lightly by the sporting masses. Behind the gothic charade of the fantastic is the fantastic itself, ever ready, again as in "Howe's Masquerade," suddenly to assert itself, independent and separate from the effort to enlist it in games and merriment—or in stories. Hawthorne will not say if Robin is dreaming. Nor will he say if it matters. He only says that he does not know and cannot tell us. Robin cannot understand that once he has accepted his place within the manufactured world of the town, once he has become a reveler among revelers, infected by the "contagion" (p. 230) and "mental inebriety" (p. 229) that control the mob, he has no more "fix" (p. 223) on his reality than before, when he was outside the dream, hampered by his naive literalism. The dream world, to which Robin now laughs his raucous assent, is not the real world playing at make-believe. Rather it is the juxtaposition of two unmergible planes of reality, which, according to the laws of Hawthornean metaphysics, cannot occupy the same place at the same time. The dream element of Hawthorne's world is made nightmarish by the fantastic, overwhelming and imprisoning the ordinary, despite the citizens' smugness that it is the other way around. That is the danger of careless, excessive fictionalization, in life as in literature.

Robin's haughty laugh of rejection signals his imprisonment in his new and equally presumptuous way of seeing. Just before the pageant rolls by, the gentleman asks Robin if he will "recognize" Major Molineux in the crowd (p. 227). By the end of the tale, Robin believes that he has met his kinsman (p. 230). But he has only met what Hawthorne calls the "spectre of his kinsman" (p. 229). This is the carefully designed image of Major Molineux that has been fashioned "by the great [inebriate] multitude" (p. 229). Robin, like Brown, sees only what some other imagination has shaped for him. Just as he imagines that the dream and the world are one and the same, he believes that the specter coincides perfectly with a solid and unambiguous presence. But Robin has not really met the "large and majestic person" with the "strong, square features, betokening a steady soul" whom the narrator produces from behind the tar-and-feather mask. He cannot see the man "majestic still in his agony," the victim of "counterfeited pomp . . . senseless uproar [and] frenzied merriment, trampling all on an old man's heart" (pp. 228–30). The specter at the heart of the dream world contains a real human being. But Robin sees only the Major's specter. And like his Puritan ancestor, he judges that specter on external appearances only, as an object lesson for himself.

At the end of the story Robin is not a substantially better interpreter of the world. For the world, according to Hawthorne, is neither reality pretending at dream nor dream overtaking reality but the separate existence of the visionary within the real and the real within the visionary. In "My Kinsman, Major Molineux" (as in "Howe's Masquerade"), Hawthorne represents historical and contemporary reality, not as veiled or mantled, but as disguised. As in Cooper's *Spy* it is a comic, even ludicrous masquerade. As in Melville's *Billy Budd*, it has dire implications for America's relationship to itself and to the world. In this charade of history, none are privileged perceivers. No one is able, finally, to make the masquerade coincide perfectly with his or her own views of reality. Hawthorne's point is that no one stands outside reality, outside history. Failing to realize this, Robin cannot achieve a meaningful perspective or point of view. The reason for Robin's failure is inextricably bound with the political circumstances of the drama in which he finds himself. The American Revolution, in Hawthorne's view, was not a revolution in perception. It was only a pivoting around on an unacknowledged axis of vision that could not establish itself in relation to reality.

As in *The Spy*, taking a stand that differentiates between one reality and another can liberate the mind to a genuine independence. Like the equivalent moment in "Lady Eleanore's Mantle," the American march to independence is manifested in "My Kinsman, Major Molineux" as an uncontrollable disease. It is an insane hatred of English heritage that, refusing to orient itself to that tradition, attempts to break with and bury the past. It becomes a revolution in the objects but not in the modes of perception. Not surprisingly the nation that supplants the colonies largely duplicates what has gone before. The controlling spirit of this new world is the gentleman, who guides and protects Robin's initiation in this supposedly new reality. The gentleman embodies the rational intelligence (not unlike the enlightenment consciousness represented in *Wieland*) that will train a new generation of Americans to their independence. But the gentleman hauntingly replicates the authority from which Robin and the people have apparently just freed themselves. He appears to be all consolation for the suffering Robin, a new father figure who will help Robin rise in the world, but he exerts an oppressive control no less restrictive than the British crown, represented by a Molineux or a Hutchinson. "Will you be kind enough to show me the way to the ferry?" Robin beseeches him twice after the parade has disappeared (pp. 230–31). "No, my good friend Robin, not to-night at least," he replies. "Some few days hence, if you continue to wish it. . . . Or, if you prefer to remain with us, perhaps as you are a shrewd youth, you may rise in the world, without the help of your kinsman, Major Molineux" (p. 231). The gentleman simply substitutes the creed of youth and the self-made man for the system of formal rank and patronage that has been overthrown (note how Robin's entry into the city recalls Franklin's as recorded in his *Autobiography*). He refuses to assist Robin in leaving, effectively preventing him from doing so. And when he echoes Robin's signal word *shrewd* and offers the quintessential Franklinesque advice that Robin can rise in the world without his kinsman, he seals Robin's imprisonment in a false vision of the relationship between independence and history.

In *The Corporeal Self* Sharon Cameron suggests, temptingly, that "the tale teaches Robin to be terrified of any source of power not his own. . . . That one has a place in the world is an idea the story rebukes. . . . Place cannot be assigned. . . . Robin must rise without his kinsman's help. He must rise in a world where bodies cannot be partialized, where meanings are not external."[22] The point of the story, I think, is the opposite. Robin cannot rise in the world without his kinsman's help. And he must discover a place from which to witness and observe the revolution, no matter how dizzying it is. Indeed, if he is not simply to become an object of that revolution but rather to make revolution into his subject, as Hawthorne has made it into his, he must discover his own point of view. This point of view depends on his being able to read the allegory and accept and respect it with historical eyes.

Hawthorne begins his story by opposing romance history to Hutchinson's "long and dry detail of colonial affairs." Historical romance, for Hawthorne, acknowledges the dream that is part of reality. But it also accepts the historical reality of a world that seems no more than a dream. Historical romance establishes a point of view that is controlled by its place within the subjectivities of reality but that accepts the tangible separateness of a historical past outside interpretation. Above all, it chooses to acknowledge its difference and distance from the past. It does not impose the logic of the present on the past or dismiss the past as utterly naive and indefensible. Rather it grants the past its own place, its own point of view, just as legitimate as its own.

Robin and the American patriots believe that they must eliminate their kinsmen to achieve their freedom. Therefore, their freedom, Hawthorne insists, consists of perceptual illusion: inebriation, contagion, frenzy. Hawthorne, however, recognizes and respects his kinsman, all his kinsmen. He acknowledges them—Hutchinson, Molineux, and Robin; Mather, Doane, and Brown; and Minister Hooper/Cooper/Hooker—as his own.[23] Each one is "My Kinsman." Each one is owned as a singular personality, despite the multiple compoundings of history's inevitable repetitions and maskings. Only by accepting the facts and figures of ancestry, as well as history's claims to perceptual difference, can the individual accede to whatever freedom human perceivers may possess. This point of view might be more restricted and less relaxed than the man-in-the-moon's informed and even affectionate "Oho" (p. 230). But it is a valuable point of view nonetheless.

History's veils, like reality's, will never be dislodged. It is imprudent and impertinent to try. All that one can do is to put oneself back into the past, listen to its echoes, and then to repeat, with some marginally greater wisdom, perhaps, but from behind the veil, which is the present's as much as the past's, within one's own limited shrewdness, just the words the past has spoken. "My Kinsman," says Robin, says Hawthorne, says the reader. To own the past exceeds even revealing the kinsman behind the mask (un-masking him). It is, for a time, to take up residence behind the veil, assume the same mask. The gentleman's last words, which conclude the literal story, and which close and seal it like a book of scripture in the ominous future he ironically prophesies, differ dramatically from Hawthorne's. "You may rise in the world without the help of *your* kinsman, Major Molineux," advises our gentleman friend. This is not even what Robin says, albeit with a lack of real certainty, perhaps even questioningly, before he is cut off and his words undercut by the gentleman. It is not what the narrator asserts, even more emphatically, more insistently, in the title of the story to which the gentle-man's words return us. The words "Major Molineux" that conclude the story do not, as the gentleman would wish, disown "My Kinsman." Rather, in repeating the words of the title, forcing the reader back to the beginning—of the story, of the history, of the origins of family and nationhood and storytelling—Hawthorne acknowledges the relations on which self and his-tory depend. Language and history are undoubtedly indeterminate. They are highly susceptible to being undercut, denied, and disowned. Nonetheless, Hawthorne does not balk at speaking his acknowledgment into existence. "Major Molineux" is "My Kinsman" whether he wants it or likes it or not.

Redemption and Renewal from the Historical Point of View: Romance in the Cinema House of the Seven Gables

"Young Goodman Brown," "Edward Randolph's Portrait," "The Minister's Black Veil," "Lady Eleanore's Mantle," and "My Kinsman, Major Molineux" simultaneously explore and reproduce the blurred boundaries separating text from world and self from other. The texts' blurring of these boundaries has made historical romance seem like a model of undecidability. But the historical romances self-consciously register the world's indeterminacy and their own in order to establish both the need for and the possibility of decidability. This decidability is linked, as it is for Cooper in *The Spy*, to the decision to confess the lack of neutrality that inheres in any neutral ground. Like *The Spy*, Hawthorne's historical romances admit origins outside themselves. The histories they tell defy the incorporative properties of fiction. Furthermore, these historical narratives position veils, much like the veils of fiction, that perplex the interpretive process. They do not, however, abandon the text to the endless subjectivity of the imagination. Instead, they establish the necessity for declaring a position or point of view in relation to what one sees and interprets, and they make the task of literature, in part, the definition of a point of view. In the historical romance tradition, a text must do more than speak about or around a problematics of being and writing. It must speak to historical and cultural issues, as well as theoretical issues, and to an audience that would hold a writer responsible for his or her words.

Stanley Cavell's vivid description of his own swerve away from the undecidability of literary texts speaks for the American tradition, which also negotiates between the necessities of fictional indeterminacy and the claims of history and the world. "To call [a] matter undecidable," explains Cavell,

> may be just a way of affirming that the words "can" be taken . . . various ways . . . or a way of denying that you have this responsibility. . . . Nothing in words will distin-

guish the real (referential?) from the dream (nonreferential?) occasion, and this difference is again not up for decision. . . . That such a thing is not up for decision is the pivot on which skepticism turns. . . . To conclude that such issues are undecidable would be to decide that the conclusion of skepticism is true, that we never know so certainly but that we can doubt. This . . . trivializes the claim of the skeptic, whose power lies not in some decision, but in his apparent discovery of the fact that we cannot know; at the same time it theatricalizes the threat, or the truth, of skepticism: that it names our wish (and the possibility of our wishing) to strip ourselves of the responsibility we have in meaning (or in failing to) one thing, or one way, rather than another.[1]

The American historical romances keep the skeptical inquiry poised on the dilemma that cannot be resolved. They understand the intangibility of meaning. In these works, every thought, every word, displaces and substitutes for another word or preword that cannot be recovered. This Derridean "scene of writing,"[2] however, is contained by what Cavell has called the "scene of instruction in words."[3] This is the moment when individuals claim responsibility for their language, their fictions, their history, and for what Paul de Man has called their nothingness.[4] However undecidable, these things come to us in a place (a scene) that is historical and geographical as well as psychical. In describing the action that might be taken in relation to the "always already" quality of language,[5] Cavell also penetrates to the core of American historical romance. "Words come to us from a distance," explains Cavell;

> they were there before we were; we are born into them. Meaning them is accepting that fact of their condition. To discover what is being said to us, as to discover what we are saying, is to discover the precise location from which it is said; to understand why it is said from just there, and at that time. The art of fiction is to teach us distance—that the sources of what is said, the character of whomever says it, is for us to discover.[6]

If Poe is the romancer who figures the indeterminacy of the purloined letter, which always conceals meaning,[7] Brown, Cooper, Hawthorne, and Melville in the nineteenth century and Fitzgerald, Hemingway, Faulkner, Doctorow, and Updike in the twentieth define a distinctly divergent historical romance tradition. This tradition resists the undecidability of literature. It explicitly does not invent a new symbolic or transcendental or romantic language. Instead, letter for letter, it takes upon itself the existing language and gives it meaning. The fictional spell of historical romance literally derives from an American alphabet that the text does not discard. Charles Feidelson has said of *The Scarlet Letter* that "as a single letter, the most indeterminate of all symbols, and first letter of the alphabet, the beginning of all communication, Hawthorne's emblem represents a potential point of coherence within a manifold historical experience."[8] In Cavell's terms it represents an acknowledgment, not only of origins but of one's responsibility for those origins and for the conditions of human utterance. The word *responsibility* is not out of place in a discussion of Hawthorne, Cooper, Melville, or Faulkner. "The burden of Hawthorne's fictions," says Roy Harvey Pearce, "is to teach us that we must learn to live in, to be responsible to and for, a world which we never made . . . or at best did not intend to make."[9] This issue of responsibility, of a burden similar to and yet also significantly more concrete and moral than the burden of our own subjectivity, which forms the central concern of many contemporary readings of American fiction,[10] is essential to the historical romance tradition. It is the central insight, leading to the affirmations and acknowledgments of such stories as "Edward Randolph's Portrait," "Lady Eleanore's Mantle," "The Minister's Black Veil," and "My Kinsman, Major Molineux." It also provides the concept of redemption and renewal at the end of *The House of the Seven Gables.*[11]

THE NATURE OF HISTORY

The optimistic conclusion of Hawthorne's second full-length romance has troubled many readers of the book. Almost no one mistakes Holgrave's hysterical antihistoricism for the author's attitudes about history. Holgrave's conversion to conservatism is a logical extension of Hawthorne's own historiographical position. Yet the book's optimism seems seriously to misrepresent the book's major premises. Michael Davitt Bell has suggested that it undercuts "the tragic implications of Hawthorne's many statements about the perpetuity of evil."[12] Several critics have described a historiography consonant with the conclusion,[13] but the end of the book does strike one as painfully cheery and glib, reminiscent of Clifford's insane statements about ascending spirals and transcendentalized realities. The moral that Hawthorne announces at the beginning of the book is "the truth, namely, that the wrong-doing of one generation lives into the successive ones, and divesting itself of every temporal advantage, becomes a pure and uncontrollable mischief" (p. 2). Somewhere along the line that moral seems to have been lost.

While Hawthorne utters the moral his novel seems to discard, he explains the point of view from which his book is to be understood. The terms of the romantic definition and this point of view justify the story's happy ending. "The point of view in which this Tale comes under the Romantic definition," writes the author in his most famous statement about romance, "lies in the attempt to connect a by-gone time with the very Present that is flitting away from us. It is a Legend, prolonging itself, from an epoch now gray in the distance, down into our own broad daylight, and bringing along with it some of its legendary mist" (p. 2). The perpetuity of evil and the romantic process of literature follow the same dynamics of expression, yet they yield diametrically opposite results. The reader should wonder, then, if there is a distinction between the two processes that changes the moral tenor of Hawthorne's romance, allowing for the concluding images of redemption and renewal.

From the romantic perspective, present and past occupy the same temporal ground. The present, which is "flitting away," is forever in the process of becoming the past. Similarly, the past, which prolongs itself from the "distance" into "broad daylight," "bringing along with it . . . its legendary mist," is constantly pushing forward to become present. It is always presenting itself to view, making itself present to consciousness. These are the temporal dimensions of Hawthorne's "neutral territory" between the real and the imaginary.[14] Like this neutral territory or Cooper's neutral ground, the conditions of past in present and present in past obliterate distinctions. Nothing is what it seems. Every reality hides and is hidden by another reality. Meaningful perception, therefore, requires that we register the differences spectrality would extinguish. Seeing in a trans-temporal world demands that we maintain a sense of past as different from present. Like our kinsman Robin Molineux, taking our place in the world means self-consciously assuming a point of view stable enough and yet flexible enough to accommodate and respond to other competing points of view.

Hawthorne's tale "comes under the romantic definition" not simply because it reproduces the world's blend of the real and the imaginary, the present and the past, but because Hawthorne chooses to place his story under this defining lens. He decides to connect the past with the present, adopting a historical-romantic point of view to make sense of a dualistic and multi-leveled universe. The House of the Seven Gables is about the selection of conscious points of view, the chosen angles of perception, and the visual processes and acts of interpretation that secure accurate seeing. Whether or not knowledge of the past is pragmatically useful or can predict progressive or retrogressive, cyclical or linear, directions, historical consciousness is essential to the act of perception itself. Free will, according to Hawthorne, and the redemption and renewal that it can bring about, depend on establishing and preserving a point of view.

In "Young Goodman Brown," Hawthorne explores history's role in promoting consciousness of the world's spectrality. History, he suggests, positions one within the imperatives of a skeptical dilemma that cannot be resolved. Out of this irresolution moral consciousness and sympathy evolve. In "Edward Randolph's Portrait," and other stories that place history behind the veil, Hawthorne represents the maneuvers by which history can preserve our distance from what we see and interpret. Acknowledgment in these stories becomes affirmation when it exceeds self-congratulation. In *The House of the Seven Gables*, Hawthorne presents history in yet another of its aspects: as a photograph or (anachronistically) as a motion picture. Like Edward Randolph's portrait, this picture mimetically verifies the reality of a world no longer present. It also exposes the lens and the angle of vision, the eye and the I, through which reality is viewed. It locates the point of view necessary to seeing, on which the moral tenor of our relationship to the world depends. The novel's four main characters—Hepzibah, Clifford, Phoebe, and Holgrave—each suffer from a failure to locate vision within an appropriate point of view. In the course of the book, each acquires control over life in proportion to his or her acquisition of this point of view. Proper vision, the book suggests, double-exposes the world. It mingles here and there and then and now. Only a further exposure of point of view can distinguish the one from the other and determine what seeing will mean.

In "The Flight of Two Owls," Hawthorne explores the relationship between historical consciousness and perception, and he points to the need for self-consciously assuming a definite and stable point of view. In typical allegorical fashion, Hawthorne portrays the train as a microcosmic mirror world. The train ride is a life's journey in miniature. The "mimic" universe of the train station, with its "arched entrance," "large structure," and "breadth" hauntingly evoke the house of the seven gables. The world inside the train mimics the world of the mercantile Hepzibah, the romantic Clifford, and the formerly political but now sleeping judge. This, as Hawthorne puts it, is "life itself":

> Some, with tickets in their hats . . . had plunged into the English scenery and adventures of pamphlet-novels, and were keeping company with dukes and earls. Others, whose briefer span forbade their devoting themselves to studies so abstruse, beguiled the little tedium of the way with penny-papers. . . . Boys, with apples, cakes, candy, and rolls of variously tinctured lozenges—merchandize that reminded Hepzibah of her deserted shop—appeared at each momentary stopping-place . . . New people continually entered. Old acquaintances—for such they soon grew to be, in this rapid current of affairs—continually departed. Here and there, amid the rumble and tumult, sat one asleep. Sleep; sport; business; graver or lighter study;—and the common and inevitable movement onward! It was life itself! (Pp. 255–57)

This is another example of Hawthorne's romantic inversions of dream reality and the world of quotidian truth. "Am I awake? Am I awake?" wonders a startled Hepzibah. "Clifford! Clifford! Is not this a dream?" Clifford answers, "A dream, Hepzibah! . . . On the contrary, I have never been awake before!" (pp. 255–56). The experience appears indeterminate. It does not seem to matter whether events take place in the world or in the mind. But, as in "Young Goodman Brown" and "My Kinsman, Major Molineux," it does make a difference whether what we see is a dream or a reality. Hepzibah and Clifford must determine what kind of vision is revealed to them and therefore how to interpret what they see.

For Hepzibah and Clifford the clarification of the romance vision is more complicated than it was for Brown and Molineux. The slice of life revealed on the train is not the only, or even the primary, scene that Hawthorne puts before them. Hepzabah and Clifford, we are told, are "drawn" by the train "into the great current of human life." They are "swept away with it, as by the suction of fate itself" (p. 256). The train, which contains "the common and inevitable movement onward" of "life itself," also travels through a universe of history and time that provides its own allegory in motion:

> [L]ooking from the window, [Hepzibah and Clifford] could see the world racing past them. At one moment, they were rattling through a solitude; —the next, a village had grown up around them; —a few breaths more, and it had vanished, as if swallowed by an earthquake. The spires of the meeting-houses seemed set adrift from their foundations; the broad-based hills glided away. Everything was unfixed from its age-long rest, and moving at whirlwind speed in a direction opposite their own. (P. 256)[15]

Hepzibah and Clifford can cope, at least minimally, with the "fluctuating waves" of "republican" life in the nineteenth century (p. 38). They can register, if only partially, the fairly straightforward activities of "sleep; sport; business [and] study" that occur within the "interior" of their contemporary moment (pp. 255–57). They cannot, however, begin to fathom the larger progression of time and history that contains them and their world and that carries them forward together. They cannot perceive themselves as a part of the flux and flow exhibited in the world outside.

Hepzibah and Clifford are simply rushed into the life force that contains them. They do not, like Hawthorne, choose to make themselves a part of the historical motion of the train. They do not self-consciously reflect on where and how they stand in relation to it. Hepzibah and Clifford simply do not know how to view the spectacular and unceasingly cinematic qualities of time. The world is racing past them. Villages and houses appear and disappear, as if the world were in constant motion. It does not occur to Hepzibah and Clifford that they too are in motion, that as the world changes, so do they.

It is not difficult to understand Hepzibah's and Clifford's problem. The passage of time, the "common and inevitable movement onward," is as complex to calculate as the motion of a body caught in a "rapid current of affairs" and moving forward at locomotive speed: "A party of girls, and one young man, on opposite sides of the car, found huge amusement in a game of ball. They tossed it to-and-fro, with peals of laughter that might be measured by mile-lengths; for, faster than the nimble ball could fly, the merry players fled unconsciously along, leaving the trail of their mirth afar behind, and ending their game under another sky than had witnessed its commencement" (p. 257). Life, like the game of ball, is motion within motion, time-frame within time-frame. The activities of "sleep; sport; business . . . study," or the tossing of a ball define human existence within one temporal framework only. But the game of ball takes place in a moving vehicle. The game of life takes place in hurtling time and space, in history. Of this historical relativity, Hepzibah and Clifford, like the ball players, are largely unconscious. They do not understand that the present moment is constantly being left behind in the past. Nor can they see that something of the past moment has been transported forward. Like the moving ball, a human life moves simultaneously along two intersecting axes. And Hepzibah and Clifford, like the ball players, cannot record both motions at once without being caught in a dizzying whirl as dangerous as reducing time to a single dimension.

Hepzibah and Clifford experience the world's spectrality without being able to interpret it. They cannot put it in perspective and use it as strengthening and sustaining point of view. Emerson's *Nature* describes the situation of the "time-stricken" Pyncheons:

Certain mechanical changes, a small alteration in our local position, apprizes us of a dualism. We are strangely affected by seeing the shore from a moving ship, from a balloon, or through the tints of an unusual sky. The least change in our point of view gives the whole world a pictorial air. A man who seldom rides, needs only to get into a coach and traverse his own town, to turn the street into a puppet-show. The men, the women—talking, running, bartering, fighting,—the earnest mechanic, the lounger, the beggar, the boys, the dogs, are unrealized at once, or, at least, wholly detached from all relation to the observer, and seen as apparent, not substantial beings. What new thoughts are suggested by seeing a face of country quite familiar, in the rapid movements of the railroad car . . . In a camera obscura, the butcher's cart, and the figure of one of our own family amuse us. So a portrait of a well-known face gratifies us. . . . In these cases, by mechanical means, is suggested the difference between the observer and the spectacle—between man and nature. . . . man is hereby apprized that whilst the world is a spectacle, something in himself is stable.[16]

"This transfiguration [of] material objects," Emerson goes on to suggest, is also the task of literature.[17]

Emerson, unlike Hepzibah and Clifford, understands the importance of point of view in this process of transfiguration. Emerson has prepared his reader to resist the egocentricity that the spectacle of nature confers on individual perceivers. "The frivolous make themselves merry with the Ideal theory," he explains, "as if its consequences were burlesque; as if it affected the stability of nature. It surely does not." Though idealism can reduce "the earnest mechanic, the lounger, the beggar" to spectacle or puppet, Emerson "resist[s] with indignation any hint that nature is more short-lived or mutable than spirit." "The broker, the wheelwright, the carpenter, the tollman" enjoy equal claims. They "are much displeased at [any other] intimation."[18] Emerson continues,

> I own there is something ungrateful in expanding too curiously the particulars of the general proposition, that all culture tends to imbue us with idealism. I have no hostility to nature, but a child's love to it. I expand and live in the warm day like corn and melons. Let us speak fair. I do not wish to fling stones at my beautiful mother, nor soil my gentle nest. I only wish to indicate the true position of nature in regard to man . . . The advantage of the ideal theory over the popular faith is this, that it presents the world in precisely that view which is most desirable to the mind.[19]

Emerson is concerned with position and view. He is interested in a relationship between the self and the world that can preserve, not destroy, a child's love and enable the individual to expand and live.

For Emerson, as for Hawthorne, the point of view by which human beings see nature is prevented from dematerializing reality by the self-conscious recognition that one is occupying a point of view. One chooses this point of view because it is "more desirable to the mind." The point of view outside the spectacle of nature is as insubstantial as nature itself. Nature presents the world in this view in order to enforce this realization. "Nature," Emerson suggests at the beginning of his discussion of idealism, "is made to conspire with spirit to emancipate us."[20] Hepzibah and Clifford intuit that the world is spectacle or dream and that they are not. They do not, however, entertain the "noble doubt,"[21] which would enable them to chart the path back from skepticism to an acknowledgment of the world's reality and hence their own. In order to exist within the world, Hepzibah and Clifford must deny duality. Hepzibah decides the skeptical dilemma by dematerializing the present and reasserting the stable physicality of the past. Clifford chooses an opposite route. He dissolves the past, so that reality can be an eternal, "visionary and impalpable Now, which, if you once look closely at it, is nothing" (p. 149). Both directions doom the Pyncheons to a partial vision that is no vision at all.

Hawthorne looks to the past for a point outside himself by which to judge his own point of view and to establish that the world always exists under a point of view. Hepzibah prefers images of the past because they fix reality beyond the disruptions of transience. The "fixed idea," Hawthorne explains, is "madness":

> Fast and far as they had rattled and clattered along the iron track, they might just as well, as regarded Hepzibah's mental images, have been passing up and down Pyncheon street. With miles and miles of varied scenery between, there was no scene for her, save the seven old gable-peaks, with their moss, and the tuft of weeds in one of the angles, and the shop-window, and a customer shaking the door, and compelling the little bell to jingle fiercely. . . . This one old house was everywhere! It transported its great, lumbering bulk with more than railroad speed, and set itself phlegmatically down on whatever spot she glanced at. The quality of Hepzibah's mind was too unmalleable to take new impressions. (P. 258)

The problem with Hepzibah's fixation is not that she sees the same old house everywhere. The house of those many compass "points" (p. 5) is in historical Salem as well as in the Salem of Hawthorne's book, in the title and in the text, in the scene of the novel and in the novel's own scenes of allegorical or mental duplication. This particular scene is mirrored several times, both before and after chapter seventeen, just as its characters reflect one another as well as figures from the past. All rambles in the world duplicate each other, all scenes are the same scene, inevitably photographed through the single lens of the individual mind from slightly different gables or angles in different lights and shades. Hence Holgrave's game with the daguerreotypes of Colonel/Judge Pyncheon. But if this is the case, if the world is an endlessly self-reflecting mirror, it is critical to know where one stands in this mirror world and where the reflective process begins and ends.

Hawthorne diagnoses Hepzibah's optical ailment as "near-sightedness." Hepzibah needs "so to concentrate her powers of vision as to substitute a firm outline of the object, instead of a vague one" (p. 34). Like Robin Molineux, she must replace an unresolved image or an image of duality with uniformity and clarity. Staring through blurry eyes at the "stern features" of Colonel Pyncheon's portrait, Hepzibah tries to bring the picture into focus. The "strange contortion of the brow" (p. 33), through which she attempts to stabilize her image of the past, ironically reproduces the portrait's own proud and presumptuous puritanical scowl. "Face to face" with the picture (p. 33) or "gazing at herself in a dim looking-glass, and perpetually encountering her own frown within its ghostly sphere" (p. 34), Hepzibah fine-tunes vision into unreflective and unself-conscious mirroring endlessly replicated. Like Reuben Bourne, Hepzibah erases the distance between then and now.

Fixated on the dead past, Hepzibah becomes a mirror of that past. She makes herself dead to the world, wishing she were "in the old family-tomb, with all [her] fore-fathers" (p. 44). Incapable of bringing the world into focus, Hepzibah wants nothing less than to vanish, to enter a realm in which no images baffle her understanding. She prefers that the world never enjoy "another glimpse of her." She will "minister to the wants of the community unseen, like a disembodied divinity, or enchantress, holding forth her bargains to the reverential and awe-stricken purchasers, in an invisible hand" (p. 40). Her flight from the house, which puts her aboard the transcendental express, represents a grand effort to disappear: "she was fain to shrink deeper into herself . . . as if in the hope of making people suppose that here was only a cloak and hood, threadbare and woefully faded, taking an airing in the midst of the storm, without any wearer!" (p. 255).

Caught in the midst of the skeptical dilemma, Hepzibah commits herself either to ideality or materiality. She cannot, however, suffer any doubt in the matter. "Any certainty" is "preferable" to a "feeling of indistinctness and unreality" (p. 255). Either she is Hepzibah Pyncheon, proprietress of the house of the seven gables, or she is Hepzibah Pyncheon, the old maid "hucksteress" of a cent shop (p. 38). The image of the one necessarily precludes the image of the other, as if two images cannot occupy the same space at the same time. But of course they can and they must. Hepzibah has not yet learned about still photography's double exposure, certainly not about pictures in motion, in which the illusion, as from a train, that everything else is in motion and the self is stable masks the fact that it is the self that moves in time while the shifting spectacle of the movies consists only of a series of still images inducing the illusion of motion.

If Hepzibah suffers from a blinding entrenchment in the past, Clifford suffers total exclusion from it. Hepzibah is nearsighted. Clifford is amnesiac. Clifford's "mysterious and terrible Past . . . had annihilated his memory," leaving "a blank Future before him [and] this visionary and impalpable Now, which, if you once look closely at it, is nothing" (p. 149). Clifford's problem, however, is a version of Hepzibah's. He lacks a viewpoint that would allow him to interpret and to act. Long before he takes the train ride that affords him one last opportunity to define his relation to history and time, Clifford sits at the arched window of the house of the seven gables, and viewing the spectacle before him like a spectator in a theater, he fails to comprehend the world's fluidity and its relation to himself:

A cab; an omnibus, with its populous interior, dropping here-and-there a passenger, and picking up another, and thus typifying that vast rolling vehicle, the world, the end of whose journey is everywhere and nowhere;—these objects he followed eagerly with his eyes, but forgot them, before the dust, raised by the horses and wheels, had settled along their track. As regarded novelties . . . his mind appeared to have lost its proper gripe and retentiveness. Twice or thrice, for example, during the sunny hours of the day, a water-cart went along by the Pyncheon-house, leaving a broad wake of moistened earth. . . . With the water-cart Clifford could never grow familiar; it always affected him with just the same surprise as at first. His mind took an apparently sharp impression from it, but lost the recollection of this perambulatory shower, before its next re-appearance, as completely as did the street itself. . . . Nothing gives a sadder sense of decay, than this loss or suspension of the power to deal with unaccustomed things and to keep up with the swiftness of the passing moment. (Pp. 160–61)

Clifford wishes to jump from the window into the crowd. "Had I taken that plunge, and survived it," he says, "methinks it would have made me another man! Possibly, in some sense, Clifford may have been right. . . . Perhaps . . . he required nothing less than the great final remedy—death!" (p. 166). Like Hepzibah, Clifford wants to close the distressful gap between himself and the world. To close that gap, Hawthorne informs us, is death.

Clifford's problem is a failure of memory to hold onto images and to project them in proper relation to the self. This is a failure of historical imagination. At the end of the book an "old, dreamy recollection" haunts him, but the "mystery" is "just beyond the grasp of [his] mind" (p. 315). He cannot "recall" or "remember" the "secret spring" that would release the lost Pyncheon "will," which is both a literal document and a metaphor for the resolve Clifford lacks (p. 315). The philosophy of history that Clifford articulates in "The Flight of Two Owls" is a mad historiography of forgetfulness. It is a philosophy of flight, from the real and the remembered. Clifford resolves the noble doubt by dismantling reality altogether. "There is a certain house within my familiar recollection," confesses Clifford, "and it were a relief to me, if that house could be torn down, or burnt up, and so the earth be rid of it, and grass be sown abundantly over its foundation" (pp. 261–62). "The railroad," he suggests, "is destined to do away with those stale ideas of home and fireside" (p. 259). "What can be any man's inducement to tarry in one spot? . . . Why should he make himself a prisoner for life in brick, and stone, and old worm-eaten timber?" (p. 260). Like Hepzibah, Clifford knows that the railroad has represented the world in a different light: "These railroads . . . are positively the greatest blessing that the ages have wrought out for us. They give us wings; they annihilate the toil and dust of pilgrimage; they spiritualize travel" (p. 260). But, also like Hepzibah, he cannot see what the railroad is showing him.

Clifford imagines that he is defining historical progress: "all human progress is in a circle; or, to use a more accurate and beautiful figure, in an ascending spiral curve"; "the past is but a coarse and sensual prophecy of the present and the future" (pp. 259–60). But his historiography, in the tradition of akedian heroes, reverses historical progression and unwrites history. "The farther I get away from [the house]," Clifford explains, "the more does the joy, the lightsome freshness, the heart-leap, the intellectual dance, the youth, in short—yes, my youth, my youth!—the more does it come back to me" (p. 262). Humankind, according to Clifford, is to return to a "nomadic" state (p. 259), while literature, we might infer from Hawthorne's references to *Pilgrim's Progress* and pilgrimage generally, is to unwrite itself into an earlier mode. It is no wonder that the girls drop their ball in the middle of his discourse (p. 260). Clifford's philosophy of history has reversed the forward moving direction of history. It has erased history, made it disappear.

FROM THE FATAL POINT OF VIEW

It is only "a moment afterwards [that] the train—with all the life of its interior, amid which Clifford had made himself so conspicuous an object— was gliding away in the distance, and rapidly lessening to a point, which, in another moment, vanished. The world had fled away from these two wanderers" (p. 266). Hepzibah and Clifford have decisively missed the point. Thinking they can flee from the world, the world flees from them. The railroad has taken Hepzibah and Clifford nowhere at all. It has only reinforced their sense of helplessness and entrapment. "Do with me what you will," Clifford says to Hepzibah. "Oh, God!" prays Hepzibah, "Have mercy on us!" (pp. 266–67). Relinquishing the gifts of Emersonian transcendentalism, Hepzibah and Clifford return to the dismal fatalities of history that Hawthorne announced in the beginning of the book and from which there is, for them, no escape. In *The Senses of Walden*, Stanley Cavell explores in relation to Thoreau what this fate that overtakes them might mean. Fate, writes Cavell, interpreting Thoreau,

> is an idea of something controlled from beyond itself, toward a predetermined end or within predetermined confines. We did not get such an idea from nature, because what we find in nature is recurrence . . . nature has no destiny beyond its presence; and it is completely autonomous, self-determined. So we must be projecting the idea onto nature . . . Then the idea comes from our own sense of being controlled from outside. *Walden's* concept for this is that of the *track*, and the most extended image of it is the new railroad.

Thoreau's choice of image, and Cavell's discussion, offer insights into Hepzibah's and Clifford's situation. Like Hawthorne, Thoreau would put human beings aboard the railroad and have them recognize their transcendental relationship to the world. "When I hear the iron horse make the hills echo with his snort like thunder," he writes, "it seems as if the earth had got a race now worthy to inhabit it. If all were as it seems, and men made their elements their servants for noble ends." But, "what happens instead," explains Cavell, "is that men will mythologize their forces, as they always have, project them into demigods, and then serve their projections." "We have constructed a fate, an *Atropos*, that never turns aside," Cavell quotes Thoreau. And Cavell continues, "what we have constructed is fate itself. That it never turns aside is merely what the word fate, or rather Atropos, means. And we are not fated to it; *we* can turn. We can learn a lesson from the railroad, as we can from the rest of what happens, if we can for once learn something that does not merely confirm our worst fears instead of our confidence."[22]

What we can turn toward, according to Cavell, is at once the world and the self as Emerson and Thoreau define them. We are spectators, not only of the world, which we must understand as an object existing independently of our perception, but of ourselves, making the self what Cavell calls "the scene of occurrence." Like Cavell's idea of the scene of instruction in words, the scene of occurrence is not a coarse confounding of undecidable meanings (doublings infinitely reflected or the spectacular world endlessly adrift). Rather it is the separation between the self and the world and between the self and itself, which simultaneously establishes an interpretive point of view, individual identity, and moral relatedness.[23] Riding on the train, realizing the spectrality of the world and the stability of the self, Hepzibah and Clifford might have discovered themselves and their relationship to the world. But the discovery of self and its relatedness requires one more turnaway. It insists that we also occupy a point of view outside ourselves, on the landscape, as it were, watching the train that goes whizzing by. Hepzibah and Clifford cannot turn away from their fixated vision. Seeing nothing, they become a scene of nonoccurrence, living death.

The scene of nonoccurrence, in which there is no one who can see, and nothing to be seen, is Hawthorne's definition of death. Death is the ultimate fate to which, in Hawthorne's view, human beings like Hepzibah and Clifford surrender. It is the fate to which they will themselves in their attempt to make the self synonymous with the world—as in Clifford's desire to jump from the arched window or Hepzibah's wish to retreat to the ancestral tomb. In the chapter "Governor Pyncheon," Hawthorne explores the interdependence between existential reality and imaginative perception. Sustaining life, suggests Hawthorne, hinges on more than understanding the particular point of view by which past and present, object and meaning are related. It depends on having a point of view. "Governor Pyncheon" records events concurrent with "The Flight of Two Owls." It is the lens that, projecting their flight as the loss of consciousness and the surrender to historical fatality, reveals the importance of point of view itself.

The chapter opens: "Judge Pyncheon, while his two relatives have fled away with such ill-considered haste, still sits in the old parlor, keeping house, as the familiar phrase is, in the absence of its ordinary occupants" (p. 268). While Hepzibah and Clifford have fled into the world of time and space and life, only to discover that flight from one place is flight from any place to nowhere, the judge remains stationary, solitary, and still. In the absence of the house's ordinary occupants, he is keeping house. But to keep house in this sense, remaining in the same place and infinitely reiterating one's point of view, ironically produces the consequences of flight. Judge Pyncheon's "gaze" is even more "fixed" than Hepzibah's (p. 268). He is even more "forgetful" than Clifford (cf. pp. 271, 273, 274). "Time" has literally become "a matter of no moment" to him (p. 271). He is quite literally dead.

Unlike the rest of the book, "Governor Pyncheon" is not about the present or the past or their relationship. It is about a future that will never be. It is about the disrelation caused by Hepzibah's and Clifford's brands of ahistoricity. The chapter title itself proclaims this essential ahistoricity. The day which "was to have been such a busy day" will never happen (p. 270). There will never be a "Governor Pyncheon." The chapter explores the hypothetical consequences of the unwriting of history, were it really possible to stop the "great world-clock of Time," to get off the train, or never to get on it. Judge Pyncheon embodies a death that is not simply the conclusion of life, marking an end to a journey or process. He represents the death that is the eclipse of the world, the annihilation of the conscious perception on which our relationship to phenomenal reality, our lives in reality, depend.

The judge's death would appear, at first, an ordinary phenomenon, not much different from the darkening of evening: "[T]he twilight is glooming upward out of the corners of the room. The shadows of the tall furniture grow deeper, and at first become more definite; then, spreading wider, they lose their distinctness of outline in the dark gray tide of oblivion, as it were, that creeps slowly over the various objects, and the one human figure sitting in the midst of them" (p. 276). But this is no common night, no typical death:

The gloom has not entered from without; it has brooded here all day, and now, taking its inevitable time, will possess itself of everything. . . . Fainter and fainter grows the light. It is as if another double-handfull of darkness had been scattered through the air. . . . There is still a faint appearance at the window; neither a glow, nor a gleam, nor a glimmer—any phrase of light would express something far brighter than this doubtful perception, or sense, rather, that there is a window there. Has it yet vanished? No!—yes!—not quite! . . . The features are all gone; there is only the paleness of them left. And how looks it now? There is no window! There is no face! An infinite, inscrutable blackness has annihilated sight! Where is our universe? All crumbled away from us; and we . . . that go sighing and murmuring about, in quest of what was once a world! (Pp. 276–77)

The scene reveals death as its own kind of forgetting and forgetfulness (oblivion), "taking its inevitable time" and possessing itself of everything. It also dramatizes the relationship between our awareness of death and our capacity for sustaining consciousness. All that intervenes between the gloom and the world is "doubtful perception." But when this doubt is decided, what remains is either only the world's window or the soul's, that is, no world and no self at all. Life, Hawthorne insists, depends on the capacity to project a spectacle that a competent spectator can witness. It depends equally on the world's windows and the "windows into consciousness," which are the eyes and the soul of human beings. When either of these windows disappears, the world that once was also disappears.

As Emily Dickinson so memorably put it, very likely thinking of this scene in Hawthorne's novel,

I heard a Fly buzz—when I died—
The Stillness in the Room
Was like the Stillness in the Air—
Between the Heaves of Storm—

The Eyes around—had wrung them dry—
And Breaths were gathering firm
For that last Onset—when the King
Be witnessed—in the Room—

I willed my Keepsakes—Signed away
What portion of me be
Assignable—and then it was
There interposed a Fly—

With Blue—uncertain stumbling Buzz—
Between the light—and me—
And then the Windows failed—and then
I could not see to see—. (No. 465)[24]

Like Hawthorne's romance, Dickinson's poem probes the essential interdependence of world and self. It discovers how the assumptions of a transcendent soul, thinking itself separate from and in control of the world's phenomena, delivers the self, not to a vision of God or salvation, but to total perceptual eclipse, which annihilates all vision and insight. For Dickinson, as for Hawthorne, the windows that fail are simultaneously the literal windows of the room, the eyes, and the soul. When all these windows fail the narrator can no longer "see to see": to see physically whatever there is to see, physically or spiritually; or to see any reason to see physically or spiritually. There is simply no "scene of interpretation," no "scene of occurrence." All that remains is the "Fly." Or, more accurately, all that remains is the fly's "uncertain stumbling Buzz," which interposes itself between the light and the self.

Dickinson's persona, like Hawthorne's characters, would eliminate perceptual doubt through a transcendent revelation: a vision of a house or of the disappearance of a house or the appearance of a savior. The price of this attempt to substitute vision for reality is not the elimination of perceptual doubt but its grotesque materialization. The fly decides the noble doubt by eliminating the point of view that causes uncertainty in the first place. "What!" exclaims Hawthorne to his dead judge: "Thou art not stirred by this last appeal? No; not a jot! And there we see a fly—one of your common house-flies, such as are always buzzing on the window-pane—which has smelt out Governor Pyncheon, and alights now on his forehead, now on his chin, and now, Heaven help us, is creeping over the bridge of his nose, towards the would-be chief-magistrate's wide-open eyes! Can thou not brush the fly away? Art thou too sluggish? . . . Art thou too weak?" (p. 283). Judge Pyncheon will not, in Cavell's terms, turn aside. He will not brush the fly away. The fly seals his fate.

What remains for Dickinson and Hawthorne in the absence of the skeptical dilemma is an "infinite, inscrutable blackness." This is the opposite of a universe or world because it annihilates sight and because it withdraws the scene of this world wherein we witness, scrutinize, and judge. Like Hepzibah's and Clifford's flight from history, the judge's withdrawal from life has caused the world itself to flee. Left behind are only the undecipherable and unknowable, unscrutinizable ghosts of the world's immateriality and, equally horrible, the world's insistent and demoralizing materiality. Like Minister Hooper hanging a veil before his face in order to awaken in his parishioners a consciousness of evil, only to discover that he has annihilated sight and insight both, so Judge Pyncheon, placing before his vision a vision of wealth and power, finds that vision cancels vision. It blocks out the light as effectively as the housefly, the baalzebub,[25] that will, in the end, assume lordship over all.

ROMANCE, REDEMPTION, AND RENEWAL

Hawthorne's historical romantic art establishes the independent existences of the world and the self and sets the stage on which mutuality and independent perception occur. The relationship between Holgrave's (or Hawthorne's) art and the problems of skepticism, fate, and subjectivity can be deduced, by analogy, from Cavell's discussion of American film, which carries forward his concern with these subjects in the American tradition and links the issue of photography to history:

> At some point the unhinging of our consciousness from the world interposed our subjectivity between us and our presentness to the world. Then our subjectivity became what is present to us, individuality became isolation. The route to conviction in reality [in expressionism and romanticism] was through the acknowledgment of the endless presence of self. . . . Photography overcame subjectivity in a way undreamed of by painting . . . by *automatism*, by removing the human agent from the task of reproduction. . . . The reality in a photograph is present to me while I am not present to it; and a world I know, and see, but to which I am nevertheless not present (through no fault of my subjectivity), is a world past.[26]

The relationship between viewer and viewed confirms the essential neighborliness of the relationship between self and world, and self and self, which Cavell describes in *The Senses of Walden* and which he links to historical consciousness itself:

> The implied presence of the rest of the world, and its explicit rejection, are as essential in the experience of a photograph as what it explicitly presents. . . . The world of a moving picture is screened. . . . A screen is a barrier. What does the silver screen screen? It screens me from the world it holds . . . And it screens that world from me . . . I am present not at something happening, which I must confirm, but at something that has happened, which I absorb (like a memory). In this, movies resemble novels, a fact mirrored in the sound of narration itself, whose tense is the past.[27]

Movies resemble historical romances in their "tense" and in the way that they "screen" past from present. Drawing the veil that divides them, they imply both the presence and absence of a world and a self, not through the endlessly dissolving subjectivities of the self but through the world's own intractable presence.

Holgrave and Phoebe are the heroes of Hawthorne's romance because they wed past to present, moral responsibility to guilt, and Puritanism to Transcendentalism, not through some kind of ineffable process but through their own rigorous commitment to history and the world. The triumph they prophesy is not, as has often been assumed, a change in the course of history, erasing the perpetuity of evil announced at the beginning of the book. Rather, perceiving the intermingling of past and present as itself proffering a version of noble doubt, they ride the perpetuity of evil into a vision of an Eden in a fallen world. Holgrave and Phoebe, albeit only partially, correct the optical deficiencies of their families. They establish a romantic, cine-magraphic point of view. The instrument of Phoebe's and Holgrave's re-demptive vision is the new and special art of photography, which projects the world through a historical romantic point of view not unlike that expressed by Hawthorne's own book.

Holgrave and Phoebe are not born with these Emersonian gifts of sight. Through the better part of the book, both of them suffer from perceptual disabilities closely related to those of Hepzibah, Clifford, and the Judge. Like Clifford, Holgrave, for example, feels nothing but disdain for the past. "The house, in my view," he says early in the book, "is expressive of that odious and abominable Past. . . . I dwell in it for a while, that I may know the better how to hate it" (p. 184). Like Hepzibah, his daguerreotypes suffer from a problem of nearsightedness. Both Holgrave and Hepzibah try to bring an unclear world into focus and to fix it in stable images. Hepzibah, we are told, "needed a walk along the noonday street, to keep her sane" (p. 59). But apparently simple daylight, such as Hawthorne discusses in his preface, provides no antidote, for the lack of clarity inheres in daylight. "I make pictures out of sunshine," explains Holgrave, "Most of my likenesses do look unamiable; but the very sufficient reason, I fancy, is because the originals are so. There is a wonderful insight in heaven's broad and simple sunshine." (p. 91). Because he wants to eliminate the past from his art, Holgrave, like Hepzibah, can see only fate's scowl, the "frown" or "sneer" that Hawthorne tells us he keeps at bay through his own kind of romantic art (p. 41). A "family," claims Holgrave, must "forget all about its ancestors" (p. 185). It must imagine the present separate and exempt from the conditions of the past. But as Hawthorne indicates in his presentation of Clifford's mad his-toriography, to do this is to misperceive the world and to endanger oneself. Early on, Holgrave cannot understand the irony of Hepzibah's reference to "old Maule's ghost" because he cannot, in his sunny vision, recognize that ghost in himself. Later, he unself-consciously pokes fun at Phoebe's mistak-ing his photograph of Judge Pyncheon for a picture of her "Puritan ancestor" (p. 92). He does not realize that Phoebe, like her cousin Hepzibah, has intuited something about the relationship between past and present that he does not yet understand. Because of his unwillingness to entertain the shadows, to see in the house what he imagines is to be pictured only outside the house, Holgrave reduces himself to the unenlightened, unethical, uncommitted spectatorship of a Clifford at his arched window. "You talk as if this old house were a theatre," Phoebe accuses him, "I do not like this. The play costs the performers too much—and the audience is too cold-hearted." To which Holgrave replies, "I cannot help fancying that Destiny is arranging its fifth act for a catastrophe" (pp. 217–18). Merely observing the world's spectacle, Holgrave loses his ability to see and matter and act in this world. "Lawless" or with a "law of his own" (p. 85), he has become an "inmate" of the house, "a lodger in a remote gable . . . with locks, bolts, and oaken bars" on his prison door (p. 30). Like Clifford, who is similarly incarcerated, he thereby forfeits the possibility of love and life. Holgrave is literally "morbid" (p. 218); and the scene concludes with Phoebe's emphatic departure: "Good bye, then . . . good night and good bye!" (p. 218).

Phoebe also does not see properly at the beginning of the book. She therefore cannot help Holgrave with his vision or communicate to him his and the world's mutual spectrality. Like Clifford, Phoebe knows little about the past. She has never heard of Clifford, or perhaps only "heard the name." She has "not been brought up a Pyncheon" (p. 74–75). She correctly notes the similarity between Holgrave's daguerreotype of the Judge and the portrait of Colonel Pyncheon, but she mistakes that photograph for a simple copy of the original portrait. Holgrave assures her that "had you looked a little longer . . . you would have seen other differences" (p. 92). Hawthorne reinforces this point when Phoebe finally meets the Judge and suffers from a version of the original misperception: "the fantasy would not quit her, that the original Puritan . . . had now stept into the shop. . . . Could the two personages have stood together before her eyes," Hawthorne insists, "many points of difference would have been perceptible" (p. 120).

Phoebe, who is sunshine personified, sees, like Holgrave, only in "broad daylight." She therefore cannot see "points of difference." As she continues to reside in the house, however, "a change [grows] visible" and "life does not look the same" (p. 214). Finally, at the climactic moment, shadow and light both penetrate her vision:

> [C]oming so suddenly from the sunny daylight [Phoebe] was altogether bedimmed in such density of shadow as lurked in most of the passages of the old house. . . . [But] before her eyes had adapted themselves to the obscurity, a hand grasped her own, with a firm, but gentle and warm pressure . . . the sunshine came freely into all the uncurtained windows of this room, and fell upon the dusty floor; so that Phoebe now clearly saw—what, indeed, had been no secret . . . to whom she owed her reception. (P. 300)

With shadow obscuring daylight and sunshine illuminating shadow, Phoebe and Holgrave can finally "see to see." At first Holgrave hesitates in showing the daguerreotype to Phoebe. "It was like dragging a hideous shape of death into the cleanly and cheerful space before a household fire, where it would present all the uglier aspect, amid the decorousness of everything about it." "Yet," Holgrave realizes, "it could not be concealed from her; she must needs know it" (p. 302). And know it she does: "This is death!" she says immediately, "Judge Pyncheon dead" (p. 302).

Phoebe, however, is not the only beneficiary of the mutual infiltration of light and dark:

> Could you but know, Phoebe, how it was with me, the hour before you came! . . . A dark, cold, miserable hour! The presence of yonder dead man threw a great black shadow over everything; he made the universe, so far as my perception could reach, a scene of guilt, and of retribution more dreadful than guilt. The sense of it took away my youth. I never hoped to feel young again! The world looked so strange, wild, evil, hostile; . . . But, Phoebe, you crossed the threshold; and hope, warmth, and joy came in with you! The black moment became at once a blissful one. (P. 306)

Like the "owl, bewildered in the daylight," which is Hawthorne's story, and unlike the owls who have fled the house, Phoebe must hasten back to her "hollow tree" (p. 268). When she gets there she sees a black-and-white photograph, which is itself a technical structure of light and shadow and innumerable "points of difference." The subject of this photograph is the scene of perceptual eclipse and of guilt and retribution that Hawthorne describes in "Governor Pyncheon," which is itself a psychological or philosophical portrait of the events of the preceding chapter. Like the railroad scene, the picture mirrors life, threatening the collapse into repetition and duplication, which is the death of consciousness itself. "This is death,"exclaims Phoebe, identifying the picture's subject, but also characterizing its own potentially deathly character. But the daguerreotype Phoebe examines has been crafted by a romantic historian who has himself become aware of the relationship between dark and light and points of difference. As readers of a printed text, we do not have Holgrave's photograph in our hands. Therefore we cannot say how, graphically, it communicates this awareness. But Hawthorne's strong suggestion is that the difference between the first daguerreotype of Judge Pyncheon and the second has to do largely with Holgrave's relation to his art. The first daguerreotype is made in "broad daylight" by a Pyncheon enemy. The second picture arises from a "feeling" that cannot be described, an "indefinite sense of some catastrophe, or consummation," which compels the young artist, who is now in love with a Pyncheon, to use "the means at [his] disposal to preserve [a] pictorial record of Judge Pyncheon's death." This record is "a point of evidence that may be useful to Clifford." It is also a "memorial valuable" to himself (p. 303). Holgrave's art, in other words, incorporates all of the shadows, including those that sunshine can never dispel. He takes their point and understands the moral obligation they imply. His picture is a record that preserves the past, memorializes it. It declares his acknowledgment of what is therein represented and his commitment to what his record has preserved.

When Hawthorne explains that he has written his novel under the "aspect" of the house, he means much the same thing (p. 5). In his romance, he has preserved the record of a house that he has in no way invented but for which he is finally responsible. Because he has written in the umbrage of the house, under its aspect, its shadows will darken his work, even after he has illuminated them and projected what they conceal. The lights and the darks thus incorporated do more than mimetically reproduce the world's unfathomable mixture of good and evil. They position the artist in a particular relation to his vision. They determine how he will act as a result of where he stands. The end of the book is not a giddy, weak-minded endorsement of Clifford's historiography of the ascending spiral. It is, rather, an announcement of an authorial point of view that has been earned by a commitment to what has been depicted. Hawthorne's moral is not that everything depends on how you see it. It is that you can win the right to look at things in a certain way. Hawthorne earns his right to his romance of history for the same reasons that Phoebe and Holgrave earn their right to their romance of love.

The Eden that Hawthorne establishes at the end of the novel is not like the promised land or the paradise that, for American protagonists from the Wielands through the Bournes through the McCaslins, substituted for a postlapsarian, fallen America. Hawthorne's Eden is only America. It exists as a consequence of and in the continuity of history:

> And it was in this hour, so full of doubt and awe, that the one miracle was wrought, without which every human existence is a blank. The bliss, which makes all things true, beautiful, and holy, shone around this youth and maiden. They were conscious of nothing sad nor old. They transfigured the earth, and made it Eden again and themselves the two first dwellers in it. The dead man, so close beside them, was forgotten. At such a crisis, there is no Death; for Immortality is revealed anew, and embraces everything in its hallowed atmosphere. (p. 307)

For a moment, Holgrave and Phoebe are, like Hepzibah, Clifford and the Judge, unconscious. Like Clifford and the Judge, they have forgotten everything, including Death. The moment is a blissful one for Holgrave and Phoebe. But Hawthorne knows, and Phoebe and Clifford have learned, how dangerous such transports can be, how easily the bliss can dissolve into the death that is, after all, what immortality is all about. "This hour," they fully understand, exists under the aspect of "doubt and awe." That doubt and awe cannot be dispelled. No sooner have Phoebe and Clifford entertained their moment of perilous unconsciousness, then "the heavy earth-dream settle[s] down again" (p. 307). It enfolds Holgrave and Phoebe in its uncertainty, its oldness, its heaviness—finally, its life: "Now let us meet the world . . . Let us open the door at once" (p. 307).

For life is the condition of doubt and awe that must be affirmed. Only for Hepzibah and Clifford is the Eden that Holgrave and Phoebe create at the conclusion of the chapter a permanent condition. "The flower of Eden has bloomed . . . in this old, darksome house, to-day!" exclaims Clifford (p. 308). Holgrave and Phoebe, however, depart this Eden. They know that "the heavy earth-dream," which casts life under the aspect of death and the uncertainty that death implies, is the essential condition of their reality. Therefore, for Phoebe and Holgrave, human experience must always exist under the pressure of what the final chapter titles "Departure." For Hepzibah and Clifford departing on the train, or for Judge Pyncheon departing life, departure is fate, mortality, and death. It evidences the disjunction between the self and the world that seems to make vision impossible. "The world," Emerson wrote:

> proceeds from the same spirit as the body of man. It is a remoter and inferior incarnation of God, a projection of God in the unconscious. But it differs from the body in one important respect. It is not, like that, now subjected to the human will. Its serene order is inviolable by us. It is, therefore, to us, the present expositor of the divine mind. It is a fixed point whereby we may measure our departure. As we degenerate, the contrast between us and our house is more evident. We are as much strangers in nature as we are aliens from God.[28]

For Phoebe and Holgrave, who are regenerative forces, departure is precisely what opens up the possibility of a point of view. It is a faith, not unlike their love for one another, that guarantees the world's stability and their own. It promises the possibilities of redemption and renewal within the heavy earth-dream.

Departure divests Phoebe and Holgrave of certainty. It withholds the promise of the future. But departing from, they are also departing toward. Leaving something behind, they discover something else. "We are not built like a ship to be tossed, but like a house to stand," writes Emerson.[29] Phoebe and Holgrave will occupy a "house to stand." They will return to the "fixed point" on which their own identities are anchored. Departing allows them to look back on what has been. Moving forward they do not lose the past. They gain a view of it that enables them to extend it further into the future. This is Hawthorne's definition of romance. It explains the relationship, expressed in the preface, between the dynamics of a romantic art and the historiography of evil that romance transforms.

At the end of the book Hawthorne suggests that "a gifted eye" might see "fore-shadowed" in the "kaleidoscopic pictures" of Maule's well the "coming fortunes of Hepzibah and Clifford, and the descendant of the legendary wizard, and the village-maiden" (p. 319). Hawthorne's book forbears such prophesying. Nature's "prophecies," the book states, are "unintelligible" (p. 319). All that human beings can see and understand intelligibly is what has departed. Prophecy is fate. It fixes vision. It freezes life in the inevitabilities of a story that is not its own. According to Hawthorne, and other historical romancers, the American Puritans and their heirs had doomed America and its history. Their Eden had reflected the moral and historical blindness of Hepzibah, Clifford, and the Judge. Hawthorne's history, like Emerson's nature, turns vision around. It renders a point of view that balances human perception on either side of the skeptical divide, between what we can and cannot know. "In most . . . cases and contingencies," Hawthorne writes, "the individual is present among us, mixed up with the daily revolution of affairs, and affording a definite point for observation. At his decease, there is only a vacancy" (p. 309). Life is point of view; death is its absence. Yet history, as the record of life now deceased, opens up an indefinite point for observation. The historical point of view is always cancelled and yet it is always present. Indeed, like Derrida's concept of writing under erasure, history under the pressure of departure reveals the bare traces of a world. These traces are all we have to interpret. But history under the pressure of departure does not sacrifice the reality of what has been effaced. It never releases the transcendentalist tether to a world that will not depart and that, like a house to stand, requires our fully conscious and unstinting occupancy.

The marriage of Phoebe and Holgrave is not a transcendental event redeeming the world and renewing Eden. It is simply the ceremony that ensures "keeping house," not the way the patriarchal and avaricious Judge or the spinster and bachelor Pyncheons kept it, but the way it was meant to be kept, by a commitment to the processes of life and death. Early in the book the narrator explains that "tradition . . . brings down truth that history has let slip" (p. 17). This truth, which can readily slip out of our historical concerns, is the importance of tradition itself. It expresses the need to take up residence in a house and keep it. The departure from the house of the seven gables does not reverse the exile from Eden any more than it redeems the house or empties it of the ghosts that haunt it. It does not decide the undecidability of experience. "Wise Uncle Venner" "*seem[s]* to hear a strain of music." He "*fancie[s]* that sweet Alice Pyncheon . . . had given one farewell touch of a spirit's joy upon her harpsichord, as she floated heavenward from the HOUSE OF THE SEVEN GABLES" (p. 319). We cannot verify these hopes. Departing, however, does reconfirm, monumentally, insistently, emphatically, what has been there from the start, in the writer's "recollection" (p. 10), even before it appears in his story, in history before it entered his personal memory or imagination: the house itself. For Hawthorne, the house of the seven gables is a "specimen of the best and stateliest architecture of a long-past epoch" (p. 10). It is a remnant or artifact of the past, confirming the reality of the past beyond all speculation and uncertainty. The house, then, is a "scene of events" (p. 10). It is where the romance of history takes place and where the romance of love is born.[30]

8

Reading Emerson:
Fitzgerald's *The Great Gatsby*
and the Romance
of Historical Revision

Jay Gatsby, more than his predecessors in the American tradition, is blind to the meaning of history. He therefore follows the track of a historical repetition from which, in Cavell's Thoreauvian terms, he simply cannot turn aside. "You can't repeat the past," counsels Nick, who understands trains and timetables and what they suggest about human experience. Gatsby responds, incredulously, " 'Can't repeat the past? . . . Why of course you can.' He looked around him wildly, as if the past were lurking here in the shadow of his house, just out of reach of his hand. 'I'm going to fix everything just the way it was before' " (p. 111).[1] Gatsby's determination to ignore historical time, to retrieve the past in the present, and to act out the story of what might have been is the basic flaw in his tragic personality.[2] It reincarnates the desire of heroes from Charles Brockden Brown's Wieland through Faulkner's Isaac McCaslin to unwrite history and to replace it with an ideal vision or myth. This desire is for Fitzgerald, as it was for Hawthorne before him, nothing other than fate. Unlike Theodore Wieland, Reuben Bourne, Captain Vere, Grandfathers Bentley and Fortune, and Isaac McCaslin, Jay Gatsby does not envision his reality in biblical terms. Nor does he sacrifice anyone, except, like Isaac McCaslin, himself and his future progeny. But this may just be Fitzgerald's advance on the tradition that he self-consciously inherits. In the strangely sterile and childless world of Fitzgerald's "valley of ashes," Tom's and Daisy's doll-like daughter is the only child, and Tom and Myrtle adopt a puppy. The antitypological drama of the akedah, therefore, has come to be enacted within the isolated self in whom destruction and self-destruction, homicide and suicide, sacrifice and blasphemy are one and the same. In this post-Freudian era, they are also aspects of a powerful psychological repression. The result is the loss of the life in history on which future generations, that is, the continuation of history, depend. For Gatsby what is "lost" (as it will be for Hemingway's similarly "lost generation") is not only an Eden that never was but also the compensation for that lost paradise, the possibility of history, which emerges triumphant at the end of Hawthorne's *The House of the Seven Gables*.

SELF-RELIANCE VS. SELF-DESTRUCTION

In *The Great Gatsby* Fitzgerald focuses on the implicit subject of the akedian romances, which is also the central preoccupation of many of Hawthorne's historical romances as well: the relationship between the self and the world and the role of history in defining and facilitating that relationship. Fitzgerald links this relationship to the other major source of American identity, which is also a major concern of Faulkner's *Go Down, Moses:* the myth of nature that is introduced into the American tradition in the fiction of James Fenimore Cooper and which receives its most significant treatment in Emersonian transcendentalism. As early as 1937, John Peale Bishop had charged that Gatsby is "the Emersonian man brought to completion and eventually to failure."[3] He is the reductio ad absurdum of self-reliance, popularly understood. Gatsby seems to have taken Emerson at his word, that he build his own world. He believes literally that the world exists for him; that for him is the world perfect.[4] Though Gatsby is not one of the subjects of Sharon Cameron's study, he vividly recalls the problems of a regressive corporeal imagination such as she describes.[5] He is a model of what Sam Girgus, building on Quentin Anderson's notion of an "imperial self," labels a "perverted self,"[6] possibly epitomizing the final reaches of a process of American incarnation such as Myra Jehlen describes.[7] Like Young Goodman Brown, Gatsby imaginatively conceives a world, which he then projects outward as the world itself. He creates a self that becomes for him the entire range and content of that world. For Gatsby the universe is a possession of and finally an expression of self.

A "gorgeous" figure of "romantic readiness" and "hope" (p. 2), Gatsby is, however, no Goodman Brown or Reuben Bourne. He is as much the genuine hero of Fitzgerald's text (and of Nick's) as he is the object of its criticism. "Gatsby . . . represented everything for which I have an unaffected scorn," Nick confesses. He continues, "Gatsby turned out all right at the end; it is what preyed on Gatsby, what foul dust floated in the wake of his dreams that temporarily closed out my interest in the abortive sorrows and short-winded elations of men" (p. 2). What redeems Gatsby as the American hero is the Emersonianism that Fitzgerald retrieves from within Gatsby's dream,

the transcendental vision that he manages to extricate from Gatsby's dangerously solipsistic, self-sacrificial fantasy.

As in *The House of the Seven Gables*, the kind of relationship between self
and world that Gatsby creates is not what Emerson had intended. Stanley
Cavell's remarks on Emerson again serve us in good stead. Although Cavell's
discussion of "Self-Reliance" takes as its focus Emerson as writer, his obser-
vations about what constitutes the Emersonian position in relation to society
focuses the differences between Gatsby's enactment of a reductive individualism and Emerson's complexly social philosophy of self-reliance. The question of writing is not irrelevant to what separates them. One of Gatsby's
problems as he writes the universe as the text of himself is he can find no
language in which to speak that is not simply a repetition of a psychic
language, which itself expresses irretrievable and "unutterable" meanings
(pp. 112, 180). " 'Self-Reliance,' " Cavell suggests, "constitutes a theory of
writing and reading. . . . The relation of Emerson's writing (the expression
of his self-reliance) to his society (the realm of what he calls conformity) is
one, as 'Self-Reliance' puts it, of mutual aversion":

> But "Self-reliance is the aversion of conformity" figures each side in terms of the other,
> declares the issue between them as always joined, never settled. But then this is to say
> that Emerson's writing and his society are in an unending argument with one
> another—that is to say he writes in such a way as to *place* his writing in his unending
> argument . . . an unending turning away from one another, but for that exact reason
> a constant keeping in mind of one another, hence endlessly a turning *toward* one
> another. So that Emerson's aversion is like and unlike, religious conversion."[8]

Alan Trachtenberg has suggested that *Gatsby* records the shifting perspectives
or points of view of myth and history.[9] Gatsby lacks what Hepzibah, Clifford,
and Judge Pyncheon lack: the ability to maintain these perspectives or points
of view, or, in Cavell's terms, the ability both to turn away and to turn toward
the world around him. Gatsby's "religious conversion," then, is as it was for
a whole line of American protagonists: a turning inward, severing the self
from the world and eclipsing external reality.

Gatsby has an impulse to "return to a certain starting place and go over it
all slowly" so that he could find out why "his life [has] been confused and
disordered" (pp. 111–12). The slow and self-conscious reordering of a life to
create a better self is, perhaps, the central impulse of both historical analysis
and psychoanalysis. Hemingway's *The Sun Also Rises*, as we shall see, is
indebted to Fitzgerald's novel for this theme. Self-reflection leads the self
into history and, as in *The House of the Seven Gables*, it permits art or
authorship to occur. In *The Great Gatsby*, Nick is the student of Fitzgerald's

Cavellian "scene of instruction in words."[10] Like Holgrave, he learns, in Cavell's sense, to "place" his writing within a process of social aversions. And he becomes what Alan Trachtenberg has called the "historical voice" of the novel.[11] He learns to identify the differences that create meaning, and he learns to speak.

Gatsby, however, wants literally to "recover something" in the past, a self-conceived idea of self and not a real or historical self (p. 111). Gatsby's religious conversion, unlike Emerson's, is an immaculate self-conception of self. His American dream is like a Freudian nightmare, replicating what is repressed, concealing its meanings, and preventing any mechanism for change. Each incarnation of Gatsby's vision, from the national self-conception on which it is based, to the personal self-conception, to the neo-Platonic love, which further reproduces that self-conception, reductively translates or restates nothing more than an ineffable and untranslatable idea, remaining forever beyond the powers of speech or action.

Although the passages that record Gatsby's (and America's) fixation with self and the speechlessness to which it delivers them are lengthy, it is difficult to grasp the book's central psychoanalytic and historical-romantic insights without recording a portion of these texts. The description of Gatsby's falling in love with Daisy is reprinted below. It is the record of the "idea of himself . . . that had gone into loving Daisy" (p. 111), which he is trying to recover because, as the second passage below demonstrates, it duplicates (or, in the manner of Faulkner, it twins) this idea of himself. The third passage reveals an echo of an even earlier historical impulse on which both Gatsby's self-conception and his Platonic love depend:

> One autumn night, five years before, they had been walking down the street when the leaves were falling, and they came to a place where there were no trees and the sidewalk was white with moonlight. . . . Out of the corner of his eye Gatsby saw that the blocks of the sidewalks really formed a ladder and mounted to a secret place above the trees—he could climb to it, if he climbed alone, and once there he could suck on the pap of life, gulp down the incomparable milk of wonder. . . . He knew that when he kissed this girl, and forever wed his unutterable visions to her perishable breath, his mind would never romp again like the mind of God. . . . At his lips' touch she blossomed for him like a flower and the incarnation was complete. (P. 112)

> The truth was that Jay Gatsby of West Egg, Long Island, sprang from his Platonic conception of himself. He was a son of God—a phrase which, if it means anything, means just that—and he must be about His Father's business, the service of a vast, vulgar, and meretricious beauty. (P. 99)

> [As] the moon rose higher the inessential houses began to melt away until gradually I became aware of the old island here that flowered once for Dutch sailors' eyes—a

vanished trees, the trees that had made way for Gatsby's house, had once pandered in whispers to the last and greatest of all human dreams; for a transitory enchanted moment man must have held his breath in the presence of this continent, compelled into an aesthetic contemplation he neither understood nor desired, face to face for the last time in history with something commensurate to his capacity for wonder. . . .

Gatsby believed in the green light, the orgiastic future that year by year recedes before us. It eluded us then, but that's no matter—tomorrow we will run faster, stretch out our arms farther. . . . And one fine morning—

So we beat on, boats against the current, borne back ceaselessly into the past. (P. 182)[12]

These are among the most thrilling, deeply stirring passages in Gatsby. Yet what all three explore is the psychosexual regression of the transcendentalizing ego. Dependent on neo-Platonic conceptions, *Gatsby* is a special kind of Platonic love story, which, like *The Sun Also Rises*, examines idealism's threat to physical love.[13] Upending the physical world, Gatsby imagines himself ascending to heaven, which is a barely disguised version of the maternal breast. This heaven is also the "secret place" from which all human life emerges. Gatsby's vision is "unutterable." It is preverbal and too horrible to be spoken. It is the psyche's primal scene transcendentalized. He must, then, deny it by wedding it to Daisy's "perishable breath." Gatsby on some level desires to link himself to sexuality and mortality. His self-conception denies this consciously, but when Daisy later contracts a cold, she becomes even more attractive to him. Yet Gatsby idealizes Daisy, immortalizing her perishable breath, as Hawthorne's Giovanni does his Beatrice's.[14] For Gatsby, breath does not evidence mortality. It is not, as it is for Whitman, inhalation and exhalation. Rather it is spirit pure and simple. Critics have accused Gatsby of materializing the transcendental.[15] Gatsby, however, is so enamoured of his transcendental vision that not even the love of a woman can recall him from it. It completes, rather than interrupts, the incarnation of self. Gatsby must transform Daisy into the virginal counterpart of himself, or into the maternal source of his own self-conception. He kisses her in order to suck on the impalpable pap of life, gulping down the milk of wonder that nourishes his vision.

Gatsby's love for Daisy replicates the hopeless self-centeredness of his neo-Platonic conception of self. His love is like an embrace of dreams (pp. 99–100), denying sexuality even as it indulges it, safely leading to no evidence of sexual desire or, even worse, sexual union. Gatsby is both parentless and childless ("his imagination had never really accepted . . . his parents" [p. 99]). If other heroes in the akedian line of American romance sacrifice their progeny on the rock in order to transcend reality, Gatsby sacrifices himself by discarding the "rock of the world" altogether.[16] He believes in "the unreality of reality, a promise that the rock of the world was founded securely on a fairy's wing" (p. 100). In one tremendous act of imagination, he disowns both of his parents and engineers or invents what can only be described as an immaculate self-conception. He forswears mother as well as father.[17] To this self-conception he is religiously "faithful to the end" (p. 99).

If Gatsby is his own father and his own God, he is also his own son. Sleeping in the embrace of dreams Gatsby is "contemptuous" of women (p. 99). His relationship to Cody, by whom he is "employed in a vague personal capacity" as "mate, skipper, secretary, and even jailor" (p. 101), is at least latently homosexual (they meet on Little Girl Bay). The eternally adolescent Gatsby falls in love, therefore, not with a woman but with another version of his own "self-absorption" (p. 99). Because this vision flowers from within him, he can safely deflower it. He can protect himself from the same contagions of sexuality and biological connectedness from which his initial self-incarnation also attempts to free him. Like many a Faulkner hero he falls in love with his sister-twin. And, like Reuben Bourne, he would, by eliminating the son, erase all evidence of his existence as a flesh and blood man caught up in the confusions and moral dilemmas of a real world. Gatsby does Reuben one step better by not bearing offspring. But his incomprehension of, let alone inability to accept, Daisy's daughter reveals his essential discomfort with the idea of children. Gatsby would purify history back to the essential paradigm, which, relocated within the world of self, can mean only self-incarnation and self-crucifixion.[18]

Gatsby's sexual repression is as conventional as repressions come. It splits sexuality and love and preserves the wife separate from the whore. But this sexual repression is not peculiar to Gatsby. Specifically, it recapitulates an essential aspect of American experience as Fitzgerald understood it.[19] The American revision of the Old Testament was a flight from history, which in Fitzgerald's view was also a flight from biological time and place. Repressing their own primitive and therefore unacceptable physical urges, the American Puritans in Fitzgerald's view had substituted the divine text for human textuality. Indeed, they had substituted textuality for sexuality. Although Fitzgerald's novel primarily probes another set of American texts, namely those of Emersonian transcendentalism, Fitzgerald's critique begins in his recognition that the ahistorical messianism of the Puritans represented America's original psychosexual repression. Gatsby's vision of the "blocks of the sidewalks [forming] a ladder and [mounting] to a secret place above the trees" recalls the vision of another dreamer whose identity is lightly veiled behind the name Jay Gatsby as it is behind the name of the other American character whose identity and destiny are also closely linked to Gatsby's, Ja(y)ke (Jacob) Barnes:

> And Jacob went out from Beer-sheba, and went toward Haran. And he lighted upon the place, and tarried there all night, because the sun was set; and he took one of the stones of the place, and put it under his head, and lay down in that place to sleep. And he dreamed, and behold a ladder set up on the earth, and the top of it reached to heaven; and behold the angels of God ascending and descending on it. And, behold, the Lord stood beside him, and said: "I am the Lord, the God of Abraham thy father, and the God of Isaac. The land whereon thou liest, to thee will I give it, and to thy seed. And thy seed shall be as the dust of the earth. . . . And in thee and in thy seed shall all the families of the earth be blessed. (Gen. 28. 10–14)[20]

Gatsby's strangely imprecise version of Jacob's dream evokes the same relationship between biblical promise and American misperception that circulates throughout American fiction. Like Jacob's ladder, Gatsby's ladder also reaches from the earthly to the spiritual. It also concerns the urgency of the seed and of the future blessing that seed may insure. But Gatsby's ladder secures no place on earth. Therefore, it promises no inheritance for his never-to-be-born children. The angels in Jacob's vision go up and come down again. Gatsby ascends never to return to earth. The biblical Jacob changes his name to Israel to move history forward. James Gatz changes his name to Jay Gatsby and finds himself headed in the wrong direction, away from a New Testament James to an Old Testament Ja(y)cob, whose role he misunderstands and misperforms.

The source of Gatsby's problem lies in the psychosexual dimensions of his vision, which he cannot recognize and control. Like his close relative, Jake Barnes, who is similarly sterile and without heirs, and their mutual prototype Jacob (and like Reuben born of Jacob), Gatsby will fall in love. But whereas Jacob will accept the passionate along with the ideal, Jay Gatsby will not. The biblical Jacob realizes destiny through sexuality. He weds not one woman, but two. He fathers the offspring of many. Jay Gatsby, however, will wed only a vision of perishable breath, the perishability of which he will deny. In this "valley of ashes, a fantastic farm where ashes grow like wheat into ridges and hills and grotesque gardens; where ashes take the forms of houses and chimney and rising smoke," God is a blind and mindless advertisement for mechanical optics (p. 23). He prophesies profit, and his prophet is a bootlegger and a gangster. Therefore the "dust of the earth" that would, in the Old Testament, seed and populate the world, has become nothing more than literal ash, culminating in the holocaust of death at the end of the book.

This holocaust, in which Gatsby himself perishes, originates in Gatsby's initial self-conception, which itself mirrors the processes of sterile and illegitimate birth in America itself. America, for its original settlers, was the promised land. It was Eden, the fresh, green breast of the new world. America was not a place of biological origination. Rather, it was the virginal source of pristine self-conception, endlessly nurturing dreams and visions and repelling the advances of the Toms of this world (as Gatsby would have Daisy do). But this view of America repressed the psychosexual urge of the seed that is at the heart of the biblical text. And when that urge expressed itself, as it must, in the beating of Gatsby's heart (p. 112; cf. p. 99) or in the beating of boats against the current, it had to be attributed to a source outside the perfect self. Therefore, America was a prostitute or whore. She pandered to the eyes that could not admit they ravished her. She yielded herself to the rape that the nation could not confess.[21]

No wonder America, thus assaulted, had given birth to a bastard breed of degenerate Tom Buchanans and Meyer Wolfsheims. America as the Dutch sailors founded her is a kind of hermaphroditic whore, endlessly self-conceiving. Thus self-authored, America had been made to defile her own virginity. She had been made, in a sense, to destroy herself. Tom and Wolfsheim are the illegitimate heirs of this self-conceived virgin-whore. So is Gatsby, this "poor son-of-a-bitch" (p. 176), who is also the son of a God whose business (and worship) is the "service of a vast, vulgar, and meretricious beauty." Gatsby is America's final lover. He is also, with Tom, her ultimate destroyer. He is America herself. Gatsby's transcendentalization of reality and Tom's materialization of it mirror each other. For Tom, as for Gatsby, Daisy is the virgin whore (he slaps Myrtle across the face when she mentions her name), but when Daisy is the virgin for Tom she is the whore for Gatsby. It is no accident that in this America of total self-absorption and self-expression Daisy is driving the car that kills Myrtle Wilson, another wife/prostitute, virgin/whore (her sister swears that she is "completely happy with her husband [and] had been into no mischief whatever" [p. 164]). Tom and Gatsby (and with them, Wilson) conspire in America's self-destruction. Myrtle's "left breast," embodying her sexual and maternal potential, "swinging loose like a flap," "giving up [her] tremendous vitality" and "mingling her blood with the dust" concludes the love affair that began with the Dutch sailors and the green breast of the new world. But the phallic vehicle of death, which hurls itself "out of the gathering darkness" in the form of the "light green" car (p. 138) that is earlier likened to a "green leather conservatory" (p. 64), has been put into the hands of Daisy of the "green light at the end of [the] dock" (p. 182). Daisy, herself an embodiment of the green breast, has taken over the phallic impulse. When she kills Myrtle she in some sense also kills herself. Not surprisingly, the conclusion to this holocaust is the death of Gatsby/America itself. The god who in the penultimate moment of the story has been left "watching over nothing" (p. 146), finally perishes with the vision that was from the beginning a self-annihilating vision of nothingness.

Borne back ceaselessly into the past of its own preverbal, preconscious origins, America/Gatsby discovers that total incarnation, total completeness, is absolute nothingness. "At his lips' touch she blossomed for him like a flower and the incarnation was complete," Fitzgerald writes of the moment that Daisy and Gatsby seal their fatal, because wholly self-referential, relationship (p. 112). And he concludes: "he must have felt that he had lost the old warm world, paid a high price for living too long with a single dream. He must have looked up at an unfamiliar sky through frightening leaves and shivered as he found what a grotesque thing a rose is and how raw the sunlight was upon the scarcely created grass. A new world, material without being real, where poor ghosts, breathing dreams like air, drifted fortuitously about . . . [sic] like that ashen, fantastic figure gliding toward him through the amorphous trees. . . . [A]nd the holocaust was complete" (pp. 162–63). As in *The House of the Seven Gables*, vision cancels vision, and when the windows of the world fail, and even the sky becomes unfamiliar, it is no longer possible to see.

TO SEE TO WRITE

The matter of vision in America, as both Hawthorne and Dickinson had also realized, is not an accidental metaphor for the pattern of idealization or regressive fantasy that had dispossessed America of its history. The rape of America had been perpetrated by the "Dutch sailors' eyes," that is, not merely by a process of intellectualization or interpretation, but by a coveting of the sight, a belief in the direct, unmediated rights of possession, which is reminiscent of the belief in visible sanctity and the evidence of the senses in Brown's *Wieland*. In Fitzgerald's semiotics of history, Dr. T. J. Eckleberg has supervised the "transcendent effort" of the "valley of ashes" (p. 23), and America has lived under the sign of the optician for longer than Americans might care to admit. The mammoth sexual repression of the American dream originated not in the psyche or in the heart or even in the sexual organs but in the eye itself. It is Ralph Waldo Emerson who makes the I/eye the organ of American generation. But if for Emerson the eye is the medium of dispossession, whereby physical sight is transformed into "insight"[22] in order to effect a new kind of spiritual ownership, for Gatsby, as for a great line of American seers going back to the original Dutch sailors, the eye is the organ of possession pure and simple. This is Emerson: "The charming landscape which I saw this morning is indubitably made up of some twenty or thirty farms. Miller owns this field, Locke that, and Manning the woodland beyond. But none of them owns the landscape. There is a property in the horizon which no man has but he whose eye can integrate all the parts, that is, the poet. This is the best part of these men's farms, yet to this their warranty-deeds give no title."[23] This is not the philosophy of Jay Gatsby, whom we first meet "come out to determine which share was his of our local heavens" (p. 21). Gatsby is a literalist for whom property does not mean quality but ownership. What he sees when he looks at the world is what he might possess. And owning all, he sees nothing. Like the similarly avaricious Judge Pyncheon, he literally becomes nothing.

"What the early radical Emerson was excited about," suggests Quentin Anderson in *The Imperial Self*, "was the primacy of the individual, who can alone realize the claims of spirit." That individual, Emerson knew, would have to be a "particular creature" in order to "incarnate the whole." This is "incarnation from the human point of view. God can be manifest only in that which is a particular, not in generic humanity, not in a second Adam. Our humanity inheres in our distinctiveness."[24] In resolving himself backwards out of time and out of his own biological and psychological maturation, Gatsby does not achieve distinctiveness, but the generic humanity that Emerson would transcend. Placing a grotesque materiality before his vision, materiality itself comes to be identified as the enemy. And so he loses the world to the ghostly presences that overtake the material and that consequently he himself must join. As many critics have noted, Gatsby is myth personified. He has forfeited a human point of view, through which the incarnation of myth might become the individuality of the historical self. This is not the relationship to history or to the world that Emerson proposes as he ties the human imagination and nature together in a relationship of shifting spectacularity. Gatsby is an embodiment of "romantic readiness" and the "capacity for wonder" (pp. 2, 182). He doesn't recognize, as Owl Eyes puts it, that he is also a "poor son-of-a-bitch," who can only be about his father's business, which is the business of generation and reproduction. Like Hawthorne, Fitzgerald takes his story, like an owl, back into the shades of a dark vision that no optical machinery can correct. Like Emerson, he preserves the tug between the body and the spirit. He allows the imagination to drift away from the physical only to return to it once again. "I only wish to indicate the true position of nature in regard to man," Emerson wrote, "wherein to establish man all right education tends; as the ground which to attain is the object of human life, that is, of man's connection with nature."[25] When Gatsby attempts to deny biology and society, he, like Hepzibah and Clifford in *The House of the Seven Gables*, loses his ground. He loses his connection with nature, and with it, his vision. He makes himself into a blind god, looking out of no face, who, seeing nothing, is "watching over nothing" (p. 146). If Emerson becomes a transparent eyeball, who becomes nothing and sees all, Gatsby becomes a lensless pair of glasses, who, becoming everything, sees nothing (pp. 22–23).

In "Being Odd, Getting Even," Stanley Cavell has described the philosophical structure of thought through which Emerson avoids the dangerous and blinding self-deification Gatsby achieves:

> That human clay and the human capacity for thought are enough to inspire the authoring of myself is, at any rate, what I take Emerson's 'Self-Reliance,' as a reading of Descartes's cogito argument, to claim. I take his underlying turning of Descartes to be something like this: there is a sense of being the author of oneself that does not require me to imagine myself God (that may just be the name of the particular picture of the self as a self-present substance), a sense in which the absence of doubt and desire of which Descartes speaks in proving that God, not he, is the author of himself is a continuing task, not a property, a task in which the goal, or the product of the process, is not a state of being but a moment of change, say of becoming—a transcience of being, a being of transcience.

Individuality, Cavell insists, depends on "self-conscious" "becoming."[26] This is "incarnation from the human point of view," according to Quentin Anderson. It is the recognition, as Emerson puts it in *Nature*, that "spirit, that is, the Supreme Being, does not build up nature around us but puts it forth through us, as the life of the tree puts forth new branches and leaves through the pores of the old."[27] This putting forth or building up is what Gatsby does not do. From the moment of his transcendental self-conception through his love affair with Daisy to his final vigil outside Daisy's house, Gatsby withdraws into the moment before becoming. Imagining himself God, as had many an American hero before him, he resolves himself back into nothing. Pure seeing becomes "eternal blindness" (p. 23). It becomes spiritual, and finally physical, death. The life that unravels from Gatsby's initial self-conception is a reductive mirror of the psychological and historical archetypes that inevitably structure all human existence. In becoming history, these archetypes could bestow personal identity and meaning. In becoming myth, they go no place at all.

Gatsby is "plagiaristic" (p. 1). Listening to Gatsby, Nick says, was like "skimming hastily through a dozen magazines" (p. 67). Gatsby has cut all the pages of his American textbooks. He has not, however, opened their covers and read them. Owl Eyes thinks Gatsby knows just how far to go. But Fitzgerald realizes that Gatsby hasn't gone far enough. Like Tom, Gatsby "nibble[s] at the edge of stale ideas" (p. 21). In particular, he misreads Emersonian transcendentalism. He misunderstands the text of American individualism and offers in its stead a reductive new text of an unbecoming American self. If Emerson would cure retrospection, Gatsby would institutionalize it, so that all we can ever see is the duplication of human experience. Gatsby threatens to destroy with his vision of self the possibility of vision. "After Gatsby's death," Nick explains, "the East was haunted for me . . . beyond my eyes' power of correction" (p. 178). "I feel that nothing can befall me in life," Emerson wrote, "no disgrace, no calamity (leaving me my eyes), which nature cannot repair."[28] Without vision, there is only the fate of endless repetition, which overtakes Gatsby as it did Reuben Bourne, Young Goodman Brown, and the Pyncheons.

We are boats against the current, Fitzgerald concludes. We are borne back, as opposed to being borne forward or simply being born, ceaselessly into a past that is itself being swept back into an earlier vision or incarnation of an unobtainable, perhaps wholly visionary, "always already" condition of consciousness. Fitzgerald suggests, however, that "we beat on." This beating on, against the current that drives us into a preconscious past, is at the heart of Fitzgerald's story, as it is at the heart of its narrator. Like the "orgiastic future" of Gatsby's repressive fantasies, the "thrilling, returning trains" of Nick's youth represent the transports of a not wholly containable sexual desire.[29] But the "thrilling, returning trains," also establish a rhythm of departure and return that, like the similar tension at the conclusion of *The House of the Seven Gables*, is the birth into consciousness and life.

Nick in many ways duplicates the most salient features of Gatsby's American myth of newness and self-origination.[30] He has come East to be "a guide, a pathfinder, an original settler": "I had that familiar conviction that life was beginning over again with the summer," he confesses (p. 4). Nor is Nick unwilling to clasp his incarnation, his goodly "Jordan," to his breast (p. 81). Nick, who is childlike and potentially childless and is having his own troubles with women, is strongly attracted to Gatsby.[31] He is not immune to the lure of Gatsby's erotics of unbirth and of the speechlessness it implies: "Through all he said, even through his appalling sentimentality, I was reminded of something—an elusive rhythm, a fragment of lost words, that I had heard somewhere a long time ago. For a moment a phrase tried to take shape in my mouth and my lips parted like a dumb man's, as though there was more struggling upon them than a wisp of startled air. But they made no sound, and what I had almost remembered was uncommunicable forever" (p. 112). Nick might indeed be only another incarnation of Gatsby and of the American problem he represents. Nick's immediate response to what Gatsby says exactly imitates Gatsby's own psychosexual repression and his speechlessness. Nick's mouth and lips struggle, almost sucking, with an idea that will not take shape.

But if Gatsby lives in the embrace of dreams, Nick is attracted to a woman who is "clean, hard, [and] limited," a woman "who dealt in universal scepticism": "Unlike Gatsby and Tom Buchanan, I had no girl whose disembodied face floated along the dark cornices and blinding signs, and so I drew up the girl beside me, tightening my arms. Her wan, scornful mouth smiled, and so I drew her up again closer, this time to my face" (p. 81). Gatsby clings to "the old warm world" of his infantile desires (p. 162). Nick, however, abandons the "warm center of the world" (p. 3). He wills himself born into the world, refusing to remain speechless. He understands what Phoebe and Holgrave learn in Hawthorne's novel: there is a difference between the dangerous, one-way journey back to the beginning of time and the thrilling, returning, trains of youth, which image Emerson's commitment constantly to return to the society from which he would also depart:

> One of my most vivid memories is of coming back West from prep school and later from college at Christmas time. . . . I remember the fur coats . . . and the chatter of frozen breath . . . and the matchings of invitations . . .
>
> When we pulled out into the winter night and the real snow, our snow, began to stretch out beside us and twinkle against the windows, and the dim lights of small Wisconsin stations moved by, a sharp wild brace came suddenly into the air. We drew in deep breaths of it as we walked back from dinner through the cold vestibules, unutterably aware of our identity with this country for one strange hour, before we melted indistinguishably into it again.
>
> That's my Middle West—not the wheat or the prairies . . . but the thrilling returning trains of my youth. (Pp. 176–77)

Watching snow and light disappear outside the windows of the train, Nick, like Hepzibah and Clifford, confronts the spectrality of a universe that is, in Emerson's words, "aloof" and "afloat."[32] But Nick feels the insistent tug of the world. He breathes in "deep breaths" of "sharp, wild," bracing air and thrills to the discovery of life. He discovers not a new world but his own identity. When he "broods" on the "old, unknown world" (p. 182) he produces neither scripture nor philosophy but "history" (p. 5). There is only an ironic, wistful relationship between his chronologies, written on the back of a train timetable, and the biblical chronicles and genealogies they play-fully parody: "From East Egg . . . came the Chester Beckers and the Leeches, and a man named Bunsen, whom I knew at Yale, and Doctor Webster Civet . . . And the Hornbeams and the Willie Voltairs . . . And the Ismays and the Chrysties," and the chronicle concludes, "All these people came to Gatsby's house in the summer" (pp. 61–63).

Nick's revision of Gatsby's story records his inheritance and acknowledg-ment and finally authoring of the texts that Gatsby denies. The story of Nick Carroway is the story of an artistic becoming, a putting forth of new life, and a new building up of history. Nick rejects Gatsby's dream because he knows, in this post-Freudian era, that like all dreams it records a fantasy of denial. Like the "intimate revelations of [all] young men, or at least the terms in which they express them" it is both "plagiaristic and marred by obvious suppressions" (p. 1). Nick tells a story that is not the transcription of a dream, whether Gatsby's, America's, or his own. He records a history that resists the transferences and deferrals of meaning which Gatsby's story enacts. This does not mean, however, that Nick subscribes to some simple, straightforward notion of truth like the newspaper accounts of Gatsby's death. These jour-nalistic reports, like the newspaper article in Faulkner's Go Down, Moses or like Tom's "Rise of the Colored Empires" (p. 13), are the opposite of Gatsby's ecstatic vision. But, like Gatsby's dream, they also reduce reality to its "simplest form." Like the ghosts that Gatsby creates, they are "grotesque," not because they mistake the material for the transcendental but because they are "circumstantial, eager, and untrue" (pp. 164–65).

But finding himself "on Gatsby's side, and alone," recognizing, like Holgrave, his place in what has occurred and his responsibility to it, Nick chooses to speak, despite the dangers that speaking entails. "From the mo-ment I telephoned news of the catastrophe to West Egg Village, every surmise about him, and every practical question, was referred to me. At first I was surprised and confused; then, as he lay in his house and didn't move or breathe or speak hour upon hour [like Judge Pyncheon], it grew upon me that I was responsible, because no one else was interested—interested, I mean, with that intense personal interest to which every one has some vague right at the end" (p. 165). The Great Gatsby is finally concerned with speaking a truth that is neither a replication of a dream vision that exists in an inarticulatable condition of displaced meaning, nor a simple and there-fore false statement of substantive fact. Rather, Gatsby is about a truth that recognizes the limitations of human speech and yet still undertakes to speak. This is a truth that in Cavell's terms places itself in relation to the world. It is the truth of history.

The issue of truth threads the book, from Nick's admission that he is one of the only truly honest people he knows, to the much more complex moments when Fitzgerald plays with the truth of Gatsby's biography (Nick swinging helplessly from utter disbelief to total acceptance of Gatsby's story). Its most dramatic formulation comes when Tom explains to Nick that he told Wilson the truth, and Nick, the storyteller, understands that "there was nothing I could say, except the one unutterable fact that it wasn't true" (p. 180).[33] Like a series of writers from Cooper on, Fitzgerald understands that truth consists neither in the statement of an apparently irrefutable fact ("I told him the truth," Tom declares) nor in the endless subversion of statements of fact, saying nothing (p. 180). It consists of carefully chosen words and gestures that one enacts because one knows that one is responsible, if only to the human relationships that responsibility implies. "I shook hands with him," Nick goes on. "It seemed silly not to" (p. 181). Nick's gesture may not, like Gatsby's, be "gorgeous" (p. 2). But it is a gesture, both to Tom and to Gatsby, that bespeaks commitment and responsibility—truth.

Nick stresses Tom's and Daisy's "vast carelessness": "It was all very careless and confused. They were careless people, Tom and Daisy—they smashed things and creatures and then retreated back into their money or their vast carelessness, or whatever it was that kept them together, and let other people clean up the mess they had made" (pp. 180–81). Nick is nothing if not careful: "I wanted to leave things in order and not just trust that obliging and indifferent sea to sweep my refuse away" (p. 178). But carefulness, being responsible, means more than taking care or being orderly; it also means caring. Caring is what keeps Nick's lies to Gatsby's father from being simple untruths. It prevents a universe of strangely repeating actions and words from dissolving into nothingness, allowing that universe to be born into commitments, meanings, and words. How else can we account for Fitzgerald's ability to contain, decorously and powerfully, within the covers of his remarkable tragedy, such wildly overflowing repetitions of language, action, and meaning?; the car accident in Gatsby's driveway, with its "amputated wheel" (p. 55), for example, which is picked up in Nick's and Jordan's discussions of driving (p. 59), and is brought to a horrid conclusion in the death of Myrtle Wilson and her amputated breast? There are broad, almost grotesque puns on the "green light" as traffic signal and transcendent vision, and, through the "green light" transformed into a "green car," there is the logic of identity between Myrtle Wilson's torn breast and the "green breast of the new world."[34] Critics frequently comment on the great care Fitzgerald took in structuring this novel. It is, by many accounts, one of the most perfect books in the English language.[35] Artistically ordering things, Fitzgerald, like Nick, wants morally to "leave things in order" (p. 178).

Despite its severe criticism of Gatsby and the American dream, *The Great Gatsby* is Fitzgerald's romance of America. Gatsby, not Nick, is its romantic hero. Many critics have commented on the paradox of Nick's and Fitzgerald's celebration and condemnation of Gatsby, which they associate, rightly, with the transformation of Gatsby's vision into Nick's text.[36] What informs that text and shines through Gatsby's failures is the Emerson whom Fitzgerald (through Nick) restores to the American dream. Nick can say without contradiction, as quoted above, that "Gatsby, who represented everything for which I have unaffected scorn . . . turned out all right at the end" (p. 2). *Gatsby* achieves its great strength through its author's awareness that Gatsby's failure results not from his "romantic readiness" and "hope," which are Emerson's "extraordinary gift[s]" to Gatsby (as they are Gatsby's extraordinary gifts to Nick [p. 2]), but from his lack of commitment to the society that Emerson never lets slip away. Like Emerson, Nick does not take his "scepticism for granted" (p. 46). He is always in the position of turning and returning to society.

Nick's relationship to America is like Fitzgerald's. "I look out at it," says Fitzgerald, "and I think it is the most beautiful history in the world. It is the history of me and of my people. And if I came here yesterday . . . I should still think so. It is the history of all aspiration—not just the American dream but the human dream and if I came at the end of it that too is a place in the line of the pioneers."[37] Unlike Cooper's pioneers, or Hawthorne's in "Roger Malvin's Burial," or Faulkner's in *Go Down, Moses*, Fitzgerald's pioneer does not grandly inaugurate a new history, divorced from everything that has gone before. Like Nick, who is a guide, pathfinder, and settler, and who in loving Gatsby accepts his romantic readiness and hope, he simply, quietly, inherits it. Moreover, he takes responsibility for this new history. He places it on the timetables of history. The "last and greatest of all human dreams," Nick knows, is always behind us, because it is by definition the last of humankind's many dreams, greatest only by comparison. There are no absolutes here, only the relative knowledge of a continuous series of dreams and events that sweeps us forward into a future indistinguishable from the past except by chronology, by the place of events within the historical chain. This is Fitzgerald's *Great* Gatsby. Hemingway has not yet written his "Greater Gatsby."[38] Therefore, like his narrator, coming "back home" again (p. 178), Fitzgerald takes his place "in the line of pioneers."

A P(ROPHETIC) S(CRIPT)

Out of inheritance and acknowledgment issues the truth of America, which is neither a reduction to the simplest, grotesque, circumstantial, eager, and untrue form of a newspaper account, nor an ineffable transcription of an unutterable nonlanguage. Fitzgerald does not, as some critics have assumed, rage against an ahistorical Emerson, whose philosophy of the transcendental self had produced the tragedy of a Great Gatsby. Instead, he retrieves the Emersonianism that history has misread and lost. He turns to Emerson as a part of an ongoing American conversation that Gatsby, who has never read his American textbooks, is unwilling or unable to have. Emerson is himself part of the American history that Gatsby ignores. Emersonian transcendentalism is a philosophy of history in which a growing, maturing, becoming self comes into being through the tension between the pull to the past and the push toward the future. Gatsby decides this tension in favor of an orgiastic future totally divorced from the past that ironically therefore reproduces the past. Nick endures the tug and gains the future Gatsby loses. For Fitzgerald, as for Hawthorne, history under the pressure of departure enables us to acquire the past as the site of life and creativity from which a new present can emerge. Fitzgerald takes his place in history, because he knows it is the only place that individuals can inhabit or from which they can speak.

Given one's place in the line of pioneers, one can only speak from a position of departure, about, as Faulkner puts it, what "Was." For Fitzgerald, as for Hawthorne in *The House of the Seven Gables*, prophecy is unintelligible or, in Fitzgerald's language, unutterable. No one can know what lies in the future, though historians, constructing histories retrospectively and yet writing them as ongoing narratives, can certainly seem prophetic enough. But historians are false prophets, because what they say is true only through hindsight. It is the presumption of retrospective wisdom to write histories and historical fictions illuminated by the knowedge of what is to come. Retrospective wisdom, in Emerson's view, prevents insight and an original relation to nature.[39] Historical romance knows that, boats against the current, we are borne back ceaselessly into a psychological, linguistic, national past that we mistake for an image of the future. We imagine that we are directing the course of history as if we were authors and not mere copiers of the book. This was the error of America's antitypological literalists. By making American history coincide with a biblical story, they had converted history into false and fatal prophetic fulfillments.

How does one avoid this fate? How do we become the authors of lives grounded in history as opposed to objects of fatalistic fantasies? Some of the following details from *The Great Gatsby* are merely suggestive. Others are wholly imponderable, unutterable. Yet they are impossible not to record. Composed in 1925, during the rise of fascism in Europe (Tom is reading "The Rise of the Colored Empires"), about American history and the promised land, about history and repetition, they hint at the relationship between history and fate that Fitzgerald describes. Gatsby's death is described as a "holocaust" (p. 163); Meyer Wolfsheim is a Jew who whistles "The Rosary" (p. 171) and is associated with the American Legion (p. 172). Wolfsheim wears human molars for cufflinks (p. 73) and his company is "the Swastika Holding Company" (p. 171).

One cannot say that *The Great Gatsby* predicts the events of World War II. Fitzgerald might well have sensed where European antisemitism was leading (the swastika was a symbol of that antisemitism before the Germans began to use it in the early 1920s),[40] but he could not have predicted the holocaust and such gruesome details as the use of human molars as jewelry. Only the future could produce Hitler's atrocities. The book, however, suggests a relationship between fate and the failure to turn aside from myth or the unwillingness to read critically the texts we casually quote.[41] John Updike may not have been the first writer in the American tradition to associate a certain perversion of Emersonianism with social repression and fascism:

> From the Oversoul to the *Übermensch* to the Supermen of Hitler's Master Race is a dreadful progression for which neither Emerson nor Nietzsche should be blamed. . . . Totalitarian rule offers a warped mirror in which we can recognize, distorted, Emerson's favorite concepts of genius and inspiration and whim; the totalitarian leader is a study in self-reliance gone amok. . . . The extermination camps are one of the things that come between us and Emerson's optimism."[42]

But to say that totalitarian rule offers a warped mirror of Emerson is to say no more than that individuals construct their own fate. In *Gatsby*, fate is the consequence of the carelessness (the lack of taking care and the lack of caring) that causes the "accidental course with its accidental burden" (p. 162). The coincidence of the events of history and the details of Fitzgerald's novel suggest that careful analyses of texts help us identify historical processes. Careless inattention allows fantasy to materialize into doom.

History is distinguished from fate by the ability to see and read and finally to write. "I see now that this has been a story of the West, after all," Nick realizes (p. 177). He means that Gatsby's story is the story of the Western world and its failure to take care. Becoming responsible for the West, Nick learns to escape from fate into history. Cavell suggests that Emerson's "Self-Reliance" offers a theory of reading and writing. Fitzgerald's *Gatsby* also offers such a theory.

In "Hope Against Hope," Cavell takes Updike to task for associating Emerson with fascism. In *The Great Gatsby*, Fitzgerald dramatizes the problem Cavell discusses. "I shun father and mother and wife and brother when my genius calls me," Cavell quotes Emerson, in the passage to which Updike's critique alludes. "I would write on the lintels of the door-post, *Whim*. I hope it is somewhat better than whim at last." Gatsby seems to be that Emerson, shunning mother and father and wife, writing "on the lintels of the door-post, *Whim*." According to Cavell, Emerson's whim refers to his devout, Christlike resistance to the forces of social conformity (aversion as conversion).[43] Gatsby, however, like Updike's perverted Emersonians, misunderstands the relationship between individual whim and social commitment. Gatsby misreads the text of Emersonian individualism, as he misreads Emerson's interpretation of the Cartesian cogito. He thus transforms himself not into a transcendental self but into an unreal and impoverished deity. It is not Gatsby who writes "whim." Rather it is the "impersonal government" whose "whim" sends Gatsby off to war (p. 149).

Collecting imponderables, I cite the following highly suggestive but possibly accidental reference to Emerson's whim in *The House of the Seven Gables*. The passage occurs just before Hepzibah's and Clifford's flight:

"Come, come, make haste [says Hepzibah]; or he will stand up like Giant Despair in pursuit of Christian and Hopeful, and catch us yet."

As they passed into the street, Clifford directed Hepzibah's attention to something on one of the posts of the front-door. It was merely the initials of his own name, which with somewhat of his characteristic grace about the forms of the letter, he had cut there, when a boy.[44]

Like so much of what is wrong with Clifford, his attempt to write whim on the lintels of his doorpost fails because he carves out only a minimalistic and empty emblem of self. Clifford and Hepzibah, who is similarly wrapped up in her own image, are Christianity and hope endlessly in flight, like Gatsby, from a despair that they cannot escape. They have failed to address despair in the appropriate terms or letters. "Whim," suggests Cavell, "is exactly to *write*." To write is not to carve one's initials on the doorposts or to inscribe oneself, Gatsby-style, onto a dream. To write is to add one's words to a reality in which words matter. Emerson's hope is grounded in his commitment to the world: "I hope it is somewhat better than whim at last." Clifford's and

Gatsby's hope is an escape from reality. Making themselves the objects, not the authors, of someone else's less hopeful and reverent whims, they convert history into fate.

Nick might also succumb to fate. Desiring to see the world in uniform and at moral attention forever (p. 2), he might also convert Emersonian individualism into fascism. Though Gatsby enacts the perversion of Emersonianism, he also contains the seeds of romantic readiness, which can retrieve Emersonianism. Like Gatsby, like all human beings, Nick is also borne back into the past of his psychosexual origins, of his desire for undifferentiated oneness with the world, of his unending and all-consuming egotism. But, with the help of Gatsby's inspiration, Nick beats his way forward to a future that does not simply repeat the past. Acknowledging the past, remembering, revising, and rewriting it, he makes Gatsby's story his own and moves history one step forward. Nick has his vision, and it is a lot like the vision Emerson (and Gatsby) have promised: "As the moon rose higher the inessential houses began to melt away until gradually I became aware of the old island here that flowered once for Dutch sailors' eyes—a fresh, green breast of the new world . . . commensurate to his capacity for wonder. . . . . tomorrow we will run faster, stretch out our arms farther. . . . [sic] And one fine morning—So we beat on, boats against the current, borne back ceaselessly into the past." "As when the summer comes from the south," Emerson concludes *Nature*, "the snow-banks melt and the face of the earth becomes green before it, so shall the advancing spirit create its ornaments. . . . The kingdom of man over nature . . . he shall enter without more wonder than the blind man feels who is gradually restored to perfect sight."[45]

The melting that restores green is recreated in the final passage of Fitzgerald's novel. What Nick sees with perfect sight is not a vision he creates from nothing or an expression of wonder commensurate with self, but a vision he recreates. He recreates this vision, not *without* wonder (meaning puzzlement as well as amazement), but without *more* wonder than the blind man restored to perfect sight. Seeing is not to manufacture vision but, as in Hawthorne's *House of the Seven Gables*, to correct it, to be made capable of perceiving what has always been there. The condition of not seeing is blindness, where blindness (again as in Hawthorne's novel) is another word for fate. Seeing, in other words, is to move from a position that we acknowledge to be blindness or fate to one of action or occurrence. It is to take our place in the world, to enter the process of historical re-visions and re-turnings, and from that position to speak.

In *Gatsby*, the choice is not between an Emersonian and a historical self, a choice between Gatsby and Nick. Rather it is the choice of Emerson (and Hawthorne, Thoreau, and Dickinson) as history, and of Emersonianism as a philosophy of historical and natural relationships. For this reason, despite its criticism of the American dream, *The Great Gatsby* is Fitzgerald's great romance of America. It is his testimony to an Emersonianism that continues to restore us to perfect sight and freedom. From Fitzgerald's point of view, this is wonder enough.

The Sun Also Rises:
Hemingway's New Covenant
of History

The Sun Also Rises[1] is Hemingway's "Greater Gatsby / (written with the friendship of F. Scott FitzGerald) / (Prophet of THE JAZZ AGE)."[2] Critics have pointed out that *The Great Gatsby* was "on [Hemingway's] mind in April 1926, when he had finished the revised typescript."[3] Fitzgerald read and revised Hemingway's manuscript before it went to press.[4] These two texts were written within a year of each other by two of the three writers who dominated early twentieth-century American literature. Hemingway and Fitzgerald shared a deep personal and professional relationship. Both intended to be spokesmen for their generation. Thus the relationship between *The Great Gatsby* and *The Sun Also Rises* in and of itself provides fascinating material for scholarly investigation. But Hemingway's explicit recasting of *The Great Gatsby*, a novel about the reading and writing and rewriting of texts, creates a special density of fictional-historical meaning. "A writer's job is to tell the truth," writes Hemingway in *Men at War*.[5] Like Fitzgerald's truth in *Gatsby*, Hemingway's truth in *The Sun Also Rises* concerns the truth of writing. It deals with the difference between the easily stated and therefore trivial and reductive claims of journalistic and historical fact, and the essentially unverifiable and unutterable insights of psychology and philosophy. None of these kinds of writing is literature. Unacknowledged intuitions and longings, as in the case of Gatsby, can produce the semblance of a literary text. But they are finally plagiaristic. They suppress more than they reveal. In Hemingway's novel, as in Fitzgerald's, truth lies between psychotic fantasy and historical accuracy. Truth requires reading, interpreting, and acknowledging the texts of both the world and the self. Knowing the truth, one is able to author a historically conscious and yet romantic text of one's own.

JAKE'S AUTOBIOGRAPHY

Reading, interpreting, and acknowledging the texts of the world and the self are the main issues raised in the opening pages of *The Sun Also Rises*.

Nowhere was Fitzgerald more actively involved in the crafting of Hemingway's novel than in these pages. At his suggestion, Hemingway cut an additional sixteen pages, the "whole biography of Brett Ashley and Mike Campbell and the autobiography of the narrator Jake Barnes." "There is nothing in those first sixteen pages," Hemingway explained, "that does not come out, or is explained, or re-stated in the rest of the book."[6] One large biographical section remains, however: the story of Robert Cohn, which opens the book.[7]

Much critical attention has been paid to Cohn's role in the novel. Some critics agree with Mark Spilka that "Cohn and Pedro are extremes for which Barnes is the unhappy medium." Others see Cohn as the absolute antithesis of Jake and therefore the novel's villain; others claim him as the book's unqualified hero, revealing the deep flaws in Jake's philosophy.[8] Clearly Cohn excites special interest, however we finally understand his relationship to Hemingway's themes. The opening pages more than contribute to Cohn's special status in the book. Cohn, however, is more than a foil against which to measure the main protagonist. Hemingway allows the pages on Cohn to open his novel because they begin Jake's book as well as his own. These pages raise an issue that is crucial throughout the book: the difference between the reductive transcriptions of life that we variously call journalism or (auto)biography or fantasy and the carefully constructed writing we call literature. Hemingway's aesthetics dictate that actions and personalities be demonstrated, not described. Hence, Hemingway withdraws those details that, in his view, are not directly dramatic.[9] Jake's lack of psychological and literary sophistication makes this restraint impossible. Jake, a journalist, writes in descriptive prose, which exposes unacknowledged psychological fixations.

Jake's autobiographical narrative consists of a psychological fantasy in which neurosis has overtaken literature and the story has resisted consolidation into a work of art. In Hemingway's story, Jake Barnes and Robert Cohn and the stories they tell, or that are told about them, enact the book's major themes. They also dramatize the failure of certain kinds of storytelling, like Jake's, to achieve dramatic objectivity and literary power. In Jake's story, characters and events signify unconscious, uncontrolled projections and repressions. Jake's portrait of Cohn is one such projection. In this description Jake imagines qualities he himself does not possess. He is boxing champion, lady's man, successful writer. However, Jake also reveals feelings of emotional inadequacy, effeminacy, and impotence, which he consciously represses. The disjunction between authorial and narrative texts is important. Hemingway begins not simply writing a novel, but rewriting his protagonist's autobiography. Thus he dramatizes the difference between the mindless and uncritical repetitions of life and literature, which conceal and distort, and the revisionary texts that interpret repetition, creating the possibility not only for psychological health but for artistic maturity as well.

With its astute psychoanalysis of Jake and Cohn and the lost generation reaching in one direction, and its biblical title, epigraph, and allusions reaching in another, *The Sun Also Rises*, like *The Great Gatsby*, intends nothing less than a theory of the relationships of psychological, biblical, historical and literary texts. Hemingway wishes to reveal how the great American novel will have to be written. He wants to state what its subject will have to be when it is written, indeed as it is being written (or rewritten) by Hemingway himself.[10] When Hemingway claims that his novel is a "Greater Gatsby," he isn't joking. Hemingway, therefore, does more than play psychoanalyst to his tormented protagonist, or psychoanalytic critic to his heavily burdened story. By slanting information, juxtaposing scenes, and altogether revising Jake's story, he does not intend, as one critic has argued, to trap the narrator.[11] Rather he wishes to reveal and correct his hero's psychological distortions so that he can transform fantasy into art. Like Fitzgerald, he wishes to perform the role of social critic and historian. He wants to be the writer of the romance not of Jake Barnes but of America. Hemingway superimposes Jake's story on a set of biblical and historical narratives, suggesting that Jake's problems, like Gatsby's, represent a general crisis in American literature and culture. He produces from behind Jake's autobiography, which itself hides behind the story of Robert Cohn, another story of which Jake's story and Cohn's (like Gatsby's) are unconscious replications. This, as we have seen, is the story of America's quest for the promised land. In Hemingway's view, as in the akedian tradition, this quest represents a serious misreading of the scriptural texts on which America had constructed its self-identity. It subsequently leads to miswriting American history and literature. This miswriting Hemingway would now repair.

The dancehall scene in chapter three illustrates the repression, projection, and consequent misrepresentation that characterize Jake's storytelling through much of the novel and that he mistakes for social commentary, journalism, and art[12]:

> A crowd of young men, some in jerseys and some in their shirt-sleeves, got out. I could see their hands and newly washed, wavy hair in the light from the door. The policeman standing by the door looked at me and smiled. They came in. As they went in, under the light I saw white hands, wavy hair, white faces, grimacing, gesturing, talking. With them was Brett. She looked very lovely, and she was very much with them. . . . And with them was Brett.
> I was very angry. Somehow they always made me angry. I know they are supposed

to be amusing, and you should be tolerant, but I wanted to swing on one, any one, anything to shatter that superior, simpering composure. (P. 20)

Jake's disgust is not without warrant, but what really infuriates Jake is that, in spite of their being effeminate, if not homosexual, these young men, like Cohn (whom Jake describes for two chapters), are physically potent and can compete for Georgette and, especially, for Brett. The haunting refrain that punctuates the description is atypical of Jake's (or Hemingway's) usually clipt and unemotional style: "With them was Brett . . . she was very much with them . . . And with them was Brett." Coupled with Jake's fixation on the young men's "hands," their "white hands," and their "newly washed, wavy hair," their "wavy hair," the refrain hints at psychological motivations that Jake's composed, surface narration refuses to confess. Jake cannot admit the intense agony occasioned by his feelings for Brett. "What's the matter with you?" Cohn asks immediately following the above scene. "You seem all worked up over something." "Nothing," Jake answers. "This whole show makes me sick is all" (p. 21; cf. p. 123). As if the repression were not obvious enough, Hemingway further fuels the reader's sense of Jake's denial by having him repeat the word "sick" that in the scene with Georgette refers directly to Jake's war injury (p. 15).

Denying to himself what he feels, Jake fixates on a scene that directly provokes his jealousy. The young men are with Brett in a way that Jake cannot possibly be with her (the biblical connotations of the word *with* foreshadow some of the book's concern with Old Testament issues). But the scene also duplicates the impossibility of Jake's and Brett's relationship. The homosexual young men are also not with Brett in any sexual sense. Jake fears he is as asexual as they are, perhaps even as homosexual. His fascination with their hands and hair betrays this suspicion, which is further reinforced by the androgynous quality of Brett's sexual appeal (her hair is brushed back like a boy's). The homosexual aspects of human personality and their role in even heterosexual love concern Hemingway as it concerned Fitzgerald. Jake has a distorted mirror relationship to the world, distinguished by jealousy and repression. It functions through a complex projection in which Jake simultaneously identifies with and rejects the objects of his perception. This relationship characterizes a large part of his text.

Unedifying duplication—the doubles that seize Jake's attention and the constant repetitions of action—creates the stalled, inert quality of much of Jake's storytelling. Unaware of his suspicions about himself, Jake cannot read the mirror image his consciousness produces. He thus repeats that image, endlessly, both in action and in words. Just a few pages and a short while later, Jake for no apparent reason describes "Ney's statue standing among the new-leaved chestnut-trees in the arc-light." A veritable icon of repressed sexuality and violence emerges: "There was a faded purple wreath leaning against the base. I stopped and read the inscription: from the Bonapartist Groups, some date; I forget. He looked very fine, Marshal Ney in his top-boots, gesturing with his sword among the green new horse-chestnut leaves. My flat was just across the street" (p. 29).[13] Jake fixates uncomprehendingly on the mirror image. His text is strangely schizophrenic, echoing his split and self-denying consciousness. Alternately impotent and ecstatic, it splices together the tense restraint of a dull, elementary school prose style ("I stopped and read . . . I forget. . . . My flat was just across the street") with the luscious romantic extravagance and lyricism of the "new-leaved chestnut trees in the arc-light," the "faded purple wreath leaning against the base," and "Marshal Ney in his top-boots, gesturing with his sword."[14] Moments like these, which reveal Jake's severe psychological disorientation, punctuate the book with a chilling regularity.[15] They separate Jake's blindly fixated, repetitive text from Hemingway's dramatic narrative. The problem is not that Jake's story repeats life. Hemingway's novel also repeats life, his own as well as Jake's. But whereas Jake repeats an image he cannot interpret and control, Hemingway critically rewrites that image. His text mirrors Jake's but it also dramatizes it. It forces the mirror image away from static representation, or rerepresentation, toward dynamic, critical commentary.

Jake's presentation of Cohn's history represents both the most extended example of Jake's failed art and the most fully developed authorial revision of Jake's story. It reveals not only Jake's psychological weakness but his cultural-historical ignorance. In Jake's story, Cohn, like the young men and Marshal Ney, is a projection of self. But Cohn's story is more than a personal narrative. It is the story of the American dream and its failure. And it also reflects the story of the heroic volunteer in the war to end all wars, Jake Barnes. Cohn's romantic idealism and his faith in America articulate an American fantasy to which Jake, for all his protestations, is no stranger. Jake's is no private, personal neurosis. It is a condition of Americanness, for reasons of repression and projection, of misreading and miswriting, related to Jake's and Cohn's personal and authorial failures.

There are many parallels between Jake and Cohn. Readers of the book have noted that both are writers and American expatriates roaming around Europe (often in tandem) and that both are tortured by desires for sexual fulfillment, which they cannot satisfy, making them both, by a loose but meaningful definition, desexed (Jake's literal impotence is evoked by the comparison between Cohn and a steer, while the physical aspect of his injury is conjured up quite graphically by Cohn's "flattened" nose [p.3]. One wonders about Jake's reference to his "flat" opposite Marshal Ney's sword [p. 29]). Both are also in love with Brett Ashley, who seduces, abuses, and abandons them both; both have "combat" records: Jake as a soldier in World War I, Cohn as a boxer who before his college days went to military school; both are sportsmen and tennis partners. Jake expresses his admiration for boxing in his comment about the Ledoux-Kid fight and in his statement that the bull has "a left and a right just like a boxer" (p. 139). (Extraliterarily, Hemingway, too, admired the art of boxing, and within the novel itself Bill valorizes that attitude.)

What is extaordinary about these parallels (which have caused Hemingway criticism to fly about in diametrically opposed directions) is that the otherwise sensitive and perceptive Jake does not recognize them. For the first hundred pages of his narrative, Jake is unaware of the jealousy that generates his interest in Cohn and that contaminates his description of him. Jake cannot show Cohn "clearly" (p. 45), because he cannot see him clearly. "I was blind, unforgivingly jealous of what had happened to him," he finally confesses. "I certainly did hate him!" (p. 99). Jake often criticizes Cohn for appropriate reasons. But he does not fundamentally understand the sources of his ire or the relevance of his criticisms to himself. Consequently he composes a blind and hateful, repressed and angry text, which blinds its author as it would its readers to the mirror it holds up to its author.

In Jake's view, as in Hemingway's, Cohn invalidates his success as a boxer by using his skill, as he uses his status as a writer and a lady's man, in order to "counteract [his] feeling of inferiority and shyness" (p. 3). Jake does not see that he has assumed the pose of a cynic, a verbal pugilist, for similar reasons. Jake represses his anger in life: "I was very angry. Somehow they always made me angry. . . . I wanted to swing on one, any one. . . . Instead I walked down the street and had a beer" (p. 20; cf. p. 39). In a similar way, his text displaces rage into irony and sarcasm. The book begins innocently enough. "Robert Cohn was once middleweight boxing champion of Princeton." But the bitterness surfaces immediately—and irrelevantly. "Do not think that I am very much impressed by that as a boxing title, but it meant a lot to Cohn" (p. 3).[16]

Like Cohn, Jake the journalist enjoys the "authority of editing" (p. 5). He desires control over his life through the act of editing it in his text. This desire for control is not objectionable. In fact, it represents an irreducible Hemingway virtue; and it points to one of the major theses of the book, that one needs to read and write and rewrite, endlessly, the text of one's life. But as the bullfighting sections reveal, the revisions that produce art are matters of daring confrontation and not of pencil and paper deletions. One must be able to read the mirror of one's writing and distinguish the unconscious duplications of projection and repression from the intentional and interpretive repetitions of art. Jake correctly "mistrust[s] all frank and simple people, especially when their stories hold together" (p. 4). A flawless, cohesive narrative, even when it reports factual truth (as in the case of Cohn's story about college) surely signals psychological dishonesty. And eventually such transparent simplicity must yield to bitterness and irony (p. 8). Hemingway, like Fitzgerald, is concerned with the complicated matter of truth. Jake does not, at the beginning of his text, recognize the false seamlessness of his own story.

AUTOBIOGRAPHY AND HISTORY

Jake's inability to read and rewrite his text represents for Hemingway a failure in narrative sensibility reaching deep into American culture. Behind the text of Jake Barnes resides the text of Robert Cohn. And behind the story of Robert Cohn lurks the story of the American dream, the myth of the new promised land, perhaps even the new Eden, in the new world. Cohn's failure to realize his place in the American paradise, like Gatsby's, reveals a failure of the American dream more complex than Cohn's failure of assimilation might suggest. In the scene in which Cohn begins to fall in love with Brett Ashley, the same essential paradox of the American situation that expressed itself in Gatsby's regressive and self-destructive love for Daisy forces its way to the surface of the text, identifying the cultural dimensions not only of Cohn's problems but of Jake's as well.

Following the dancehall scene, this scene once more portrays Jake's psychological condition. But the language in which Hemingway has Jake reveal his repression leads in directions more startling than individual pain. The scene begins with Jake looking at Cohn looking at Brett: "She stood holding a glass and I saw Robert Cohn looking at her. He looked a great deal as his compatriot must have looked when he saw the promised land. Cohn, of course, was much younger. But he had that look of eager, deserving expectation" (p. 22). Ostensibly Jake relates this incident in order to further illuminate Cohn, whom he ridicules for a kind of adolescent eagerness that he associates with Cohn's Jewishness. But Jake's jealousy and repression immediately reveal themselves: "Brett was damned good-looking. She wore a slipover jersey and a tweed skirt. . . . She was built with curves like the hull of a racing yacht, and you missed none of it with that wool jersey" (p. 22). Jake fixates on a scene that, arousing his sexual longings for Brett, causes him both to satisfy and reject his desire by displacing it onto someone else. But when Jake, in an apparently antisemitic slur, compares Cohn to his "compatriot" looking at the "promised land," a new area of meaning intrudes into the text. In this passage, which pictures characters looking at and looking like each other, emphasizing, that is, the ways in which individuals reflect and mirror one another, the word *compatriot* must be seen as referring equally to another compatriot of Cohn's, who is also, if not literally older, at least emotionally older than Cohn, who similarly lusts after Brett, and who is even more Moseslike than Cohn. That compatriot is Jake himself, who expresses the same eagerness for the "damned good-looking" Brett that he attributes to Cohn. Unlike Cohn, Jake never does enter the promised land.[17]

More striking than the passage's psychoanalysis of Jake and Cohn, in which Jake identifies so strongly with Cohn as to assume even his Jewishness, is the commentary on Americanness that emerges. If Jake suddenly reflects Moses, longing for the denied promised land, he also, as the text reminds us a few sentences later, recalls the biblical Jacob: "I've promsied to dance this with Jacob," Brett says to Cohn, "You've a hell of a biblical name, Jake" (p. 22).[18] Jacob's relationship to Rachel, denied to him for fourteen years, strongly evokes Jake's own situation in relation to Brett. Jake's wound may even recall the wound to Jacob's thigh, received when he wrestles with the angel. Furthermore, the situation as a whole echoes the related echoing of the Jacob passage in *The Great Gatsby*, where Gatsby dreams of his promised land and conceives a passion for the woman who is its incarnation. Like Brett, or like the lover in the A. E. W. Mason story that Jake reads later, while dozing or dreaming, Daisy is also withheld from Gatsby.

The importance of delay or deferral, in their current philosophical meanings, cannot be ignored here. The story of Moses, which is the primary textual occasion for the unraveling of the many intertextual allusions enfolded in *The Sun*, grows out of the story of Jacob in a complexly indirect way. Specifically, the story of Jacob that names Jacob as Israel and ensures his handing-on of the covenant, culminates in the loss of the promised land. It necessitates the exodus by which the promised land is, arduously, tortuously, regained—almost. For Moses never does enter the promised land. In the five books of Moses, the Israelites themselves do not enter the promised land. As literary characters, they remain poised before it in eternal expectation. By tentatively recalling these biblical stories of Jacob and Moses, Hemingway, like Fitzgerald, redirects the force of his analysis from simple psychological or even sociopsychological description to a complex historical and literary discussion of the conception and birth of American identity. The Old Testament, in Hemingway's view, recognized the importance of delay and deferral. It depended on delay and deferral for its own dramatic action. But these delays and deferrals were not, even in the Old Testament, just temporal measurements or psychological disappointments. Like the paradox of the akedah, they represented that unbridgeable space between truth and its apprehension, the space between human and divine logic that human beings could not close.

In rewriting the scriptures as American history, American authors had eliminated the quality of deference, the attitude toward God that is represented in this Old Testament history of an asymptotic arrival in the promised land. Like Fitzgerald's Dutch sailors, Americans, in Hemingway's view, wanted to possess the land absolutely, totally, immediately. Simultaneously, however, they denied the biological and sexual longings that the desire for possession revealed. Though the characters of the Old Testament defer to God and to the story in its entirety, they are never shy about acting in response to their passions, sexual and otherwise. Hemingway signals his awareness of this fact when he associates the promised land with Brett, whose hull-like curves recall Fitzgerald's own association of sexuality with national destiny (Fitzgerald's boats and the "green breast of the new world"). Jacob, for example, is variously motivated by greed, lust, and pride when he usurps his brother's birthright, deceives his father-in-law, desires one sister over the other, and prefers one of his sons.[19] Similarly, Moses is at times a fearful and uncertain leader who finally gives vent to a wrath that expresses, as in "Roger Malvin's Burial," a simple human frustration and not a divine calling.

Throughout the Bible, the patriarchs are punished for being human. But they are also promised the recompense that will come, despite time and deferral, over generations, indeed through their own generative potencies as men. Both wife and son are temporarily withheld from Jacob. But Jacob gains his Rachel. He recovers Joseph, in Egypt, where Moses will be born. Moses never enters the promised land. But his progeny do, even if it is in the moment after the story of the exodus officially closes. The tradition of textual explication that applied these stories to the American context had purged the scriptures of their painful delays and deferrals. When the American Puritans crossed over the border into the promised land, they began to violate the many boundaries or bournes separating the human and the divine. They initiated a process of literalistic and repressive misreading that they handed on to their descendants. They denied the most radical and spiritually important deferral of all: the relocation of the promised land from the physical geography of a place named Israel to the spiritual domain of the saved church. Morally we cannot excuse Hemingway for his antisemitic portrait of Cohn. But what generates Hemingway's interest in the Jew is that he reincarnates salient features of America's Puritan past. Cohn's Jewishness reveals Hemingway's essential suspicion about the retrogressive literalism of American Christianity. Cohn resembles the "reverted" and "backward" looking Hebrews of Longfellow's "Jewish Cemetery at Newport" who are themselves types of Old Testament Puritans, recalcitrantly insisting on repeating a history long since revised and replaced.[20] He recalls Melville's "Puritan" Zionist in *Clarel*, who takes the next logical step and leaves the promised land of America for Palestine itself and who, predictably enough, perishes there with his family.

Jake's experience recalls life's inevitable frustrations. Yet he stands on the brink of a salvation that can and will come despite disruptions and postponements. Indeed, it will come because of his willingness to accept the conditions of deferral. Like Nick, Jake comes to realize that in everything we say or do there is something not said, not done, that must also be taken into account. Despite this, human beings must remain committed to sexuality, to the potential for generation and therefore for creating history, which they may never be able totally to control. Jake's situation obviously differs from Nick's. His is the situation of the most painful deferral of all. But Jake's is only an extreme case of a general human situation. The expatriate American drifting through Roman Catholic Europe knows in his heart that there are other compensations to be had, including the solace of the church. As inheritor of an American Puritan past, however, as distant from the church as a Jew might be, he cannot immediately understand what comfort the church might offer. It will take a "religious [that is, Catholic] festival" (p. 153) to release Jake from his Puritan prejudices and allow him to resume his Roman Catholic identity. This identity will return him to an incarnational view of the universe (p. 72).[21] For Hemingway the bullfight is the church of the modern world; Montoya is its priest; and Jake himself will become the author of its new scripture. Ecclesiastes is the key text in Jake's rewriting of American biblical history.

Hemingway once announced that the hero of his novel was the earth, its theme, that the earth endureth forever.[22] *The Sun Also Rises* reinstates the psychological and human implications and the intertextual (historical and typological) dimensions of the Old Testament text that America's ahistorical typologizing had erased. And it suggests that the American version of biblical and national history represented a repression and a blind repetition closely resembling Jake's misdirected storytelling in the early portions of the book. It recognizes in American Puritanism a denial of an incarnational and sacramental (Roman Catholic) world in which divinity might be discovered within the physical universe itself. Puritanism ignored New Testament facts of redemption. It preferred to leap from the Old Testament to the testament of America and from there to the testament of self. In so doing, it explicitly devalued the natural world in which truth could be made accessible to human consciousness. Like Eliot, Hemingway points to a dissociation of sensibility that he lays at the feet of the American Puritans.

In the book of Ecclesiastes Hemingway finds both the interpretive counterforce to the story of the promised land and the engagement with the earthly and the physical that for him secures the meaning of life in this world. This is the passage from which Hemingway borrows his title and one of his epigraphs:

> What profit hath a man of all his labor which he taketh under the sun? One generation passeth away, and another generation cometh: but the earth abidst forever. . . . The sun also ariseth, and the sun goeth down, and hasteth to his place where he arose. . . . The wind goeth toward the south, and turneth about unto the north; it whirleth about continually, and the wind returneth again according to his circuits. All the rivers run into the sea; yet the sea is not full; unto the place from whence the rivers come, thither they return again.[23]

By its process of severe eliminations and its pessimistic pronouncements, Ecclesiastes reverses some of the major premises of Moses's narrative journey. Instead of focusing on the national fulfillment that comes despite delays and deferrals, it focuses on those deferrals themselves. All human striving is vanity. It is a striving after wind. Ecclesiastes is about the endless repetition of natural events, the circularity of human experience in which human error repeats and redoubles upon itself. The knowledge of the divine and the commitment to God can extenuate life's painful conditions. But, according to Ecclesiastes, no ecstasy of revelation or messianic triumph necessarily concludes this life. And yet, Ecclesiastes insists, the sun also rises. The earth endures forever. (The author of the austere Ecclesiastes reputedly also wrote the sensuous and celebratory Song of Songs.)

For Hemingway, Ecclesiastes presents the relationship between the human and the divine that America failed to establish. It is a poem about deferral that does not diminish the power and importance of the physical universe. Ecclesiastes, in Hemingway's view, emphasizes fullness rather than fulfillment. It dwells on sexual generation and not the generations of Jacob. Its sun is an astronomical sun and not a son who acts as an instrument of covenantal destiny; its wind a wind that is not spirit and does not breathe life into the universe, but that circulates endlessly, "according to his circuits."[24] Here is a river that is not the place where a savior is set afloat to be found again and to set into motion the final sweep of history, or to be baptized and launched into a life everlasting, but which is a natural phenomenon, emptying itself, flowing on, and filling up again. Ecclesiastes portrays the universe's own potential for rich, stupendous survival and endless renewal, within the straitened circumstances of a limited universe. The circularity of natural phenomena does not have to end in meaningless redundancy and mindless replay. It can enable self-reflection and self-analysis to evolve into self-knowledge and self-control.

The lostness of Gertrude Stein's "lost generation," Hemingway suggests, was at least in part attributable to a misreading of the spiritual paradigms on which America constructed its self-identity, as it substituted the generations of the patriarchs, culminating in itself, for the vital generations of life. The American myth removed America from human history. Ironically, though its intentions were otherwise, it took America outside nature as well. It located a finale to history's endless cycles, called that climax America, and settled back into an atemporal or transhistorical existence that it called Eden. But in so locating paradise, Hemingway insists, and in gracefully instituting itself within its domain, America dispossessed itself of the lessons of experience that were born of the loss of paradise. It divested itself of the rich, procreative sexuality of the world itself. The biblical text never denies that sexuality. Indeed the sexual urge always promotes cosmic destiny despite history's delays and disruptions. In misunderstanding this, America made itself vulnerable to a lostness even more dire than the original fall from innocence. For America lost the earth and its compensations. It withdrew itself from generation in the most important sense of the word; hence from regeneration as well.

Juxtaposing Genesis and Exodus with Ecclesiastes highlights an important fact about the biblical text that the American authors of new scriptural history failed to perceive. The pattern of repetition and redoubling so extensively developed in Ecclesiastes is a basic feature of the five books of Moses as well.[25] Indeed, Old Testament repetition anticipates the typologizing of Old Testament materials. But in the typological view—and this is the crucial problem for Hemingway—the futility of human endeavor was overtaken by a decisive climax, in Christ, or, for the Americans, in America as well as in Christ. This, in Hemingway's view, halted the infinite incrementalism of the Old Testament text. The possibility for continuing interpretation, the fact that the text propagates a commentary on itself, provides the key to Hemingway's interest in the biblical materials. It is an interest that we might, invoking both old and new schools of criticism, call midrashic.[26] It accounts for the avowed optimism of what might well have been an overwhelmingly pessimistic text, a Hemingway *Waste Land*.[27] But, though *The Sun Also*

Rises, like *The Great Gatsby*, invokes Eliot's *Waste Land* vision, it also, like *Gatsby*, imagines something beyond the wasteland. For Hemingway, religious and artistic consciousness and the possibility of a new covenant of history come together in the bullfight.

THE NEW SCRIPTURE OF NATURE

Hemingway's novel of restatement, in which Hemingway tells the story of Jake Barnes, who tells the stories of himself and Robert Cohn, which themselves reformulate the story of the American dream, suggests that it is only in self-aware repetition, accompanied by the achievement of an inner self-control accommodating the knowledge of deferral, that the cycling of human experience becomes more than repressive déjà vu. Throughout Hemingway's novel experiences, statements, characters, and stories double each other with an almost hysteria-inducing regularity. (Like *Gatsby*, this is a novel of "things-by-pairs," suggests one critic.)[28] "I've been so miserable," Brett whines early in the book (p. 24) to the ever-sympathetic Jake; only to echo herself later: "I'm so miserable" (p. 64). And in perhaps the most terrifying occurrence of dreamlike replay, Jake's and Brett's final car ride repeats their first moment together in the novel (though with a significant difference). Fishing trips, bullfights, and swimming episodes reincarnate each other, as do scenes and conversations around diningroom tables and in bars. Robert Cohn, as I suggest, doubles Jake Barnes, as does Romero later in the book, and as many of the characters repeat or reflect one another.[29]

But Jake does not see the duplications his story records. "I had that feeling of going through something that has all happened before," Jake reports early in the novel. "I had the feeling as in a nightmare of it all being something repeated, something I had been through and that now I must go through again" (p. 64). Such a moment of déjà vu is not self-knowledge and self-reflexive commentary. It is, rather, an effort of the mind to forget what it has unconsciously remembered.[30] It is repression, of the kind that characterizes much of Jake's narrative enterprise. Significantly, this moment of repressed awareness of his almost warlike march to the pulsations of Brett's sexual rhythms is accompanied in the text by the meaningless beat of the drummer, whose voiceless hypnotic power is represented in the story by the mechanical sign ". . . . . . " repeated three times (p. 64). Jake is victim to a drum beat he is powerless to stop. This beat is reproduced maddeningly in the staccato of his text. He cannot control the nightmarish repetition of experience, which is represented in the novel both by the literal reenactment of events and, more nightmarishly, by Jake's recastings of his own emotions as the

feelings and thoughts of others. Because he has not yet penetrated to meaning and self-knowledge he is a poor interpreter of the nightmare that has
become his life and art. Like Gatsby, who is also directed by the "drums of
his destiny,"[31] Jake yields to a fate that has decidedly militaristic overtones.

The problem of psychological and artistic control results, for Hemingway,
from an inability to get the story right. From both Jake's and Hemingway's
points of view, the wrong kinds of texts are being published (p. 8). Even more
troubling, those who cannot write texts also do not know how to read them:

> [Cohn] had been reading W. H. Hudson. That sounds like an innocent occupation
> but Cohn had read and reread "The Purple Land." "The Purple Land" is a very
> sinister book if read too late in life. It recounts splendid imaginary amorous adventures
> of a perfect English gentleman in an intensely romantic land, the scenery of which is
> very well described. For a man to take it at thirty-four as a guidebook to what life holds
> is about as safe as it would be for a man of the same age to enter Wall Street direct from
> a French convent, equipped with a complete set of the more practical Alger books.
> Cohn, I believe, took every word of "The Purple Land" as literally as though it had
> been an R. G. Dun report. You understand me, he made some reservations, but on
> the whole the book to him was sound. It was all that was needed to set him off. (P. 9)

The reference here to "The Purple Land" (alliteratively suggesting the same
"promised land" of which Cohn is also enamored), and to Wall Street,
Horatio Alger, and the French convent, set up allusions to the issues, public
and private, that circulate in the book as a whole. These are issues of the
American dream, biblical metaphor, and psychological wholeness. (If green
is the visionary color for Fitzgerald's novel, purple—associated with Marshal
Ney and the Hudson book—serves the same purpose here.) The passage
specifically links these problems to the matter of textual misinterpretation.
Cohn fails as an interpreter of texts because he reads and rereads his "Bible"
in the tradition of Puritan literalism. Like the American Puritan now shown
for the Jew he really is, he believes perversely in the purple, promised land
that has, in Christianity, already been superseded. (I think here, again, of the
Longfellow poem.) Robert Cohn is the priest or Hebrew *cohen*[32] or perhaps
a "convent" nun or monk (suggesting some of Hemingway's and Jake's
suspicions about Cohn's sexuality), who imposes a rigidly spiritual and
therefore destructively naive perception of reality on a complex, sexually and
emotionally charged universe. Cohn cannot read critically or self-
consciously. In the portrait of the "splendid imaginary amorous adventures
of a perfect English gentleman in an intensely romantic land," he cannot
discern the critical reflection of himself.

Though Jake comprehends Cohn's failure as a writer and reader, he does not see that he himself also fails to read texts correctly. His story of Cohn, down to such details as the English-gentleman-like Cohn's amorous adventures and the well-described scenery, is a self-portrait. But Jake too does not see himself implicated by what he reads or writes:

> It was a little past noon and there was not much shade, but I sat against the trunk of two of the trees that grew together, and read. The book was something by A. E. W. Mason, and I was reading a wonderful story about a man who had been frozen in the Alps and then fallen into a glacier and disappeared, and his bride was going to wait twenty-four years exactly for his body to come out on the moraine, while her true love waited too, and they were still waiting when Bill came up. (P. 120; the name A. E. W. Mason, with initials preceding the family name ending in *son*, recalls the author of "The Purple Land," W. H. Hudson and thus links the two scenes)

Jake gives no clear evidence that he is aware that the Mason novel symbolically evokes his own situation, though by having Jake collapse levels of reference when he says that "they," the characters in the Mason story, were still waiting when "Bill" came up, Hemingway signals that the story and the reality are significantly related. Jake cannot understand why he recalls this moment. Nor can he "utilize" (to pick up the gist of Bill's and Jake's pseudo-biblical conversation) the insights that a self-conscious reading of the novel might have afforded. Later in the scene, Jake explicitly, and falsely, denies his feelings for Brett, with disturbing consequences (pp. 123–24).

Again, Jake's experience, like his biblical progenitor's, explicitly recalls the "toil and struggle" recorded in the original biblical encounter. But the scriptural struggle, Geoffrey Hartman has argued, can itself be a "struggle for the text":

> What interests me are the fault lines of a text, the evidence of a narrative sedimentation that has not entirely settled, and the tension that results between producing one authoritative account and respecting traditions characterized by a certain heterogeneity. In Scripture, despite doubled stories and inconsistencies, there is a sometimes laconic, sometimes wordy, but always imperious unity. In Jacob's combat that unifying tension reaches a peculiar pitch . . .
> And when he saw that he prevailed not against him, he touched the hollow of his thigh, and the hollow of Jacob's thigh was strained, as he wrestled with him. And he said, Let me go . . .
> There is something twisted here, because while it is Jacob who is wounded, it is his antagonist who immediately pleads for release.[33]

Hartman speculates as to how we might reconstruct the process of textual decentering. What is most important for understanding Hemingway's involvement in the biblical materials is Hartman's conclusion:

The universality of Jacob's combat with the angel lies, finally, in that struggle for a text—for a supreme fiction or authoritative account stripped of inessentials. . . . It centers on a sparse and doubtful set of words, handed on by an editorial process which in its conflations or accommodations could seem to be the very antithesis of the unmediated encounter it describes. . . . The accreted, promissory narrative we call Scripture is composed of tokens that demand the continuous and precarious intervention of successive generations of interpreters, who must keep the words as well as the faith.[34]

For Hemingway the bullfight is the new testament, the psychologically, spiritually, and artistically potent text of the modern world. The bullfight encodes the struggle for authority and faith. Not everyone will be able to understand and accept this new law: "The Biarritz crowd did not like it. They thought Romero was afraid [and they] preferred Belmonte's imitation of himself or Marcial's imitation of Belmonte" (pp. 217–18). But it is a text to which Jake can and does respond. At San Sebastian Jake will win back his birthright and his name. He will regain his ability to interpret language and to speak and write.[35]

The bullfight completes the process of psychological purging begun in Romero's (and by extension, Jake's) fistfight with Cohn (p. 219). Psychological health precedes artistic success. But the bullfight is more than psychotherapy. Because Romero is able to integrate his emotions and bring them to bear on the one perfect object, he converts psychological force into artistic, sexual, and religious power. There is no repression here, no fantasy overtaking life:

> Pedro Romero had the greatness. He loved bull-fighting, and I think he loved the bulls, and I think he loved Brett. Everything of which he could control the locality he did in front of her all that afternoon. Never once did he look up. He made it stronger that way, and did it for himself, too, as well as for her. Because he did not look up to ask if it pleased he did it all for himself inside, and it strengthened him, and yet he did it for her, too. But he did not do it for her at any loss to himself. (p. 216)

Romero loves the bull and identifies with it, but he does not mistake the bull for himself. He does not project himself onto it and see himself reflected in it. He remains separate and in control. There is no akedian temptation here. Romero maintains a purity of perception in relation to the bull. Conversely, then, he retains an integrity of self; no distorting legend, no competing text, contaminates his performance.

Romero accepts both his basic aggressivity and his pervasive sexuality (which is not differentiated into homosexuality or heterosexuality). Therefore, he is able to convert the same internal forces that cause Jake so much irresolvable pain into love. Romero and the bull and, by implication, Brett, whom Romero is also courting, are joined together as one by the phallic sword. The sword is activated (not immobilized as in the statue of Marshal Ney) in an assault and a seduction as loving as they are violent: "The bull wanted it again. . . . Each time he let the bull pass so close that the man and the bull . . . were . . . one . . . for just an instant he and the bull were one, Romero way out over the bull, the right arm extended high up to where the hilt of the sword had gone in between the bull's shoulders. Then the figure was broken. There was a little jolt as Romero came clear" (pp. 217–18). Romero uses his sword not only to unite himself with the bull, who stands also for Brett, but also to protect himself from it. The bullfight acknowledges the violence of sexuality. It accepts the life-and-death aspects of love, and their dangers, and therefore the necessary resistance to them in the context of heterosexual love. Hence, the bullfight images for Hemingway, and for Jake, perfect art, life, love, and religion.

The faith that bullfighting expresses is the faith of "aficion," "passion" (p. 131), that link between the physical and the spiritual that has, in Jake, as in America, broken down.[36] If Robert Cohn is the priest of a God-centered Jewish-Puritanism that, in Hemingway's view, has purified the scriptures of sexuality and sacramentalism, Montoya is the priest of the physical, man-and-beast-centered paganism of bullfighting. Ironically recalling the tradition of religion in America, Montoya administers "a sort of oral spiritual examination" (p. 132) to potential members of his church of the elect. But Montoya's spiritual examination involves "putting [his] hand on the shoulder . . . nearly always . . . the actual touching." Its prayer is "Buen hombre" (p. 132). The homosexual overtones are obvious and therefore the ceremony is "embarrassed" (p. 132). But the religion of bullfighting, in which one male assaults another, more masculine male with a phallic weapon, demands the total acceptance of oneself and one's indeterminate sexuality. (In the case of Romero's bullfight the sexual situation is even more complex, since the bull also stands for an androgynous Brett, while Romero doubles for an impotent Jake.) Jake knows the value of the religion of bullfighting. "Nobody ever lives their life all the way up except bull-fighters," he explains (p. 10). But, until the final segment of the book, Jake cannot sustain the faith of bullfighting. He cannot overcome his embarrassed love for men as well as for women (witness the strained affection in his relationship to Bill), or risk the emotional and physical self-destruction with which this religion (like all religions) threatens him. The biblical Jacob had to wrestle with an angel and be touched in the thigh or touch the angel's thigh in order to secure God's covenant.[37] The Old Testament thus hints that the competition for creative authority between man and God is sexual in nature. Jake's wound recalls Jacob's wound. It also recalls the wound in the loins of the mythical Fisher King.[38] Whatever the source of the threat to one's sexuality, one must discover a way of surviving the injury, of deflecting the blow and returning it (and oneself) to one's maker, without sacrificing oneself in the process.

The bullfight and the trip to San Sebastian it inspires initiate a process of recovery that restores Jake to manhood and psychological and artistic well-being. These events release Jake's creative powers and enable him to author an emotionally valid and yet not psychologically obsessed story. In this story, author, narrator, and protagonist enjoy a unity of voice and purpose that, like the sacred trinity of Romero, the bull, and Brett, demonstrate the unifying power of art. Jake is only a spectator at the bullfights. He is a reader of the text. In San Sebastian, however, he is actor and interpreter both. He undergoes a mystical, ritualistic immersion to confront, finally, his sexuality and his mortality. Diving down to the "green and dark" bottom of the ocean, eyes open (in contrast to his usually drunken "blindness" or his being "blind" to his feelings about Robert Cohn [p. 99]) (or his own likeness to Cohn's "near-sightedness" [p. 3]), "trying to swim through the rollers, but having to dive sometimes," Jake swims "slowly" and "steadily," floating and turning, consenting like Romero with his body to a rhythm outside his control (pp. 237–38; cf. p. 217). He exults in a physical pleasure that intensifies the undifferentiated and potentially destructive sexuality of the bullfight, producing a threatening autoeroticism.[39] As in every gesture, sexual or otherwise, there is the painful delay.

But like Romero controlling the locality of the fight, Jake learns to control his swim and concentrate the sexual overflow of the text. Like the bullfight, the swim and the telling of it become strong enough, self-confident enough, to reclaim and legitimize even the possibility of homosexuality. This possibility, coupled with desire for Brett, occasioned Jake's flight into repressive denial and sterility in chapter three. It led Jake to the frozen and impotent statue of Marshal Ney and to the stalled text of the early portions of the book. The account of the swim celebrates the solitary confrontation between a man and himself, a man and his death. Jake mounts the threat of his own weakness and possible destruction and, like Romero, comes clear.[40]

The "smooth waves" of his mind, which once pushed him in spite of himself, toward emotional cleansing (p. 31), are now within Jake's control and are converted into usable knowledge and an artistic moment. Like Romero performing two separate bullfights and displaying a dual consciousness in relation to himself and the bull, himself and Brett, and Brett and the bull, Jake swims twice and repeats those two events in his writing. These repetitions represent the difference between raw experience or raw psychology and self-referential, self-knowing, and self-controlled experience and knowledge. They suggest the difference between the text of one's life and the commentary on that text, which is the text of one's writing. Earlier, the many repetitions and doublings had represented blind reenactments and moral confusion.[41] Toward the book's end, however, repetition comes to signal the same possibility for meaning's own increment that Old Testament repetition represents. Jake has been a puppet playing out a pantomime directed by Brett, jerking back mindlessly like a toy boxer on a string (p. 35) to Brett's every pull of the threads that bound him. After his swim, Jake directs the action (pp. 239–47). Emerging from the waves, Jake is purged of Cohn, of Romero, and of the ghosts of self-doubt and wish-fulfillment that have haunted his life and his text. His doubles have been banished. He is his own man. What Jake does at the end of the novel he does for himself. When Brett's telegram arrives, also twice, Jake is ready and able to respond and to acknowledge the meaning of his response. He responds, as it were, also twice:

LADY ASHLEY HOTEL MONTANA MADRID ARRIVING SUD EXPRESS TOMORROW LOVE JAKE.
   That seemed to handle it. That was it. Send a girl off with one man. Introduce her to another to go off with. Now go and bring her back. And sign the wire with love. That was it all right. I went in to lunch. (p. 239)

Like his earlier self, Jake signs his telegram with love and goes in to lunch. He repeats himself, as he repeats Cohn and Romero. But his words do not mean what they seem to mean. The voice that clarifies the complexity of Jake's language is not Hemingway's or a distorted echo of one of Jake's doubles. It is his own. This is repetition not as déjà vu or repression or projection but as self-knowledge and self-control. For this reason, Jake, and not Cohn or Romero, is Hemingway's hero. Jake's commentary on his own telegram changes its meaning. The telegram thus rendered is not mushy and naive. Nor is it unintentionally bitter, like the opening of Jake's text. Rather it is tense, controlled, deliberately angry and yet still able to bear the signature of love. It is, like Hemingway's novel, text and necessitated commentary both. Jake may never be wholly free of the Robert Cohn part of himself that signs his telegrams with love. But he can now acknowledge that part of himself and deal with it. He can convert love into a formal signature, signifying only what he would have it mean.

   In the final moments of the book, Jake, in his own voice, frames and analyzes the neurotic denial mechanisms that have operated in much of his earlier text. " 'Oh, Jake,' Brett said, 'we could have had such a damned good time together.' . . . 'Yes,' I said. 'Isn't it pretty to think so?' " (p. 247). Romero has "ruined" Cohn and "wiped [him] out" (pp. 203, 243), but Jake has eliminated him from his consciousness and hence from his novel. By acknowledging the inevitability of projection and fantasy, Jake converts the image of Romero from that of a paralyzing projection, such as Cohn had been and as Romero too could become were Jake to fixate on it, into a usable one. This is a projection that readies the self for action.[42] The bulk of the pages after Jake leaves Spain are remarkably free of any projections of self, as Jake proceeds to the independence of mind and voice that denotes the artist and not the patient. The final image of the book, however, neatly inserted between Brett's fantasizing that "we could have had such a damned good time together" and Jake's penetrating irony, "Isn't it pretty to think so?" represents one, final, fleeting image of self. Unlike the earlier projections, however, this one does not subjugate and debilitate Jake's consciousness: "Ahead was a mounted policeman in khaki directing traffic. He raised his baton. The car slowed suddenly pressing Brett against me." As Carole Vopat has suggested, the policeman is "the projection of that part of Jake's self capable of arresting his destructive impulses."[43] Moreover, this projection avoids projection's psychological perils. As Jake and Brett settle back all too easily into their relationship of make-believe lovers ("We sat close against each other. I put my arm around her and she rested against me comfortably"), Jake retrieves an image of himself by which he is able to mount the emotions and complexities of his relationship to Brett. The policeman mounted on a horse recalls Romero mounting the bull and Jake mounting the waves. His raised baton resurrects Romero's sword, both of them intimating the sexual potency, violence and aggression, self-protectiveness, and finally consolidated maleness that facilitate rather than destroy the possibility of love.[44] These are necessary parts of Jake's vision of himself, however impossible their absolute attainment. Whatever the forces of delay and deferral, however agonizing they are to bear, to be a man means for Hemingway the willingness to take control. To be a writer means to speak the truth in all its barely articulatable complexity. "The car slowed suddenly pressing Brett against me," Jake reports. The rhythm orchestrated by the policeman's baton is totally unlike the compulsive, meaningless ". . . . . ." of the drummer. The baton slows the car (Romero fights slowly, Jake swims slowly, Hemingway's text unfolds slowly), allowing Jake to regain his composure. That composure takes the form of the words pronouncing the book's final, measured message: "Isn't it pretty to think so." In their terse restraint, their self-awareness, their self-composed power (turning a question into a statement of fact), these words represent Jake's triumph as a man and as a writer.

Jake's narration has been both a fantasy projection of the qualities he would have liked to possess, as well as a nightmare rendering of his life's story. At the beginning of the novel Jake reads texts—his own and others'— inattentively. By the end, however, he has become the kind of artist-critic Hemingway has been all along. He is capable not only of reading texts but of writing them as well. *The Sun Also Rises* is not simply one more story about America's lost generation. Rather it is the story of generation and regeneration, of the growth from type and archetype and stereotype into artistic and textual maturity. Jake begins his novel with the language of adolescent rage. He concludes it with a commentary that is Hemingway's as well as his own. Fantasy has become art; America's biblical origins have been rediscovered and revised; and, from Hemingway's point of view, the great(er) American novel has been written.

10
Seeking the Shores of Self:
E. L. Doctorow's *Ragtime*
and the Moral Fiction
of History

In *The Sun Also Rises*, Hemingway, taking his cue from Fitzgerald, associates the ahistoricity of the American imagination with a severe sexual repression. This repression, according to both writers, had created conditions of acute cultural sterility. But in associating sexuality with writing, Hemingway is not salaciously groping for a glib analogy between acts of creativity, nor he is trying facilely to compensate his protagonist for his impotence, applying to a reductive Freudian (or Petrarchan) formula whereby women beget children and men beget texts. Rather he is exploring both the sexual act and its literary correlatives in terms of the processes of delay and deferral that frustrate both sexual and literary creativity, especially in their interrelation. The sexual psyche is insatiable. It is also largely unutterable. It will never be susceptible of total description or expression. Language itself creates its own painful barriers to fulfillment. No truth, whether of our sexual natures or of another psychological, political, cultural, or historical self, will ever achieve more than approximate expression. Truth or knowledge can only be reached, if at all, by approximation. Just as biological generation depends on the completion of the sexual act, so artistic meaning resides in the attempt— necessarily orgiastic—to reach the future. This future eludes us. In the painful case of Hemingway's hero, it is absolutely unattainable. Yet Jake's condition is only an extreme metaphor for our own. What life consists of, therefore, is beating against the current, so that we are born(e) consciously like Nick and Jake, into history itself. This history is not reality per se, but as in *The House of the Seven Gables*, reality under the pressure of departure. It is *current*, not in the sense of its being present (that is, either being contemporary or being here) but in the sense of its being a part of the fluidity of generation, moving toward some distant but creative arrival. Historical ro-

185

mance is the written record of the struggle to arrive and of the commitment to generation. This concern with a procreative, regenerative relationship between the self and the world is the subject of E. L. Doctorow's *Ragtime* and John Updike's *Rabbit is Rich.*[1]

ABSENT HISTORY AND THE ESCAPE INTO FANTASY

Since contemporary American fiction has been interpreted as an extreme-case celebration of the indeterminate literary text, and since *Ragtime* is highly susceptible to this kind of reading,[2] it is appropriate to approach the conclusion of this book with some remarks on Doctorow's novel. *Ragtime* confirms American fiction's continuing commitment to exploring the undecidability of literary meaning and to placing that indeterminacy within the claims of history. If for Fitzgerald, Hemingway, and Faulkner it is enough for literature to record the morally determinant differences between fantasy and history, for Doctorow fiction itself must become a part of the historical process. Doctorow's moral fiction of history is intended directly to effect social and moral change.

Doctorow's *Ragtime* is one of the twentieth century's great inheritors of the historical romance tradition. Like Cooper's *Spy*, many of Hawthorne's stories and novels, and Melville's *Billy Budd*, the book records genuine historical events. It incorporates real people and real controversies into its story, and it assumes responsibility for interpreting the history that it traces. *Ragtime*, however, stretches believability beyond mimetic realism. The coincidental intermingling of characters defies reason. The young boy's prophecy at the beginning of the book and its inverted replication at the end of the novel, in the mind of the historical Houdini, is eerie and indeterminate. The ghostly scene of Father's death and arrival in heaven is purely gothic. *Ragtime* observes problems of skepticism and indeterminacy through the lens of history.

Considering the intensity of its interest in history, it is remarkable that *Ragtime* begins the storytelling process in the vacuum created by an absent history. The novel starts at the moment when a particular historical reality fails to occur. As in *The Great Gatsby*, *The Sun Also Rises*, and *Go Down, Moses*, the reason for this failure is a blocked or aborted sexual act. The appearance of Henry Houdini interrupts Mother's and Father's weekly coitus and sets into motion the main action of the story. This action, which coincides with the rest of Doctorow's text, can be understood as a fantasy of the young boy's imagination. In turn it records the various fantasies of the other characters, whose relationships to reality have also been interrupted.

The absent history opens the space in which a fantasy of reality, or a fiction, emerges. Doctorow understands the importance of opening this space: it will become, in the course of his book, a mechanism for moral and social change. But, like Hemingway, he also knows that fantasy's displacement of reality is dangerous. For Doctorow, the difference between valid fiction and escapist fantasy is the way in which the space of fiction is filled. It hinges on whether or not the fantasizer can recover the historical thread that has been severed and on how he or she recommits his or her fiction to the historical realm that has been vacated. The characters of the book, like Jake in *The Sun Also Rises*, escape history into a fantasy that unself-consciously and painfully mirrors the entrapment from which they are in flight. The author, however, empties out a space in which a considered and self-critical fiction of history can be born. Reuniting history and fiction at the end, in the vision of World War I that has been overtaking the characters from the beginning of the novel, but which has gone unremarked and is therefore also absent, he brings his text back into the responsibilities and constraints of time and place.

Doctorow encodes the presence of history in the text in order to subject the text to the conditions of reality from which it represents a (temporary) escape. Like Hawthorne, he throws a net around the text, cordoning off the range and direction and depth of the novel's fantasy. Doctorow does this through the curious device of the young boy's prophecy of World War I. The young boy, of course, cannot possibly know that the war is going to occur. Prophecy is a dishonest form of historical narrative. But the prophecy is also a communication from a voice outside the world of the novel. It writes into the book the author who is excluded from the fictional world because, like the history that the novel also absents, he occupies a different and discontinuous ontological plane. Prophecy thus becomes the ultimate recognition of and tribute to the world outside the novel. At the end of the book, prophecy will have been realized. This occurs, however, not because of some fatalistic predeterminism, such as we have seen acted out before in American fiction. Rather it suggests the powerful primacy of historical reality, the boundaries that history places on the imagination. As Doctorow's fiction is also the young boy's fantasy (the fantasy coincides with the rest of Doctorow's novel), it suggests how a certain consciousness of history (that is also revealed in the form of the young boy's prophecy) can prevent fantasy from becoming a self-consuming absorption in self. Historical consciousness effects a relationship with the world that is both imaginative and moral.

Like most of the characters in *Ragtime*, Mother and Father flee the reality of difference and change which is the uninterrupted intercourse of history. Houdini's interference with their sexual act only exposes and finalizes the series of flights that characterizes their relationship. "There was no sign from Mother that [the sexual intercourse] was now to be resumed. She fled to her garden. . . . In the meantime the whole household girded for [Father's] departure [to the north pole]. . . . The next morning everyone rode down to the New Rochelle railroad station to see Father off' (pp. 13–14). Father's escape from the world of mother's well-bred sexual delicacy and restraint delivers him into a world of sexual fantasy. Like Gatsby's or Jake's fantasies, Father's expresses powerful and unanswered sexual needs and equally potent sexual fears. It represents an escape that breaks the bonds of community and makes human experience painfully indeterminate and morally ambiguous.

At the north pole, in the hiatus between historical and personal identity, at a distance remote from rational and social habit, Father is forced to confront, without context and outside history, the absolute "terrors of [the] universe" (p. 83). This "continuous night" (p. 83), the "uninterrupted flow of . . . darkness" (p. 81), corresponds to the psychosexual center of his own being that the civilized society of New Rochelle has kept in careful check. (Like his family, the community *girds* his loins.) In his fantasy Father confronts his repressed sexuality. This would be fine if Father knew how to interpret his psychological processes and deliver them back to conscious control. But relocating the basic tensions of his nature within the fantasy world causes only further absenting, a deeper escape. Not only does it increase his distance from his sexuality, but it divorces him from the reality and history which are sexuality's only viable, palpable means of expression:

> There seemed in this icebound winter night a force that gripped you by the neck and faced you into it. The Esquimo families lived all over the ship, camping on the decks and in the holds. They were not discreet in their intercourse. They cohabited without even undressing, through vents in their furs, and they went at it with grunts and shouts of fierce joy. One day Father came upon a couple and was shocked to see the wife thrusting her hips upwards to the thrusts of her husband. An uncanny animal song came from her throat. . . . The woman was actually pushing back. It stunned him that she could react this way. . . . He thought of Mother's fastidiousness . . . and found himself resenting this primitive woman's claim to the gender. (p. 84)

Father cannot survive the confrontations at the pole of his being. Like Hemingway's Jake, he cannot connect the fantasy with his psychological and historical life. Therefore, he cannot meaningfully incorporate it back into the sense of a continuous self—continuous, not least, with the world it inhabits and cohabits—from which it has escaped. Father proves "not the sturdiest member of the expedition," not from a "lack of heart . . . but from the tendency of his extremities to freeze easily. . . . Pieces of Father froze very casually" (p. 89). Father's vulnerable sexuality proves his undoing.

In order to keep himself "under control" (p. 83), to keep account of the "uninterrupted flow of twilight darkness" (p. 81) that threatens to engulf him in his own primitive and repressed impulses, Father does what educated western men, including the fathers of the American experience whom the adventurer Father recalls, have always done. Like the journalists in Fitzgerald's, Hemingway's, and Faulkner's novels, he tries to document his experience. He applies to the "system of language and conceptualization [that] proposed that human beings, by the act of making witness, waranted times and places for their existence other than the time and place they were living through" (pp. 83–84). This kind of historical record, it seems, can purchase immortality and sanity with a single scratch of the pen. "The Esquimos, who had no system but merely lived here, suffered the terrors of their universe. Sometimes the Esquimo women would unaccountably tear off their clothes and run into the black storms howling and rolling on the ice. Their husbands had forcibly to restrain them from killing themselves" (p. 83). Father does not go insane. There is no better evidence for the need to restrain sexuality and to relocate life's terrors in the written record where it can do no harm and where it can verify and stand witness to the continuity of human life.

But Father barely outlives his experience. His death smacks of a suicidal impulse like the Esquimos'. Father's control is purchased at the price of his sexuality. Therefore, it makes his written record an empty, meaningless gesture. Reducing truth to a bare minimum of notations, it is a pantomime or parody of historicization, like the newspaper accounts of Gatsby's death or the ledgers in *Go Down, Moses*. Doctorow captures the essential aridity of Father's historical record when he imagines Father's arrival in heaven. Even more than Gatsby's heaven, Father's is only a sterile duplication of the dry, empty, frustrating world of sand and shore (*Gatsby*'s valley of ashes) that has kept Father perpetually at the edge of discovery: "Poor Father, I see his final exploration. He arrives at the new place, his hair risen in astonishment, his mouth and eyes dumb. His toe scuffs a soft storm of sand, and he kneels and his arms spread in pantomimic celebration, the immigrant, as in every moment of his life, arriving eternally on the shore of his Self" (p. 368). Father's final expedition mirrors the blind, dumb, futile, and egocentric explorations of his life. It delivers him back to what he has always sought, but, because it was the unnamed, unacknowledged object of his quest, he has never himself discovered in a meaningful way. His existence has always been a dumb pantomime, an ironic celebration, like his fireworks, of an unachieved glory. Arriving eternally on the shore of self, he can discover nothing but the most vacuous and empty scene of interpretation.

This is where Father's exploration to the pole of being takes him. It leaves him astonished and dumb, incapable of returning home as anything more than the ghost he becomes when finally, literally, he reaches the other side of history. Father's epistolary historical journal fails as historical art because it buries history, absents it, in an escape from reality that makes history a fantasy. Father's letters, his historical record, exist a pole away from his essential historical being. They are "delayed transmission[s]" (p. 81), which arrive too late to redress the gap between the sexual and the psychological. They are another form of coitus interruptus, in which Father spills the seed that might provide a genuine issue of self, an offspring or heir to yield the only kind of immortality allowed within history's biological kingdom. For a short while Father escapes into an adventure that fantasizes and finally dissipates his repressed fears and desires. He consummates the suspended sexual act, not completed with Mother, with an Esquimo woman. But because he cannot admit the reality of that sexual escape, credit its historical existence, it remains locked inside the fiction his history has become. The sexual act remains impotent to place his historical being outside the relocated fantasy world. It produces no offspring, and his true heir, the young boy, soon becomes somebody else's son.

While Father is escaping from Mother and her denial of his sexual being, Mother is similarly entering her own dream of sexual and reproductive fulfillment—and denial. Without actually engaging in the sexual act, she bears (home) the black baby, who in its brownness represents for her the same earthy sexuality that the Esquimos represent in Father's fantasy. Like Father, Mother flees the actual life of her asexual sterility into a sexuality from which she is strangely protected by its status as fantasy. Mother has committed the only kind of adultery her polite society allows her. But the effect of her fantasy of passionate betrayal is as total as if she had actually taken a lover. For a while she continues to receive Father into her bed. She temporarily imagines Father capable of living up to her expectations of passion. But Father will literally be replaced. After his death (which is itself a consequence of his and her untethered and mutually exclusive fantasies), Mother marries the Jewish immigrant socialist Tateh. She adopts both the brown baby and Tateh's beautiful and sensuous daughter, for whom her own well-bred New York son has already conceived a passionate affection.

The consequence of Mother's and Father's separate and irreconcilable flights from genuine sexuality into sexual fantasy is that their world comes to exclude the possibilities of genuine procreation and historical renewal. "When Father returned to New Rochelle he walked up the front steps of his home, passed under the giant Norwegian maples and found his wife holding a brown baby in her arms" (p. 123). Everything is the same—the town, the

home, and the giant Norwegian maples. And yet everything is utterly transformed. Mother is holding in her arms the brown baby that represents the
product of both of their sexual fantasies without its being the result of their
sexual union or even the union of their fantasies—that is, of their dreams
and aspirations for each other and for their society. The brown baby, a blend
of Black and Esquimo perhaps, separates rather than unites them. The son
of the black radical Coalhouse Walker, who represents the new history that
the white community actively tries to thwart, he ultimately causes Father and
Mother to enter into their period of dissolution.

Because Father denies his sexuality and divorces it from his life, Father
returns from the pole in a permanent state of limpness, associated with the
tendency of his extremities, including certain delicate members of his body,
to freeze easily. Tearfully childlike, he discovers a son who has turned into
a man in his absence. On Mother's bedside there is "a pamphlet on the
subject of family limitation" (p. 127). Father wanders through the house
"finding everywhere signs of his own exclusion" (p. 123). Even the "mirror
in his bath [gives] back the gaunt, bearded face of a derelict, a man who
lacked a home" (pp. 123–24). He also lacks the vitality of manhood that
provides the basis for a home: "he was shocked by the outlines of his body,
the ribs and clavicle, white-skinned and vulnerable, the bony pelvis, the
organ hanging there redder than anything else. At night, in bed Mother held
him and tried to warm the small of his back [but] it was apparent to them
both that this time he'd stayed away too long" (pp. 123–24).

The danger of flight, of fantasy, is that one might stay away too long.
Delay is one thing, but permanent deferral is another. In one's absence a new
reality could intervene to one's permanent exclusion. Father is disinherited
because of his unwillingness to enter history. He is absented from history by
a history that must come into being, whatever his strategies of withdrawal.
This new history excludes him. A manufacturer of fireworks all his life, he
is killed when he enters the real world of firearms of which his toys (like his
expeditions) are fanciful and futile denials. (He is aboard a ship that looks
back to his earlier polar voyages.) From the moment of the interrupted sexual
act, Father and Mother suspend themselves dangerously between fantasy and
history. Only Mother, who awakens to the sexual passion that creates history,
returns alive to keep the real world going.

THE RAGTIME RHYTHM OF HISTORY AND ART

As in *The Sun Also Rises*, art is not irrelevant to the potency that preserves
history. The narrative that contains the history of Mother's and Father's

fantasies is itself a fantasy that springs from the consciousness of their son. His desire to dispense with a restrictive reality reflects his parents's desire to flee. It causes him to conjure the disruptive appearance of Henry Houdini in the first place:

> Across town the little boy in the sailor suit was suddenly restless and began to measure the length of the porch. . . . He felt that the circumstances of his family's life operated against his need to see things and to go places. For instance he had conceived an enormous interest in the works and career of Henry Houdini the escape artist. But he had not been taken to a performance. . . . [T]he little boy stood at the end of the porch and fixed his gaze on a bluebottle fly traversing the screen in a way that made it appear to be coming up the hill from North Avenue. The fly flew off. An automobile was coming up the hill from North Avenue. . . . [It] was Henry Houdini, the famous escape artist. (Pp. 7–9)

Houdini's "unexpected visit" (p. 13) out of which the entire novel unfolds, or, perhaps, for which it substitutes, as Houdini substitutes for the fly, results from a restless shifting of position that changes the young boy's angle of vision. It occurs when a rupture in the natural rhythm of events allows the escape into fantasy or art which, in this case, is the novel itself (not only does the young boy's fantasy essentially coincide with the whole of Doctorow's narrative but it is the boy who eventually becomes the son and heir of Tateh the artist). But there is clearly a difference between the fantasies of Mother and Father and of the young boy. Whereas Father's and Mother's egocentric and self-denying fantasies essentially displace the historical world with the self, the young boy's historical romantic story (the novel *Ragtime*) pushes outward from self to world. Like the movies of which he is so enamored, his story represents self-divestment, self-sacrifice, and a commitment to social reality, which ultimately effects its own changes on that reality.

Ragtime seems to many readers an indeterminate fantasy, much like the many fantasies of escape it records. Repeating, rephrasing, reinvesting themes and motifs, it seems, in the great tradition of much American fiction, to obscure the differences between people, places, and events, undermining the distinctions between fiction and history.[3] The evidence for this view is overwhelming: identities overlap; characters mirror each other and echo each other's words; and they repeat each other's actions, replicating each other's essential principles of being. Father, for example, is echoed by Tateh. Both share the role of father, and Mother marries both of them, literally converting Tateh into the father of Father's son. Coalhouse Walker and Younger Brother duplicate each other as radical soulmates (the anachronism of Walker's black power philosophy mirroring events still in the future, while Booker

T. Washington, who also represents an aspect of Walker, reflects events in the black past). Emma Goldman looks in one direction to Evelyn Nesbitt, in the other to Walker and Younger Brother, and in her Jewishness, also to Tateh. Houdini recalls the explorer Father but also the reincarnationists Morgan and Ford, who are themselves flipsides of the same coin. The historical figures Houdini, Emma Goldman, and Pierpont Morgan circulate comfortably in the fictional world of Father, Mother, Younger Brother, and Little Boy. More disconcerting, the fictional Houdini and the factual one inhabit the same text and reflect each other. Adding even further to the book's ontological indeterminacy, the fictional characters echo autobiographical details, thus representing history in still another key. Doctorow's narrative voice might seem the ultimate instance of a self-realizing ego, such as Father's. It seems to authorize a world that it claims to be reality itself.

But like Fitzgerald's boats against the current, Doctorow's book generates a tension between its backward-looking and forward-moving impulses. Recognizing the tendency of the past to draw one back into the primal fantasies of asexual being, the book pushes irreversibly forward into the inevitabilities of time and unforeseen change. The book's four parts trace a development from a static, jigsaw replication of social stasis, which is an indeterminate silhouette of reality, to a dynamic involvement in the radical consequences of a clearly felt historical direction, which in the final pages makes the book itself a part of the historical process. For Doctorow a major subject of art is its relationship to time and change, history and society. The power of the novel derives from its ability to receive and sustain change and to transfer it back to society. The book opens with the interruption of the sexual act, which eventuates in a double dissolution of family and history, fantasy substituting for life in the minds of the characters. It concludes, however, with a marriage joining Christian and Jew, upper and lower classes, and producing a multiracial family. It thus becomes an image of America's new historical reality, which the book itself, transcending cultural stereotypes, helps to create.[4] In *Ragtime*, sexuality and art meet in the creation of history.

Like Tateh's silhouette portraits, the opening of Doctorow's novel silhouettes a world of white, conservative, male-dominated affluence against the dark background of black, immigrant, female impoverishment. Doctorow's silhouette, like Tateh's, conveys "textures, moods, character, despair" (p. 51). But its tensions derive not from articulated and dynamic depths of portraiture but from sterile juxtapositions of stark antitheses. These juxtapositions expose painful contradictions. They also, however, freeze them into hopeless impotence. "There were no Negroes. There were no immigrants," the book begins. "Apparently there *were* Negroes. There *were* immigrants," it continues a few sentences later (pp. 4–5). The statements identify a painful paradox of the American reality. But they do not offer alternatives or solutions or meaningful interpretations. They do not even provide a place or space in which meaningful interpretation or discussion can occur. They close down interpretive possibility: the statements are too bare to sustain the kind of commentary necessary to effect significant social or artistic debate.

The problem with the silhouette is that it favors the egocentric and indeterminate potentialities of art. For the perceiver or reader, the silhouette is an unoccupied territory (as opposed to the kind of neutral territory that concerns so many American writers), which can contain, wholly and without contradiction, any meaning an interpreter might want to demand of it. It is not incidental to the aesthetic qualities of the silhouette that it is often commissioned and purchased as an image of self. The indeterminacy and concern with self reflected in the silhouette are direct consequences of how the silhouette is crafted. Fashioned by the strong hand of the artist literally cutting out an image of the world, it places that image in bold and unrelieved opposition to everything the artist does not wish to consider. The silhouette eliminates the details and relations that invite discussion and interpretation and even sympathy. The silhouette is an unanswered and perhaps unanswerable cry of despair, trapping a stagnant reality in a static outline of that reality. What is wrong with the silhouette is not only its lack of realism, its effacement of social reality, but also its lack of interpretive space. Like fantasy, the silhouette opens up a place in reality for the imagination to consider. But what the imagination considers when it looks at the silhouette, as when it examines its fantasies, is often only itself.

According to Doctorow the problem with photographic journalism is significantly related to the deficiencies of the silhouette. Like the newspaper accounts in *Gatsby, The Sun Also Rises,* and *Go Down, Moses* (or like Father's journals), the photographs of social reformer Jacob Riis produce reductive images of reality. Riis "went around climbing dark stairs and knocking on doors and taking flash photos of indigent families in their dwellings. He held up the flash pan and put his head under the hood and a picture exploded. After he left, the family, not daring to move, remained in the position in which they had been photographed. They waited for life to change. They waited for their transformation" (p. 20). Similarly, Riis's "color maps of Manhattan's ethnic populations," gray for Jews, red for Italians, blue for Germans, black for Africans, green for Irish, form a "crazy quilt of humanity," painfully forced and inappropriately gay (p. 21). This frantic montage conceals pain beneath its colorful geometry of alleged social realities. It produces no basis for social change. When Riis presents his case for housing for the poor to Stanford White, presumably armed with these photographs and maps, he fails to win the support that he needs. The art forms of the reformer-reporter simply re-form the world and report its news. They ignore the violent internal explosions and human pain that initiate the artistic moment. "That evening White went to the opening night of *Mamzelle Champagne* . . . a serious heat wave had begun to kill infants all over the slums" (p. 22). Art is implicated here at all levels. White's decision to spend the evening at the revue while infants die emphasizes a failure in Riis's stifling reformed art. And White himself will be one of the casualties of the misuse of art, when the self-dramatizing husband of a theatrical lady kills him at the performance.

Emptied of detail, the silhouette conveys repeating and repeatable outlines that cancel the urgencies of social reality. It is an empty fantasy of the world, reproducing flat shapes and figures that are often reproductions of the outlines of self. Doctorow, then, must discover some alternative to the silhouette. He has to release his own book from the silhouette's deadening power. The second part of *Ragtime* (p. 123) opens with the return of Father, an image much like a silhouette. It is an image so unexceptional, so much of a piece with everything that we know and expect of Mother and Father, that were it not for one totally startling, incongruous detail, the presence of the brown baby, it would function simply to reconfirm the blank stability of a changeless reality, the endless repeatability of the archetypical human story. Here is the static, totally unremarkable snapshot of the return home to the perduring homestead. It records Father's fantasy of homecoming, Mother's fantasy of maternity. But in the intersection of the two irreconcilable fantasies, a new picture emerges. The brown baby prevents the picture from resolving into a conservative, featureless portrait cancelling social diversity. Like his biological father in the social history that follows, this baby focuses attention on what defies fantasy and makes it not only unrealistic but immoral. The black background that once served only to highlight the disproportionate totality of the white silhouette will, like the brown baby in this vignette, leap to the foreground and activate the otherwise frozen picture. As foreground and background displace one another, portraiture will begin to achieve a frantic vitality capable of effecting social change: the writing into the picture of black characters as major figures is, even in the sixties and seventies, evidence of dramatic social transformation. The rhythm of *Ragtime*, then, is not the rhythm of repetition. It is, as its title suggests, the rhythm of ragtime. According to *Webster's New Collegiate Dictionary*, this is a "rhythm characterized by strong syncopation in the melody with a regularly accented accompaniment," where *syncopation* is "a temporary displacement of the regular metrical accent . . . caused typically by stressing the weak beat." The first weak beat that is self-consciously stressed in this book is the black baby. Once struck, this note takes the book off in a new direction.

If the commanding form of the first part of the novel is the silhouette, the operational mode of the second part is the movies. This is the silhouette animated, the fantasy in flight from itself, the ragtime rhythm of strong and weak beats, lights and shadows, projected onto the screen. The movies capture the essential vitality of life that can never be conveyed in a silhouette or in a still photograph. But the movies do more than this. *The House of the Seven Gables* suggests some aspects of the relationship between historiography and cinematic technique. From the moment that Doctorow introduces the house as the major set of his story, *The House of the Seven Gables* cannot be far from our minds. For Doctorow, as for Hawthorne, the movies represent reality under the pressure of departure. The movies are fantasies of reality that first acknowledge and then control the forces of subjective perception. They screen a world of images that is, for the moment, reality. But they do not reduce the world to its spectral performance.[5] Like fantasy or the silhouette, the movies open up an imaginative place within social reality. Like historical romance, however, they recognize the relationship between invented story and inherited reality, self and other.

The movies realize the potential of photography to transcend the endless subjectivity and dematerialization of silhouetting. The young boy is the interpreter of silhouettes. His spiritual father is the silhouette artist himself, the man who later becomes the novel's maker of movies. The boy's perception of life begins in his contemplation of the static and frozen image that accentuates sameness because it excludes the details that locate difference. But the boy does not remain enslaved to the silhouette. His imagination, which is richly fed by a "discarded treasure" (p. 133), his grandfather, instinctively gravitates toward the "discarded" thing itself (p. 131). This is the silhouette, which has been acquired and cast aside by Evelyn Nesbitt and Younger Brother out of an egocentric sentimentality wholly consonant with what the silhouette represents. In retrieving this discarded thing, the young boy also recovers the life within the carved out space that the silhouette has also discarded. This is the image of the young girl in "the posture of someone who might run at any moment" (p. 131) with whom he falls in love (cf. p. 104).

The theory of metamorphosis that fascinates the boy does not argue for the simple substitution of one thing or person for another or the reemergence of the self after death (as do the reincarnationist philosophies of Ford and

Morgan, which are the subjects of the third part of the novel). Reincarnation is a metaphor for history's changelessness, its silhouetting of recurring motifs. Metamorphosis, on the other hand, insists on a principle of
transformation, of change. This is what Riis's photographic subjects await
and what his photographs cannot achieve. It is what the movies effect.
"The forms of life," Ovid teaches him, are "volatile" (p. 132). Volatility
means the capacity for self-sacrifice, self-divestment. Seeing that the
"world composed and recomposed itself constantly in an endless process of
dissatisfaction" (p. 135), the boy is able to leave himself open to life's
changes. He actively seeks those changes in himself. Gazing into a mirror
that might only reflect back an image of self, he searches for evidences of
personal "change." This is not "vanity," as his mother supposes. It is not
an attempt, like his father's, at a static image of "self-duplication" that
endlessly reproduces the self. Rather the boy endeavors to discover a dynamic "self-duplication" that signals self-awareness, self-consciousness:
"He would gaze at himself until there were two selves facing one another,
neither of which could claim to be the real one. The sensation was of
being disembodied. He was no longer anything exact as a person. He had
the dizzying feeling of separating from himself endlessly" (p. 134), as if he
were himself a moving picture of the sort that draws him to that other
mirror of life, the cinema. The boy would be a spectator, in Thoreau's
terms, of his own scene of interpretation. This is what Cavell calls the
scene of instruction in life and language.[6]

The boy "liked to go to the moving picture shows downtown at the
New Rochelle Theatre on Main Street. He knew the principles of photography but saw also that moving pictures depended on the capacity of
humans, animals, or objects to forfeit portions of themselves, residues of
shadow and light which they left behind" (p. 133). For the young boy the
movies represent and respect transformation in its largest terms. They
represent and respect otherness. Tateh's most powerful motion picture
success is precisely about this other America that the citizens of New
Rochelle or the silhouette would conceal. The our gang series is "about a
bunch of children who were pals, white black, fat thin, rich poor, all
kinds, mischievous little urchins who would have funny adventures in
their own neighborhood, a society of ragamuffins, like all of us, a gang,
getting into trouble and getting out again" (p. 369). The motion pictures
are constructed out of silhouettes. They convey the same stark antitheses
and unmediated oppositions as the silhouette: white/black, fat/thin, rich
/poor (cf. "There were no Negroes." "Apparently there *were* Negroes").
Yet the movies, in animating these oppositions, focus on the activities of

life that differentiate one moment from the next. These are the moments that invite and foster reader (or viewer) response. They are the moments that finally cause social action.

Like the black man's ragtime, the immigrant's movies literally, historically, democratize American culture. They are, therefore, in and of themselves, forms of positive moral change. They provide what static and stabilizing images cannot, the possibility for sympathetic self-divestment and identification with the other. The movies suggest that art must also be self-sacrificing and self-forfeiting. As dramas in which the real identities of the actors who act out the various roles matter, the movies force to the surface of the visual text the identities of real human beings whose realness cannot for a moment be forgotten and whose individuality is not hidden behind the blind mask of the silhouette.[7] Doctorow's novel approaches replicating this mingling of the fictional and the real that characterizes the movies. Like film, Doctorow's novel is a transparency. It does not simply represent life. It attempts to incorporate into the representation the human presence that is life and that is therefore not subject to endless authorial interpretation or viewer subjectivity. Fictionalize as he might, a Pierpont Morgan or a Henry Ford exists to defy his authorial control. The ontological confusion between the fictive and the real is not intended to subvert the reader's faith in history. Rather, like the spectral performance in "Young Goodman Brown" it provides the occasion for qualifying one's confidence in the ability of the imagination to create its own world separate and distinct from the world in which it exists.

A moral fiction of history is what the young boy as artist achieves in the text that Doctorow calls *Ragtime*. It is an art form that he inherits directly from Tateh. But it is an artistic achievement that Tateh himself must learn through the inadequacies of his own earlier medium of expression, the silhouette. The young boy is not only Tateh's artistic heir. He is also, in a Wordsworthian manner, his spiritual father. Tateh must learn to incorporate the child's insights on mutability and on the importance of the discarded thing into his art in order to make it responsive to and responsible for the social reality in which it exists. Tateh's first artistic success is pointedly a moving picture book that depicts a scene in which the young boy and not the artist himself participates. This book of the ice skaters looks back to an earlier moment in the text, when Mother, Younger Brother, and the boy go skating. Mother and Younger Brother see the scene as a beautiful image of social harmony in which they can achieve a flawless, graceful balance. It is for them a silhouette of social stability. The boy, however, perceives the fragility and fleetingness of the image that the socially dominant population would attempt to cut into the world. "The boy's eyes saw only the tracks made by the skaters, traces quickly erased of moments past, journeys taken" (p. 135). In this scene, only the boy perceives the transcience of human existence. He alone understands the ways in which the tracks of rote tradition are only ephemeral traces revealing loss and disappearance and the impermanence of social convention.[8]

The world of the skaters is the world from which Tateh and the girl are excluded. This is the world of endlessly repeating and duplicating social maneuvers that preserve and perpetuate social elitism. The girl can enter this world only through the magic of the artist's moving picture book, which not only invites her participation but which also invests her with imaginative control over the world of privilege and joy: "She held the little book and governed the pages with her thumb and watched herself skating away and skating back . . . returning, pirouetting and making a lovely bow to her audience" (p. 141). In creating his moving picture book, Tateh does not abandon the method of silhouetting that, like the "cut-cut of the skate blades on the ice" (p. 135), carves out static, impersonal images of social reality. He accepts the force of the silhouette and of the social conformity that it implies. He takes his art one step further, however, discovering how art itself can conspire to break the force of social stability. He combines the silhouettes, a hundred and twenty of them, to make them record the subtle changes that inevitably distinguish one picture from another over time. Tateh discovers what Holgrave can only barely approximate when he juxtaposes portraits of Judge and Colonel Pynchon and of the living and dead judge. The pirouetting silhouette is cinema.

As the boy had intuited, motion pictures represent a willingness to allow some other consciousness to fill the imaginative space they leave behind. They represent endless realignments of points of view:

> Tateh had drawn pickets, stark figures with their feet in the snow. . . . He switched to lettering. All for one and one for all. He felt better. At night he took home scraps of paper, oak tag, pens and India ink, and to take the child's mind off their troubles he began to entertain her with silhouette drawings. He created a streetcar scene, the people getting on and off. She loved it. She leaned it against her bed pillow and looked at it from different angles. This gave him an inspiration. He did several studies of the streetcar and when he held them together and flipped the pages it appeared as if the streetcar came down the tracks from a distance and stopped so that people could get on and off. His own delight matched the girl's. She gazed at them with such serene approval that he had a fever to create for her. He brought home more scrap paper. He imagined her on ice skates. In two nights he made a hundred and twenty silhouettes on pages not bigger than his hand. He bound them with string. (Pp. 140–41)

Tateh's art begins as social protest. It represents a tendency to perceive the world through silhouettes, stereotypes, and slogans (slogans being a verbal approximation to silhouetting). Soon, however, his art begins to express a desire to ease individual suffering, to entertain and to please. As Tateh moves from the art of politics (his posters) to the politics of art (his silhouette books), he begins to realize that change, to be effective, does not necessarily have to be revolutionary. It might be continuous, subtle, and on a small scale. It might have to do with angles of perception (recall the young boy's shifting of position that gives way to the fantasy of the novel), made manageable in a miniature volume bound together with nothing more than string.

This artistic expression of social change cannot remain a private experience. Fearing that he might be able to do "nothing more for [his daughter] than make pictures," that they might just go on this way "in varying degrees of unrealized hope" (p. 141), Tateh goes out into the world to sell his art and secure for her the real world behind the fictive image. Even art must do something more than state an idea. It must enter the world. It must join itself to history:

> Thus did the artist point his life along the lines of flow of American energy. Workers would strike and die but in the streets of the cities an entrepreneur could cook sweet potatoes in a bucket of hot coals and sell them for a penny or two. . . . All across the continent merchants pressed the large round keys of their registers. The value of the duplicable event was everywhere perceived. . . . At Highland Park, Michigan, the first Model T automobile built on a moving assembly line lurched down a ramp and came to rest in the grass under a clear sky. (Pp. 153–54)

Doctorow explicitly links Tateh's art to the great industrial revolution in manufacture. But if in a democracy like America, capitalism and art are related in fundamental ways, they are still by no means the same thing.[9] Ford is a self-concerned, complacent boor who sees no problem in creating a machine that can "replicate itself endlessly" and who can easily conclude from "these principles . . . the final proposition of the theory of industrial manufacture—not only that the parts of the finished product be interchangeable, but that the men who build the products be themselves interchangeable parts" (p. 155). Tateh, on the other hand, is motivated by social and private dissatisfaction to reproduce, with painstaking care, little pictures of reality, which with their small, unpretentious claims, invite identification and sympathy and thus promote social progress. Ford's Model T's and the movies are both big business, but they are not the same business. Ford's philosophy of manufacture and the historiography of reincarnation that this philosophy incorporates are the fantasies of self-duplication that Tateh's movies, animating the silhouette, displace. Eliminating the need for the other, and the sexual union by which self and other join, Ford's theory of industrial reproduction creates, like Father's journals, a history of a single self arriving endlessly on the sterile shores of his own being.

Pierpont Morgan clearly shows up the difference between Tateh's medium of entrepreneurship and Ford's, which is also his own:

> Has it occurred to you that your assembly line is not merely a stroke of industrial genius but a projection of organic truth? After all, the interchangeability of parts is a rule of nature. . . . [I]ndividuation may be compared to a pyramid in that it is only achieved by the placement of the top stone. . . . I do not think you can be so insolent as to believe your achievements are the result only of your own effort. . . . [The gifted] are with us in every age. They come back, you see? They come back! (Pp. 168–72)

Morgan's philosophy of history could be mistaken for a version of Kantian idealism. He constructs a view of history as cumulative achievement moving inevitably forward toward greater pinnacles of success. For him, the collective human accomplishment far surpasses the success of any one individual. But as he is himself already the "top of the business pyramid," his historiography becomes merely an un-Whitmanesque celebration of self. History, for Morgan, as for Father, records the eternal duplication of self, of himself, his own perpetual reemergence through time and space (which he calls reincarnation). Progress, such as he conceives it, is always controlled by the aristocratic few, indeed by the same aristocratic few of whom Morgan himself is the top of the line. Morgan's historiography is summed up nicely by what one critic has called "marching backward into the future."[10] His philosophy of reincarnation recalls Holgrave's and Clifford's ascending spiral curve in The House of the Seven Gables.[11] It is associated by Doctorow with selfishness, immaturity, and a desire to fold history back onto itself to reveal at its center the essential primacy of self.

Though couched in sophisticated, scholarly language, Morgan's theory of reincarnation is nothing more than aristocratic snobbism and self-centeredness. This fact is driven home by Ford's spontaneous and extraordinarily crude revision of Morgan's philosophy: "Exceptin the Jews," he says, "The Jews. . . . They aint' like anyone else I know" (p. 168).

> If I understand you right . . . you are talking about reincarnation. . . . Reincarnation is the only belief I hold. . . . I explain my genius this way—some of us have just lived more times than others. So you see, what you have spent on scholars and traveled around the world to find, I already knew. And I'll tell you something, in thanks for the eats, I'm going to lend that book to you. Why, you don't have to fuss with all these

> Latiny things. . . . [Y]ou don't have to pick the garbage pails of Europe . . . just to find out something that you can get in the mail order for two bits! (Pp. 173–74)

Ford's restatement of Morgan's philosophy exposes the historiography of reincarnation as a fantasy of the supreme and immortal self escaping reality into its own distorted and sterile delusions.

This is also what Houdini, who is the occasion of the book's opening fantasy, reveals. Houdini understands the finality of death and change. He has gone "all over the world accepting all kinds of bondage and escaping. He was roped to a chair. He escaped. He was chained to a ladder. He escaped. . . . He escaped . . . He escaped . . . He escaped. He was buried alive in a grave and could not escape, and had to be rescued. Hurriedly, they dug him out. The earth is too heavy, he said gasping" (pp. 7–8; cf. p. 227). Nonetheless Houdini is obsessed with the idea of resurrection. He forgets the finality of death and attempts, with literalistic absurdity, to resurrect his dead mother. The remembrance stones he leaves on his mother's gravestone begin to form their own "kind of pyramid." His professional life becomes a grotesque effort to realize the same old Egyptian secrets of immortality and resurrection that obsess Morgan and Ford. Desperately he attempts to actualize the possibilities of rebirth. He is "buried and reborn, buried and reborn" (p. 234) in a painful parody of resurrection.

The blast from the firehouse station down the block from the theater in which Houdini is performing, which sends his terrified audience scurrying from his performance, points to the difference between real life and Houdini's maddening inability to "distinguish his life from his tricks" (p. 234). His efforts to reincarnate himself or his mother represent a childish indulgence. The moment Coalhouse Walker's real grievances burst on the scene, Houdini's trivializing escapist magic loses the affection of his audience (p. 239). Indeed, the Jewish Erich Weiss ought to have intuited the terrible inappropriateness of the Egyptian world of pyramids and pharoahs and eternal life to the people of the promised land. The nature of the American obsession with Egypt, apparently so quaint and harmless as to manifest itself in wallpaper and drapes, is revealed in the young boy's fantasy, wherein Sarah is a "Nubian princess now captured for a slave" (p. 178). No wonder an "unseasonably warm breeze" with a "breath of menace" blows the "window curtain in the Egyptian dining room" (p. 213) while Walker voices his complaint against the white fire chief, and the family advises him to walk away from it. Escape from bondage and the acquistion of the promised land were important to American blacks, as they had been to Jews during the escape from slavery in Egypt. Set in the heartland of America's pharaonic fantasy—Pierpont Morgan's Manhattan estate—Booker T. Washington's prayer, "Oh Lord . . . lead my people to the Promised Land. Take them from under the Pharoah's whip" (p. 327) can only reverberate, like the Negro spiritual in *Go Down, Moses*, with painful irony. Enslavement, whether of blacks or of immigrants or of women, has become an American way of life. America plays a dangerous game when it resurrects Egypt in the promised land. The third part of the book, which follows fast and heavy on the heels of Coalhouse Walker's revenge, unmasks the awful fallacies of the reincarnationist philosophy and the dangers of America's infantile indulgence in it.

The painful violence of Coalhouse Walker's revenge shatters the world of fantasy in which the majority of the characters exist. But Walker's raw, unmitigated realism does no more than reinstate the essential confusion between fantasy and history in reverse. Walker demands that white society "restore" what has been taken from him (p. 212). "I want the infamous Fire Chief of the Volunteers turned over to my justice. . . . I want my automobile returned to me in its original condition" (p. 243). But changing the possessors of power does not change the principles of power and its corruption:

> By eight in the morning a truck carrying all the interchangeable parts for a Model T [arrived]. . . . As the crowd watched . . . First Chief Conklin . . . piece by piece dismantled the Ford and made a new Ford. . . . By five in the afternoon, with the sun still blazing in the sky over New York, a shining black Model T Ford with a custom pantasote roof stood at the curb . . . two hours later Coalhouse Walker Jr. came down the stairs . . . with his arms raised. . . . Inside the Library, Father heard the coordinated volley of a firing squad. (Pp. 341–50)

It is as impossible to revise history as it is to escape it:

> Even to someone who had followed the case form the beginning, Coalhouse's strategy of vengeance must have seemed the final proof of his insanity. By what other standard could the craven and miserable Willie Conklin, a bigot so ordinary as to be like all men, become Pierpont Morgan, the most important individual of his time? With eight people dead by Coalhouse's hand, horses destroyed and buildings demolished, with a suburban town still reverberating in its terror, his arrogance knew no bounds. Or is injustice, once suffered, a mirror universe, with laws of logic and principles of reason the opposite of civilization's? (P. 311)

Like the Giant fool (p. 267), who misunderstands the rules of the social game, Coalhouse Walker, in a tradition of black activism anticipated by Faulkner's *Go Down, Moses*, unwittingly reproduces the structure of thought that has disenfranchised and mocked him. Coalhouse Walker's violence fails because, like so much else in the book, it ignores the irreversibility of history. It reflects a private vendetta conceptualized wholly in terms of self. He wants *his* car returned as it was. Walker does not manage to link his vision of personal justice to larger social claims and aspirations. He does not comprehend what will essentially distinguish the black power movement of the sixties. This is the movement toward the celebration of ethnic separateness and difference, which, like Tateh's movies or like the ragtime music Walker plays but doesn't understand, will transform American social structure. Coalhouse Walker is not, as some critics have charged, an anachronistic relocation of the black power movement. He replicates a stage of social thought as yet incapable of dislodging social conservatism in America. Like Father, Ford, Morgan, Houdini, and other characters in the book, Coalhouse Walker is still seeking the shores of self; like the maps and diagrams, baseball and ice-skating and silhouetting that show social conformity, he can imagine only a single game plan, different only in that it puts him, and not someone else, at the center. Reincarnation and the interchangeability of parts are Morgan's and Ford's philosophies of social oppression. Even the ragtime pianist Walker plays their tune.

The artform of ragtime/*Ragtime* is the metamorphic artform of the discarded thing. It is the composition created by the pressure of the outside notes. The shape that Doctorow's historical fiction assumes is not the image of a self controlling its vision of the world and hence controlling the shape that the world assumes. There is neither a strong first-person narrator in the book nor even a stable omniscient narrator whose vision the book reproduces. Rather the book is like a motion picture in which historical figures, like actors, create a presence independent of authorial control. In fiction as in life, characters, themes, and events can seem like duplications of each other, silhouettes temporarily filled in by one set of details or another. However, in time and in history they are their own unique realities, whose independence and individuality must be respected. In Doctorow's world, there is no reincarnation, no interchangeability of parts that is not the effect of the most inhuman form of social authoritarianism. And when the egocentric fantasies of self dictate social reality, when the self's fictions substitute for world history, the result can only be the obliteration of the free, democratic interaction of self and world.

The young boy is the inheritor of the new social history created by the wedding of Mother and Tateh, the conflagrations of Coalhouse Walker's black rebellion, and the social upheavals of World War I. He is the heir of Tateh's cinemagraphic art and of Coalhouse Walker's ragtime. Staring at that same blue fly that stands between the light and a number of American dreamers whom we have met, the boy experiences the moment of visual eclipse that can signal either the death of consciousness or the birth of art. Seeing beyond the fly, he envisions a world that can actually call a world into being. Doctorow's novel does not displace history with fiction. It carefully preserves the pressure of the historical on the fictional. It subordinates authorial consciousness to the world from which it derives and to which it must rejoin itself. Though the story proceeds from the young boy's desperate and largely undirected desire to escape history and enter into the fantasy world of an escape artist, it manages its escape in such a way that it does not sacrifice history or substitute the self for a world of others. It reinterprets history and brings it to bear on the individual imagination.

Like Doctorow, the boy writes a fantasy that becomes a historical romance. This fantasy interrupts the course of his family's history. It controls that history until the final moments of the book when the era of ragtime runs down, leaving its characters in the middle of World War I and its readers back in whatever contemporary moment they are a part of. But there is within that fantasy another story. This is the story of a historical reality that neither Doctorow nor the young boy invents. It is the text's own prophetic, that is, historically informed, awareness of its relationship to historical reality. As history is set into Doctorow's novel as an aspect of its fictional texture, it also frames the novel. The boy's prophecy of World War I not only reveals what will happen at the end of this particular novel, but it also creates a common area of knowledge that reader and text share even before the author creates his fictive world. Readers come to this story knowing what is going to happen. Therefore, they demand that the book fulfill certain criteria of truthfulness.

The prophecy of the assassination of Archduke Ferdinand is first articulated by the young boy to Houdini. It is recalled, tentatively, when Houdini meets the archduke, and it is more emphatically remembered and verified at the end of the story, when Houdini recognizes the truth of the prophecy. It represents an alternate mode of fantasy imagination that is the obverse of a coitus interruptus: "The little boy had followed the magician to the street and now stood at the front of the Pope-Toledo gazing at the distorted macrocephalic image of himself in the shiny brass fitting of the headlight. . . . Warn the Duke, the little boy said. Then he ran off" (p. 11). Whatever the claims of the fantasizing imagination or the desires of the soul searching for immortality, history overtakes us. It is determined by forces that cannot be interrupted just because some imagination or other wills it so. The events of World War I will occur, whatever strategies of escape Houdini or Father or Mother or the young boy, or his surrogate, the author, devise. But history is not the blind, mechanical repetition of experience, grotesquely materializing the self's own worst fantasies. As the young boy stares at the macrocephalic image of himself in the car, in the middle of what is his own fantasy of escape, he recognizes the primary egocentricity and distortion of his imagination. Immediately, instinctively, he corrects the impulse to recreate the material world in his own image. He turns his fiction away from himself and back to the world outside. He will warn the world in what danger it stands when people will see nothing but themselves, whether over eternities of time or within a single historical moment. He thereby releases himself from the self-destructive fates of a line of American heroes. He enters history, which is not fate, imposed from on high, but the collective enterprise of human society. History contextualizes without determining our lives.

Doctorow's subject, like Hawthorne's in "Young Goodman Brown" or "My Kinsman, Major Molineux," is the freedom of the world from the impositions of the imagination—that is, he is concerned with the conditions of a philosophical skepticism, in which undecidability must be entertained as part of a commitment to historical reality. The boy's parting words to Houdini introduce Doctorow's brand of romance fiction. Like any fiction, the boy's fantasy reverses the standard positions of fact and fancy. It interrupts the normal flow of events, but it also interprets that flow, interrupting the interruption. It opens a window in the fiction that sucks the story back into the world outside it, just as the world outside it had provided, in the form of a bluebottle fly, a hole in its own universe out of which the story itself could explode. At the end of the book, the relationship between fact and fiction is reversed. The story returns back through its own openings into the world of history. Hanging upside down over Times Square, Houdini, of whom the young boy is a younger, purer version perceives his disrelation to reality: "He was upside down over Broadway, the year was 1914, and the Archduke Franz Ferdinand was reported to have been assassinated. It was at this moment that an image composed itself in Houdini's mind. The image was of a small boy looking at himself in the shiny brass headlamp of an automobile" (p. 365). In the moment to which this one looks back, a breach is effected on the quotidian world. The imagination (the young boy's and Doctorow's) fills in the space. The factual Houdini is sucked into the fictional world and made to function there as of no more historical validity than the purely fictional Mother, Father, and young boy. In the final moments of the book, however, the process is reversed. Fiction does not create history. Rather history creates fiction. Though the moment recorded in the book may be fictional, the Houdini that hangs at its center is not. Broadway, the year 1914, the assassination of the archduke all exist irrespective of the novel. Houdini, a historical person, in his historical moment, is seen to compose an image in his mind. This image is not of his historical reality but of the fiction of Doctorow's novel. The mirror world of fiction folds back on itself to reveal the historical world that had earlier folded back on itself to expose a fiction at its center. Like Hawthorne, Doctorow does not confound the indeterminacies of history and fiction and their relationship. He traces a pattern of moral consequence whereby history and fiction, each charting its own stories, must nonetheless reveal each other, depicting not so much their interdependency as the moments at which they disengage themselves from, and recommit themselves to, each other. For Doctorow, this is the moral fiction of historical romance.

A NOTE ON JOHN UPDIKE'S *RABBIT IS RICH*

In a series of American fictions I call historical romances, individual texts are illuminated by the larger literary tradition in which they participate. In order to suggest how far the net of the American historical romance tradition can be flung, without sacrificing the intensity of filiation that is important in establishing how any tradition functions, a brief look at one more text is warranted. This text might seem to have nothing to do with the tradition of historical romance, but it enters into this two-hundred-year-long conversation in American fiction in powerful ways.

John Updike's *Rabbit Is Rich*[12] is *not* a historical romance. It is not even historical fiction. This last of three books narrating Rabbit's biography from early manhood to approaching middle age is, however, deeply invested in its historicity. Not only does it draw into itself constant references to the social and political reality outside the novel (as do *Rabbit, Run* and *Rabbit Redux*), but it claims its fictional predecessors as its own history. The trilogy itself constitutes an American social history of the 1950s, 1960s and 1970s.[13] *Rabbit Is Rich* creates fictional history. Like *Ragtime*, however, *Rabbit Is Rich* does not begin with history but with an absent history. This absent history develops into the dangerous, obsessive fantasies that control much of the action of the book. What Harry Angstrom lacks at the beginning of the novel and what he gains at the end is a historical self.

In *Rabbit Is Rich* the appearance of Rabbit's illegitimate daughter, if she is indeed his daughter, that is, if his former mistress did not abort the only product of their sexual union, provides the unwritten text, the imaginary history, into which Rabbit continuously retreats. This imaginary history hovers around the story largely unspoken. Like Father in *Ragtime*, Harry is seeking the shores of himself, though Rabbit, unlike Father, is a hopelessly middle-class landlubber. For Harry, as for Father, the flight into the fantasy of sexual potency and youth delivers him back into a history of arrested psychosexual development not unlike Gatsby's, Jake's, or Ike's. His flight from genuine history echoes the flights of American protagonists from Reuben Bourne to Ike McCaslin.[14]

Like Gatsby, Harry Angstrom attempts to free himself from the implications of time and place by converting history into myth. Myth, Harry believes, bestows power. But the novel reveals that his myths are only childish reproductions of what was never more than a sterile fairy tale of reality:

> Running out of gas, Rabbit Angstrom thinks as he stands behind the summer-dusty windows of the Springer Motors display room watching the traffic go by . . . But they won't catch him . . . because there isn't a piece of junk on the road that gets better mileage than his Toyotas, with lower service costs. Read *Consumer Reports*, April issue. That's all he has to tell the people when they come in. And come in they do, the people out there are getting frantic, they know the great American ride is ending. . . .
>
> He owns Springer Motors. . . . Or rather he co-owns a half-interest. . . . But Rabbit feels as though he owns it all, showing up at the showroom day after day, riding herd on the paperwork and the payroll, swinging in his clean suit in and out of Service and Parts where the men work filmed with oil and look up white-eyed from the bulb-lit engines as in a kind of underworld. (Pp. 3–4)

Approaching middle age, Harry reads images of his own "dwindling energy" (p. 12) in the outside world. Harry, too, is "running out of gas," or so he fears (p. 55). Nothing, therefore, could be more natural than Harry's projection of his own anxieties onto the world. But, like Jake Barnes in *The Sun Also Rises*, Harry cannot read the mirror of his mind. He articulates his perception in such a way as to exempt himself from the conditions that his inner consciousness recognizes. He endows himself with the energy he fears he lacks. Vampirishly, his myth exploits the world's dwindling energy to fuel its own fantasy of omnipotence. For other Americans the great American ride is coming to an end. For Harry it is just beginning. For him the American myth remains intact, because it is and always has been the story of himself. Imagining himself a cowboy of the original American ride, Rabbit sees himself as combining the resilience, independence, and resourcefulness that defy the bleak facts of contemporary sociopolitical reality. Like Ford or Morgan in *Ragtime*, Rabbit believes in the constant resurrection and reincarnation of a superior self. Therefore, he pins old basketball photos of himself on the wall (p. 4).

Like Gatsby, Harry wants to make the world conform to a neo-Platonic conception of self, though Harry's idealism, unlike Gatsby's, has acceded totally to the materialism of a Tom Buchanan. He therefore creates the world in his own image and acts out all of the roles by himself. For Harry, the ideal child, who would prove his virility and insure his immortality without threatening to disrupt the perfect solipsism of his world, is also the ideal wife, who would satisfy and supplement his sexual authority. Harry accepts neither his wife, Janice, nor his son, Nelson, as his real family. Neither one of them perfectly enough reflects him. Neither one can insure his immortality and potency. Each one insists on a psychological and physical separateness that threatens the perfect equilibrium of his Gatsby-like incarnation of self and the fantasy world in which that self exists.

Harry thus retreats into the fantasy of the illegitimate daughter who is also the perfect lover. Simultaneously realizing all of his desires, this fantasy wholly expresses Harry's gigantic self-love without imposing any of the moral or human considerations of real life. Since his daughter is "illegitimate," she does not threaten him with legal patrimony. Because there is even a question as to whether she is his daughter, she does not threaten him with the responsibilities of biological inheritance. And since she is only theoretically his lover (and his daughter), she protects him from the implications of incest of which self-love (as Faulkner suggests and as Harry must unconsciously understand) is one variety. She ensures an unbroken simultaneity between self and world that biology and history threaten to disturb.

In *Ragtime*, Houdini enters the text at the moment that the young boy has articulated his denial of the world. In *Rabbit Is Rich*, Harry's illegitimate daughter, if she is his daughter, intrudes on the story just after Rabbit has defined the book's major subjects as "energy" and "escape" and has confronted his own great fear: the "blanks," the "patches of burnt-out gray cells where there used to be lust and keen dreaming and wide-eyed dread" (p. 13). The car that "swings in" from "the world of asphalt beyond" into the "muted aquarium air" of his "sunken ship" of a showroom (p. 13) pierces Harry's consciousness of the dead weight of a barren world and provides the stuff on which his imaginative life broods. The wateriness of the image conjures the recesses of an explicitly sexual consciousness. The girl appears "milky-pale and bare-legged and blinking in the sunshine. . . . A little touch of the hooker about her looks. The way her soft body wants to spill from these small clothes, the faded denim shorts and purple Paisley halter" (pp. 13–14). She is a sexual fantasy (later Harry will masturbate while thinking about his daughter's "milky serene disposition" [p. 191]). She causes a "buried bell" to ring in Harry's memory (or is it in his desire?), as he "imagines he feels an unwitting swimming of her spirit upward toward his" (p. 14). "Those chunky eyesockets [remind] him of somebody" (p. 17). That somebody is not only the girl's mother, Ruth, who is herself associated with a more virile period in Rabbit's life, but also Harry himself. She reminds him of his own sexual vitality, which he has begun to forget. She is "a mystery arrived at this time of his own numb life, death taking his measure with the invisible tapping of that neighborhood hammer" (p. 47). In the "mirror" of the "innocent blue in her eyes," he sees "his" own eyes (pp. 22–23). He sees himself potent, whole, intact—experiencing sexual ecstasy. Like Father, Harry exists in the moment after coitus interruptus. Harry vaguely senses that his problem has something to do with sex. He doesn't, however, realize that the only place to complete the sexual act is in the real world, and that sex in the real world means family, children and the responsibilities of history. Until he can reunite his fantasy with his absent history, Rabbit will know no sexual rest. He will find no genuine completion of self.

But Harry resists history. "When you think about the dead," he explains at the beginning of the book, "you got to be grateful. . . . The great thing about the dead, they make space" (pp. 4–5). The problem with the living, especially your own seed, is that they take up room. There is "not enough room in the world," Harry complains. "People came north from the sun belt in Egypt and lived in heated houses and now the heat is being used up, just the oil for the showroom and offices and garage has doubled since '74 when he first saw the Springer Motors books and will double in the next year or two again" (p. 226). To live in history, in time, is to relinquish space, to give up heat. And the source of the problem is the law of nature, the biology of sexuality. "Seed, so disgustingly much of it, Nature [is] such a cruel smotherer" (p. 47). "Seed that goes into the ground invisible and if it takes hold cannot be stopped, it fulfills the shape it was programmed for, its destiny, sure as our death, and shapely" (p. 23; cf. p. 86). "There's no getting away; our sins, our seed, coil back" (p. 33). Unless the seed can be prevented from growing, or, better still, be transplanted to a world where self and other do not occupy mutually exclusive places, biology and history must signal death and the extinction of self.

Updike contemplates the tension between fathers and sons, which concerns Hawthorne as well. He recognizes all too vividly that Nelson's aggression against his father's car (pp. 105–107) and his father's business (pp. 164–70) is aggression against his father. Reciprocally, Harry's reactions in both of the above incidents provide occasions for Harry to act out his own hostilities toward his son. Harry's relationship to Nelson painfully dramatizes the unspeakable horrors of the fantasy of infanticide, which assumes grotesque proportions in the Rabbit trilogy because of the actual (albeit accidental) death of Harry's daughter at her mother's hands. The specter of infanticide is reinforced by the death of the daughter-substitute Jill in *Rabbit, Redux*, a death that Nelson blames on his father. But like Hawthorne and Fitzgerald, Updike focuses the problem of family and mortality in terms of a conflict between the self-referential imagination and the demands of biology and history. In Updike's novel, Harry struggles to preserve both his place in his home, family, and business and his self-emplacement within a fantasy of omnipotence, virility, and immortality.

Harry's attempt to escape history by rewriting or transposing or relocating it fails. The illegitimate daughter Annabelle cannot legitimately convey Harry back into the historical world from which his fantasy has broken loose. This is true not simply because of some legalistic or moral or biological definition of illegitimacy, but rather because the fantasy of the illegitimate child exists on a different ontological plane. Annabelle is illegitimate not only as a child and lover but also as an extension of self into the world. She is fantasy, not history. Therefore, to bring her into the family discussion, is as Janice suggests, "disgusting . . . dis*gust*ing" (p. 72). Harry wisely promises to "never mention it again." Nonetheless "this ghost of his alone" (p. 72) continues to haunt his vision throughout the novel.

Harry's illegitimate daughter does not finally incarnate his vital fertility, either biological or imaginative. Instead, she images or projects the deadening impotence of a denied sexuality. In order to reenter history and gain his manhood, Harry must realize this. If at the beginning of the novel Rabbit's fantasy overwhelms his reality, swinging in from a place beyond memory into his mythic kingdom of self, by the end of the book Rabbit reverses direction and drives his mythic identity directly into his fantasy vision. Harry deliberately invades the "lie" that characterizes his reality (p. 435). He confronts, once and for all, the relationship between his fantasy and his reality.

Many elements crowd the opening passage, producing the mythic dimensions of Harry's fantasy. At the end, a similar complex of images produces a larger-than-life quality to Harry's odyssey of inward pilgrimage.[15] Allusions to the past, like the "spray-painted SKEETER LIVES," and the fact that he is going to visit his former mistress, associate the drive most fundamentally with a kind of remembering. The "blacks [that] stared out from under the neon signs, JIMBO'S *Friendly* LOUNGE and LIVE ENTERTAINMENT and ADULT ADULT ADULT, as he slid by in virgin blue grapeskin" (p. 435), suggest that this remembering has to do with Harry's adolescent sexual imagination. The car, which is so explicitly phallic that it has its own foreskin/grapeskin, symbolizes Harry's infantile sexuality. Sliding by Rabbit is protected from sexual contact. He is kept prophylactically safe and pure.[16]

The oddly biblical references to "Jesus," the "Savior," and to "Galilee" (p. 435), toward which he is heading, imply that this purity is pseudo-religious. As in *Gatsby*, they intimate the problems of a falsely conceived neo-Platonic journey. Even his former mistress's name hints at the complexities of the moment. Ruth is one in the line of descent leading, through a number of illegitimate sexual alliances (Ruth and Boaz, Reuben and Tamar, David and Bathsheba) to the birth of Christ. The trip to salvation knows no simple route. And yet, as Hemingway suggests in *The Sun Also Rises*, out of mistaken turns and detours, salvation can be achieved.

Harry's interview with Ruth achieves whatever measure of salvation human beings can achieve in this world. Once Rabbit has pushed through from the world of reality into the "loving void" of his fantasies, once he no longer avoids confronting his fantasy as fantasy and allows himself to die to the living reality that his fantasy denies, Rabbit discovers both the hellish underside of fantasy, which fantasy carefully conceals, and its nurturing potential. "As with dying there is a moment that must be pushed through, a slice of time more transparent than plate glass; it is in front of him and he takes the step, drawing heart from that loving void" (p. 437). The explicitly sexual language here brings forward the repressed motives of his car ride. Harry is searching for some way to retrieve his lost sexuality, to return to the mature love his fantasizing has sacrificed. The encounter with Ruth brings him face to face with the grotesqueness of his fantasy of the daughter-lover. Only by symbolically concluding his relationship with Ruth, bringing to sexual climax their suspended relationship, can Rabbit regain his manhood and free himself of his infantile sexual delusions. Rabbit must learn that sexual relations are just that: *relations*. They have to do with recognizing and accepting the other.

In the first scene of the novel Rabbit thinks he recognizes in the eyes of his illegitimate daughter a vital and virile image of himself. Here, in one of the final moments of the book, "Rabbit recognizes, buried under the wrinkles and fat . . . those known eyes [of his former mistress] blazing out alive" (p. 438). These eyes proudly assert Ruth's vitality, not Harry's. They defy his claims of relatedness to her and her daughter. The scene turns on the horror of recognizing how the claims and needs of the self depend on crediting the otherness of others. "Stuck on yourself from cradle to grave," Ruth accuses Harry, "you're nothing but me, me and gimme, gimme" (pp. 441, 442). Like Father, Harry is still seeking the shores of self. He is stuck on himself from cradle to grave, asserting himself by absorbing everything into himself. "Who said you could look at those?" (p. 441), Ruth demands of Harry, recognizing, as he examines the family photos, that Harry is not willing simply to admire other people and their possessions. Harry, Ruth knows, covets all of life's images and experiences. The scene recalls an earlier moment in the book when, sneaking a glance at his friends' pornographic photos of themselves, Harry so possesses them that he brings himself to orgasm in their bedroom. Ruth is right to insist that this is her family: "Mine and not yours," she says (p. 441). Harry doesn't agree: "The girl," he says. "She's mine. She's the baby you said you couldn't stand to have the abortion for. . . . Tell me about our girl" (pp. 442–43).

The text never tells us whether Ruth is lying when she claims Annabelle is not Harry's daughter. But it doesn't really matter. Harry discovers at Ruth's that to possess the world's images and to have them confirm one's own being in the world one must assume responsibility for those images. This means assuming responsibility, Hawthorne- and Faulkner-style, both for what he has done and what he has not done, what he has fashioned in his own image and what has assumed a life of its own, independent of him. The moment Harry offers Ruth "deferred payments" (p. 447) for the child, he acknowledges his responsibilities to Ruth, whether her daughter is his or not. When Ruth refuses those payments, she releases Harry from his debt. His "surge of relief" climaxes the scene (p. 447). The frustration induced by the coitus interruptus that has been his life is dissipated. Both he and Ruth are released back into life, out of the paralyzing consequence of indecision and incompletion: "In his surge of relief he stands. She stands too, and having risen together their ghosts feel their inflated flesh fall away" (p. 447). Spiritual ascension climaxes unfulfilled sexual desires. The ghosts of the past have achieved their consummation. In the process, Harry and Ruth give birth to something (their inflated flesh falls away). With Ruth's help, Harry's descent into the hellish underside of his fantasy vision bears him back, not to the paradise that his fantasy of a daughter-lover had promised to provide him, but to the purgatory of real wives and real children that is his life in this world.

Harry experiences one final moment of restless doubt: he "pops a Life Saver into his mouth and wonders if he should have called her bluff on the birth certificates. Or suppose Frank had had another wife, and Scott was his child by that marriage? If the girl was as young as Ruth said, wouldn't she still be in high school?" (p. 450). But Harry must accept his loss. He acknowledges what he cannot possess and cannot be: "But no. Let go. God has never wanted him to have a daughter" (p. 450). Having said no, Harry achieves what he has desired, what he has been waiting for from the beginning. For if God never wanted Harry to have a daughter, either his and Janice's or his and Ruth's, He does seem to have wanted him to have a granddaughter:

As Harry resettles himself in one of his silvery-pink wing chairs in front of the game, he can hear the old lady clumping on her painful legs directly above his head, inspecting, searching out the room where she might some day have to come and stay. He assumes Pru is with them, but the footsteps mingling on the ceiling are not that many, and Teresa comes softly down the one step into his den and deposits into his lap what he has been waiting for. Oblong cocooned little visitor, the baby shows her profile blindly in the shuddering flashes of color jerking from the Sony, the tiny stitchless seam of the closed eyelid aslant, lips bubbled forward beneath the whorled nose as if in delicate disdain, she knows she's good. You can feel in the curve of the cranium she's feminine, that shows from the first day. Through all this she has pushed to be here, in his lap, his hands, a real presence hardly weighing anything but alive. Fortune's hostage, heart's desire, a granddaughter. His. Another nail in his coffin. His. (Pp. 466–67)

Harry finally achieves the place, the home and the patrimony, from which he felt himself excluded and that he sought throughout his dislocated and fantastic odyssey. Fantasy is not excluded from this final portrait. Harry is enveloped by silvery pink wings as illusive and evasive as the fairy wings that sustain Gatsby's visions. Pru's descent into Harry's den echoes an undefined ominousness that circulates throughout the book. But the baby's presence, though "hardly . . . anything," is real. The baby verifies Harry's presence as well, not by reflecting or mirroring him, as he wanted his wife and son and illegitimate daughter to do, but by setting herself in opposition to him. The baby has her own strength. "She has pushed to be here." Not only does her being not include his, but she disdains and denies him. She is decidedly "feminine." "She knows she's good." But the baby is finally his. This is so, if for no other reason than that she is his son's daughter. She is the hostage of genetic fortunes that cannot be willed or fantasized away. It is no accident that Harry views her through "the shuddering flashes of color jerking" from the Son(y). Even more importantly, however, she is his because he chooses to acknowledge her as his. The second "His" in the passage above transforms possession into acknowledgment. She is his because she is "a real presence hardly weighing anything but alive . . . His." But she is his also because, though she signals his death as well as his life ("Another nail in his coffin. His"), Harry chooses to call her his. Harry's acceptance transforms possession by acknowledging the simultaneous impossibilities of total possession, on the one hand, and of not possessing at all, on the other. Possession is itself an impossible fiction. But it is a fiction without which the historical life cannot continue. The "real presence hardly weighing anything but alive" turns fantasy back onto and then into historicity. She is a real presence, a kind of miracle of transubstantiation. Enveloped in fairy wings, holding this visitor cocooned in mystery, her eyes closed and still not quite conscious of the world, Harry, like the baby, pushes through, out of the world of fantasy into history.

As in the long tradition of historical romances in which Updike's novel takes its place, historical consciousness means acknowledging the past and taking one's place in a world created by that past. Reality is the barest of presences. In many ways it is more like fantasy than fact, indistinguishable from all other fantasies. But reality isn't a fantasy. It is the only real presence human beings ever know. The ethical realism of American historical romance is to accept the world as belonging both to oneself and to others. Thus, faithful skeptics all, we commit ourselves to the common enterprise of history and romance.

Notes

Chapter 1

1 James Fenimore Cooper, *The Spy: A Tale of the Neutral Ground*, ed. James H. Pickering (Schenectady, N.Y.: New College and University Press, 1971), p. 7. All references to the novel are to this edition and appear in parentheses in the chapter.

2 Ibid., p. 24.

3 W. H. Gardiner, "Review in *North American Review*, July 1822," in *Fenimore Cooper: The Critical Heritage*, eds. George Dekker and John P. McWilliams (London: Routledge and Kegan Paul, 1973), p. 58. Michael Davitt Bell, *The Development of American Romance: The Sacrifice of Relation* (Chicago: Univ. of Chicago Press, 1980), pp. 16–22, surveys the early critical doubts as to America's suitability as a fictional landscape.

4 In "Fictions of Factual Representation," *The Literature of Fact: Selected Papers from the English Institute*, ed. Angus Fletcher (New York: Columbia Univ. Press, 1976), pp. 21–44, Hayden White discusses the separation of history from fiction in the nineteenth century. Mark A. Weinstein, "The Creative Imagination in Fiction and History," *Genre* 9 (1976):263–77 provides a good survey of the history of the relationship between fact and fiction from Scott to the present. See also David Levin, *History as Romantic Art: Bancroft, Prescott, Motley, and Parkman* (New York: Harcourt, Brace, and World, 1959). The list of criticism on historical fiction is lengthy. The major studies are presented during the course of this book.

5 In "Concepts of the Romance in Hawthorne's America," *Nineteenth-Century Fiction* 38 (1984):426–43, Nina Baym argues persuasively that the terms *romance* and *novel* were used almost interchangeably, and that where differences were noted between the two forms, no consistent pattern of differentiation can be detected. Hawthorne, of course, does insist on a difference, and Baym discusses this on pp. 438–43. Michael Davitt Bell's discussion of many of the same issues dwells on the distrust of fiction/romance (*Development of American Romance*, esp. pp. 7–36).

6 Wolfgang Iser, *The Implied Reader: Patterns of Communication in Prose Fiction from Bunyan to Beckett* (Baltimore: Johns Hopkins Univ. Press, 1974), pp. 82–83; and Bell, *Development of American Romance*, p. 15. See also Murray Krieger, "Fiction, History, and Empirical Reality," *Critical Inquiry* 1 (1975):335–60. In *Visionary Compacts: American Renaissance Writings in Cultural Context* (Madison: Univ. of Wisconsin Press, 1987), Donald Pease discusses the reconciliation between the romantic and the historical in somewhat different terms.

7 Writes John P. McWilliams, "Astute contemporaries recognized that the main thrust of Cooper's writings had been his desire to serve as spokesman and guardian for the unformed republic. The *Memorial of James Fenimore Cooper* reveals that Cooper was valued chiefly as an historian of American culture and character, a graphic and passionate chronicler of the American frontier, not as a romancer nor as a social critic, but as a combination of the two. In the letters and speeches preserved in the *Memorial*, Bancroft, Prescott, R. H. Dana, Parkman, and Bryant all insist upon Cooper's importance as a national historian in fiction. Prescott's evaluation is representative: 'surely no one has succeeded like Cooper in the por-

traiture of American character, taken in its broadest sense, of the civilized and the uncivilized man, or has given such glowing and eminently faithful pictures of the American scenery. His writings are instinct with the spirit of nationality, shown not less in those devoted to sober fact than in the sportive inventions of his inexhaustible fancy' " (*Political Justice in a Republic: James Fenimore Cooper's America* [Berkeley: Univ. of California Press, 1972], p. 3). See also Levin, *History as Romantic Art*.

8 Morris Dickstein has described a decidedly alternative line in the development of the novel that favors the fanciful flights of the popular imagination over the more grounded, realistic uses of imagination that have come to represent the major canon ("Popular Fiction and Critical Values: The Novel as a Challenge to Literary History," in *Reconstructing American Literary History*, ed. Sacvan Bercovitch [Cambridge, Mass.: Harvard Univ. Press, 1986], pp. 29–66).

9 Iser, *Implied Reader*, pp. 81–100. Iser quotes Scott on p. 84. See also George Lukács, *The Historical Novel*, trans. Hannah and Stanley Mitchell (1937); reprint, London: Merlin Press, 1962), p. 42, and Weinstein, "Creative Imagination."

10 See "The Custom-House," *The Scarlet Letter*, in *The Centenary Edition of the Works of Nathaniel Hawthorne*, ed. William Charvat et al., 14 vols. (Columbus: Ohio State Univ. Press, 1962–80), 1:36.

11 Barbara Foley, *Telling the Truth: The Theory and Practice of Documentary Fiction* (Ithaca: Cornell Univ. Press, 1986), p. 153. For a similar view, see Robert Clark, *History, Ideology and Myth in American Fiction, 1823–52* (London: Macmillan, 1984), esp. pp. 16–19.

12 Myra Jehlen, *American Incarnation: The Individual, the Nation, and the Continent* (Cambridge: Harvard Univ. Press, 1986), discusses the special literalness of the American relationship to the land; as do Annette Kolodny, *The Lay of the Land: Metaphor as Experience and History in American Life and Letters* (Chapel Hill: Univ. of North Carolina Press, 1975), and Sharon Cameron, *The Corporeal Self: Allegories of the Body in Melville and Hawthorne* (Baltimore: Johns Hopkins Univ. Press, 1981), pp. 54–58.

13 See Hayden White, *Metahistory: The Historical Imagination in Nineteenth-Century Europe* (Baltimore: Johns Hopkins Univ. Press, 1973); Krieger, "Fiction, History, and Empirical Reality"; Mas'ud Zavarzadeh, *The Mythopoeic Reality: The Postwar American Nonfiction Novel* (Urbana: Univ. of Illinois Press, 1976); Robert Scholes, *Structural Fabulations: An Essay on the Fiction of the Future* (Notre Dame, Ind.: Univ. of Notre Dame Press, 1975); Jerome Klinkowitz, *The Self-Apparent Word: Fiction as Language/Language as Fiction* (Carbondale: Southern Illinois Univ. Press, 1984); John Hollowell, *Fact and Fiction: The New Journalism and the Nonfiction Novel* (Chapel Hill: Univ. of North Carolina Press, 1977); and John Hellman, *Fables of Fact: The New Journalism as New Fiction* (Urbana: Univ. of Illinois Press, 1981).

14 See Foley, *Telling the Truth*; Clark, *History, Ideology and Myth in American Fiction*; Bell, *Development of American Romance*, and Bell, "Arts of Deception: Hawthorne, 'Romance,' and *The Scarlet Letter*" in *New Essays on The Scarlet Letter*, ed. Michael J. Colacurcio (Cambridge: Cambridge Univ. Press, 1985), pp. 29–56. Related to these claims is Philip Fisher's intriguing study, *Hard Facts: Setting and Form in the American Novel* (New York: Oxford Univ. Press, 1985), in which he argues that certain popular novels in the nineteenth century did the "cultural work" of stabilizing and incorporating "nearly ungraspable or widely various states of moral or representational or perceptual experience" (pp. 3–5). The historical romances, I believe, performed cultural work of a similar variety. But they make explicit the process of incorporation Fisher describes.

15 See my own work on Poe in "Poe's Gothic Idea: The Cosmic Geniture of Horror," *Essays in Literature* 3 (1976):73–85.

16 "An Approach Through History," in *Towards a Poetics of Fiction*, ed. Mark Spilka (Bloomington: Indiana Univ. Press, 1977), p. 24.

17 Harry B. Henderson, III, *Versions of the Past: The Historical Imagination in American Fiction* (New York: Oxford Univ. Press, 1974), pp. 54–56.

18 This observation is developed powerfully in *The Crucible*, by Arthur Miller. See my essay

"History and Other Spectres in Arthur Miller's *The Crucible*," *Modern Drama* 28 (1985): 535–52.

19 The relationship between secrecy and literary meaning has, of course, been most deftly and extensively treated by Frank Kermode in *The Genesis of Secrecy: On the Interpretation of Narrative* (Cambridge, Mass.: Harvard Univ. Press, 1979).

20 James Pickering details the extent of Cooper's knowledge of the neutral ground in his edition of the text, pp. 14–20.

21 According to Eric Partridges's *Dictionary of Slang and Unconventional English*, ed. Paul Beale (London: Routledge and Kegan Paul, 1984), it is not clear when the use of the word *fanny* as a slang expression for bottom came into common usage in English. It is in use from "ca. 1860" but "perhaps much earlier." What commentators do agree on is that it derives from the sexy females of eighteenth-century British fiction who are called Fanny. That allusion, I think, is sufficient to warrant our reading Fanny's name as something of a sexual joke.

Chapter 2

1 Rosemary M. Laughlin, "Godliness and the American Dream in Winesburg, Ohio," *Twentieth-Century Literature* 13 (1967):97–103, notes the recurrence of the image in all five works. Alan Axelrod, *Charles Brockden Brown: An American Tale* (Austin: Univ. of Texas Press, 1983), pp. 61–64, has traced the source of the Abraham-Isaac motif in *Wieland* to a German epic that appeared in America in 1778 as *The Trial of Abraham*. Axelrod argues that the episode relates to Brown's concern about the impact of the wilderness on American religion and culture. A discussion of the Abraham-Isaac motif in Faulkner that is relevant to our discussion generally is John T. Irwin, *Doubling and Incest/Repetition and Revenge: A Speculative Reading of Faulkner* (Baltimore: Johns Hopkins Univ. Press, 1975), pp. 125–35, who discusses the sacrifice of the son in terms of the father's aggression against his own father.

2 References to *The Prairie: A Tale* are to the Riverside Press edition (Cambridge, 1872) and appear in parentheses in the text.

3 In "Temple in the Promised Land: Old Testament Parallels in Cooper's *The Pioneers*," *American Literature* 57 (1985): 68–78, Daryl E. Jones discusses America's failed biblical promise. Compare with Eric J. Sundquist's discussion of Cooper's suspicions about the American Eden in *Home as Found: Authority and Genealogy in Nineteenth-Century American Literature* (Baltimore: Johns Hopkins Univ. Press, 1979). Barton Levi St. Armand discusses *The Spy* in terms of the Old Law and the New in "Harvey Birch as the Wandering Jew: Literary Calvinism in James Fenimore Cooper's *The Spy*," *American Literature* 50 (1978): 348–68.

4 All references to *Wieland* are to the Doubleday edition (New York, 1962) and appear in parentheses in the text.

5 David Lee Clark, *Charles Brockden Brown: Pioneer Voice of America* (Durham, N.C.: Duke Univ. Press, 1952), pp. 168–69, argues the first case. Larzar Ziff, "A Reading of *Wieland*," *PMLA* 77 (1962): 51–57 argues the second. For readings compatible with Clark's, see Bernard Rosenthal, "The Voices of *Wieland*," in *Critical Essays on Charles Brockden Brown*, ed. Bernard Rosenthal (Boston: G. K. Hall, 1981), pp. 104–25, who suggests that the book is an argument against "the danger of morality based on revealed religion" (p. 104); Harry R. Warfel, *Charles Brockden Brown: American Gothic Novelist* (Gainesville: Univ. of Florida Press, 1949); and Alan Axelrod, *Charles Brockden Brown*, pp. 65–69. For a reading supportive of Ziff's see Michael T. Gilmore, "Calvinism and Gothicism: The Example of Brown's *Wieland*," *Studies in the Novel* 9 (1977):107–18. Emory Elliot treads a middle position in *Revolutionary Writers: Literature and Authority in the New Republic, 1725–1810* (Oxford: Oxford Univ. Press, 1982), pp. 228–33.

6 "The Black Cat," in *The Collected Works of Edgar Allan Poe: Tales and Sketches, 1843–1849*, ed. Thomas Ollive Mabbott (Cambridge: Harvard Univ. Press, 1978), pp. 849–50.

7 Michael Davitt Bell, *The Development of American Romance: The Sacrifice of Relation* (Chicago: Univ. of Chicago Press, 1980), p. 51.

8 Nina Baym, "A Minority Reading of *Wieland*," *Critical Essays*, ed. Rosenthal, pp. 95–99.

9 On the critical assessment of Brown's attack on reason see Donald Ringe, *Charles Brockden Brown* (New York: Twayne, 1966). See also Ziff, "A Reading of *Wieland*."

10 Michael T. Gilmore has discussed at length the resonances of the biblical fall in *Wieland* in his essay on "Calvinism and Gothicism." On the Adamic myth of the American, see R. W. B. Lewis, *The American Adam: Innocence, Tragedy and Tradition in the Nineteenth Century* (Chicago: Univ. of Chicago Press, 1955). See also David W. Noble, *The Eternal Adam and the New World Garden: The Central Myth in the American Novel since 1830* (New York: George Braziller, 1968).

11 Edmund Morgan, *Visible Saints: The History of a Puritan Idea* (Ithaca: Cornell Univ. Press, 1963). See also Sacvan Bercovitch, *The Puritan Origins of the American Self* (New Haven: Yale Univ. Press, 1975), and Michael J. Colacurcio, *The Province of Piety: Moral History in Hawthorne's Early Tales* (Cambridge: Harvard Univ. Press, 1984), pp. 283–313 (on "Young Goodman Brown").

12 Alan Axelrod, *Charles Brockden Brown*, pp. 66–75, traces a different, non-Puritan religious lineage for Wieland through Quakerism and Enthusiasm. I believe Brown was interested in the origins of eighteenth-century American religious experience, such as the Great Awakening, in Puritan history. For Brown, as for Hawthorne, Quakerism exposed certain unresolved contradictions within Puritanism itself. See Michael Colacurcio's reading of Hawthorne's "Gentle Boy" in *Province of Piety*, pp. 160–201.

13 Barbara Kiefer Lewalski, "Typological Symbolism and the 'Progress of the Soul' in Seventeenth-Century Literature," in *Literary Uses of Typology from the Late Middle Ages to the Present*, ed. Earl Miner (Princeton: Princeton Univ. Press, 1977), pp.79–114.

14 Ann Kibbey, *The Interpretation of Material Shapes in Puritanism: A Study of Rhetoric, Prejudice, and Violence* (Cambridge: Cambridge Univ. Press, 1986), pp. 2, 7. Kibbey's discussion provides a theological context in which to understand some of Sharon Cameron's arguments about the corporeality of certain American protagonists in *The Corporeal Self: Allegories of the Body in Melville and Hawthorne* (Baltimore: Johns Hopkins Univ. Press, 1981). Cameron identifies Wieland briefly as one of those American corporeal selves who cannot distinguish between inner and outer (pp. 8–9). Kibbey's work also informs Myra Jehlen's thesis concerning incarnational tendencies within American imagination generally (*American Incarnation: The Individual, the Nation, and the Continent* [Cambridge: Harvard Univ. Press, 1986]).

15 Michael T. Gilmore, *The Middle Way: Puritanism and Ideology in American Romantic Fiction* (New Brunswick, N.J.: Rutgers Univ. Press, 1977).

16 See Colacurcio's discussion of "Young Goodman Brown" in *Province of Piety*, pp. 283–313.

17 See my essay on Miller's play, "History and Other Spectres in Arthur Miller's *The Crucible*," *Modern Drama* 28 (1985):535–52.

18 Bernard Rosenthal, "The Voices of *Wieland*," locates some of the qualities of the religious beliefs of Wieland, Sr., that I am calling Puritan. Rosenthal concludes that Brown "was writing a polemic novel—regarding *all* varieties of religious experience" (p. 108).

19 Richard Reinitz, "The Separatist Background of Roger Williams' Argument for Religious Toleration" in *Typology and Early American Literature*, ed. Sacvan Bercovitch (Amherst: Univ. of Massachusetts Press, 1972), p. 109; and Perry Miller, *Roger Williams: His Contribution to the American Tradition* (New York: Atheneum, 1966), p. 151. On Williams as a separatist seeking the wholly pure church, see also *The Puritans: A Sourcebook of Their Writings*, ed. Perry Miller and Thomas H. Johnson, 2 vols. (New York: Harper and Row, 1963), 1:214–15

20 Williams, "The Bloudy Tenant Yet more Bloudy," quoted in Bercovitch, "Typology in Puritan New England: The Williams-Cotton Controversy," *American Quarterly* 19 (1967):177. See also Bercovitch's discussion of Williams in *Puritan Origins of the American Self*, pp. 109–10.

21 In "The Separatist Background of Roger Williams' Argument for Religious Toleration," Richard

Reinitz links Williams' separatism and his use of typology (*Typology and Early American Literature*, ed. Bercovitch, pp. 107–37).

22 On the pervasive influence of Puritanism during this period, see Alan Heimert, *Religion and the American Mind from the Great Awakening to the Revolution* (Cambridge: Harvard Univ. Press, 1968), whose ideas are discussed and amplified in Mason I. Lowance, Jr., "Typology and Millennial Eschatology in Early New England," in *Literary Uses of Typology*, ed. Miner, pp. 228–73.

23 On Brown's background in Locke, see Arthur Kimball, *Rational Fictions: A Study of Charles Brockden Brown* (McMinnville, Ore.: Linnfield Research Institute, 1968). See also Mason I. Lowance, Jr., " 'Images or Shadows of Divine Things' in the Thought of Jonathan Edwards" in *Typology and Early American Literature*, ed. Bercovitch, pp. 223–38.

24 See John F. Lynen, "Benjamin Franklin and the Choice of a Single Point of View," in *The American Puritan Imagination: Essays in Revaluation*, ed. Sacvan Bercovitch (Cambridge: Cambridge Univ. Press, 1974), pp. 173–95; Perry Miller, "From Edwards to Emerson," *Errand into the Wilderness* (New York: Harper and Row, 1956), pp. 184–203; and Mason I. Lowance, Jr., "From Edwards to Emerson and Thoreau," in *The Language of Canaan: Metaphor and Symbol in New England from the Puritans to the Transcendentalists* (Cambridge, Mass.: Harvard Univ. Press, 1980), pp. 277–95.

25 In *The Law of the Heart: Individualism and the Modern Self in American Literature* (Austin: Univ. of Texas Press, 1979), Sam B. Girgus describes what he calls a "perverted self" which is a painfully distorted version of Quentin Anderson's "imperial self." See Anderson's *The Imperial Self: An Essay in American Literary and Cultural History* (New York: Alfred A. Knopf, 1971). I will return to these concepts in my discussion of *The Great Gatsby*.

26 "Young Goodman Brown," in *The Centenary Edition of the Works of Nathaniel Hawthorne*, ed. William Charvat et al., 14 vols. (Columbus: Ohio State Univ. Press, 1962–80), 10:77, where Brown speaks of his "good works, to boot."

27 On the historical incident on which Brown bases Wieland's actions, see Axelrod, *Charles Brockden Brown*, pp. 53–59. John Greenleaf Whittier discusses this incident in an essay which appeared in 1848, reprinted in *Critical Essays*, ed. Rosenthal, pp. 65–67.

Chapter 3

1 Karl Keller, "Alephs, Zahirs, and the Triumph of Ambiguity," in *Literary Uses of Typology from the Middle Ages to the Present*, ed. Earl Miner (Princeton: Princeton Univ. Press, 1977), pp. 274–314. Keller argues that, while some nineteenth-century American authors, like Emerson and Thoreau, positively reinvest typological structures in their works, substituting the oversoul for God, other writers, like Hawthorne, Melville, and Dickinson, subvert the structure of typological thought and develop a mode of ambiguity instead.

2 Perry Miller, "Introduction," *The Puritans: A Sourcebook of Their Writings*, ed. Perry Miller and Thomas H. Johnson, 2 vols. (New York: Harper and Row, 1963), 1:41–55 (the phrase appears on p. 44); Charles Feidelson, Jr., *Symbolism and American Literature* (Chicago: Univ. of Chicago Press, 1953), pp. 77–94; Sacvan Bercovitch, *The Puritan Origins of the American Self* (New Haven: Yale Univ. Press, 1975).

3 Bercovitch, "Typology in Puritan New England: The Williams-Cotton Controversy Reassessed," *American Quarterly* 19 (1967): 181–82; and *Puritan Origins*, pp. 112–13. See also Mason I. Lowance, Jr., *The Language of Canaan: Metaphor and Symbol in New England from the Puritans to the Transcendentalists* (Cambridge, Mass.: Harvard Univ. Press, 1980).

4 Mather is quoted in Ursula Brumm, *American Thought and Religious Typology* (New Brunswick, N.J.: Rutgers Univ. Press, 1970), p. 43. The passage is from his *Figures or Types of the Old Testament* (1673). In *Radical Discontinuities: American Romanticism and Christian Consciousness* (Rutherford, N.J.: Fairleigh Dickinson Univ. Press, 1983), pp. 20–21, Harold P. Simonson discusses the evolution of historical typology. See also the essays reprinted in two major collec-

tions on typology: Sacvan Bercovitch's *Typology and Early American Literature* (Amherst: Univ. of Massachusetts Press, 1972), and Earl Miner's *Literary Uses of Typology*. See also Lowance, *Language of Canaan*, chaps. 1, 2. The discussion of the development of the typological tradition perhaps most relevant to our purposes is in Erich Auerbach's seminal essay "Figura," in *Scenes from the Drama of European Literature* (Minneapolis: Univ. of Minnesota Press, 1984), pp. 19–43.

5 Edmund Morgan, *Visible Saints: The History of a Puritan Idea* (Ithaca: Cornell Univ. Press, 1963). See also Lowance, *Language of Canaan*.

6 Not all literary works in the American tradition that use the Abraham-Isaac motif are akedian romances. Mary E. Wilkins Freemans' *Pembroke* (New York: Harper and Bros., 1894) uses the figure in relation to a religiously fanatical mother who sacrifices her son, but it is not, I think, an akedian romance. Another story that might, however, be included in the list of akedian romances is Hawthorne's "The Gentle Boy," which also involves the sacrifice of a son, by no less than two sets of parents. Also O'Connor's *The Violent Bear It Away*.

7 *The Centenary Edition of the Works of Nathaniel Hawthorne*, ed. William Charvat et al., 14 vols. (Columbus: Ohio State Univ. Press, 1962–80), 10. All references to "Roger Malvin's Burial" are to this edition and appear in parentheses in the text. My discussion of "Roger Malvin's Burial" is indebted throughout to Michael Colacurcio's reading in *The Province of Piety: Moral History in Hawthorne's Early Tales* (Cambridge: Harvard Univ. Press, 1984), pp. 107–30.

8 Ely Stock, "History and the Bible in Hawthorne's 'Roger Malvin's Burial,' " *Essex Institute Historical Collections* 100 (1964):289. Lowance discusses both Mather's typological and antitypological strategies at length in *Language of Canaan*.

9 See Robert J. Daly, "History and Chivalric Myth in 'Roger Malvin's Burial,' " *Essex Institute Historical Collections* 109 (1973): 99–115.

10 See Michael Colacurcio's discussion of these issues in *Province of Piety*, and cf. Diane C. Naples, "Roger Malvin's Burial—A Parable for Historians?" *American Transcendentalist Quarterly*, 13 (1972): 45–48. Sharon Cameron's reading of "Roger Malvin's Burial" provides, I think, the philosophical, Wittgensteinian counterpart to Colacurcio's analysis (*The Corporeal Self: Allegories of the Body in Melville and Hawthorne* [Baltimore: Johns Hopkins Univ. Press, 1981], pp. 137–44).

11 On Malvin's culpability in the tragedy, see Daly, "History and Chivalric Myth."

12 See Stock, "History and the Bible in Hawthorne's 'Roger Malvin's Burial.' " For another reading of the story that views the end as expressing Reuben's expiation, see John R. Byers, Jr., "The Geography and Framework of Hawthorne's 'Roger Malvin's Burial,' " *Tennessee Studies in Literature* 21 (1976):11–20.

13 On Hawthorne's use of biblical materials, see Stock, "History and the Bible in Hawthorne's 'Roger Malvin's Burial' "; Byers, "The Geography and Framework of Hawthorne's 'Roger Malvin's Burial' " (who discusses the use of the Jacob/Rachel/Laban motif); W. R. Thompson, "The Biblical Sources of Hawthorne's 'Roger Malvin's Burial,' " *PMLA* 77 (1962):92–96; and Burton J. Fishman, "Imagined Redemption in 'Roger Malvin's Burial,' " *Studies in American Fiction* 5 (1977):257–62. On the debate about whether the story is intended to confirm the need for sacrifice or oppose it, see Fishman, "Imagined Redemption."

14 See Colacurcio, *Province of Piety*, p. 126.

15 Compare with Robert Alter, *The Art of Biblical Narrative* (New York: Basic Books, 1981).

16 See Bercovitch, *Puritan Origins*, pp. 136 ff.

17 My quotations are from the *Pentateuch and Haftorahs: Hebrew Text, English Translation, and Commentary*, ed. J. H. Hertz (London: Soncino Press, 1981).

18 Feidelson, *Symbolism and American Literature*, p. 87.

19 The Hebrew is even more complex on this point than the English translation. At the end of the passage an important place naming occurs: "And Abraham called the name of that place Adonaijireh: as it is said to this day: 'In the mount where the Lord is seen' " (Gen. 12.14). The word *yireh* which means "is seen" is the same word that appears in Gen. 12.8 and is translated

in English as "will provide Himself" but which literally means "will see for Himself," *yireh lo*. The word *yireh* also appears when the ram is seen caught in the thicket.

20 *Pentateuch and Haftorahs*, ed. Hertz, pp. 201–02.

21 Again the Hebrew emphasizes what is less powerful but nonetheless present in the English. The Hebrew for "take now" is peculiar in that the imperative "take" is followed by the Hebrew particle *nun aleph* which means, "I pray thee" which indicates that "God was speaking to Abraham 'as friend to friend.' " Also the "repetition" in "thy son, thine only son, whom thou lovest, even Isaac" "indicates the intense strain that was being placed upon Abraham's faith, and the greatness of the sacrifice demanded" (*Pentateuch and Haftorahs*, ed. Hertz, p. 74).

22 Feidelson, *Symbolism and American Literature*, pp. 77–94.

23 Robert Hollander, "Typology and Secular Literature: Some Medieval Problems and Examples" in *Literary Uses of Typology*, ed. Miner, pp. 3–19.

24 Colacurcio, *Province of Piety*, p. 126.

25 "What," asks Sharon Cameron, "is Reuben's confusion, father-in-law with self, son with father-in-law? What is Reuben's sin? What is the tale's subject?" According to Cameron, the "subject . . . is the denial of relations" that constitutes an escape from history: "Allegorical conception would transport Roger Malvin . . . to an ahistorical place (where death does not exist) . . . with Reuben . . . tagging along after" (*Corporeal Self*, pp. 138–40).

26 Relevant here is Gloria Ehrlich's observation that Reuben's killing his son may represent an act of revenge against Roger, leaving Roger heirless ("Guilt and Expiation in Roger Malvin's Burial," *Nineteenth-Century Fiction* 26 [1971]: 377–89). See also John T. Irwin, *Doubling and Incest/Repetition and Revenge* (Baltimore: Johns Hopkins Univ. Press, 1975), pp. 125–35, who discusses the sacrifice of the son in terms of the implied aggression against the father. Cameron suggests that Reuben "will not go near the dead man, for to go near him is to be him" (*Corporeal Self*, p. 140).

27 Colacurcio, *Province of Piety*, p. 126, and Fishman, "Imagined Redemption," pp. 257–62.

28 George P. Landow, "Moses Striking The Rock: Typological Symbolism in Victorian Poetry," in *Literary Uses of Typology*, ed. Miner, pp. 323, 331.

29 It is interesting to speculate that Emily Dickinson had Hawthorne's story in mind when she wrote her own commentary on the Mosaic type in "A Wounded Deer—leaps highest—" (no. 165) (*The Poems of Emily Dickinson*, ed. Thomas H. Johnson, 3 vols. [Cambridge, Mass.: Harvard Univ. Press, 1976]). As in Hawthorne's rendering of the typological moment, Dickinson focuses on how the Smitten Rock conceals the true meaning of the experience. George Landow notes the Dickinson poem's use of the typological material but does not explore its subversion of the tradition ("Moses Striking the Rock," pp. 338–39). See also Keller's discussion of this poem, "Alephs, Zahirs," p. 308.

30 One cannot help but recall the strange hieroglyphic Hebraic shapes in Poe's "Arthur Gordon Pym." Poe's purloined letters, as they have been amply discussed by deconstructive critics, seem to have interested Hawthorne as well. See "Seminar on 'The Purloined Letter,' " trans. Jeffrey Mehlman, *Yale French Studies* 48 (1977).

31 There is a magnificent midrash that is appropriate here. From the moment of the akedah until her death, Sarah disappears from the biblical text. The rabbinic explanation for this is that the horror of the potential sacrifice was so great that for all intents and purposes she died with Isaac on the rock. It is extremely unlikely Hawthorne would have known such an interpretation. But if the rabbis could read the text this way, Hawthorne may have also recognized the story's human implications for the mother.

Chapter 4

1 See Michael J. Colacurcio, *The Province of Piety: Moral History in Hawthorne's Early Tales* (Cambridge, Mass.: Harvard Univ. Press, 1984), p. 128, and Ann Ronald, "Roger Malvin's Grandson," *Studies in American Fiction* 12 (1984):71–77.

2 References to *The Prairie: A Tale* are to the Riverside Press edition (Cambridge, 1872) and appear in parentheses in the text.

3 References to *Billy Budd, Sailor* are to the Harrison Hayford and Merton M. Sealts, Jr., edition (Chicago: Univ. of Chicago Press, 1962) and appear in parentheses in the text.

4 Perhaps the most intriguing treatment of Vere is Barbara Johnson's deconstructive reading in *The Critical Difference: Essays in the Contemporary Rhetoric of Reading* (Baltimore: Johns Hopkins Univ. Press, 1981), pp. 79–109. Johnson's position on the impossibility of making absolute and impartial determinations even (or especially) in the political realm is, I believe, enhanced by the context of antitypological literalism that informs Melville's story. See also Milton R. Stern, *The Fine Hammered Steel of Herman Melville* (Urbana: Univ. of Illinois Press, 1957), p. 214, and Edgar A. Dryden, *Melville's Thematics of Form: The Great Art of Telling the Truth* (Baltimore: Johns Hopkins Univ. Press, 1968), pp. 209–16.

5 See preface, printed in *Billy Budd, Foretopman*, in *Herman Melville: Selected Tales and Poems*, ed. Richard Chase (New York: Holt, Rinehart and Winston, 1966), pp. 289–90.

6 The most penetrating and thorough analysis along these lines is Laurance Thompson's "Divine Depravity," in *Melville's Quarrel with God* (Princeton: Princeton Univ. Press, 1952), pp. 355–414.

7 On Vere's behavior see Peter A. Still, "Herman Melville's *Billy Budd*: Sympathy and Rebellion," *Arizona Quarterly* 28 (1972):39–54 and Leonard Casper, "The Case against Vere," *Perspective* 5 (1952):146–52.

8 This is the fate of the "civil, honest man," about whom Michael Wigglesworth writes in *The Day of Doom*.

9 See Michael Davitt Bell's excellent discussion of Melville and the idea of revolution in *The Development of American Romance: The Sacrifice of Relation* (Chicago: Univ. of Chicago Press, 1980), pp. 195–245.

10 Alan Heimert, *Religion and the American Mind from the Great Awakening to the Revolution* (Cambridge, Mass.: Harvard Univ. Press, 1968); and Mason I. Lowance, Jr., "Typology and Millennial Eschatology in Early New England," in *Literary Uses of Typology from the Late Middle Ages to the Present*, ed. Earl Miner (Princeton: Princeton Univ. Press, 1977), pp. 228–73. A similar idea informs Michael Colacurcio's reading of Hawthorne's "My Kinsman, Major Molineux," concerning the gentleman who sits with Robin on the church steps while the pageant rolls by (*Province of Piety*, pp. 130–55).

11 Preface to *Billy Budd*, in *Herman Melville: Selected Tales*, p. 289.

12 References to "Godliness" are to *Winesburg, Ohio* (New York: Viking, 1960). References to "A View of the Woods" are to *Everything that Rises Must Converge* (New York: Farrar, Straus and Giroux, 1965). They appear in the text in parentheses.

13 David Eggenschwiler, *The Christian Humanism of Flannery O'Connor* (Detroit: Wayne State Univ. Press, 1972), p. 70.

14 All references to *Go Down, Moses* are to the Vintage edition (New York: Random House, 1973), and appear in parentheses in the text.

15 The criticism dealing with Faulkner's use of and relationship to biblical materials in *Go Down, Moses* is vast. Major contributions in this field include: John W. Hunt, *William Faulkner: Art in Theological Tension* (Syracuse: Syracuse Univ. Press, 1965); James M. Mellard, "The Biblical Rhythm of *Go Down, Moses*," *Mississippi Quarterly* 20 (1967):135–47; Jessie McGuire Coffee, *Faulkner's Un-Christlike Christians: Biblical Allusions in the Novels* (Ann Arbor, Michigan: UMI Research Press, 1971); J. Robert Barth, "Faulkner and the Calvinist Tradition," in *Religious Perspectives in Faulkner's Fiction: Yoknapatawpha and Beyond*, ed. J. Robert Barth (Notre Dame: Univ. of Notre Dame Press, 1972), pp. 11–34; Harold J. Douglas and Robert Daniel, "Faulkner's Southern Puritanism," also in *Religious Perspectives*, ed. Barth, pp. 37–51; John Pilkington, "Nature's Legacy to William Faulkner," in *The South and Faulkner's Yoknapataw-pha: The Actual and the Apocryphal*, eds. Evan Harrington and Ann J. Abadie (Jackson: Univ. Press of Mississippi, 1979), pp. 104–27; and Stuart James, "The Ironic Voices of Faulkner's *Go*

Down, Moses," South Dakota Review 16 (1978): 80–101. On compulsion-obsession in the novels, see Irving Malin, *William Faulkner: An Interpretation* (Stanford: Stanford Univ. Press, 1957) and John T. Irwin's *Doubling and Incest/Repetition and Revenge: A Speculative Reading of Faulkner* (Baltimore: Johns Hopkins Univ. Press, 1975), who also deals with the Abraham-Isaac motif in Faulkner (pp. 125–35). In *The Fragile Thread: The Meaning of Form in Faulkner's Novels* (Amherst: Univ. of Massachusetts Press, 1979), p. 135, Donald M. Kartiganer argues that "The Bear" "makes clear the difficulty of translating faith into action, but it never challenges the accuracy of the particular historical pattern Ike sets up or the ideas of a single truth which is the theoretical basis of what he does." *Go Down, Moses*, I believe, refutes the idea of the "particular" pattern.

16 The relationship between Faulkner and Cooper has elicited some commentary. See, for example, John Pilkington, "Nature's Legacy to William Faulkner," and Otis B. Wheeler, "Faulkner's Wilderness," *American Literature* 31 (1959): 127–36. The more sustained subject of analysis, however, has been Faulkner and Emerson. See Irving D. Blum's "The Parallel Philosophy of Emerson's *Nature* and Faulkner's *The Bear*," *ESQ: A Journal of the American Renaissance* 13 (1958):22–25, and Irving Howe's *William Faulkner: A Critical Study* (New York: Vintage Books, 1962).

17 Hunt, *William Faulkner*, pp. 146–47, 155. See also Cleanth Brooks, "Faulkner's Vision of Good and Evil"; Herbert A. Perluck, " 'The Bear': An Unromantic Reading," in *Religious Perspectives*, ed. Barth, pp. 173–98; T. H. Adamowski, "Isaac McCaslin and the Wilderness Imagination," *The Centennial Review* 17 (1973):92–112; James, "Ironic Voices," and William Van O'Connor, "The Wilderness Theme in Faulkner's 'The Bear,' " in *William Faulkner: Three Decades of Criticism*, ed. Frederick J. Hoffman and Olga W. Vickery (Ann Arbor: Michigan State Univ. Press, 1960), pp. 322–31.

18 Stanley Sultan, "Call Me Ishmael: The Hagiography of Isaac McCaslin," *Texas Studies in Literature and Language* 3 (1961):61.

19 The great test case of whether one can rewrite Christian history from the Ishmaelite side is Melville's *Moby Dick*.

20 Faulkner seems to have anticipated a more contemporary interest in black adaptations of American religious language and thought. See, for example, David Howard-Pitney's "The American Jeremiad and Black Protest Rhetoric, From Frederick Douglass to W. E. B. Du Bois, 1841–1919," *American Quarterly* 38 (1986): 481–92. In *Beyond Ethnicity: Consent and Descent in American Culture* (N.Y.: Oxford Univ. Press, 1986), Werner Sollors has traced the pervasive use of the America-as-promised land motif in American black writers (pp. 40–65: "Typology and Ethnogenesis). Moving in the other direction, Barbara Foley ("History, Fiction, and the Ground Between: The Uses of the Documentary Mode in Black Literature," *PMLA* 95 [1980]:389–403) has described the influence of black writing on the contemporary American documentary novel, which is a descendant of the historical romance. Exploring the black expression of some of the motifs that I am describing in this study would, I think, yield fascinating insights into the continuities and divergences of the black and white traditions of American writing. But it is an undertaking that unfortunately lies outside the boundaries of my present undertaking.

21 Thadious M. Davis, *Faulkner's "Negro": Art and the Southern Context* (Baton Rouge: Louisiana State Univ. Press, 1983), p. 14.

22 H. R. Stoneback, "Faulkner's Blues: 'Pantaloon in Black,' " *Modern Fiction Studies* 21 (1975): 241–46, identifies sources for the story in Southern blues songs that were sung by both black and white Southerners.

23 See Darwin T. Turner, "Faulkner and Slavery," *The South and Faulkner's Yoknapatawpha*, ed. Harrington and Abadie, pp. 62–85; Charles D. Peary, *Go Slow, Now: Faulkner and the Race Question* (Eugene: Univ. of Oregon Books, 1971); Walter Taylor, "Faulkner's Pantaloon: The Negro Anomaly at the Heart of *Go Down, Moses*," *American Literature* 44 (1972): 430–44; Myra Jehlen, *Class and Character in Faulkner's South* (New York: Columbia Univ. Press, 1976);

Thadious M. Davis, *Faulkner's "Negro": Art and the Southern Context*; and Dorothy L. Denniston, "Faulkner's Image of Blacks in *Go Down, Moses*," *Pylon* 44 (1983): 33–43.

24 "Faulkner and the Negroes," in *Faulkner: A Collection of Essays*, ed. Richard H. Brodhead (Englewood Cliffs, N.J.: Prentice-Hall, 1983), pp. 50, 56.

25 Darwin T. Turner, "Faulkner and Race," in *The South and Yoknapatawpha*, ed. Harrington and Abadie, pp. 91–95. See also Sandra D. Milloy, "Faulkner's Lucas: An 'Arrogant, Intractable, and Insolent Old Man,' " *CLA Journal* 28 (1984): 393–405.

26 Jehlen, *Class and Character*, p. 99.

27 Terence Martin, "The Negative Structures of American Literature," *American Literature* 57 (1985): 1–22.

28 Davis, *Faulkner's "Negro"*, p. 14.

29 See John Barth, *The End of the Road* (New York: Avon, 1958), p. 66, "The world is everything that is the case."

30 Joseph Brogunier has located the historical documents on which the Commissary records are based ("A Source for the Commissary Entries in *Go Down, Moses*," *Texas Studies in Literature and Language* 14 [1972]: 545–54).

31 Carl E. Rollyson, "Faulkner as Historian: The Commissary Books in *Go Down, Moses*," *Markham Review* 7 (1978): 31–36.

32 Among the best attempts to define the work's structure are Mark R. Hochberg, "The Unity of *Go Down, Moses*," *Tennessee Studies in Literature* 21 (1976): 58–67; Joanne V. Creighton, *William Faulkner's Craft of Revision: The Snopses Trilogy, "The Unvanquished," and "Go Down, Moses"*, (Detroit, Mich.; Wayne State Univ. Press, 1977); John L. Cleman, " 'Pantaloon in Black': Its Place in *Go Down, Moses*," *Tennessee Studies in Literature* 22 (1977):170–81; Weldon Thornton's "Structure and Theme in Fitzgerald's *Go Down, Moses*," in *William Faulkner: Critical Collection*, ed. Leland H. Cox (Detroit, Mich.: Gale Research, 1982), pp. 328–68; and John L. Selzer, " 'Go Down, Moses' and *Go Down, Moses*" *Studies in American Fiction* 13 (1985):89–96. On the publication history of *Go Down, Moses*, see James B. Carothers, *William Faulkner's Short Stories* (Ann Arbor, Mich.: UMI Research Press, 1985), pp. 87–89, who quotes Faulkner as stating, "I always thought it was a novel"; Joanne V. Creighton, *William Faulkner's Craft of Revision*, and Weldon Thornton, "Structure and Theme in Faulkner's *Go Down, Moses*" in *William Faulkner: A Critical Collection*, ed. Leland H. Cox (Detroit, Mich.: Gale Research, 1982), pp. 328–68.

33 John Selzer argues correctly that one of the reasons *Go Down, Moses* must be read as a novel and not as a collection of short stories is that, while Stevens comes off fairly sympathetically in the short story "Go Down, Moses," he is viewed much more severely in the context of the novel as a whole (" 'Go Down, Moses' and *Go Down, Moses*," *Studies in American Fiction*). Stuart James points out that by "all of hit" Mollie really means all of it and not just what Stevens thinks he knows ("Ironic Voices").

34 Quoted from *Afro-American History: Primary Souces*, ed. Thomas R. Frazier (N.Y.: Harcourt, Brace and World, 1970), p. 92.

Chapter 5

1 Wolfgang Iser, *The Implied Reader: Patterns of Communication in Prose Fiction from Bunyan to Beckett* (Baltimore: Johns Hopkins Univ. Press, 1974), pp. 1–29 ("Bunyan's *Pilgrim's Progress*: The Doctrine of Predestination and the Shaping of the Novel").

2 Jacques Derrida, "Freud and the Scene of Writing," in *Writing and Difference*, trans. Alan Bass (Chicago: Univ. of Chicago Press, 1978), p. 211.

3 In *The Rhetoric of American Romance: Dialectic and Identity in Emerson, Dickinson, Poe, and Hawthorne* (Baltimore: Johns Hopkins Univ. Press, 1985), Evan Carton has taken up the issue of the origination and originality of American texts (p. 151). I recur to Carton's book below.
     On the indeterminacy of fiction see Wolfgang Iser's "Indeterminacy and the Reader's Response

in Prose Fiction," in *Aspects of Narrative: Selected Papers from the English Institute*, ed. J. Hillis Miller (New York: Columbia Univ. Press, 1971). Iser develops his ideas further in *The Act of Reading: A Theory of Aesthetic Response* (Baltimore: Johns Hopkins Univ. Press, 1978). On nineteenth-century American fiction's anticipation of contemporary critical theories see Kenneth Dauber, "Criticism of American Literature," *Diacritics* 7 (1977): 55–66; John Carlos Rowe, *Through the Custom-House: Nineteenth-Century American Fiction and Modern Theory* (Baltimore: Johns Hopkins Univ. Press, 1982); and Russell Reising, *The Unusable Past: Theory and the Study of American Literature* (New York: Methuen, 1986).

4 Richard Poirier, *A World Elsewhere: The Place of Style in American Literature* (New York: Oxford Univ. Press, 1966), p. 6

5 Michael Davitt Bell, *The Development of American Romance: The Sacrifice of Relation* (Chicago: Chicago Univ. Press, 1980), p. 148. Bell's study extends the ideas of earlier critics such as Richard Chase, *The American Novel and Its Tradition* (New York: Doubleday, 1957); Perry Miller, "The Romance and the Novel," *Nature's Nation* (Cambridge, Mass.: Harvard Univ. Press, 1967) and *The Raven and the Whale: The War of Words and Wits in the Era of Poe and Melville* (New York: Harcourt, Brace and World, 1965); and Joel Porte, *The Romance in America: Studies in Cooper, Poe, Hawthorne, Melville, and James* (Middletown, Conn.: Wesleyan University Press, 1969). Other books that define American romance are Michael T. Gilmore, *The Middle Way: Puritanism and Ideology in American Romantic Fiction* (New Brunswick, N.J.: Rutgers Univ. Press, 1977); Edwin M. Eigner, *The Metaphysical Novel in England and America: Dickens, Bulwer, Melville, and Hawthorne* (Berkeley: Univ. of California Press, 1978); Sam B. Girgus, *The Law of the Heart: Individualism and the Modern Self in American Literature* (Austin: Univ. of Texas Press, 1979); Harold Peter Simonson, *Radical Discontinuities: American Romanticism and Christian Consciousness* (Rutherford, N.J.: Fairleigh Dickinson Univ. Press, 1983); Samuel Chase Coale, *In Hawthorne's Shadow: American Romance from Melville to Mailer* (Lexington: Univ. Press of Kentucky, 1985); and David Van Leer, "Hester's Labyrinth: Transcendental Rhetoric in Puritan Boston," *New Essays on The Scarlet Letter*, ed. Michael J. Colacurcio (Cambridge: Cambridge Univ. Press, 1985), pp. 57–100. Eigner's introduction, pp. 1–12, nicely complements Bell's. The title of Bell's book alludes to Henry James's discussion of the romance in his preface to *The American*. See also Bell's essay "Arts of Deception: Hawthorne, 'Romance,' and *The Scarlet Letter*" in *New Essays on The Scarlet Letter*, ed. Colacurcio, pp. 29–56. For a different kind of history of the romance, which concerns the development of the novel itself as it wrestled with the conflict between reality and art and moved in the direction of fantasy, bringing forward and collecting certain impulses of popular as opposed to classical art, see Morris Dickstein's "Popular Fiction and Critical Values: The Novel as a Challenge to Literary History," in *Reconstructing American Literary History*, ed. Sacvan Bercovitch (Cambridge, Mass.: Harvard Univ. Press, 1986), pp. 29–66.

6 Evan Carton, *Rhetoric of American Romance*. Carton's book develops along lines suggested in Richard Brodhead, *Hawthorne, Melville, and the Novel* (Chicago: Univ. of Chicago Press, 1973) and moves them in a more contemporary, deconstructive direction.

7 Robert Clark, *History, Ideology and Myth in American Fiction, 1823–52* (London: Macmillan Press, 1984); John P. McWilliams, Jr., *Hawthorne, Melville, and the American Character: A Looking-Glass Business* (Cambridge: Cambridge Univ. Press, 1984); Michael T. Gilmore, *American Romanticism and the Marketplace* (Chicago: Univ. of Chicago Press, 1985); Philip Fisher, *Hard Facts: Setting and Form in the American Novel* (New York: Oxford Univ. Press, 1985); Richard Brodhead, *The School of Hawthorne* (New York: Oxford Univ. Press, 1986; Barbara Foley, *Telling the Truth: The Theory and Practice of Documentary Fiction* (Ithaca: Cornell Univ. Press, 1986); and Donald Pease, *Visionary Compacts: American Renaissance Writings in Cultural Context* (Madison: Univ. of Wisconsin Press, 1987). A classic study in this field is still William Charvat's *The Profession of Authorship in America, 1800–1870*, ed. Matthew J. Bruccoli (Columbus, Ohio: Ohio State Univ. Press, 1968). Many of the new

historicist readings build on more traditional historical studies such as Roy Harvey Pearce, "Romance and the Study of History" in *Hawthorne Centenary Essays*, ed. Roy Harvey Pearce (Ohio State Univ. Press, 1964), pp. 221–44 and *Historicism Once More: Problems and Occasions for the American Scholar* (Princeton: Princeton Univ. Press, 1962); and Charles Feidelson, Jr., "The Scarlet Letter," also in *Hawthorne Centenary Essays*, pp. 31–77. As one critic has so succinctly put it, "loneliness and symbolic settings, either before the Civil War or after it, have not been in conflict with profound literary attention to historical realities and social issues" (Cushing Strout, *The Veracious Imagination: Essays on American History, Literature, and Biography* [Middletown, Conn.: Wesleyan Univ. Press, 1981], p. 95). For historical analyses of some of the writers discussed in this book, see Michael J. Colacurcio, *The Province of Piety: Moral History in Hawthorne's Early Tales* (Cambridge, Mass.: Harvard Univ. Press, 1984); David Van Leer, "Hester's Labyrinth," in *New Essays on The Scarlet Letter*, ed. Colacurcio; Carol Marie Bensick, *La Nouvelle Beatrice: Renaissance and Romance in "Rappaccini's Daughter"* (New Brunswick, N.J.: Rutgers Univ. Press, 1985); Myra Jehlen, *Class and Character in Faulkner's South* (New York: Columbia Univ. Press, 1976); John P. McWilliams, Jr., *Political Justice in a Republic: James Fenimore Cooper's America* (Berkeley: Univ. of California Press, 1972); and Brian Way, *F. Scott Fitzgerald and the Art of Social Fiction* (New York: St. Martin's Press, 1980).

8 Barbara Foley (*Telling the Truth*), Robert Clark (*History, Ideology and Myth in American Fiction*), and Michael Davitt Bell (*The Development of American Romance* and "Arts of Deception," in *New Essays on The Scarlet Letter*, ed. Colacurcio).

9 See again Evan Carton's dialectical argument in *Rhetoric of Romance*.

10 All references to "Young Goodman Brown" are to *The Centenary Edition of the Works of Nathaniel Hawthorne*, ed. William Charvat et al., 14 vols. (Columbus Ohio: Ohio State Univ. Press, 1962–80), 10, and appear in parentheses in the text.

11 See, for example, Q. D. Leavis, "Hawthorne as Poet," *Sewanee Review* 59 (1951): 179–205; Roy Male, *Hawthorne's Tragic Vision* (Austin: Univ. of Texas Press, 1957); Harry Levin, *The Power of Darkness: Hawthorne, Poe, and Melville* (London: Faber, 1958); and Reginald Cooke's "The Forest of Goodman Brown's Night: A Reading of 'Young Goodman Brown,'" *New England Quarterly* 43 (1970): 433–81.

12 Frederick Crews, *The Sins of the Fathers: Hawthorne's Psychological Themes* (New York: Oxford Univ. Press, 1966), pp. 27–29.

13 See, for example, Hyatt Waggoner, *Hawthorne: A Critical Study* (Cambridge: Harvard Univ. Press, 1955), pp. 50–51, and Michael Davitt Bell, *Hawthorne and the Historical Romance of New England* (Princeton: Princeton Univ. Press, 1971), p. 79.

14 Male, *Hawthorne's Tragic Vision*, p. 79; see also Hyatt Waggoner, *Hawthorne: A Critical Study*, pp. 50–51 and Darrel Abel, "Black Glove and Pink Ribbon: Hawthorne's Metonymic Symbols," *New England Quarterly* 42 (1969): 163–80.

15 Crews, *Sins of the Fathers*, p. 27.

16 Bell, *Hawthorne and the Historical Romance of New England*, p. 77. Despite his concern with Hawthorne's use of history, Bell's overestimation of the psychological elements of the story finally compromises his historical interpretation. "Young Goodman Brown," he writes, is "a forceful example of what Hawthorne felt Puritanism had become in New England. . . . His expedition into the forest becomes a way of getting back at his ancestors for his own sense of inferiority" (p. 77).

17 Compare with Darrell Abel's suggestion in "Black Glove and Pink Ribbon" that for Hawthorne "every reading of facts, every version of 'truth,' is an arbitrary determination" (p. 173). Harold Simonson reviews a whole range of criticism concerning Hawthorne's ambiguity in *Radical Discontinuities*, pp. 47–48. Roy Male discusses Abel's ideas in "Hawthorne's Literal Figures," in *Ruined Eden of the Present: Hawthorne, Melville, and Poe: Critical Essays in Honor of Darrel Abel*, ed. G. R. Thompson and Virgil L. Lokke (West Lafayette, Indiana: Purdue University Press, 1981), pp. 71–92.

18 Colacurcio, *Province of Piety*, pp. 283–313.

19 David Levin, *In Defense of Historical Literature: Essays on American History, Autobiography, Drama and Fiction* (New York: Hill, 1967).

20 Levin, *In Defense of Historical Literature*, p. 92. Compare with Daniel Hoffman, *Form and Fable in American Fiction* (New York: Oxford Univ. Press, 1961), p. 155.

21 Compare with Abel, "Black Glove and Pink Ribbon," p. 173 and Taylor Stoehr, " 'Young Goodman Brown' and Hawthorne's Theory of Mimesis," *Nineteenth-Century Fiction* 23 (1969): 393–412.

22 Colacurcio, *Province of Piety*, pp. 19–20.

23 Colacurcio, *Province of Piety*, p. 294 and David Levin, "Shadows of Doubt: Specter Evidence in Hawthorne's 'Young Goodman Brown,' " *American Literature* 34 (1962) 344.

24 Colacurcio, *Province of Piety*, p. 300.

25 Millicent Bell points out that artists are often rendered as witches or magicians in Hawthorne's fiction (*Hawthorne's View of the Artist* [N.p.: State Univ. of New York Press, 1962], pp.78–91).

26 Perhaps the most bold application of Hawthorne's understanding of history, reapplying the same Puritan situation and yet reading onto it still another historical reality, is Arthur Miller's *The Crucible*. I discuss this in "History and Other Spectres in Arthur Miller's *The Crucible*," *Modern Drama* 28 (1985): 535–52.

27 Bell, *Development of American Romance*, p. 139.

28 Roy Harvey Pearce, *The Continuity of American Poetry* (Princeton: Princeton Univ. Press, 1961).

29 Emerson, *Nature*, in *Nature, Addresses, Lectures: The Complete Works of Ralph Waldo Emerson*, 12 vols. (Boston: Houghton, Mifflin, 1903; rpt. New York: AMS Press, 1968), 1:76 (hereafter cited as *Nature, Works*). Thoreau, *Walden: Or, Life in the Woods* (New York: Holt, 1961), pp. 1–2.

30 Emerson, "History" in *Essays: First Series*, in *Works*, 2:11.

31 Quentin Anderson, *The Imperial Self: An Essay in American Literary and Cultural History* (New York: Alfred A. Knopf, 1971), p. 17.

32 Anderson, *Imperial Self*, p. 17.

33 Emerson, *Nature*, *Works*, 1:47.

Chapter 6

1 Compare with Nina Baym, *The Shape of Hawthorne's Career* (Ithaca: Cornell Univ. Press, 1976), p. 26.

2 Cameron, *The Corporeal Self: Allegories of the Body in Melville and Hawthorne* (Baltimore: Johns Hopkins Univ. Press, 1981), and Jehlen, *American Incarnation: The Individual, the Nation, and the Continent* (Cambridge: Harvard Univ. Press, 1986). See also John T. Irwin's thesis in *American Hieroglyphics: The Symbol of the Egyptian Hieroglyphics in the American Renaissance* (New Haven: Yale Univ. Press, 1980). Evan Carton also deals with this subject, most astutely, in relation to Hawthorne in *The Rhetoric of American Romance: Dialectic and Identity in Emerson, Dickinson, Poe, and Hawthorne* (Baltimore: Johns Hopkins Univ. Press, 1985), p. 184. See also David Van Leer's statements about the corporeal and incarnational qualities of language—and about Hawthorne's responses to them—in "Hester's Labyrinth: Transcendental Rhetoric in Puritan Boston," in *New Essays on The Scarlet Letter*, ed. Michael J. Colacurcio (Cambridge: Cambridge Univ. Press, 1985), pp. 57–100.

3 All references to the story are to *The Centenary Edition of the Works of Nathaniel Hawthorne*, ed. William Charvat et al., 14 vols. (Columbus: Ohio State Univ. Press, 1962–80), 11, and appear in parentheses in the text.

4 See Michael Colacurcio's discussion of "Alice Doane's Appeal" in *The Province of Piety: Moral History in Hawthorne's Early Tales* (Cambridge: Harvard Univ. Press, 1984), pp. 78–93.

5 The story does not, I think, chronicle "the narrator's discovery of how to write American Gothic," as Nine Baym has claimed in *Shape of Hawthorne's Career*, p. 38. For a general

discussion of Hawthorne's narrative strategies in this story see Charles Swann, " 'Alice Doane's Appeal': Or, How to Tell a Story," *Literature and History* 5 (1977):4–25.

6 My readings of "Edward Randolph's Portrait," "Lady Eleanore's Mantle," "The Minister's Black Veil," and "My Kinsman, Major Molineux" assume a familiarity with Colacurcio's densely packed and extensive historical analyses of these works. To integrate and respond to Colacurcio's readings at every moment would have considerably (and unnecessarily) lengthened my own comments, and therefore I have incorporated Colacurcio's readings only in key instances. Evan Carton's approach to Hawthorne's historical tales, especially on "The Legends of the Province House" (which contain "Edward Randolph's Portrait" and "Lady Eleanore's Mantle"), in *The Rhetoric of American Romance*, is also extremely valuable. As Carton's work focuses more on the structure of Hawthorne's relationship to history than on the historical content of the stories, it shares my own emphasis on historical consciousness as separate from historical analysis as such. Carton's approach and my own differ, however, in the degree to which the specificity of historical events (as charted by Colacurcio) enters into my readings and determines their configuration. All references to "Edward Randolph's Portrait" are to the *Centenary Edition*, 9, and appear in parentheses in the text.

7 Hawthorne might well write here a version of what he has Grandfather say in "Grandfather's Chair": "when you want instruction on [certain] points you must seek it in Mr. Bancroft's History. I am merely telling the history of a chair" (*The Whole History of Grandfather's Chair, Centenary Works*, 6:33).

8 Colacurcio, *Province of Piety*, pp. 406–23.

9 All references to "The Minister's Black Veil" are to *Centenary Edition*, 9, and appear in parentheses in the text.

10 Richard Harter Fogle, *Hawthorne's Fiction: The Light and the Dark* (Norman: Univ. of Oklahoma Press, 1952), p. 39.

11 Colacurcio, *Province of Piety*, pp. 314–85; quotation on p. 322.

12 Colacurcio, *Province of Piety*, pp. 328, 331, 345. See esp. pp. 331 ff., 371 ff., which discuss Hooper's fixation on self.

13 For this view of Hawthornean allegory, see Colacurcio, "The Politics of Allegory," *Province of Piety*, pp. 424–48; Bell, *Development of American Romance*, p. 139; Van Leer, "Hester's Labyrinth"; and Carol Marie Bensick, *La Nouvelle Beatrice: Renaissance and Romance in "Rappaccini's Daughter"* (New Brunswick, N.J.: Rutgers Univ. Press, 1985).

14 Auerbach, "Figura," in *Scenes from the Drama of European Literature* (Minneapolis: Univ. of Minnesota Press, 1984), pp. 29, 47, 53, 52, 54, 57. Auerbach discusses the relationship between figura and type on pp. 47–48.

15 *The Scarlet Letter*, in *Centenary Works*, 1:4.

16 The problem of intimacy is a major concern of *The Scarlet Letter*. It is explored most compellingly (though in opposite ways) by Kenneth Dauber in *Rediscovering Hawthorne* (Princeton: Princeton Univ. Press, 1972), and by David Leverenz, in "Mrs. Hawthorne's Headache: Reading *The Scarlet Letter*," in *The (M)other Tongue: Essays in Feminist Psychoanalytic Interpretation*, ed. Shirley Nelson Garner, Claire Kahane, and Madelon Sprengnether (Ithaca: Cornell Univ. Press, 1985), pp. 194–216.

17 On the history of the perverted self as a version of the American self, see Sam B. Girgus, *The Law of the Heart: Individualism and the Modern Self in American Literature* (Austin: Univ. of Texas Press, 1979).

18 *Centenary Works*, 11:13. The comment continues: "Yet, his avocations were not so vain as our philosophic moralizing. In this world we are the things of a moment."

19 References to "Lady Eleanore's Mantle" are to *Centenary Works*, 9, and will appear in parentheses in the text. As usual, Colacurcio, *Province of Piety*, pp. 424–48, provides a detailed analysis of the tale's historical resonances. He argues that the story attacks the politicization of allegory.

20 References to "My Kinsman, Major Molineux" are to *Centenary Works*, 11, and appear in parentheses in the text.

21 See Nina Baym, *Shape of Hawthorne's Career*, p. 33.

22 Sharon Cameron, *The Corporeal Self: Allegories of the Body in Melville and Hawthorne* (Baltimore: Johns Hopkins Univ. Press, 1981), pp. 144–55. In *Historicism Once More*, Roy Harvey Pearce discusses other bodily transformations in Hawthorne's text, such as the representation of "William Molineux, a well-to-do radical Boston trader, an organizer and leader of anti-Loyalist mobs" in the Major Molineux of the story. And he concludes as follows: "His friend of the night . . . urges him to stay on. For perhaps, being a shrewd youth, he may rise in the world even without his kinsman, Major Molineux. But can he? we ask. For through the William Molineux whose name they share, Robin and his kinsman are one, as through the history we share, we are one with them too" (*Historicism Once More: Problems and Occasions for the American Scholar* [Princeton: Princeton Univ. Press, 1962], p. 145). See also P. L. Abernathy, "The Identity of Hawthorne's Major Molineux," *American Transcendentalist Quarterly* 31 (1976):5–8. Pearce's reading of the story is, I think, more reflective of Hawthorne's purposes than is Cameron's.

23 On the minister's multiple identity, see Colacurcio, *Province of Piety*, p. 360.

Chapter 7

1 Stanley Cavell, "Being Odd, Getting Even: Threats to Individuality," in *Reconstructing Individualism: Autonomy, Individuality, and the Self in Western Thought*, eds. T. C. Heller, M. Sosna, and D. E. Wellbery (Stanford: Stanford Univ. Press, 1986), p. 311. See also Cavell's *The Claim of Reason: Wittgenstein, Skepticism, Morality, and Tragedy* (Oxford: Oxford Univ. Press, 1979), esp. pp. 327 ff.

2 Jacques Derrida, "Freud and the Scene of Writing" in *Writing and Difference*, trans. Alan Bass (Chicago: Univ. of Chicago Press, 1978).

3 Cavell, "Being Odd, Getting Even," p. 307.

4 Paul de Man, "Criticism and Crisis," *Blindness and Insight: Essays in the Rhetoric of Contemporary Criticism*, 2d ed. (Methuen, 1983), p. 19.

5 See Derrida, "Freud and the Scene of Writing," p. 211.

6 Stanley Cavell, *The Senses of Walden* (New York: Viking Press, 1972), p. 63. Compare with Cavell "Being Odd, Getting Even," p. 287.

7 See "The Seminar on 'The Purloined Letter,' " trans. Jeffrey Mehlman, *Yale French Studies* 48 (1977).

8 "The Scarlet Letter," in *Hawthorne Centenary Essays*, ed. Roy Harvey Pearce (Columbus: Ohio State Univ. Press, 1964) p. 36; cf. David Van Leer, "Hester's Labyrinth: Transcendental Rhetoric in Puritan Boston," in *New Essays on The Scarlet Letter*, ed. Michael J. Colacurcio (Cambridge: Cambridge Univ. Press, 1985), pp. 57–100: "The tendency to corporealize concepts (not to say incarnate them) has been natural since at least the time of Descartes. But negation is the inevitable result of all such reifications. The only effective defense against the process is not to mystify reality through a pseudospiritual pursuit of the Actual in the unfamiliar, but to refuse altogether to describe the ineffable. Whether or not life is a prison, it is something that must take place within rules and limits—the custom-houses of history, society, and language" (pp. 87–88). As Feidelson puts it, "Reality in 'The Custom-House' is history" ("The Scarlet Letter," p. 36).

9 Roy Harvey Pearce, "Romance and the Study of History," in *Hawthorne Centenary Essays*, ed. Pearce, p. 222.

10 See for example Kenneth Dauber, *Rediscovering Hawthorne* (Princeton: Princeton Univ. Press, 1972) and Evan Carton, *The Rhetoric of American Romance: Dialectic and Identity in Emerson, Dickinson, Poe, and Hawthorne* (Baltimore: Johns Hopkins Univ. Press, 1985).

11 All references to *The House of the Seven Gables* are to *The Centenary Edition of the Works of Nathaniel Hawthorne*, ed. William Charvat et al., 14 vols. (Columbus: Ohio State Univ. Press, 1962–80), 2. They appear in parentheses in the text.

12 Michael Davitt Bell, *Hawthorne and the Historical Romance of New England* (Princeton: Princeton Univ. Press, 1971), pp. 214 ff., 220. In *The Development of American Romance: The Sacrifice of Relation* (Chicago: Chicago Univ. Press, 1980), pp. 181–82, Bell describes the book as marking the collapse of the romance tradition.

13 Roy Male, *Hawthorne's Tragic Vision* (Austin: Univ. of Texas Press, 1957), pp. 122–24, for example, argues that the book is about the "interpenetration of the past and the present," "the history of the house . . . a record of continuity and change." Hyatt Waggoner, *Hawthorne: A Critical Study* (Cambridge: Harvard Univ. Press, 1955), and John Gatta, Jr., "Progress and Providence in *The House of the Seven Gables*," *American Literature* 50 (1978): 37–48, claim, respectively, that the book is about progress or progress measured against providence. See also Richard Harter Fogle, *Hawthorne's Fiction: The Light and the Dark* (Norman: Univ. of Oklahoma Press, 1952), pp. 122–39.

14 *The Scarlet Letter, Centenary Works,* 1:36.

15 As Jonathan Arac has pointed out, "the world 'racing past them' offers a view of history like that of time-lapse photography" ("The House and the Railroad: *Dombey and Son* and *The House of the Seven Gables*," *New England Quarterly* 53 [1978]: 3–22).

16 *Nature* in *Nature, Addresses, and Lectures: The Complete Works of Ralph Waldo Emerson,* 12 vols. (Boston: Houghton, Mifflin, 1903; rpt. New York: AMS Press, 1968), 1:50–51 (hereafter cited as *Nature, Works*).

17 *Nature, Works,* 1:51–54.

18 *Nature, Works,* 1:48–49.

19 *Nature, Works,* 1:59.

20 *Nature, Works,* 1:50.

21 *Nature, Works,* 1:47.

22 Cavell, *Senses of Walden,* pp. 94–96.

23 Cavell, *Senses of Walden,* p. 100.

24 *The Complete Poems of Emily Dickinson,* ed. Thomas H. Johnson (Cambridge, Mass: Harvard Univ. Press, 1983). I discuss Dickinson's poem in terms relevant to this discussion of *The House of the Seven Gables* in *Emily Dickinson and the Life of Language: A Study in Symbolic Poetics* (Baton Rouge: Louisiana State Univ. Press, 1985), pp. 169–74.

25 Hebrew: *baal* or lord, *zebub,* or fly. See also my reading of Dickinson's "Before I got my eye put out," *Emily Dickinson,* pp. 117–21.

26 Stanley Cavell, *The World Viewed: Reflections on the Ontology of Film, Enlarged Edition* (Cambridge, Harvard Univ. Press, 1979), pp. 22–23; see also p. 18: "The [photographic] image is not a likeness; it is not exactly a replica, or a relic, or a shadow, or an apparition either, though all of these natural candidates share a striking feature with photographs—an aura or history of magic surrounding them."

27 Cavell, *The World Viewed,* pp. 24–26.

28 *Nature, Works,* 1:64–65.

29 *Nature, Works,* 1:48.

30 Since this chapter is already so indebted to the writings of Stanley Cavell I cannot forbear making one further connection with his work. In *Pursuits of Happiness: The Hollywood Comedy of Remarriage* (Cambridge, Mass.: Harvard Univ. Press, 1981), Cavell describes a series of films, deriving from the tradition of Shakespearean romance, about couples who separate and remarry, as the woman, under the tutelage of the male, becomes an independent self capable of engaging in the conversation of wedded life. It occurs to me that Hawthorne's *Romance* of Holgrave and Phoebe might be the first such American comedy of remarriage. Not only do Holgrave and Phoebe (who is Holgrave's student in life) marry, but in so doing, they effect the remarriage or at least the reunion of two other couples: Alice Pyncheon and Matthew Maule (with whom they are closely associated) and that original couple of marriage and "converse sweet" whose Eden they recreate, Adam and Eve.

Chapter 8

1 All references to *The Great Gatsby* are to the Scribner edition (New York, 1925) and appear in parentheses in the text.

2 Much *Gatsby* criticism has touched, of course, on Gatsby's lack of historical consciousness and on the tragic consequences of his American dream. See William Troy, "Scott Fitzgerald—The Authority of Failure," in *F. Scott Fitzgerald*, ed. Arthur Mizener (Englewood Cliffs, N.J.: Prentice-Hall, 1963), pp. 20–24; A. E. Dyson, *"The Great Gatsby: Thirty-Six Years After,"* in *F. Scott Fitzgerald*, ed. Mizener, pp. 112–24; Kermit W. Moyer, *"The Great Gatsby:* Fitzgerald's Meditation on American History," in *Fitzgerald/Hemingway Annual* 4 (1972):49, also reprinted in *Critical Essays on F. Scott Fitzgerald's The Great Gatsby*, ed. Scott Donaldson (Boston: G. K. Hall, 1984), pp. 215–28. See also the following essays in Mizener's *F. Scott Fitzgerald:* Lionel Trilling, "F. Scott Fitzgerald," pp. 11–19; Wright Morris, "The Function of Nostalgia: F. Scott Fitzgerald," pp. 25–31; and John Henry Raleigh, "F. Scott Fitzgerald's *The Great Gatsby*," pp. 99–103. Edwin Fussell captures the major elements of the ongoing discussion when he writes that "Fitzgerald's basic plot is the history of the New World . . . more precisely, of the human imagination in the New World. It shows itself in two predominant patterns, quest and seduction. The quest is the search for romantic wonder. . . . [T]he seduction represents capitulation to these terms. Obversely, the quest is a flight: from reality, from normality, from time, fate, death, and the conception of *limit"* ("Fitzgerald's Brave New World," in *F. Scott Fitzgerald*, ed. Mizener, p. 43). See also John F. Callahan, *The Illusions of a Nation: Myth and History in the Novels of F. Scott Fitzgerald* (Urbana: Univ. of Illinois Press, 1972), pp. 3–61.

3 Kermit W. Moyer quotes Bishop's comment which originally appeared in "The Missing All," *Virginia Quarterly Review* 13 (1937), in *"The Great Gatsby:* Fitzgerald's Meditation on American History," in *F. Scott Fitzgerald*, ed. Mizener, p. 43.

4 *Nature*, in *Nature, Addresses, Lectures: The Complete Works of Ralph Waldo Emerson*, 12 vols. (Boston: Houghton Mifflin, 1903; rpt. New York: AMS Press, 1968), 1:76 (hereafter cited as *Nature, Works*).

5 Sharon Cameron, *The Corporeal Self: Allegories of the Body in Melville and Hawthorne* (Baltimore: Johns Hopkins Univ. Press, 1981).

6 Quentin Anderson, *The Imperial Self: An Essay in American Literary and Cultural History* (New York: Alfred A. Knopf, 1971), and Sam B. Girgus *The Law of the Heart: Individualism and the Modern Self in American Literature* (Austin: Univ. of Texas Press, 1979), pp. 24 ff., 112–13.

7 Myra Jehlen, *American Incarnation: The Individual, The Nation, and the Continent* (Cambridge, Mass.: Harvard Univ. Press, 1986). See also John T. Irwin, *American Hieroglyphics: The Symbol of the Egyptian Hieroglyphics in the American Renaissance* (New Haven: Yale Univ. Press, 1980), pp. 113–14.

8 Stanley Cavell, "Hope Against Hope," *The American Poetry Review* (January-February 1986):9–13.

9 Alan Trachtenberg, "The Journey Back: Myth and History in *Tender Is the Night*," in *Experience in the Novel: Selected Papers from the English Institute* ed. Roy Harvey Pearce (New York: Columbia Univ. Press, 1968), pp. 132–38.

10 Stanley Cavell, "Being Odd, Getting Even: Threats to Individuality," *Reconstructing Individualism: Autonomy, Individuality, and the Self in Western Thought*, eds. T. C. Heller, M. Sosna, and D. E. Wellbery (Stanford: Stanfor Univ. Press, 1986), p. 307.

11 Trachtenberg, "The Journey Back," *Experience in the Novel*, ed. Pearce, p. 36.

12 For readings of these passages consonant with my own, see, for example, Robert Sklar, *F. Scott Fitzgerald: The Last Laocoon* (New York: Oxford Univ. Press, 1967); John Callahan, *The Illusions of a Nation*, (pp. 19–20); and Keath Fraser, "Another Reading of *The Great Gatsby*," *English Studies in Canada* 5 (1979): 330–43; also reprinted in *Critical Essays*, ed. Donaldson, pp. 140–53. Edwin Fussell, "Fitzgerald's Brave New World," in *F. Scott Fitzgerald*, ed.

Mizener, pp. 47–50, describes Gatsby's vision of Daisy as a "parody of the incarnation." "The focus of the novel must be sexual and social for the implication of the religious implication is that Gatsby (that is, American culture) provides mainly secular objects for the religious imagination to feed on, as it also provides tawdry images for the aesthetic imagination." The green light is "the historically-corrupted religious symbol." "For Fitzgerald," and we might well add, for Hemingway and Faulkner as well, "this contemptuous repudiation of tradition, historical necessity, and moral accountability, was deluded and hubristic."

13 Many critics have cited instances in the book of "uncertain sexuality" and "impotence and bisexuality" (Keath Fraser, "Another Reading of The Great Gatsby," p. 341) and "sexual confusion" and "role reversal" (Patrician Pacey Thornton, "Sexual Roles in The Great Gatsby," English Studies in Canada 5 [1979]: 457).

14 See Michael J. Colacurcio's illuminating discussion of "Rappaccini's Daughter," in "A Better Mode of Evidence—The Transcendental Problem of Faith and Spirit," Emerson Society Quarterly 54 (1969): 12–22, in which he discusses the tale in relation to the Emersonian tradition.

15 See, for example, Kermit W. Moyer, "The Great Gatsby," and Joan M. Allen, Candles and Carnival Lights: The Catholic Sensibility of F. Scott Fitzgerald (New York: New York Univ. Press, 1978), esp. p. 102.

16 Fussell notes the religious overtones of the word rock in "Fitzgerald's Brave New World," in F. Scott Fitzgerald, ed. Mizener, p. 47.

17 Compare with Oliver H. Evans, "A Sort of Moral Attention: The Narrator of The Great Gatsby," Fitzgerald/Hemingway Annual 3 (1971): 118. In The Imperial Self, pp. 13–18, Quentin Anderson discusses the American denial of fatherhood.

18 On Gatsby as a "bogus Christ" see Joan M. Allen, Candles and Carnival Lights, p. 109. In "Who Killed Jay Gatsby?" David L. Vanderwerhen identifies George Wilson as the ghost of James Gatz and calls Gatsby's death a "psychic suicide" (Notes on Modern American Literature 10 [1979]: item 11).

19 Judith Fetterley responds to the antifeminist implications of the depiction of women and America in The Resisting Reader: A Feminist Approach to American Literature (Bloomington: Indiana Univ. Press, 1978), pp. 72–100. Fetterley captures the ambience of the book but mistakes Fitzgerald's criticism of Gatsby and the American forefathers for his own attitude toward women.

20 Pentateuch and Haftorahs, Hebrew Text, English Translation, and Commentary, ed. J. H. Hertz (London: Soncino Press, 1981).

21 The word pandered is, as more than one critic has noted, viciously loaded: R. W. Stallman, The Houses that James Built and Other Literary Studies (East Lansing: Michigan State Univ. Press, 1961), p. 125, and Fussell, "Fitzgerald's Brave New World," p. 50. For a different development of this line of argument, see Annette Kolodny's The Lay of the Land: Metaphor as Experience and History in American Life and Letters (Chapel Hill: Univ. of North Carolina Press, 1975), pp. 138–39 and Fetterley, Resisting Reader.

22 Nature, Works, 1:3.

23 Nature, Works, 1:8.

24 Anderson, Imperial Self, pp. 3, 15 and 11–12.

25 Nature, Works, 1:59.

26 Cavell, "Being Odd, Getting Even," p. 284.

27 Nature, Works, 1:64.

28 Nature, Works, 1:10.

29 Jennifer Atkinson "Fitzgerald's Marked Copy of The Great Gatsby," Fitzgerald/Hemingway Annual 2 (1970):30, records Fitzgerald's comment to Perkins in a 1925 letter that "orgiastic is the adjective for 'orgasm' and it expresses exactly the intended ecstasy."

30 Critics have expressed opposing views on the matter of Nick as narrator. For criticisms of Nick, see Gary J. Scrimgeour, "Against 'The Great Gatsby,'" Criticism 8 (1966): 75–86, and David O'Rourke, "Nick Carraway as Narrator in The Great Gatsby," International Fiction Review 9 (1982): 57–60. For a different view, see Charles Thomas Samuels, "The Greatness of 'Gatsby,'"

Massachusetts Review 7 (1966):783–94, and Jeffrey Steinbrink, " 'Boats Against the Current': Mortality and the Myth of Renewal in *The Great Gatsby*," *Twentieth Century Literature* 26 (1980): 157–70.

31 Oliver H. Evans, "A Sort of Moral Attention," p. 119, suggests that Gatsby becomes for Nick what Daisy is for Gatsby.

32 *Nature, Works*, 1:49.

33 Compare with Michael Davitt Bell's discussion of the "truth" in *The Development of American Romance: The Sacrifice of Relation* (Chicago: Chicago Univ. Press, 1980), pp. 210 ff.

34 One critic has suggested, rather elaborately, that "gonnegtion" is a pun on con-egg-tion: "Nick, like Gatsby, is . . . seeking a connection with women . . . 'gon' of 'gonnegtion' is the Greek root for seed . . . and one wonders . . . whether Carraway, which after all is a seed, isn't seeking [an] 'egg' " (Keath Fraser, "Another Reading of *The Great Gatsby*," p. 342). Another pun might be *carless and careless*.

35 See Charles Thomas Samuels's "The Greatness of Gatsby," p. 794, who states, among other things, that "In Joyce's sense of the word, *The Great Gatsby* is one of the few novels *written* in our language."

36 Marius Bewley, *The Eccentric Design: Form in the Classic American Novel* (New York: Columbia Univ. Press, 1959), p. 287, has captured the paradox of *Gatsby* beautifully: "We recognize that the great achievement of this novel is that it manages, while poetically evoking a sense of the goodness of that early dream, to offer the most damaging criticism of it in American literature. The astonishing thing is that the criticism—if indictment wouldn't be a better word—manages to be part of the tribute." Other important statements of this paradox include Arnold Weinstein, "Fiction as Greatness: The Case of *Gatsby*," *Novel* 19 (1985): 22–38, and Giles Gunn, "F. Scott Fitzgerald's *Gatsby* and the Imagination of Wonder," *Critical Essays*, ed. Donaldson, esp. pp. 229–30. Other discussions of the romantic and mythic versus the realistic elements include Richard Lehan, "F. Scott Fitzgerald and Romantic Destiny," *Twentieth-Century Literature* 26 (1980): 137–56, Leonard A. Podis, "The Unreality of Reality: Metaphor in *The Great Gatsby*," *Style* 11 (1977): 56–72, R. W. Stallman, *The Houses that James Built*, and James E. Miller, Jr., "Fitzgerald's *Gatsby*: The World as Ash Heap," *Critical Essays*, ed. Donaldson, pp. 242–58. As several critics have pointed out, many of the book's themes and motifs originate in mythic and romantic texts. See, for example, Bruce Michelson, "The Myth of Gatsby," *Modern Fiction Studies* 26 (1980–81): 563–77, K. G. Probert, "Nick Carraway and the Romance of Art," *English Studies in Canada* 10 (1984): 188–208, Keath Fraser, "Another Reading of *The Great Gatsby*," and Joseph N. Riddel, "F. Scott Fitzgerald, "The Jamesian Influence and the Morality of Fiction," *Modern Fiction Studies* 11 (1965–66): 331–50. See also John F. Callahan, *The Illusions of a Nation*, p. 15.

37 *The Notebooks of F. Scott Fitzgerald*, ed. Matthew J. Bruccoli (New York: Harcourt, Brace, Jovanovich, 1978), p. 332.

38 Cited by Matthew J. Bruccoli, *Scott and Ernest: The Authority of Failure and the Authority of Success* (London: Bodley Head, 1978), p. 54.

39 *Nature, Works*, 1:3.

40 See Frederick L. Schuman, *The Nazi Dictatorship: A Study in Social Pathology* (New York: Alfred A. Knopf, 1936), pp. 24–25. Hitler's *Mein Kampf* was published in 1925, the same year as Fitzgerald's novel.

41 See again Stanley Cavell's discussion of fate in *The Senses of Walden* (New York: Viking Press, 1972), pp. 94–96.

42 John Updike, "Emersonianism," *The New Yorker*, June 4, 1984, p. 127. See Cavell's discussion of this essay in "Hope Against Hope."

43 Cavell, "Hope Against Hope."

44 *The Centenary Edition of the Works of Nathaniel Hawthorne*, ed. William Charvat et al. 14 vols. (Columbus: Ohio State Univ. Press, 1962–80), 2.251–52.

45 *Nature, Works*, 1:76–77.

Chapter 9

1 All references to *The Sun Also Rises* are to the Scribner edition (New York, 1954) and appear in parentheses in the text.

2 Cited by Matthew J. Bruccoli, *Scott and Ernest: The Authority of Failure and the Authority of Success* (London: Bodley Head, 1978), p. 54. Discussions of the relationship between Fitzgerald's novel and Hemingway's include: Philip Young and Charles W. Mann, "Fitzgerald's *The Sun Also Rises*: Notes and Comment," *Fitzgerald and Hemingway Annual* 1 (1970): 1–13; Frederic Joseph Svoboda, *Hemingway and The Sun Also Rises: The Crafting of a Style* (Lexington: Univ. Press of Kentucky, 1983), esp. pp. 97–110; Michael S. Reynolds, "False Dawn: A Preliminary Analysis of *The Sun Also Rises*'s Manuscript," in *Hemingway: A Revaluation*, ed. Donald R. Noble (Troy, N.Y.: Whitston, 1983), pp. 115–35; Andrew Hook, "Art and Life in *The Sun Also Rises*," in *Ernest Hemingway: New Critical Essays*, ed. Robert Lee (Totowa, N.J.: Barnes and Noble, 1983), pp. 49–64; Conrad Aiken's review in the "New York Herald Tribune Books," October 31, 1926, reprinted in *Hemingway: The Critical Heritage*, ed. Jeffrey Meyers (London: Routledge and Kegan Paul, 1982); and R. W. Stallman, "Ernest Hemingway *The Sun Also Rises*—But No Bells Ring," *The Houses that James Built and Other Literary Studies* (Ann Arbor: Michigan State Univ. Press, 1961), pp. 173–93, where he states that "It's just possible that Hemingway learned how to write *The Sun Also Rises* from Fitzgerald's *The Great Gatsby*."

3 Reynolds, "False Dawn," p. 118.

4 See especially Svoboda's *Hemingway and The Sun Also Rises*.

5 Hemingway, *Men at War*, (New York: 1942), p. xv.

6 This statement is contained in a letter written to Max Perkins, reprinted in *Ernest Hemingway: Selected Letters, 1917–1961*, ed. Carlos Baker (London: Granada, 1981), p. 208. Fitzgerald himself made a similar decision concerning *The Great Gatsby*. Fitzgerald cut the story "Absolution," which records the early part of Gatsby's life, from the novel in order to "preserve the sense of mystery" (see Henry Dan Piper, *F. Scott Fitzgerald: A Critical Portrait* [New York: Holt, Rinehart, and Winston, 1965], p. 104).

7 Svoboda, *Hemingway and The Sun Also Rises*, indicates that Fitzgerald wanted even more cutting than Hemingway finally allowed.

8 Mark Spilka, "The Death of Love in *The Sun Also Rises*," in *Ernest Hemingway: A Critique of Four Major Novels*, ed. Carlos Baker (New York: Scribner, 1962), p. 23. See also James T. Farrell, "*The Sun Also Rises*," also in *A Critique of Four Major Novels*. Malvin Bachman writes in "The Matador Crucified," in *Modern American Fiction: Essays in Criticism*, ed. Walton Litz (New York: Oxford Univ. Press, 1963) that "it is Cohn for whom Hemingway reserved his most damning portrait. . . . [W]eak and self-pitying [and] woman-dominated, he was without the vital maleness which Hemingway . . . deems absolutely essential to the true man" (p. 203). "Read the novel from Cohn's point-of-view," suggests R. W. Stallman, "and you end obversely in bias against Jake Barnes and his sophomoric code and his friends who damn Cohn by it" ("Ernest Hemingway *The Sun Also Rises*—But No Bells Ring," p. 173). Harold F. Mosher, Jr., "The Two Styles of Hemingway's *The Sun Also Rises*," contains a good summary of the various statements on the Jake versus Cohn and Jake versus Hemingway controversies (*Fitzgerald/Hemingway Annual* 2 [1971]:262–73). For psychoanalytic approaches to the conflict, see Richard Hovey's *Hemingway: The Inward Terrain* (Seattle: Univ. of Washington Press, 1968), esp. pp. 71–72, and Gerry Brenner, *Concealments in Hemingway's Works* (Columbus: Ohio Univ. Press, 1983), pp. 3–24, 55–64. Another useful discussion is "Art and Life in *The Sun Also Rises*," by Andrew Hook, reprinted in *New Critical Essays*, ed. Lee. It is clear that Jake evokes large segments of Hemingway's autobiography. Baker, *Ernest Hemingway*, records the biographical details behind the story (pp. 147–55) as does Michael Reynold in "False Dawn" (p. 120) and Bertram D. Sarason, *Hemingway and The Sun Set* (Washington, D.C.: NCR, 1972).

9 On Hemingway's aesthetic theories see Carlos Baker, *Ernest Hemingway: A Life Story* (New York: Scribners, 1969), p. 170 and H. M. Halliday, "Hemingway's Narrative Perspective," reprinted in *Modern American Fiction*, ed. Litz, p. 218.

10 W. R. Stallman quotes Hemingway as having stated: "I knew nothing about writing a novel when I started [*The Sun Also Rises*], but in rewriting it I learned much" (*"The Sun Also Rises*—But No Bells Ring," p. 188).

11 See Terence Doody's fine essay, "Hemingway's Style and Jake's Narration," *Journal of Narrative Technique* 4 (1974): 212–25. In *Psychotherapeutic Approaches to the Resistant Child* (N.Y.: Jason Aronson, 1975), pp. 101–40, Richard Gardner discusses a "mutual storytelling technique" similar to the one Hemingway, I think, employs. Hemingway refers to psychiatry several times in several contexts. See Baker, *Ernest Hemingway*, pp. 435, 642–43, and Reynolds, "False Dawn," pp. 121, 124–25. Because of Hemingway's explicit interest in psychoanalyzing his narrator, it is, I think, less productive than it might be for critics to psychoanalyze Hemingway and accuse him of the traumas that afflict his protagonist. The two major psychoanalytic studies are, as I suggest, Richard Hovey's *Hemingway: The Inward Terrain* and Gerry Brenner's *Concealments in Hemingway's Works*.

12 On repression and projection and their relationship to fantasy and fictionalization see Otto Fenichel, *The Psychoanalytic Theory of Neurosis* (New York: Norton, 1945), pp. 117–67; and Anna Freud, *Writings of Anna Freud* (New York: International Universities Press, 1966), pp. 69–93 ("Denial in Fantasy" and "Denial in Word and Act"). A literary study that does not deal with *The Sun Also Rises* but whose insights into the problem of the mirroring text usefully illuminate the book is John T. Irwin, *American Hieroglyphics: The Symbol of the Egyptian Hieroglyphics in the American Renaissance* (New Haven: Yale Univ. Press, 1980).

13 E. M. Halliday describes what he calls "objective epitome" in which an object described conveys an inner state ("Hemingway's Narrative Perspective," pp. 217–18). Calling this projection lends a certain attitude toward the technique of "objective epitome," which is crucial to understanding Hemingway's purposes.

14 The sensuousness of the chestnut leaves and the arc are reinforced by the appearance of these terms in other contexts (see pp. 35 and 119). Fantasies of military prowess are familiar symptoms of repression.

15 Note the toy boxers on p. 95.

16 Compare with Jake's and Bill's conversation on irony (pp. 114–15).

17 In "Ernest Hemingway *The Sun Also Rises*—But No Bells Ring," R. W. Stallman discusses the pervasive confusions or overlappings of identities throughout the novel, associating them with the moral confusion and lack of self-identity, which are the novel's themes (pp. 185–88). Stallman also notes (in particular) that "Cohn is mockingly referred to as Moses . . . Jake is paired with Cohn, for Jake also plays the role of Moses; as historian of his expatriate clan and as the law-giver and leader of the Gentiles in Exodus from their Native Land" (pp. 187–88).

18 The fact of Jake's biblical name has evoked comment throughout Hemingway criticism. In *"The Sun Also Rises*: I: The Jacob Allusion, II: Parody as Meaning," *Ball State University Forum* 16 (1975): 50, Manuel Schonhorn suggests that the name does not, as other critics had claimed, signal the enormous gap between Jake and his biblical ancestor but rather identifies Jake's "struggle" with Jacob's. Schonhorn refers back to Alexander Tamke's study "Jake Barnes' 'Biblical Name': Central Irony in *The Sun Also Rises*," *English Record* 7 (1967): 2–7. R. W. Stallman also notes the echoes of the biblical Jacob in Jake at various points in his essay (*"The Sun Also Rises*—But No Bells Ring," p. 189).

19 Geoffrey Hartman's "The Struggle for the Text," for example, contains a good statement of Jacob's somewhat ambiguous morality (*Midrash and Literature*, ed. Geoffrey H. Hartman and Sanford Budick [New Haven: Yale Univ. Press, 1986], pp. 6–7).

20 Hemingway, I think, would have agreed with the historical-typological implications of the end of Longfellow's poem:

But ah! what once has been shall be no more!
　The groaning earth in travail and pain
Brings forth its races, but does not restore,
　And the dead nations never rise again.

Quoted from *The American Tradition in Literature*, ed. Sculley Bradley et al., shorter ed. (New York: Norton, 1974), pp. 776–78.

21 During the composition of *The Sun Also Rises* Hemingway was particularly close to the Church, in anticipation of his marriage to Hadley. See Baker, *Ernest Hemingway*, pp. 185–6. I have already suggested the importance of Roman Catholicism for Fitzgerald. It need hardly be mentioned that Eliot, through Anglicanism, also preferred a religion of ceremonies and symbols to the bare rigidity of Puritanism. At one point in the original manuscript Hemingway had Jake say that "I am spared that Protestant urge . . . to set things out . . . for the good of some future generation" (Svoboda, *Hemingway and the Sun Also Rises*, p. 102).

22 *Letters*, ed. Baker, p. 229.

23 All citations are from the Authorized Version; verses 3–7. On Hemingway's intense absorption in Ecclesiastes, see Reynolds, "False Dawn," pp. 116–17; and Svoboda, *Hemingway and The Sun Also Rises*.

24 The Hebrew word *ruah* means both wind and spirit.

25 On repetition in the Old Testament, see Robert Alter, *The Art of Biblical Narrative* (New York: Basic Books, 1981), pp. 88–113; and Bruce Kawin, *Telling it Again and Again: Repetition in Literature and Film* (Ithaca: Cornell Univ. Press, 1972).

26 Rabbinic midrash has surfaced recently in literary criticism as an exegetical method which preserves the openness of the text. For a collection of essays defining midrash and dealing with some of its implications for literary criticism, see *Midrash and Literature*, ed. Geoffrey H. Hartman and Sanford Budick.

27 Joseph Svoboda quotes Hemingway's defense of the book's optimism, *Hemingway and The Sun Also Rises*, p. 108. *Gatsby* has also been interpreted as a wasteland statement. In *The Sun Also Rises*, A Reconsideration," Donald T. Torchiana rejects Philip Young's notion that *"The Sun Also Rises* is . . . Hemingway's *Waste Land*, and Jake is Hemingway's Fisher King" (*Ernest Hemingway: A Reconsideration* [University Park: Penn State Univ. Press, 1966], pp. 87–88). He extends the idea of Dewey Ganzel that the bullfight rather than the *Waste Land* is the "proper analogy" of the book (pp. 77–103). On the relationship of Eliot's *Waste Land* to both *Gatsby* and *The Sun Also Rises* see Stallman, *"The Sun Also Rises*—But No Bells Ring," pp. 189–90.

28 Stallman, *"The Sun Also Rises*—But No Bells Ring," p. 187.

29 See again Stallman, *"The Sun Also Rises*—But No Bells Ring," pp. 185–88.

30 On déjà vu as a form of repression see Fenichel, *Psychoanalytic Theory of Neurosis*, p. 146.

31 F. Scott Fitzgerald, *The Great Gatsby* (New York: Scribner, 1925), p. 100. The references in both novels recall Thoreau's drummer, who is the measure of our transcendental individualism.

32 At one point Bill asks what the name Cohn means (p. 127).

33 Hartman "The Struggle for the Text," p. 11.

34 Hartman "The Struggle for the Text," pp. 16–17.

35 As Hartman says of Jacob's struggle with the angel, "Through this unmediated encounter, everything shady in Jacob is removed: the blessing he stole he now receives by right; and his name, tainted by his birth and subsequent behavior, is cleared. No longer will he be called Jacob, that is, Heel or Usuper, but Israel, the God-fighter" ("The Struggle for the Text," p. 8).

36 In his 1926 review of the book Conrad Aiken perceptively explains that "*Aficianado* . . . is a profounder word than fan, and suggests emotional intensities and religious zeals, not to mention psychotic fixations. . . . If one likes bull fighting, it has much the effect on one that half a course of psychoanalysis might have" (*Critical Heritage*, p. 89).

37 It is unclear in the biblical text who touches whose thigh. See Hartman, "The Struggle for the Text," p. 11.

38 Stallman notes Malcolm Cowley's comments on this (*"The Sun Also Rises*—But No Bells Ring," p. 189).

39 Hemingway's description of Jake, "Then in the quiet water I turned and floated. Floating I saw only the sky, and felt the drop and life of the swells," might well recall Whitman's description of the twenty-eight male bathers in *Song of Myself*:

> The beards of the young men glisten'd with wet, it ran
> from their long hair,
> Little streams pass'd all over their bodies,
> An unseen hand also pass'd over their bodies,
> It descended trembling from their temples and ribs.
> The young men float on their backs, their white bellies
> bulge to the sun. . .—

From *Leaves of Grass and Selected Prose*, intro. Sculley Bradley (New York: Holt, Rinehart, 1960), p. 32.

40 For a reading of the end of the book that harmonizes with my own, see Carole Gottlieb Vopat, "The End of *The Sun Also Rises*: A New Beginning," *Fitzgerald-Hemingway Annual* (1972):250.

41 Compare with Stallman, *"The Sun Also Rises—But No Bells Ring."*

42 See again Fenichel, *Psychoanalytic Theory of Neurosis*, p. 50.

43 "The End of *The Sun Also Rises*," p. 255. For a different interpretation of the policeman see Spilka, "The Death of Love," p. 25. The policeman here looks back, I think, to the policeman in Book 1 whose smile there reflects Jake's awkwardness and lack of authority.

44 The phallic suggestiveness of the baton also draws out some of the hidden meanings of Hemingway's title. Given Jake's impotence, the assurance that the sun *also* rises hints at a different form of sexual potency (of rising), which may be available to Jake himself. Hence the relevance of Hemingway's own punning comment "THE SUN ALSO RISES (LIKE YOUR COCK IF YOU HAVE ONE)," cited by Matthew J. Bruccoli in *Scott and Ernest*, p. 54.

Chapter 10

1 All References to *Ragtime* are to the Bantam edition (New York, 1976) and appear in parentheses in the text.

2 On the book as a model of repetition, see David Emblidge, "Marching Backward into the Future: Progress as Illusion in Doctorow's Novels," *Southwest Review* 62 (1977): 397–408. On the book's blurring of the distinctions between history and fiction, see Barbara Foley's excellent essay, "From *USA* to *Ragtime*: Notes on the Forms of Historical Consciousness in Modern Fiction," *American Literature* 50 (1978): 85–105, Cushing Strout's, "The Antihistorical Novel," in *The Veracious Imagination: Essays in American History, Literature, and Biography* (Middletown, Conn.: Wesleyan Univ. Press, 1981), pp. 183–96; and Geoffrey Galt Harpham's "E. L. Doctorow and the Technology of Narrative," *PMLA* 100 (1985):81–95. For a survey of the shifting attitudes toward history in historical fiction, see Mark A. Weinstein, "The Creative Imagination in Fiction and History," *Genre* 9 (1976): 263–77.

3 See Emblidge, "Marching Backward into the Future," Foley, "From *USA* to *Ragtime*," Strout, "The Anti-Historical Novel," and Harpham, "E. L. Doctorow and the Technology of Narrative."

4 Doctorow's association of blacks and Eskimos with earthiness and fertility and of Jews with sexual passion might seem racist were it not for his representation of the multiethnic family at the book's conclusion. The book initially reflects cultural prejudices and then revises them, insisting on the tension between social duplication and historical change.

5 See again Stanley Cavell, *The World Viewed: Reflections on the Ontology of Film, Enlarged Edition* (Cambridge, Mass.: Harvard Univ. Press, 1979).

6 See Stanley Cavell, *The Senses of Walden* (New York: Viking Press, 1972) and "Being Odd, Getting Even: Threats to Individuality," in *Reconstructing Individualism: Autonomy, Individuality, and the Self in Western Thought*, eds. T. C. Heller, M. Sosna, and D. E. Wellbery (Stanford: Stanford Univ. Press, 1986).

7 On the importance of the actors in the movies, see Cavell, *The World Viewed*, pp. 25–29; also pp. 179 ff.

8 The pattern of deceptive repetition depicted in skating is later picked up in the description of

baseball: the boy revels in the fact that "the same thing happens over and over" (p. 266). Father has the "illusion that what he saw was not baseball but an elaborate representation of his own problems" (p. 266). Like ice skating, and like silhouettes, photographs, and jigsaw puzzles, baseball presents the illusion of a stable, serene, joyful, democratic, fun-loving America. But as Father's own aristocratic dissatisfactions with the game first suggest, and as Pierpont Morgan's suicidal response to seeing a baseball team in Egypt reconfirms, baseball is a false image of democracy. When the "Giant fool" who is the team's "goodluck charm," actually tries to play the game, they have him "remanded to an insane asylum," where he dies (p. 267).

9 In "E. L. Doctorow and the Technology of Narrative," Harpham suggests that Ford's philosophy of the interchangeability of parts is the same as Doctorow's aesthetic philosophy. I disagree. Ford's and Morgan's philosophies contain serious moral problems that Doctorow's text both exposes and corrects.

10 See Emblidge, "Marching Backward into the Future."

11 Like the early twentieth century, the nineteenth century of Hawthorne was fascinated with ancient Egypt. See John T. Irwin, *American Hieroglyphics: The Symbol of the Egyptian Hieroglyphics in the American Renaissance* (New Haven: Yale Univ. Press, 1980).

12 Reference to *Rabbit is Rich* are to the Alfred A. Knopf edition (New York, 1981) and appear in parentheses in the text.

13 As many Updike critics have observed, *Rabbit Redux* explicitly examines three critical historical manifestations of the period: the fascination with outer space, the Vietnamese War, and the liberation movements of blacks and young people. The bibliography on Updike is still limited, but the most concentrated studies of Updike's *Rabbit* trilogy include: Robert Detweiler, *John Updike* (New York: Twayne, 1972), Richard Gilman, "An Image of Precarious Life," in *John Updike: A Collection of Critical Essays,* eds. David Thorburn and Howard Eiland (Englewood Cliffs, N.J.: Prentice-Hall, 1979), pp. 13–16; Donald J. Grenier, *John Updike's Novels* (Athens: Ohio Univ. Press, 1984), which includes a discussion of *Rabbit is Rich*; and Suzanne Henning Uphaus, *John Updike* (New York: Frederick Ungar, 1980). Detweiler suggests that while *Bech: A Book* presents "fantasy as history," *Rabbit Redux,* for example, is "critically aligned to historical world events" (pp. 152–55). Donald Grenier suggest that *Rabbit, Run* is informed by a crisis of religion, *Rabbit Redux* by the politics of the sixties, and *Rabbit is Rich* by economics (*John Updike's Novels,* pp. 84–100).

14 A number of critics have detailed Hawthorne's influence on Updike. Updike is also the F. Scott Fitzgerald of the 1960s and 1970s, sketching the social world with Fitzgerald's fidelity to human detail and embracing a romantic vision not wholly consonant with his realism.

15 Donald Grenier calls Harry a "quester in a medieval romance" and compares his experience to a "pilgrimage" (*John Updike's Novels,* p. 91). The two passages at the beginning and at the end illustrate what Detweiler aptly calls Updike's "interplay of tropes," producing an almost poemlike quality to his work (*John Updike,* p. 158).

16 For the prophylactic image I am indebted to Carl Rosen.

Index